ON-LINE ANALYTICAL PROCESSING SYSTEMS FOR BUSINESS

ON-LINE ANALYTICAL PROCESSING SYSTEMS FOR BUSINESS

Robert J. Thierauf

Robert J. Thierauf
Ph.D., C.P.A.

Q

QUORUM BOOKS
Westport, Connecticut • London

Library of Congress Cataloging-in-Publication Data

Thierauf, Robert J.
    On-line analytical processing systems for business / Robert J.
    Thierauf.
        p.   cm.
    Includes bibliographical references (p.   ) and index.
    ISBN 1–56720–099–0 (alk. paper)
        1. Management information systems.   2. Online data processing.
    I. Title.
    T58.6.T486   1997
    658.4'038'011—dc21   96–54260

British Library Cataloguing in Publication Data is available.

Library of Congress Catalog Card Number: 96–54260
ISBN: 1–56720–099–0

First published in 1997

Quorum Books, 88 Post Road West, Westport, CT 06881
An imprint of Greenwood Publishing Group, Inc.

The paper used in this book complies with the
Permanent Paper Standard issued by the National
Information Standards Organization (Z39.48–1984).

10 9 8 7 6 5 4 3 2 1

To be successful, decision makers must be able to analyze information that allows them to challenge a company's direction today as well as tomorrow. Such an approach is realizable with on-line analytical processing (OLAP) systems.

Robert J. Thierauf

Contents

viii   Contents

Figures

Preface

Typically, most management information systems have been able to handle and present data in only two dimensions—in columns or rows. This results in limited decision making. However, a new way of handling information, called *on-line analytical processing* (OLAP), helps to remove barriers for decision makers at all levels of a company. OLAP tools enable decision makers to build and work with analytical data models easily and view data in multiple dimensions. The result is that decision makers can see new relationships in data that were not possible previously.

Because decision makers are constantly looking for new patterns, they need to go beyond mere facts. For example, once a typical decision maker knows this month's sales, a series of questions is asked: What is the percent change from the previous year? What is the company's market share and its change from the previous year? What are the current selling prices and the change from the previous year? In fact, most of the information needed by decision makers is not stored in the company's database or data warehouse. It must be calculated on the fly, as specified by the decision makers at the time one or more issues arise. From this example, the need for a new approach is evident, namely, on-line analytical processing systems.

An important consideration for successful OLAP is the identification of critical success factors (CSFs) and their analysis by key performance indicators (KPIs) and financial ratios. The CSF process states that there are specific and limited numbers of areas in which satisfactory results will dramatically affect the competitive performance of a company. Depending on the strategic direction of an industry and the specific company, there are different ways of managing change and reshaping a business. The CSF process identifies what these specific needs are, and the OLAP system allows decision makers to monitor the CSFs.

Thus, by using the CSF approach, an OLAP system can provide access to selected views of information that, much like a pilot using instruments to monitor
an airplane, allow decision makers to direct their operations in an effective
manner not only for today, but also in the future.

Not only is the text designed for the practitioner, but also for the academican
in the information systems field. Systems analysts and MIS (management information system) managers will find the text helpful in understanding one of
the most important developments in information systems. Company managers,
that is, decision makers, will be particularly interested in installing their own
systems. In addition, end users in the various functional areas of a typical company can benefit from OLAP knowledge contained in this text. In a similar
manner, the book is quite suitable in an academic environment, that is, an un-
dergraduate-or graduate-level course covering the fundamentals of on-line analytical processing systems. The student will be exposed to the latest thinking on
this topic and will be given ample information for undertaking an OLAP project.
If so desired, the student's project can be linked to virtual reality. Overall, the
text is quite capable of serving the needs of both groups.

There is a logical structure to this text for a comprehensive treatment of on-
line analytical processing systems. The topical areas which are enhanced by real-
world applications where deemed appropriate, are as follows.

PART I: INTRODUCTION TO ON-LINE ANALYTICAL
PROCESSING (OLAP) SYSTEMS

In Chapter 1, the emerging need for OLAP systems is set forth, along with
the essential elements underlying them. In addition, the relationship of OLAP
to prior information systems and succeeding ones is discussed. Chapter 2 examines the types of problems uncovered and solved typically by decision makers, including reference to on-line analytical processing. The problem-solving
and problem-finding processes, which includes uncovering future opportunities,
are covered along with illustrative examples.

PART II: THE ESSENTIAL ELEMENTS OF OLAP SYSTEMS

Types of databases useful to decision makers and their staffs plus analysts in
an OLAP-operating mode are explored in Chapter 3, with emphasis on data
warehouses and multidimensional databases. In addition, the latest directions in
data communications and networking that is complementary to data needed for
OLAP systems are presented. Chapter 4 centers on OLAP software that assists
decision makers in obtaining important information from their systems. Emphasis is placed on available OLAP software from outside vendors that utilizes
multidimensional analysis to produce desired information. Many times, this information is helpful in answering a wide range of questions as they arise in the
normal course of intensive business analysis. In Chapter 5, current approaches

useful to decision makers and their staffs plus analysts in developing systems in an OLAP-operating mode are set forth. This is followed by an approach to implement and support a typical OLAP system on a day-to-day basis.

PART III: TYPICAL APPLICATIONS OF OLAP SYSTEMS

In Chapter 6, newer directions in effective strategic planning are explored along with strategic-planning applications that can benefit from the implementation of OLAP systems. The remaining chapters follow the same format. That is, Chapters 7, 8, 9, and 10 explore the newer directions that are related to marketing, manufacturing, accounting and finance, and human resources, respectively. In turn, representative applications of OLAP systems are presented to demonstrate their use under varying conditions and tie-in with virtual reality.

In a project of this magnitude, I wish to thank the following who have assisted me. First, I would like to thank the many vendors who have supplied materials that have been included throughout the text. These include Arbor Software Corporation (Sunnyvale, California); Brio Technology (Mountain View, California); Business Objects, Inc. (San Jose, California); Comshare, Inc. (Ann Arbor, Michigan); Dimensional Insight, Inc. (Burlington, Massachusetts); Kenan Technologies (Cambridge, Massachusetts); Oracle Corporation (Redwood Shores, California); Pilot Software, Inc. (Cambridge, Massachusetts); and SAS Institute Inc. (Cary, North Carolina). Second, my graduate students at Xavier University are to be commended for their comments and helpful suggestions. Most of these students are employed full-time by a number of organizations in the Midwest, where they are computer professionals. Third, I am especially thankful to Mr. Larry Schwalbach of Hankyu International Transport (USA) Inc. for helping in the development of the OLAP illustrations in the text. Fourth, but not last, a special note of appreciation is due to Mr. Eric Valentine, Publisher of Quorum Books, for his helpful suggestions in this most interesting project.

Abbreviations

ABC	activity-based costing
ACID	atomicity, consistency, isolation, and durability
AI	artificial intelligence
API	application programming interface
ASRS	automated storage and retrieval system
ATM	asynchronous transfer mode
BC/BS	Blue Cross/Blue Shield
BI	business intelligence
BIS	business intelligence system
BISDN	broadband integrated services digital network
BLOBS	binary large objects
BPR	business process reengineering
CAD	computer-aided design
CAM	computer-aided manufacturing
CASE	computer-aided software engineering
CCITT	Consultative Committee of International Telegraph and Telephone
CD-ROM	compact disks—read-only memory
CEO	chief executive officer
CIM	computer integrated manufacturing
COMMS	customer-oriented manufacturing management system
CRT	cathode ray terminal
CSF	critical success factor

DBMS	database-management system
DDP	distributed data processing
DOLAP	desktop on-line analytical processing
DP	data processing
DOS	disk operating system
DSS	decision support system
EDI	electronic data interchange
EDS	electronic data systems
EIS	executive information system
E-mail	electronic mail
EOQ	economic order quantity
ERP	enterprise resources planning
ES	enterprise solution
ESS	employee self service
4GL	fourth-generation language
GDP	gross domestic product
GDSS	group decision support system
GUI	graphical user interface
HD	hard-disk drive
HDTV	high-definition television
HR	human resources
HRMS	human resource management system
HTML	Hypertext Mark-up Language
IFIPS	International Federation of Information Processing Societies
IS	information system
ISDN	integrated services digital network
IT	information technology
JIT	just-in-time
KISS	keep it simple, stupid
KPI	key performance indicator
LAD	Latin America Division
L&D	logistics and distribution
LAN	local area network
MAN	metropolitan area network
MB	megabytes
Mbps	megabits per second
MDD	multidimensional database

MDDB	multidimensional database
MES	manufacturing execution system
MIS	management information system
MOLAP	multidimensional on-line analytical processing
MPP	massive parallel processing
MRP	material requirements planning
MRP-II	manufacturing resource planning
MSPL	Multidimensional Stored Procedural Language
ODBC	open database connectivity
OLAP	on-line analytical processing
OLE2	object linking and embedding
OLTP	on-line transactional processing
ONA	open network architecture
OOAD	object-oriented analysis and design
OODBMS	object-oriented database-management system
OOP	object-oriented programming
OSI	open systems interconnection
PAWWS	Portfolio Accounting World-Wide System
PC	personal computer or microcomputer
PCI	PepsiCola International
PIMS	profit impact of marketing strategies
PPI	purchase performance index
RAD	rapid application development
R&D	research and development
RDBMS	relational database-management system
ROI	return on investment
ROLAP	relational on-line analytical processing
SAM	strategic analysis model
SAS	statistical analysis system
SMDS	switched multi-megabit digital service
SMIS	sales & marketing intelligence system
SMP	symmetric multiprocessing
SONET	synchronous optical network
SQL	Structured Query Language
TCP/IP	transmission control protocol/internet protocol
2-D	two-dimensional
3-D	three-dimensional

TQM	total quality management
VBX	visual basic extension
VIART	virtual reality research team
VLAN	virtual local area network
VR	virtual reality
VRAM	virtual RAM
VRML	Virtual Reality Modeling Language
VRT	virtual reality toolkit
WAN	wide area network
WTK	WorldToolKit
YTD	year to date

PART I

Introduction to On-line Analytical Processing (OLAP) Systems

1

OLAP Systems Versus Other Systems

ISSUES EXPLORED

- Why do changing times demand more innovative approaches to information processing, like on-line analytical processing?
- What is the reason for including information (and knowledge) as a major resource of a typical company?
- What leverage can a typical company get from using OLAP systems?
- What is the tie-in of OLAP systems to prior information systems?
- What lies beyond OLAP systems for a typical company?

OUTLINE

CHANGING TIMES DEMAND MORE INNOVATIVE APPROACHES TO INFORMATION PROCESSING

For all sizes of organizations, including the *Fortune* 1000 companies, a new type of computer-based information system, that is, an on-line analytical processing (OLAP) system, is expanding the computer's role in everyday operations. This type of system also goes by the name of a business intelligence system (BIS), although OLAP will be used throughout this text. The primary goal of an OLAP system is to promote information-based insight and understanding by providing decision makers (from the highest level to the lowest level) with the information they need quickly, and in the form they want it. In effect, an organization-wide OLAP system challenges decision makers to evaluate the status quo. An OLAP system allows decision makers to tailor their information and knowledge requirements by discriminating according to user-defined criteria. An OLAP system is capable of making comparisons, analyzing trends, and presenting historical and current data. Unlike a traditional management information system (MIS) presentation, it can distinguish between vital and seldom-used data. An on-line analytical processing system can track and evaluate key critical success factors for decision makers, which is valuable in assessing whether or not the organization is meeting its corporate objectives and goals. In general, an OLAP system can shape an information base that decision makers can use to make better informed decisions.

As will be seen in this chapter and future ones, past management information systems basically used the computer as a means of providing information to solve recurring operational problems. A better approach today is on-line analytical processing systems, which position decision makers at the center of the information revolution. By increasing the capabilities of decision makers and by eliminating impediments to their rational functioning, an OLAP system improves the chances that an organization will achieve its goals of increased sales, profits, and so forth, by placing information and knowledge in the hands of decision makers at the proper time and place, and by providing flexibility in their choice and sequence of information analysis and in the ultimate presentation of results. From this perspective, OLAP systems provide essential information to decision makers so that they can better cope with changing times. In this chapter, not only is a background given on the essentials of information and knowledge, but also on the important features of OLAP systems. Additionally, there is a tie-in of OLAP systems with past and current management information systems, as well as continuing MIS developments.

Focus of OLAP—Challenges a Company's Status Quo

Fueling the interest in OLAP systems is going beyond the traditional approach to finding out what went wrong. In the past, a typical relational database-management system (RDBMS) query told the decision maker *what* had happened, but not *why*. The focus, then, has shifted to finding out why. In a few words, "what" is not satisfying, that is, it only provides the decision maker with an opportunity to solve today's superficial problems; whereas "why" helps the decision maker to get to the root of the problems and prevent future occurrences.

To put the OLAP concept into perspective, a sales manager, for example, wants to know why sales are down in a specific region for a specific product, and he/she would like to know if this will change in the future. The sales manager wants to know it *now*, without being subjected to IT (information technology) backlog found in most MIS departments. Needless to say, this is where OLAP comes into play. To get at OLAP information that challenges a company's status quo by asking why, there is need to go beyond extracting data from company databases for traditional two-dimensional analysis and provide the ability for managers at all levels to employ multidimensional analysis in finalizing their decisions. Or, to state it another way, the information useful to a typical manager should center around information organized to answer questions that challenge an organization's strategy today and tomorrow.

INFORMATION—A SIXTH ORGANIZATION RESOURCE
FOR DECISION MAKERS

In the past, a typical company is said to have *five* major resources: men (i.e., people), machines, money, materials, and management (the five M's). More recently, information has been added as the *sixth* resource. However, within the context of information technology, many companies regard such technology as an overhead expense, not as a valued asset. It is time that these misconceptions be turned around and that organizations can actually lower their costs, increase profits, or enhance their market image through the latest IT advancements, as demonstrated in this text for OLAP systems.

It should be noted that information derived from improved information technology can be a source of power over competition, and can be useful for not only assisting the traditional five resources in coordinating organizational activities, but also for supporting them in planning, organizing, directing, and controlling these activities from the highest management level to the lowest operational level. This provides a rationale for spending large sums of money on various types of information systems, such as OLAP systems. Even though it is not as tangible as the other five resources in justifying, it is a way of bringing them together in an economical and efficient manner. The net result is effectiveness of organization operations.

After the human element, *quality and timely business information* is a decision maker's most important resource. Generally, it is an important business asset that has been generally undervalued, underestimated, and underused. A major problem facing today's managers is the volume of information crossing their desks. It can be so voluminous as to be almost unmanageable; yet good planning and control over operations via effective decisions must be based on a steady flow of good-quality up-to-date information. Given these conditions and the accelerating pace of business changes, there arises a definite need to change their working habits. A human-computer dialogue is essential for managers to be productive and effective. The computer should not impede the managers' thought processes; rather, it should augment their capabilities and become an extension of their minds. From this view, the computer is an important means of providing essential information in an OLAP environment for answering the *whys* of a company's operations versus just the *whats*.

Relationship of Information to Knowledge

To show the relationship of information to knowledge and other levels, reference can be made to Figure 1.1, which shows important factors about each level of the summarization for data, information, knowledge, wisdom, and truth. At the lowest level, *data*, which represents the unstructured facts and figures, is at the least impact level of inputs for the typical manager. This is followed by *information* (the next level up), which is structured data that is useful for the

Figure 1.1
Relationship of Information to Knowledge and Other Levels

Level of Summarization	Definition	Problem Importance	Decision Approach	Nature of Problem
Truth	Conformance to fact or reality	Critical	Consensus	Structured to unstructured
Wisdom	Ability to judge soundly	Critical	Consensus	Unstructured
Knowledge	Obtained from experts based on actual experience	Major	Advisory Group	Semistructured
Information	Structured data useful for analysis	Major to minor	Advisors	Structured and semi-structured
Data	Unstructured facts	Minor to trivial	Individual	Structured

manager in analyzing and resolving critical problems. The use of information by the manager will be evident throughout the text.

At the next higher level, there is *knowledge*, which is obtained from experts based upon actual experience. As such, there is need to integrate a fund of information in order to see patterns and trends that enable decision makers to make the transition to insight and prediction. Essentially, this is the function of expert systems and neural networks as well as decision-support systems and on-line analytical processing systems (all of which are covered in this chapter). In a similar manner, the principal product of a consulting or a CPA firm is knowledge, as is the purpose of this text to impart knowledge about OLAP systems.

At the second highest level, *wisdom* is the ability to judge soundly. This high level of understanding involves such philosophical attributes as the awareness that the models constructed will not always hold true. Wisdom requires the intuitive ability, born of experience, to look beyond the apparent situation to recognize exceptional factors and anticipate unusual outcomes. *Truth*, the highest level, is conformance to fact or reality, and represents the lofty pinnacle of understanding. To the ultimate degree, truth is equivalent to God.

Basically, an analysis of Figure 1.1 emphasizes that, generally, decisions with the most significant ramifications for the operations of a company tend to have characteristics that are most suited to a participatory decision-making process. The decisions that are best made by an individual do not appear, in general, to have as wide-ranging or overall an organization impact. Hence, the implication of this figure is that group decision making is the way to go for quality decision making for many business situations. As the environment becomes more complex, the typical decision makers will have to call upon more resources if effective decision making is to prevail. Studies have shown a relationship between characteristics of decisions and the nature of the decision-making process. Decisions were found to be more participatory when decision quality and user acceptance was important. Participation was also preferable when the problem was complex or unstructured. Studies have shown that decisions were found to be less participatory when the manager had all the necessary information, the problem was routine or structured, or time was limited and immediate action was required.

LEVERAGING INFORMATION AND KNOWLEDGE FOUND IN OLAP SYSTEMS

If a company truly leverages information and knowledge, it should be able to accomplish the following. *First*, information and knowledge should make the organization more responsive to rapidly changing competitive conditions. This way, new opportunities may be more quickly exploited and competitive vulnerabilities may be reduced. *Second*, they allow managers and their staffs to evaluate a company's critical success factors. These factors are the ones that can make or break any company. *Third*, they should enhance the internal efficiency and productivity of the organization with emphasis on managerial productivity. This includes better coordination of the organizational functional components such as sales and marketing, manufacturing and production, distribution, support and service, finance and accounting, and administration. *Fourth*, they should improve the creativity, productivity, and effectiveness of individual decision makers as well as group decision making in the organization. This centers on providing the appropriate tools for collecting accurate and timely information; improving the analysis of the information and the quality of the decisions from it; and expediting, supporting, and monitoring the implementation of management actions and decisions. Overall, these four items center on gaining competitive advantage, leveraging a company's critical success factors, and improving organizational productivity. Due to their importance, they are discussed below.

Gaining Competitive Advantage

From past surveys of American competitiveness, the consensus is that U.S. competitiveness has deteriorated and that diminished competitiveness will hurt America's economic performance for the foreseeable future. The net result is that the current situation represents a threat to the country's standard of living and economic power. In light of these comments, there is need for organizations "to shift gears" by employing an appropriate information technology to gain a competitive advantage. It is the job of MIS management, working with top management, to bring about the needed change in the *competitive landscape* by employing the proper approach to organization-wide computing activities.

Essentially, an important thrust of this text is on the latest direction in information systems, that is, OLAP systems, whether they are on an individual or a group-oriented basis to gain competitive advantage. The technology of personal computers and data communications is changing the parameters of competition in every industry whether it is manufacturing or service oriented. Formerly, information technology was directed toward being a "storekeeper" of data and information. In today's fast-changing world, information technology has to facilitate change so that the organization remains competitive. The importance of OLAP technology as a competitive weapon in furthering the organization's objectives, goals, and strategies is no less applicable for the small- to medium-size company than for the large-size company.

Leveraging a Company's Critical Success Factors

Although the typical manager undertakes a number of roles, the accent in this text is on relating decision making to the traditional problem-solving processes plus the utilization of the newer problem-finding process to expand the manager's view of how problems can be solved and how new opportunities can be identified for implementation. In the process of making a wide range of decisions, there is need for the manager to take into account the organization's critical success factors (CSFs), that is, those factors that are critical in making or breaking the organization. The process to identify CSFs was originally defined by John Rockart of MIT in the late 1970s. (A rich discussion of these CSFs will be given in Chapter 6.) At this point, it is sufficient to say that there are a specific and limited number of areas in which satisfactory results will dramatically affect the competitive performance of an organization. Typically, these areas are the ones to be measured and evaluated. As the old saying goes, "If you can't measure, you can't manage." Similarly, "What you measure wrong, you manage wrong." Establishing the wrong measures will lead to far worse results than establishing no measures at all.

Depending on the strategic direction of an industry and the specific organization, there are different ways of managing change and reshaping a business. The CSF process identifies what these specific needs are. Also, an on-line analytical processing system can be used to monitor these CSFs. In turn, an OLAP system can be used to analyze these CSFs such that their thorough analysis leads to new and different ways to exploring opportunities for a company. This approach can result in leveraging a company's CSFs for its betterment. Thus, by using a CSF process, an OLAP system can provide access to selected views of information that allow company managers and their staffs to direct their present and future operations in an effective manner.

Improving Organization Productivity

Related to gaining competitive advantage and leveraging a company's critical success factors is the area of improving management productivity. Discussions have generally ignored the productivity of managers at the top. Attention has focused on assembly-line robots or the implementation of the paperless office, whereby the productivity of individual workers at the lower levels of an organization is increased. However, when viewed from a strictly financial perspective, the productivity of labor and clerical workers is only one element in achieving organization productivity. The financial community measures productivity in terms of return on stockholders' equity, return on capital, and other financial tests. If the management of an organization decides to launch a new product which the customer will not buy, it is irrelevant whether the workers actually assembling the product are performing their jobs efficiently. Having the right product at the right time, however, has a much greater impact on the organizational productivity than gaining an incremental improvement in labor or clerical productivity.

Because a manager makes decisions and not products per se, his or her productivity is measured by the quality and timeliness of those decisions. Accepting the fact that management decisions are at least as important to organization productivity as the automation of lower-level work leads to the conclusion that managerial productivity is worthy of a great deal of time, attention, and money. As will be seen later in the chapter, the problem with past information systems was that there was plenty of data, but the data became information only when gainfully employed in supporting decision making. This approach has resulted in managers being buried in data while forced to make important decisions in a relative vacuum of timely and pertinent information.

To overcome past information-systems problems, managers need to analyze data in order to see important trends and relationships. Generally, this can be accomplished by the utilization of multidimensional analysis within an OLAP processing mode. For these multidimensional representations to accomplish anything, they must communicate relationships—contrasts, comparisons, and trends. These are important elements of which decisions are made. The right kind of multidimensional analysis via computerized graphics overcomes the inability of tabular data to represent relationships. In view of these factors, multidimensional analysis is an important means to improve managerial productivity and, at the same time, support decision making within an OLAP environment.

THE ESSENTIALS OF OLAP SYSTEMS

As one looks around the business environment these days, one sees that layers of management have been reduced whereby managers on the whole are closer to the business, more self-sufficient, and more hands-on than ever before. Because of the greater need to make more informed decisions faster, there are a few problems, including the ones found in an approach to OLAP. Chief among these problems is the fact that most OLAP servers are extracting data from a two-dimensional relational database management system (RDBMS) and populating a multidimensional data cube. This creates data duplication and update challenges. Typically, static data cubes require users to rely on the MIS department to modify them as query needs change. The end result is that the IT backlog increases.

In light of this problem and others, there is need for a new approach to OLAP. Ideally, there is need for the decision-support process to be open, scalable, and integrated for a typical company. The *first* term (open) refers to the use of current databases with the schemas now in place. In this way, current technology investment and infrastructure can be leveraged to a company's full advantage. The *second* term (scalable) means that the user must be able to deploy OLAP solutions throughout the company, from one work group to the entire enterprise. The *third* term (integrated) means the OLAP solution should be comprehensive, that is, one place for query, analysis, and reporting. Users need to have everything in their own personnel decision tool kit working together without a need for assistance of the MIS department. Although the foregoing are the desired goals of OLAP, it is recommended that OLAP vendors prove how their solutions will meet the above criteria. An avoidance of asking how vendors will meet these underlying essentials of on-line analytical processing may prove to be detrimental to the typical company getting started on asking the *whys* of their operations as opposed to asking the *whats* only.

Accent on Multidimensional Analysis

A most important characteristic of OLAP systems is multidimensional analysis, that is, analysis that goes beyond the traditional two-dimensional analysis. Essentially, multidimensional analysis represents an important method for leveraging the contents of an organization's production data and other data stored in company databases and data warehouses because it allows users to look at different dimensions of the same data. According to research director Howard Dresner of the Gartner Group, users need OLAP tools if they spend more than 20 percent of their time analyzing data and the data is compared across more than two dimensions (such as business units, geographics, products, industries, market segments, distribution channels, and so forth).[1] As such, OLAP makes it easier to do analyses that cross departmental and even corporate boundaries.

Another way of viewing OLAP is getting a typical company out of the custom-report-writing business and into the data-cube-server building business. An OLAP data structure can be thought of as a Rubik's Cube of data that users can twist and twirl in different ways to work through "what-if" and "what-happened" scenarios to get at the *whys* of the situation. An example of multi-

Figure 1.2
A Multidimensional Analysis for Sales by Region Over a Three-Year Period

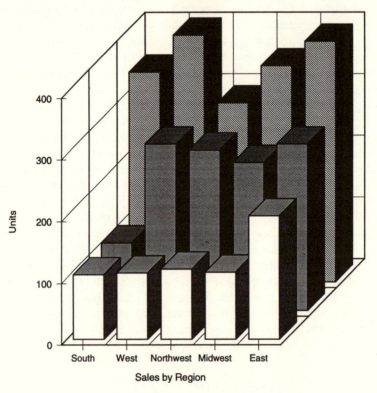

□Year 1   ▥Year 2   ▨Year 3

dimensional analysis is found in Figure 1.2, where the focus is on sales analysis by region over a three-year period.

Within an OLAP environment, the focus is on performing dictionary definition and maintenance as well as mapping flat files or relational columns to dimensions and measures. Although this may sound like a lot of work, managing one data cube beats writing a number of custom reports. Currently, some vendors provide administrative tools to get the data into the cubes in the first place, in the proper form, and on a regular basis. (Current vendors offer a number of multidimensional tools which are given in Chapter 4.) It should be noted that some of these data cubes are "real" while others are "virtual" or "open." That is, in some cases, data are replicated from the warehouse or other data source into the cube; in others, a metadata structure is built full of pointers that runs directly against a standard relational warehouse. In either case, there is need to design and maintain it.

Generally, the real cubes are more limited in size but run much faster. Most real cubes can support at least 1 or 2 GB structures, while a few claim up to 100 GB capacity. Cube size grows rapidly as the user adds dimensions because of all the cross-dimensional links. Real cubes have something of an advantage for financial analysis, which generally has fewer empty spots in the matrix. On the other hand, the virtual ones are able to handle sales and marketing analysis, which, generally, goes against larger, more spottily populated data sets. Virtual cubes have pointers, not data, so sparsity is not so much of a problem.

Utilization of OLAP Servers

Although data is found somewhere in a company's scattered databases, this does not mean that the user can get at it or that it can answer the toughest questions. From this view, there is a need for OLAP servers that can get the data out and make it mean something. Important criteria to consider when evaluating OLAP servers are the architecture, data manipulation, ad hoc reporting, links to back-end data, and security. Needless to say, it pays to keep an open mind.

Currently, all OLAP servers are multidimensional, but to varying degrees. In addition, OLAP servers traffic in aggregated data. Because an important part of an OLAP system is the capability of drilling down through the cube, the most flexible products let the user drill in any direction, skipping levels as one drills, and drilling along pathways that have not been predefined. Thus, there is a need for seamless integration with transaction-processing databases.

It is also necessary to look at the degree of multiuser support, and the ability to do time-series analysis—both trademarks of the best OLAP servers. In a similar manner, security, especially user authority, is necessary with OLAP. Many of these products let the user read and write to the cube. That can create a problem if the products do not give the user tools to control read-and-write access. The user needs tailoring and flexibility as well as support for multiple hierarchies for the same entities. Overall, OLAP servers represent an approach to answer the *whys* of users' questions in a timely manner.

Accent on Multidimensional Databases with Tie-In to Other Databases

Typically, most companies have all the data they need for on-line analytical processing in their databases or data warehouses. However, they find it difficult to get at the data since it is necessary to deal with data in multidimensional space. To assist users in getting at the data, OLAP applications make use of three different types of database structures: (1) multidimensional, (2) relational, and (3) specialized relational databases, which are explored below.

The *first* type of database is multidimensional. Its essential characteristics center on high performance for databases up to 5 Gbytes, capable of handling more than five dimensions, and typically used by a smaller number of users, as in a single department. This is the mainstay of on-line analytical processing. The *second* type is relational, which requires the database to be redesigned using star schema to achieve good performance. Relational is very good for databases larger than 5 Gbytes. However, performance declines when more than five dimensions are implemented, and is typically used by a larger number of users across multiple departments. The *third* type of database is the specialized relational which requires a front-end OLAP tool. It is designed for decision support and data warehousing. Some products require that the database be redesigned since they still treat it as relational. All of these basic database structures, along with current vendor offerings, are set forth in Chapter 3.

OLAP DEFINED

In the preceding discussion on the essentials of OLAP systems, the focus was on multidimensional analysis which looks at data from different perspectives, as defined by the end user. In order to undertake the desired analysis, the end user acts as the *front end*. In the *middle* is an OLAP server where data is retrieved from back-end databases and staged in an OLAP-multidimensional database for retrieval by front-end systems. At the *back end* are databases and data warehouses that are multidimensional, relational, or specialized relational. In a typical situation, OLAP uses a multidimensional database that reads and aggregates large groups of diverse data to analyze relationships and look for patterns, trends, and exceptions.

Based on this overview, on-line analytical processing technology gives end users easy access to large volumes of numerical data on-line. Usually, data is transferred from on-line transactional processing systems to a multidimensional database for data summarization. OLAP functions between the back-end databases and data warehouses and the front end or end user. The multidimensional engine that drives OLAP technology enables the system to analyze large volumes of data quickly. Retrieval times are aided by the use of efficient data-storage algorithms that preaggregate data, saving it in fewer places but with more intelligent directional markers.

As noted previously, a most important feature of OLAP is its drill-through capability from the highest level to the lowest level of detail. As such, OLAP is a user-friendly, quick, and flexible client/server solution that lets users drill down into information housed in databases and data warehouses for analysis. To get at the detail level, there is need for a seamless integration of these data whether they are transaction-processing databases for everyday or data warehouses for historical data. Thus, there is a need for an open architecture which allows the user to obtain the desired data for analysis from any database or data warehouse in an organization.

Based on the preceding essential features found in OLAP systems, on-line analytical processing systems can be defined as an open-systems architecture that provides the user with rapid retrieval of data from company databases and/

or data warehouses for the purpose of summarization and multidimensional analysis. Typically, the end result of the analysis is information and knowledge per user-defined dimensions for getting at the *whys* of the problem(s) under study. Where deemed necessary, a drill down and/or dice capability is utilized to get at the appropriate level of detail in the analysis.

OVERCOMING OBSTACLES TO IMPLEMENTING OLAP SYSTEMS

Although there are obvious benefits to managers and their staffs for having ready access to corporate data for multidimensional analysis, MIS managers who assist in implementing OLAP systems face a series of obstacles. Going beyond the problem mentioned previously that centered on a two-dimensional database, there is managerial resistance and apathy as well as a feeling that costs will be too high. Any one of these issues can thwart OLAP. Chief among the obstacles to implement a successful OLAP system is resistance from managers who feel threatened by what they perceive as a radical change in the way the company's data is evaluated and exchanged. In effect, the politics of OLAP systems is one of the most frequently overlooked barriers to successful implementation. Although higher-level managers are often above the politics, this generally is not true regarding subordinates who are likely to resist the system.

To complicate matters further, MIS managers responsible for implementing an enterprise-wide OLAP system are usually naive about the business problems created by it; and they are often hesitant about approaching the chief executive officer when they run into resistance. Functional-unit executives (managers responsible for specific business units) have a lot to lose from the adoption of an OLAP system, since it opens up their operations to the scrutiny of top executives. Although company politics often keeps line executives from objecting too loudly to an OLAP system, their more passive resistance is frequently described as "foot dragging."

Recognizing the potential for such subtle forms of resistance, OLAP system builders (i.e., systems analysts) stress that MIS managers must work closely with functional-unit managers and others supplying data for the OLAP system, making sure they understand the system's purpose and building in applications that will be useful to them. In addition, MIS managers encounter resistance from many middle-level managers, whose jobs involve analyzing data. They view the OLAP system as a battle for control over access to data and a possible way of getting rid of them. A company controller, for example, is used to presenting information to company executives and can easily feel threatened when that relationship is challenged. If an OLAP system is properly constructed, this individual will not be cut out, but will be able to answer specifically directed questions from managers at all levels regarding the *whys* of the company's operations.

Even if the political roadblocks and managerial apathy of implementing an enterprise-wide OLAP system are overcome, MIS managers must be able to justify the costs to get started since the system's benefits tend to be intangible, especially at first. To demonstrate why costs are justifiable, an approach might be to show a manager a vendor's demonstration of an OLAP system for him or her. Although it is easy to raise the manager's expectations by using demos, it should be noted that the demonstrations may not bear any resemblance to how data is handled within a particular company and the cost of the data handling. However, it is suggested that a prototype be built that shows a manager a specific example of how the system will analyze specific business problems that are troubling him or her currently.

PAST AND CURRENT MANAGEMENT INFORMATION SYSTEMS

Having set forth an overview of OLAP systems, it would be helpful to look at the development of management information systems over the years. Past and current MIS which are covered below are integrated MIS, real-time MIS, and distributed MIS along with their shortcomings. In turn, continuing developments of MIS will be explored in the next sections of the chapter.

For the most part, the systems in this section center on processing a company's mission-critical applications. The term *critical* generally refers to applications without which the business could not continue to operate. Traditionally, MIS mission-critical applications involve issues concerning transactionality, usually defined with the help of the ACID (for atomicity, consistency, isolation, and durability) properties. The ACID properties are what let applications handle individual transactions as individual events, in the correct order, and with the appropriate safeguards to ensure informational and processing integrity as well as automated recovery and rollback in the event of failures. From this perspective, the main focus of systems in this section is not to help decision makers per se.

Integrated MIS

Generally, past management information systems have not provided managers with the potential to offer creative solutions to an organization's problems. That is, *integrated management information systems* provided selected decision-oriented information needed by management to plan, control, and evaluate the activities of the organization. They were designed within a framework that emphasizes profit planning, performance planning, and control at all levels. Integrated MIS centered on the integration of required business information systems, both financial and non-financial, within the organization. In the past, the primary interest of information systems was developing financial statements. When an integrated MIS was installed, its *primary purpose* was the production of reports that assist management. In contrast, its *secondary purpose* was the preparation of periodic financial reports representing a byproduct of the information processed to assist in planning and controlling operations.

Although integrated management information systems rectified the problem of prior accounting-oriented systems by providing feedback in the form of reports through its various systems and subsystems, they were still deficient in one important respect—data had to be accumulated for a period of time before processing was feasible. Whether sequential or random-access files are used, there was still the problem of time lag. For this reason, all prior systems, including integrated MIS, were called *backward-looking systems*. The methods, procedures, and equipment looked to past history before reports were produced for feedback. What was needed were *forward-looking systems*—ones that look to the present and the future. Such an approach is found in subsequent management information systems, in particular, real-time MIS and distributed MIS, as discussed below. However, it should be noted that these systems do not stress leveraging information technology to gain competitive advantage or improve productivity of organization personnel for a typical organization.

Real-Time MIS

Although integrated MIS is operating in a few organizations of various sizes, it has been replaced by the implementation of *real-time management information systems*, sometimes referred to as *on-line real-time systems*. Like prior systems, they are essentially transactional processing systems that also provide essential information for management. Typical applications in such an environment include accounts receivable, airline reservation systems, bank deposit and withdrawal accounting, hotel accounting and reservations systems, law enforcement intelligence systems, patient hospital records, savings and loan deposit accounting, and stock market information.

Such systems focus on the on-line real-time concept. All data are *on-line*, that is, all data are sent directly to a computer system as soon as they come into being. The whole operation is in *real time*, which means that data are processed and fed back to the appropriate source in sufficient time to change or control the operating environment. Basically, then, any system that processes and stores data or reports them as they are happening is considered to be an on-line real-time system. Company personnel will receive a response from the system in time to satisfy their own real-time environmental requirements. The response time may range from a fraction of a second to minutes, hours, or days, depending on the attendant circumstances.

The integrated data accumulated from the many detailed on-line transactions are commonly referred to as the database elements or the organization's database. In addition to having all data collected in one place, the same inventory database, for example, may be used by a number of departments, such as manufacturing, production planning and control, inventory control, purchasing, and accounting. In another example, a database element is an employee skill number that can assist in preparing weekly payroll, referencing personnel records, filling new job openings, preparing contract negotiations, and the like. A database, then, contains elements or data bits in a common storage medium that form the foundation for operational information although a database may be physically dispersed. Because designing a structured database for accommodating the various levels of management is a formidable task, real-time MIS satisfies the needs of lower and middle management for organizing, directing, and controlling activities around the established plans, being in conformance with the organization's objectives. Although real-time MIS does respond to the managerial needs of the first two levels and does provide immediate feedback on present operations, it falls short of the information desired by top-level executives.[2] As will be seen shortly, this is not the case with decision-support systems.

Distributed MIS

Distributed MIS, commonly referred to as *distributed data processing* (DDP), is one of the major thrusts in current management information systems. These systems represent a decentralized approach to placing low-cost computing power, starting at the various points of data entry, and linking these points, where deemed necessary, with a centralized computer via a distributed communications network. Like the previous systems, their essential focus is on transactional processing of business activities at the lower level of operations while also supplying appropriate managerial information. In effect, distributed data processing is an approach to placing computing power where it is needed in an organization for efficient and economical data-processing operations. Similarly, it is a feasible alternative to centralized data processing due to the declining costs of programmable terminals, microcomputers, minicomputers, and small business computers. Because the focus of current distributed data-processing systems is placing power at the lower levels in an organization, their output generally centers on assisting lower and middle management.

An integral part of a distributed processing system is the use of data-communications equipment from the remote processors to the central-computer facility. The system allows a number of small computers to be combined to form an operational data center at more than one location. A network of these centers sharing computerized files provides a powerful data-processing capability at local and regional levels. The system provides on-line data entry to the local and regional databases for concurrent processing of multiple independent jobs. An operational data center performs the required MIS requirements of the remote site while it maintains concurrent high-speed communication with the central computer and other data centers in the network. It permits the development of network applications that can be solved by the existing MIS staff where the accent is on simplicity of operations. The system provides for generating reports within the network that give operational management control over their operations as well as for generating summary information for higher levels of management. Various network configurations can be developed by connecting network elements through communication lines. The attendant circumstances must be surveyed for the proper DDP network. In addition, to overcome objections to a large, centralized database, MIS strategists came up with the idea of *distributed databases* whereby the user's files are placed at or near the point where transactions occur. This way, the user's data are always available; the concern about data communications failures is no longer necessary.[3]

Shortcomings of Past and Current MIS for Decision Makers

As noted in the above discussion, management information systems center on producing periodic reports designed not only to recap past operations with an accent on exception items, but also to pinpoint possible control problems about current and upcoming operations for lower and middle management. Although these factors represent improvements over prior information systems, they can be viewed from a *two-dimensional* framework, that is, the computer gives a periodic answer that is indicative of what should have been done or what should be done to control operations. However, in this fast-changing world, there is a need to bring in a *third-dimensional* viewpoint, namely, that of the decision maker, who brings personal judgment, expertise, and the like to bear on the whole process of the problem. From this broadened perspective, the manager is able to get a macro view of the problem. Whereas prior MIS focuses on structured problem solving, decision-support systems extend the range of problem structure to include semistructured and unstructured problems.

CONTINUING DEVELOPMENTS IN MANAGEMENT INFORMATION SYSTEMS

Because the preceding systems are rather narrow in their perspective (two-dimensional framework), there is a need for a much broader perspective (three-dimensional framework) as found in decision-support systems (DSSs). DSS allows managers and their staffs to be at the center of the decision-making process as changes occur through the use of computer-query capabilities to obtain requested information. This is in contrast to relying on periodic-control reports, for the most part, as found in previous MIS. In the discussion to follow, decision-support systems are viewed from an individual and a group perspective as well as their tie-in with executive-information systems (EISs). It should be noted that on-line analytical processing systems are considered to be an extension of DSS and EIS. This comment should be evident in the material found throughout the text.

From a slightly different perspective, the range of management information systems can be extended to include multimedia systems, electronic-data-interchange (EDI) systems, image-processing systems, idea-processing systems, expert systems, and neural networks. All of these systems are covered separately below, along with a separate section on virtual-reality systems. Many other types of information systems could have been covered. These could have included voice-recognition systems, geographic-information systems, fuzzy systems, and chaotic systems. Also, newer systems that are currently being developed in academic research labs as well as in the business world could have been included. Space limitations narrow the range of materials presented below.

Decision-Support Systems

Essentially, an individually oriented *decision-support system* is designed to satisfy the needs of a manager at any level in a distributed data-processing environment. The system is designed to support the problem-finding (future problems related to the present) and problem-solving decisions of the manager. It incorporates features found in management information systems and in quantitative models of management science. Such a system emphasizes direct support for the manager in order to enhance the professional judgments required in making decisions, especially when the problem structures tend to be semistructured and unstructured. The use of interactive systems and CRT displays in a decision-support system are examples of this point. Emphasis is placed on helping the manager to make decisions by being at the center of the decision-making process rather than on actually making decisions for the manager. This interplay results in a total effort that is greater than the manager or computer operating independently (as in traditional MIS), thereby providing *synergistic decision making*. Also, information is presented in a useful form rather than as a mass of all information that might be useful. From this perspective, an individually oriented decision-support system builds on present management information systems as well as complements them.[4]

Since there is a move toward *group decision-support systems* (GDSS), there is a need to define such an approach. Fundamentally, group decision-support systems combine computers, data communications, and decision technologies to support problem finding and problem solving for managers and their staffs, which may also include operating personnel in the newer work environments. Technological advancements, such as electronic boardrooms, local area networks, teleconferencing, and decision-support software, have spurred an interest in this area. In addition, fundamental changes in the external environment of organizations are encouraging organizations to head in this direction. Typically, organizations currently are experiencing the emergence of a post-industrial environment characterized by greater knowledge, complexity, and turbulence. One important effect of this trend is that decision-related meetings are becoming more frequent and more important. At the same time, the decisions confronting groups are becoming more complex and must be made more quickly and with greater participation than in the past. As part of the transition into this new environment, organizations are exploring advanced-information technologies which might be employed in group meetings. Overall, group DSS has the capability to allow marketing executives, for example, to outmaneuver their competition and assist in resolving issues that center on making employees more productive.[5]

Executive Information Systems

To a degree, an extension of DSS is *executive information systems*. EIS is used mostly for highly structured reporting, sometimes referred to as status access. DSS has become almost synonymous with modeling and unstructured, ad hoc querying. Executive-information systems are aimed at senior executives who currently have few, if any, computer-based systems to assist them in their day-to-day responsibilities. EIS brings together relevant data from various internal and external sources, delivering important information quickly and in a useful way. More important, it filters, compresses, and tracks critical data as determined by each executive end user. EIS performs the conceptually simple task of informing senior executives on matters relevant to their organizational responsibilities. Unlike traditional MIS functions that focus on the storage of large amounts of information, EIS focuses on the retrieval of specific information and on status access. The emphasis is on reducing the time and effort that the executive user must expend to obtain useful information for making the organization more competitive and its employees more productive.

An executive information system can be defined in its broadest sense as one that deals with all of the information that helps an executive make strategic and competitive decisions, keeps track of the overall business and its functional units, and cuts down on the time spent on routine tasks performed by an executive. As such, an EIS is capable of providing an executive with the right information in the right format, fast enough to enable the individual to make the right decisions.[6]

Multimedia Systems

Another latest direction in leveraging information technology is *multimedia systems* that are networked. Making a video call from a PC is as easy as making a phone call. The purpose of meeting face to face on a video screen is to share work and information interactively. In this collaborative computing mode, there can be distributed meetings with co-workers and customers or vendors. Participants interact using the same documents while seeing each other on PCs. From another perspective, on-demand, stored video can be used in many different applications and environments. Video workstations located on the manufacturing floor can help workers get video reference information for complex operations. Multimedia information will help office workers receive "just-in-time" training at their desktops, that is, when it is most convenient and timely. Distributing training on the desktop will increase productivity by giving access to material without waiting for scheduled classes, and it will save travel costs. Organization communications can improve by distributing sales and business video information to employees at their desktops.

Other digital video applications promise to improve computer-based education and collaboration among medical workers. Advertising will take on a whole new look as advertisers will be able to tailor messages to specific people at the point of sale. Information video kiosks will be used in many different environments, from business to consumer applications. Travel agencies will use on-line video to show vacation spots or hotels. On-demand movies delivered to the home are possible with video-capable networks and end-user devices.

To be useful, there is a need for video applications to be networked. Only recently has networking video become practical. Networks are important because of the characteristics of multimedia data, especially the audio and video components. Multimedia has huge storage requirements relative to other kinds of data, which is a limiting factor for installation at every desktop. Most multimedia applications support work group or organization-wide activities, requiring access by many simultaneous users. In addition, future applications such as desktop videoconferencing will mandate networked solutions. Thus, networked multmedia may well prove to be an important means to leverage information technology for a company's customers, vendors, and its employees.[7]

Electronic-Data-Interchange Systems

Electronic-data-interchange systems represent the exchange of documents and transactions by a computer in one company with the computer(s) of one or more companies in an open-system environment. Prior to EDI, the data flow focused on paper documents. The paper documents, for example, were mailed by the buyer to the seller, and the seller moved the paper documents to the proper departments for appropriate processing. In turn, the buyer undertook the necessary processing as well as the receipt of the goods. In contrast, the application of EDI involves the conversion of a written document into a machine readable form so that a computer in one company can communicate directly with the computer of another company. Generally, the bulk of these documents relate to events that would generate input transactions for accounting systems to be processed into information.

EDI transmissions go from application to application between buyers and sellers without human intervention. An EDI system is involved in electronically exchanging purchase orders, invoices, payments, shipping notices, and similar transactions. In the process, staffing needs are cut by reducing paper handling, reducing errors by eliminating the need to rekey data, and improving transaction turnaround time. The net result of utilizing an EDI system is a computerized exchange of business documents in a specific format between companies. Fundamentally, an EDI system can be defined as a computer-to-computer exchange of routine paper documents, such as purchase orders, material releases, or receipt advices, by one company with other companies. This computerized information is transmitted in a standard format between a company and other companies. In an EDI system, electronically transmitted data replaces paper documents throughout a company's transaction cycle.[8]

Image-Processing Systems

From another perspective, electronic processing can be viewed only from within the organization—called *image-processing systems*—whereby electronic imaging is used to replace paper-intensive information systems. From an overall standpoint, there is an advantage to automating existing business processes with image-processing systems. That is, the present method of paper processing is replaced by capturing all data initially in an electronic form. In turn, all subsequent processing refers to the same electronic images. Also, there is a need to go a step further. There is a need to find applications for image processing that transform the business.

Organizations that have faced up to the issue of their survival can be very innovative in changing their business culture. As an example, the Xerox Corporation revolutionized its own methods of designing and manufacturing copiers when extreme competitive pressures came from Canon. Company-wide integration and systems coordination is another key to improving customer service and guaranteeing success. Procter & Gamble pulled together under the umbrella of "product delivery" three separate functions that covered suppliers, manufacturers, and finished goods delivery. In effect, image-processing systems can be a competitive edge while also making its employees more productive.[9]

Idea-Processing Systems

Generally, *idea-processing systems* are considered to be related to decision-support systems. Some in the field consider them a subset of group DSS. No matter how idea-processing systems are looked upon, they are essentially systems designed to capture, evaluate, and synthesize individual ideas into a large context that have real meaning for problem solving. From this perspective, idea generators are generally used to assist in the idea-formulation stage. To better understand this type of system, it would be helpful to examine initially the meaning of ideas. An *idea* can be thought of as a formulated thought or opinion. Ideas spring from knowledge which is essentially derived from observation of the environment in which one lives, as well as from an awareness of one's internal emotions and feelings on these observations. Knowledge implies more than observations of past experience, but also includes some form of interpretation of past experience. Ideas can be thought of as the conscious expression of these interpretations. It should be noted that ideas are separate notions that a person is conscious of, but which may or may not be relevant to any specific purpose that has been predefined.

The basic stages of an idea-processing system center on *inputs* in the form of problem statement and observation about the problem. In turn, *processing* involves idea generation and evaluation of ideas for solving the problem. The end result is *outputs*, that is, report preparation and dissemination of information about specific ideas to solve the problem. Regarding idea generation, the behavioral sciences have not been able to explain how a person's mental process operates nor how a person's knowledge is organized. However, there is ongoing research by behavioral psychologists as well as by computer scientists who are attempting to imitate such functions on a computer. Needless to say, idea-processing systems are a natural way for helping management and their staffs in gaining competitive advantage and improving employee productivity.[10]

Expert Systems

An *expert system* arrives at intelligent solutions to user queries by using the rules contained in the system's knowledge base. A *knowledge base* consists of "if–then" rules, mathematical formulas, or some other knowledge representation structure to represent the knowledge of experts in a certain domain. The expert system scans through its knowledge base to find the appropriate rules, formulas, or some other knowledge structure to apply. Knowledge for such a system is extracted from human experts (i.e., domain experts) on the subject in which the expert system is expected to specialize. The knowledge in the form of rules is then stored in the expert system's knowledge base for use when needed.

Knowledge engineers who have been trained in the techniques of obtaining knowledge from domain experts procure the knowledge necessary to develop rules, formulas, or some other knowledge structure for the problem under study. In effect, knowledge engineers develop the expert system that is designed to parallel decisions made by recognized experts in a field by acquiring knowledge about the particular problem and applying appropriate rules. Once the rules are captured and programmed, a panel of domain experts reviews the program's recommendations in a series of test cases to verify the newly designed expert system.

For typical business applications, most often the knowledge is stored in the form of "if–then" statements known as rules. This collection of rules is interpreted by an *inference engine*. Fundamentally, an inference engine navigates through the knowledge base much like a human would reason through a problem. Each rule can have one or more statements in its "if" and "then" parts. If all the premises of the "if" part holds *true*, the conclusions reached by the expert system in the "then" parts are also *true* and the rule is said to "fire." Furthermore, the conclusion of a certain rule may exist as a premise of another rule that may itself "fire" and "ignite" other rules in succession, until a final conclusion is reached.

Basically, expert systems are designed to mimic the problem-solving abilities of experts in a particular domain. Because an expert system works roughly the way human experts do, it combines factual knowledge with rules that experience teaches, that is, heuristics, and then makes inferences about the situation at hand, whether that means diagnosing the financial portfolio of a client or the cost of a new product. In light of these facts, an expert system can be defined as a computer program that embodies the expertise in a specific domain that would otherwise be available only from a human expert. It represents a codification of the knowledge and reasoning used by human experts. Once operational, it can be copied and distributed at little marginal cost to assist users whether they are experts or inexperienced personnel. From this perspective, expert systems can assist company employees in being more productive when assisting users whether they are inside or outside the organization.[11]

Neural Networks

Since an expert system contains expertise in the form of a knowledge base, the system goes through its knowledge base and picks out the most appropriate response. The real problem is that if a person queries the expert system about something outside of its knowledge domain, it cannot respond. This is where *neural networks* come into play. The key distinction between expert systems and neural networks is that neural nets do not involve specific recordings or transcriptions of someone else's thinking. Neural networks can learn from experience. Neural networks can be used in medical testing and financial applications, such as seeing patterns in stock price changes.

Neural networks supposedly imitate the way actual neurons operate in a human's brain. The brain contains 100 billion or so neurons. Axons carry a signal away from the neuron and dendrites carry the signal toward another neuron; synapses are where nervous impulses pass between neurons. Individual neurons thereby reach out to 10,000 or so other neurons. Related to the number of neurons is another item, that is, the connections per second that a neural net can make. Hardware vendors, such as Intel, are starting to show off specialized chips that increase the number of connections per second between these neurons. Intel, in fact, is claiming something like a billion-plus connections per second. Even with this increase in processing speed, neural nets still have a long way to go before they truly imitate the human brain. However, they can be useful in gaining a competitive advantage and in improving employee productivity.[12]

RELATIONSHIP OF OLAP WITH PRIOR MIS

To assist in tying together some of the information systems set forth previously for managers and their staffs, reference is made to decision-support systems and executive-information systems along with electronic spreadsheets. In turn, these approaches to information systems are related to on-line analytical processing systems. As illustrated in Figure 1.3, the typical manager is concerned with the visualization of important facts about his or her operations.

Figure 1.3

The Relationship of OLAP Systems with Prior Information Systems

	Decision-Support System	OLAP (Using Data Warehousing)
High	Merchandise Mix	Consumer Segmentation
	Market Share	Category Management
Complexity	Product Profitability	Supplier Management
	Spreadsheets	Executive-Information System
Low	Budgeting	Key-Performance Factors
	Financial Reporting	Variance Analysis
	Forecasting	Flash Reporting

Ad-Hoc   Visualization   Structured Reporting

Where visualization of operations is ad hoc for items of *low* complexity, spreadsheets are a natural for budgeting, financial reporting, and forecasting. In contrast, for items of *high* complexity where the focus is on merchandise mix (per extensive market research), market share (per marketing analysis), and product profitability (such as using venture analysis), decision-support systems can handle most situations. On the other hand, where there is a need for visualization in terms of structured reporting for items of *low* complexity, key-performance factors, variance analysis, and flash reporting are normally provided by executive-information systems. Where there is structured reporting for items of *high* complexity relating to consumer segmentation, category management, and supplier management, OLAP systems are useful for typical managers and their staffs. As such, data warehousing comes into play. From this figure, each type of information processing has its specific processing mode. For effective on-line analytical processing, the accent is on high-end computing for structured reports that tend to be complex.

GOING BEYOND OLAP—VIRTUAL-REALITY SYSTEMS

Although OLAP systems have their roots in prior information systems, this does not mean that the capability of such information technology needs to end at this point. Rather, there is a migration to something that makes the output from OLAP more meaningful and interesting to its users, namely, virtual reality (VR). The transition to this "New Age of Computing" must be carefully managed if it is to benefit the typical company. This new era will bring new levels of involvement by users, increased flexibility in their analyses, and unprecedented amounts of information to users. If the transition is not properly managed, this new era will result in a widening gap between those empowered with information technology and those without. In addition, wireless technology will play an important role in this new era, providing users with more mobility. The integration of OLAP with VR has the capability to help users think from a different perspective to enhance their decision-making skills.

Experience Via VR What OLAP Systems Display

One way to experience what OLAP systems display is to enter virtual worlds. In a virtual-reality experience, sophisticated interactive computer programs, written in Forth, C, and Pascal, put a person inside a world of computer graphics. This allows the person to treat system-generated objects almost as if they were real things. The person interacts with the environment using special clothing and fiber-optic sensors that interpret body positions as computer commands. In theory, the person can create a world limited only by his or her imagination and programming capabilities.

Computer scientists are looking into ways to use what they call "augmented" or "see through" reality. Workers would wear clear goggles with 3-D images reflected onto the lenses. The goggles would superimpose a virtual image of the desired result on a real object, so that workers would know what to do with the object without consulting manuals or blueprints. For example, an assembler inside a fuselage would see the real operations for hydraulic ducts or communications cables with a virtual image of the installed ducts or cables superimposed on them. The goggles could also reflect schematic and wiring diagrams, location of drill holes, and other information.

In a manager's world, virtual reality provides the capability to experience what the on-line processing system displays. For example, a sales manager could fly over a simulated landscape of sales by specific areas in terms of sales dollars and time periods (past year versus budgeted year). The color *red* could be used to indicate where sales efforts have been and will be lagging, and the color *green* could indicate increased sales. Also, the color *yellow* could be used to indicate that sales have changed less than 5 percent from their budgeted amounts. The end result is better quality analysis in less time. Some virtual reality experts predict that VR will eventually have an impact as great as the invention of writing. If they are wrong, it will not be for any want of ambition or confidence among pioneers in the field. The major drawbacks are the ability to write complex software programs and the speed of light, that is, the limitations of the physical world.[13]

SUMMARY

Initially, the chapter focused on the need for on-line analytical processing systems in an ever-changing business environment, followed by a discussion on information as a sixth information resource and its tie-in with knowledge. Next, the leveraging of information afforded by OLAP systems was discussed at some length. After an introduction to the essentials of on-line analytical processing systems was presented, it was defined along with potential obstacles to implementing OLAP systems. Different approaches to processing mission-critical applications were explored that have preceded OLAP systems. For the most part, previous information systems assisted managers first and provided accounting results second. Although this evolving development of information systems is still continuing as evidenced by virtual-reality systems for business, it should be recognized that OLAP systems are not the end state, but yet another stage in the ever-evolving state of information-systems technology.

NOTES

1. Lee Thé, "OLAP Answers Tough Business Questions," *Datamation*, May 1, 1995, p. 65.

2. Robert J. Thierauf, *Systems Analysis and Design of Real-Time Management Information Systems* (Englewood Cliffs, N.J.: Prentice-Hall, 1975).

3. Robert J. Thierauf, *Distributed Processing Systems* (Englewood Cliffs, N.J.: Prentice-Hall, 1978).

4. Robert J. Thierauf, *Decision Support Systems for Effective Planning and Control: A Case Study Approach* (Englewood Cliffs, N.J.: Prentice-Hall, 1982); and *User-Oriented Decision Support Systems: Accent on Problem Finding* (Englewood Cliffs, N.J.: Prentice-Hall, 1988).

5. Robert J. Thierauf, *Group Decision Support Systems for Effective Decision Making: A Guide for MIS Professionals and End Users* (Westport, Conn.: Quorum Books, 1989).

6. Robert J. Thierauf, *Executive Information Systems: A Guide for Senior Management and MIS Professionals* (Westport, Conn.: Quorum Books, 1991).

7. Jim Long and Barbara M. Baker, "Distributed Computing," *Network Computing*, November 1, 1992, pp. 22–26.

8. Robert J. Thierauf, *Electronic Data Interchange in Finance and Accounting* (Westport, Conn.: Quorum Books, 1990).

9. Robert J. Thierauf, *Image Processing Systems for Business: A Guide for MIS Professionals and End Users* (Westport, Conn.: Quorum Books, 1992).

10. Robert J, Thierauf, *Creative Computer Software for Strategic Thinking and Decision Making: A Guide for Senior Management and MIS Professionals* (Westport, Conn.: Quorum Books, 1993).

11. Robert J. Thierauf, *Expert Systems in Finance and Accounting* (Westport, Conn.: Quorum Books, 1990).

12. Franco Vitaliano, "Expert Systems and Neural Networks," *Digital Review*, June 10, 1991, p. 15.

13. Robert J. Thierauf, *Virtual Reality Systems for Business* (Westport, Conn.: Quorum Books, 1995).

2

Decision Making in an OLAP Environment

ISSUES EXPLORED

- What is the relationship of OLAP systems to improving a decision maker's *effectiveness*?
- What types of problems can be solved within the decision-making process?
- How can multidimensional analysis be utilized within a planning and control framework?
- What is the difference between the problem-solving process and the problem-finding process?
- How useful is problem finding within an OLAP-operating mode?

OUTLINE

OLAP Systems Help Improve a Decision Maker's Effectiveness
    Accent on "Information Focus"
    Need for Synergistic Interaction
Types of Problems to Be Solved
    Well-Structured Problems
    Semistructured Problems
    Unstructured Problems
Planning and Control Framework for Problems to Be Solved
    Continuum Within a Planning and Control Framework
    Multidimensional Analysis Within a Planning and Control Framework

OLAP SYSTEMS HELP IMPROVE A DECISION MAKER'S EFFECTIVENESS

Because decision making is the process of evaluating, selecting, and inititating courses of action, managers at the highest level make decisions in establishing objectives. Similarly, managers from the highest level to the lowest level make planning, organizing, directing, and controlling decisions. Decision making then is at the center of the functions comprising the entire management process. With this in mind, the fundamentals of decision making that involve solving all types of problems are investigated, along with a planning and control framework for problems to be solved. Additionally, in this chapter, problem-solving and problem-finding processes are explored as a means of assisting managers in resolving their problems and identifying future opportunities.

In the past, decision making focused on information systems that provided routine, structured, and periodic reports where standard operating procedures, decision rules, and information flows were predefined. By reducing costs, turnaround time, and so forth, as well as replacing clerical personnel, the main payoff from information systems has been improved *operational efficiency*. The relevance for managerial decision making has mainly been indirect, that is, periodic reports and access to data as contained in a centralized or decentralized database have been provided. Rather than attempt to go back and rework past information systems, organizations are finding that it is less costly and time consuming to design and implement newer information systems, like OLAP systems, for supporting specific decision processes. Managers and computers operate interactively to produce higher quality decisions.

From this perspective, the main thrust of on-line analytical processing is on decisions in which there is sufficient structure for the computer and appropriate models to be of value but where the manager's judgment is essential. OLAP extends the range and capability of the manager's decision processes to provide *operational effectiveness*. The relevance for managers is that OLAP systems do not attempt to redefine objectives, automate the decision process, or impose solutions directly. But rather, managers employ the computer's capabilities as an extension of their minds. In past information systems, the accent was on information that had been retrieved, analyzed, interpreted, and presented on a selected basis intended to foster the making of a decision. Basically, on-line analytical processing systems allow a much broader approach to decision making by using multidimensional analysis than is possible with past information systems.

Accent on "Information Focus"

To assist managers and their staffs in operational effectiveness, there is a need to have an "information focus" in order to make the best business decisions possible. Decision makers do not have the time to study a problem exhaustively or to be paralyzed by a tidal wave of data. An information focus, however, gives decision makers the specific information they need to make better decisions. Today, most business decisions center on an initial decision and ongoing reviews to determine whether the decision should be fine-tuned or possibly reversed. Each aspect requires different information. The more specifically each of them can be defined, the better will be the end result.

For example, a company's objective is to expand sales by adding a new product line. To meet this objective, decision makers have to decide, among other things, which products to add, how to structure the sales force to market the products effectively, and what distribution channels to use. Initially, they will need to know who will be buying the new products, what features the buyers are looking for, how much they cost, how the products will be priced, the size of the potential market, what the company's share of that market might be, and the sales volume that can be expected. To evaluate these decisions on an operating basis, unit sales volume and profitability figures can be compared with the initial plan on a frequent basis (say, weekly and monthly). On the other hand, decisions about target market and distribution can be assessed on a less frequent basis (say, semiannually or annually). To assist in this periodic evaluation, an OLAP system is designed to provide appropriate multidimensional analysis for decision makers.

Need for Synergistic Interaction

Because the manager's hunches, intuition, and judgment are critical in the decision-making process, an OLAP system is able to combine the computer and the managers' minds in the production of meaningful information to support their decisions. The synergistic interaction of the human aspects with the machine aspects results in more meaningful information to support the decision-making process than each operating alone. Such an approach is taken by Digital Equipment Corporation's new advanced technology group which focuses on identifying new technologies, new products, new business ideas, and new ways to get them started.[1]

In a synergistic-interactive OLAP environment, managers and their support staff can use computer output in conjunction with their judgmental abilities to change strategic, tactical, and operating plans more rapidly in order to have more cost-effective resources. They combine information and judgment for planning and decision making rather than limiting it to the areas of control for which information, by itself, has been most widely used in the past. Similarly, they can use information and judgment to evaluate performance and the organization's responsiveness to its growing and varied constituencies, to complement the profitability measurements. Finally, they can use both for tracking product and service performance on a longer-term basis. Essentially, an on-line analytical processing system can be a unifying bond that allows the company's managers to use effectively the resources at their disposal.

Closely related to this synergistic interaction is the use of color graphics to provide answers. In an OLAP environment, graphic displays allow decision makers to distill quickly the essence of large amounts of business data and reduce greatly the mass of financial reports and other paperwork they face. An effective multidimensional-graphics system can condense reams of printout into a few readily understandable graphs and charts. It is a way of sorting out meaningful information in a user-machine interface such that managers and their staffs retain control throughout the decision-making process.

Generally, "at a glance" multidimensional-graphic presentations of information allow managers and their staffs to start their thinking processes quickly. (The usual method—also the slower method—involves a lot of reading.) A "picture" may tell them immediately what they want to know. Information in this visual aid might otherwise be buried in stacks of computer-generated reports. From another viewpoint, managers and their staffs may view multidimensional analysis on a display screen and also employ a paper printout of the data to ponder later, as in problem finding (discussed later in the chapter). Based on either perspective, computer-generated multidimensional analysis is very effective for supporting decision making in an OLAP environment.

TYPES OF PROBLEMS TO BE SOLVED

Typically, an OLAP system tends to focus on solving well-structured problems. In certain situations, an OLAP system is capable of resolving semistructured and unstructured problems. The environment in which a problem exists determines its type and not whether the approach to decision making is to be on an individual or a group basis. In terms of the essential nature of problems to be solved, they are discussed below.

Well-Structured Problems

A problem is said to be *well-structured* if all of its elements can be identified and quantified in order to determine an answer. Typically, the time frame is of short duration, say, up to one year. For example, in a production allocation problem, the time available this month and next month on the first and second shifts as well as the costs to produce the products in the manufacturing departments can be identified. Also, the level of production is known based upon the forecasted sales for these months. Thus, the problem is well defined and can be solved within the parameters set forth using a quantitative approach to decision making.

Since the problem is fully structured, a computer approach is generally desirable because an appropriate mathematical or statistical model can be employed to reach a good solution. The model may well be a simple, straightforward rule or procedure or a very complex, computerized mathematical model. The approach is not as important a criterion as the ability to identify all the important parameters surrounding the problem.

Semistructured Problems

A problem is said to be *semistructured* if it contains both well-structured and unstructured elements. The time frame can range from the short run to the long run. For example, an investment problem is considered to be semistructured. From one viewpoint, a systematic search through data on portfolios and securities is required; this can be effected through retrieval, reports, and display via a CRT terminal using mathematical and statistical analytic models. At the same time, the criteria for making investments for a specific portfolio need to be left to the manager's judgment. Thus, output from the computer is combined with the portfolio manager's judgment to select appropriate securities to solve the investment problem.

Because the semistructured problem makes use of both computer decision making and human judgment, the user-machine interface is just as important as the quantitative model used. Failure to use this combined manager and computerized-model approach will generally result in reaching less favorable decisions.

Figure 2.1
The Relationship of Top-, Middle-, and Lower-Level Managers to Types of Problems (Well-Structured, Semistructured, and Unstructured)

Managerial Level	Types of Problems
	Well-Structured Problems:
Top-level manager	Manufacturing facilities problems
Middle-level manager	Budget problems
Lower-level manager	Production problems
	Semistructured Problems:
Top-level manager	Merger problems
Middle-level manager	Sales forecasting problems
Lower-level manager	Purchasing problems
	Unstructured Problems:
Top-level manager	Future anticipated new product problems
Middle-level manager	Motivational problems
Lower-level manager	Group behavior problems

Unstructured Problems

If the significant parameters of the problem cannot be identified precisely, it is said to be *unstructured*, since human intuition and judgment are generally needed to reach a decision. Typically, the rationale for the inability to identify specific parameters in the problem is that the time frame is too long, say, beyond five years. As an example, consider the problem of determining a company's personnel needs ten years hence. Because there are a large number of unknowns relating to sales and production, the net result is that the appropriate level of personnel to support these areas is also unknown. In effect, the parameters of the problem are too loosely defined to solve it with a high degree of accuracy.

If the problem is unstructured from the perspective of the executive, computerized mathematical or statistical models are generally inappropriate. To reach a decision, there is a need for meaningful experience, know-how, intuition, judgment, and past experience. This may mean taking a qualitative approach to decision making. However, *rules of thumb* (i.e., heuristic methods) may be appropriate to resolve unstructured problems. This may require resorting to hypotheses, evaluations, educated guesses, and the like. Essentially, it is problem solving under uncertainty. The attendant circumstances must be surveyed to determine whether or not heuristic methods are appropriate for solving unstructured problems.

Typical examples of well-structured, semistructured, and unstructured problems found at various managerial levels are given in Figure 2.1. Numerous other examples of these three problem types appear later in the text, that is, Part III. Also, they are related to creativity and managerial decision making.

PLANNING AND CONTROL FRAMEWORK FOR PROBLEMS TO BE SOLVED

Management activities and, in turn, decisions can be segregated into three categories: those that related to top, middle, and lower management. Decision making at these levels has varying degrees of futurity. Top management decisions involve longer time periods than those made at the lower- and middle-management levels. According to Robert Anthony, managerial activities fall into three categories:[2]

- *strategic planning*—the development of an organization's overall goals and methods for achieving them
- *management control*—the process of assuring that the organization's goals are being accomplished effectively and efficiently
- *operational control*—the process of assuring that specific tasks are being accomplished effectively and efficiently.

These three categories of managerial activities can be thought of as corresponding to activities that take place at different levels in a typical organization.

Strategic planning in most organizations is carried out by top management, that is, top-level executives. For them, the system must provide information upon which strategic plans can be soundly based. For this task, external sources of information that center on economic conditions, technological developments, competitive reactions, and like matters assume paramount importance. This information does not have to possess the greatest accuracy since strategic plans are broad rather than detailed in nature, and because they require approximate indications of future trends rather than exact statements about the past or present. The typical time frame goes beyond one year and up to five years or more.

For *management control* activities, the sources of information come from both external and internal sources. Top-level executives, for example, would be concerned about the overall financial performance of their organizations. They will therefore need internal information on quarterly sales and profits as well as those relating to competitors—external sources. In a similar manner, middle managers, that is, middle-level executives, are concerned about current and future performance of their organization units. They will need external information on important matters that affect their units, such as problems with suppliers, sales declines, or increased demand for one or more products. In addition, middle-level managers need to know about plant costs and the periodic performance of their units—internal information. The typical time frame relates to the current year.

At the bottom of the executive hierarchy, lower management, that is, lower-level executives, is concerned with information about *operational control* activities so that day-to-day operation of specific departments can be controlled. A manufacturing supervisor has to know if material wastage is exceeding the standard, if costly overruns are in the making, and if the standard time allocated to a specific job has been exceeded. Similarly, a local sales manager wants to know the number of customer calls the sales staff has made for a specific day. Accuracy of detailed information is particularly important at this level for managerial activities, since lower-level managers may find it necessary to take on-the-spot action to rectify a bad situation. Essentially, the time frame for operational control relates to daily operations but also can be related to weekly or monthly operations.

Continuum Within a Planning and Control Framework

A thorough analysis of these types of managerial activities indicates that they overlap, thereby forming a continuum. For example, the information *sources* for operational control are based largely within the organization, whereas the information sources for strategic planning are based largely outside the organization. Sources for management control will be somewhat balanced between external and internal ones. The *scope* of information is narrow and well defined for operational control, very wide for strategic planning, and in between for management control. The *level of aggregation* is very detailed for operational control, moderately detailed for management control, and summarized for strategic planning. In terms of *time horizon*, operational control relies on historical information, strategic planning relies on futuristic type of information, and management control makes use of both historical and futuristic information. The other characteristics of information, including currency, required accuracy, and frequency of use, can be interpreted in a similar manner.

Multidimensional Analysis Within a Planning and Control Framework

The adoption of a planning and control framework is a desirable way to go for any organization. However, managing technology, systems, and even information resources is no longer enough. There is need for a typical company to go beyond what was the norm in the past. The focus is on viewing decision making from a different perspective, that is, using multidimensional analysis to get at the real facts surrounding decision making. A company's ability to make effective decisions depends on many factors, such as recognizing the most important issues and opportunities, and defining optimal goals. The company must choose and involve the right participants—both people and automated information systems—when making decisions. It has to use optimal processes to make decisions; and it has to use the right information whether from employees and internal information systems or from outside sources. Many times, this approach can be effectively accomplished using multidimensional analysis found in OLAP systems.

To utilize OLAP effectively within a planning and control framework, it is highly recommended that a creative approach be undertaken from the outset. Today, creativity includes the ability to uncover new relationships utilizing multidimensional analysis, to look at the results from new perspectives, and to ask questions based on one or more previous analyses. This creative analysis may result in new perspectives or answers not envisioned through conventional problem solving or problem finding. The tie-in of creativity with multidimensional analysis is that decision makers are better able to select, analyze, and resolve difficult problems facing them throughout the organization.

Similarly, decision makers can explore many new opportunities. For example, they can determine whether to opt for radically reengineered decision-making processes or instill continuous improvement in those processes. Whether problems or opportunities are the focus of attention, managers have a natural entrée using OLAP technology to help them achieve specific objectives in their decisions.

FORERUNNERS OF PROBLEM-SOLVING AND PROBLEM-FINDING PROCESSES

Before discussing the processes to solve and/or find problems that are the focus of decision making, it would be helpful at this time to take a look at their development over the centuries. One of the oldest models for resolving problems is the "dialectic model" that was formulated by the early Greek philosophers. It was employed to discern *truth* when solving all types of problems. The dialectic model thrived because of its simplicity, that is, it was easily understood and easily employed. It was followed centuries later by the "scientific method."

The Dialectic Model

Although considered very crude in terms of today's advances in problem solving, it consisted of three basic steps. First, the *thesis* was a basic premise, statement, or belief. The purpose of the dialectic model was to either confirm the veracity of the thesis or disprove it, and act accordingly based upon the outcome. A thesis would be formulated and then subjected to the antithesis. The *antithesis* was typically the converse of the thesis. It always supported an entirely contradictory approach, purely for the sake of argument. Formal presentations of a thesis and antithesis were a popular mental sport in Greek times when orators enjoyed a high art status. The first two steps often constituted formal debate for a group, but the method could be employed for an individual. In the third step, a *synthesis* or a new understanding was reached by subjecting a thesis to its antithesis. In actuality, it was a yielding of both sides to a middle ground which embraced more truth and less absolutism. Sometimes the synthesis would acually confirm wholeheartedly the original thesis, but this in part implies a weak antithesis.

By the advent of the Italian Renaissance, the dialectic model was waning and would soon yield to the forerunner of the modern scientific method. The dialectic model may have solved many business problems centuries ago, such as "Should we sail in search of Phoenician treasure?" but it has little practical application today. It is noteworthy in that it can be held up as the first formal exercise which was used for problem analysis.

Scientific Method

Another important problem-solving model that is currently enjoying widespread usage is the popular "scientific method." Essentially, this method is employed as the chief means for both scientific as well as non-scientific research. It is commonly used in research, surveying, sampling, and testing. Because it is a proven and rigorous model, it is useful for testing a hypothesis in controlled settings, with a baseline (control case) for comparison of the outcome.

The scientific method consists of five basic steps: (1) identifying the problem to be analyzed, (2) collecting facts which are pertinent to the problem, (3) selecting one or more tentative solutions, (4) evaluating all solutions to see which one fits all of the facts, and (5) selecting the optimal solution. This method, as utilized by Charles Darwin, had these underlying tenants: a natural explanation exists for all phenomena; a solution may be supported by evidence alone (not a hypothesis) and, wherever possible, substitute actual observations for logic. As will be seen in the discussion to follow, current decision support problem-solving approaches are actually variations of the traditional scientific method to solve clearly defined well-structured problems.

TWO APPROACHES TO THE PROBLEM-SOLVING PROCESS

In a survey of the literature currently in many disciplines, a large number of approaches to solving problems would be found. Rather than try to explore and compare most of them, two approaches that are germane to the problem-solving process will be examined. The first is the *quantitative-centered approach* which is oriented more toward solving well-structured problems facing managers and which is a variation of the scientific method. The accent is on using mathematical models that optimize performance (maximize profits, minimize costs, or some other criterion) for one or more functional areas of an organization. In contrast, the second is the *decision-centered approach* which is oriented toward solving semistructured and unstructured problems. The accent is on finding a limited number of acceptable solutions to the problem under study versus many solutions. In turn, the solution is selected from this small number.

Figure 2.2
A Comparison of Steps in the *Problem-Solving Process*—The Quantitative-Centered Approach and the Decision-Centered Approach

Basic Phases	Quantitative-Centered Approach	Decision-Centered Approach
Identification	Step 1 Observation - review the phenomena surrounding the problem	Step 1 Intelligence - search the environment for conditions that call for a decision
	Step 2 Definition of the Real Problem - state the root or real problem underlying the major difficulties	
Solution	Step 3 Development of Alternative Solutions - alternatives are based on factors affecting the problem	Step 2 Design - invent, develop, and analyze possible courses of action
	Step 4 Selection of Optimum Solution - best alternative is selected, based on a thorough analysis of feasible alternatives using experimentation If deemed necessary, sensitivity analysis is used.	Step 3 Choice - evaluate courses of action and select the best one If deemed necessary, sensitivity analysis is used.
Implementation	Step 5 Verification of Optimum Solution - implementation of the optimum solution in areas that are representative of the entire company	Step 4 Implementation - place the chosen solution into operation
	Step 6 Establishment of Proper Controls - controls are used to detect how changes affect the existing solution	Step 5 Control - monitor the outcome and make the necessary adjustments

Note: There is *Feedback* from the Last Step of Both Approaches to the First Step.

Quantitative-Centered Approach

The quantitative-centered approach to the problem-solving process is an extension of the scientific method mentioned in the previous section. The scientific method was originally formulated by Francis Bacon in the sixteenth century and elaborated by John Stuart Mill in the nineteenth century.[3] Its traditional steps have been altered to accommodate the ever-changing business environment, that is, the establishment of proper controls over the final solution. As shown in Figure 2.2, the approach consists of the following six steps.

1. *Observation.* In the first step, there is a thorough observation of the phenomena surrounding the problem—the facts, opinions, symptoms, and so on. Observation may be a casual glance or a concentrated, detailed, and lengthy study, depending on the requirements of the problem. Observation is used to identify problems. The capable manager is always alert and sensitive to the presence of problems. The individual must be certain that the basic or real problem has been identified, not just the symptoms of it.

2. *Definition of the Real Problem.* The real problem that is impeding the

accomplishment of one or more desired objectives is defined in the second step. To do so, the manager should gain a deeper understanding by discussing the matter with knowledgeable people. Because defining the real problem can be a difficult task, the manager must investigate as broadly as possible the factors surrounding the problem. A thorough analysis of all the factors in collaboration with the appropriate parties should lead to a definition of the real problem.

3. *Development of Alternative Solutions.* In the third step, alternative courses of action or tentative solutions to the real problem are developed. The alternative courses of action can take the form of quantitative models that can be developed to accommodate the real-world problem. They are generally computer-oriented for a final solution. As each model is developed, deficiencies may become apparent if the model's behavior is inconsistent with that of the modeled problem. Certain models that looked promising at the outset may have to be discarded. Instead of a half dozen models, the choice might be narrowed to one, two, or three candidates.

4. *Selection of Optimum Solution.* The fourth step centers on the alternative quantitative models or tentative solutions that remain when they are evaluated in order to select the optimum one. If one fits, a solution may be obtained by using one of the *standard* quantitative models. If the mathematical relationships of the model are too complex for the standard techniques, a *custom-made* quantitative model is required. Thus, the selection of the appropriate model using experimentation is dependent on the problem's nature and complexity. Where deemed appropriate, *sensitivity analysis* can be employed to select the optimum solution. Sensitivity analysis is a way of observing output changes while varying inputs to determine their relative impact on the optimum solution.

5. *Verification of Optimum Solution.* Verification involves most or all of the target population (as defined in statistics) for the fifth step. Implementation is necessary because reaction of competitors, consumer buying habits, and comparable factors observed in the limited sample during the development of alternative courses of action (and the selection of the optimum solution) may not hold true for the target population. To verify the optimum model or solution, it must be translated into a set of operating procedures capable of being understood and applied by the personnel who will be responsible for their use. Major or minor changes must be specified and implemented.

6. *Establishment of Proper Controls.* Once action has been recommended and implemented, and the results have been interpreted, the sixth and final step establishes controls over the solution. A solution remains an optimum one as long as the factors retain their original relationships. The solution goes out of control when the factors and/or more of the relationships change significantly. The importance of the change depends on the cost of changing the present solution versus the deviation under the changed conditions from the true optimum solution.

For effective control over the model (solution), it is necessary to establish a monitoring system, preferably as a part of an MIS. This will permit *feedback* to the various managers who are responsible and accountable. Continuous monitoring through feedback provides a means for modifying the solution as external and internal conditions and demands change over time. The foregoing steps are seldom, if ever, conducted in a particular order, since there is usually a constant interplay among the steps. However, they provide a conceptual framework for the quantitative-centered approach to problem solving.

Decision-Centered Approach

Based upon the quantitative-centered approach to the problem-solving process, managers try to choose the best or optimal alternative—one that balances the costs, benefits, and uncertainties best and is therefore most likely to achieve the most satisfactory results. Optimizing a decision means making the best one available to the organization at a given time. In practice, however, managers may lack important information affecting the decision, may be under pressure to act quickly and with apparent decisiveness, or may have overlooked alternatives in the early stages of the problem-solving process. These limitations restrict decision making and thereby result in *satisficing*. The word "satisficing" means finding and selecting a satisfactory alternative (as opposed to the best one) that achieves a minimally acceptable solution.[4] There is one word of caution: managers should not select the first satisfactory alternative developed but should take the opportunity and time to develop other good, feasible alternatives.

Included in satisficing is the concept of *bounded rationality*. That is, managers often make decisions without knowing all the alternatives available to them and their possible consequences, which means that there is a limit as to how logical or rational their decisions can be. In everyday organizational life, managers make the most logical decisions they can, limited by their inadequate information and by their ability to utilize this information, thereby resulting in bounded rationality.[5] Rather than make the best or ideal decision, managers more realistically settle for a decision that will "satisfice" rather than one that will "optimize."

This satisficing approach does not mean that managers should give up trying to make the best possible decisions. It simply means that they recognize that at some point it is too expensive, time-consuming, or difficult to acquire additional information or attempt to analyze it. For example, it is more practical for a finance manager to try to decide what must be done to earn an "acceptable" level of profits than to try to "maximize" potential profits.

In light of the realities of the business world, Herbert Simon's three steps of problem solving are set forth below,[6] including a fourth step he added later. One last step has been appended by the author for a more complete decision-centered approach to the problem-solving process.

1. *Intelligence.* The first step is concerned with searching the environment for conditions that call for a decision, that is, problem recognition. It is basically a data-gathering phase in which the manager seeks information to define the

problem more clearly and provide some input to the solution process. The manager assesses the extent of the problem and obtains data to be used in the design phase.

2. *Design.* The second step centers on inventing, developing, and analyzing possible courses of action. It involves manipulation of the data obtained to develop various alternative solutions to the problem. The manager's perception of the problem is used as the data are assembled and manipulated to provide input in the development of alternatives.

3. *Choice.* In this third step, the task is one of evaluating alternatives. This phase of the problem-solving process also requires selection of the best from among the alternatives developed in the design phase. The choice is generally made under a satisficing perspective versus one of optimization. Also, *sensitivity analysis* can be employed to select the best alternative.

4. *Implementation.* The fourth step puts the chosen solution into effect. The best alternative selected in the prior step is placed into operation for better or for worse. If a good alternative has been selected, the results should be favorable. If a poor alternative has been implemented, the results will generally be poor. This step parallels step 5 of the quantitative-centered approach.

5. *Control.* The fifth step is the monitoring of the outcome and making necessary adjustments. This last step links to the first step—intelligence—by recognizing that a new problem has arisen and needs to be solved. This step is like step 6 of the quantitative-centered approach.

These steps are summarized in Figure 2.2 and related to the quantitative-centered approach. As with that approach, the decision-centered approach provides for *feedback.*

Typical Applications of the Problem-Solving Process

The reader should have no difficulty in applying the *quantitative-centered approach* to well-structured problems since this approach is widely used. As one example, it is necessary to allocate production facilities to the company's products on a least-cost basis. This problem is solvable by utilizing a standard mathematical model called linear programming from the discipline of management science which allocates production resources on a lowest-cost basis first before moving on to a higher-cost basis. Another example is the problem of allocating a number of vehicles by size to shipments for a transportation company. This problem is solvable by the transportation model from management science which solves for the proper allocation of transportation vehicles to minimize total transportation costs. Essentially, these illustrations are for relatively well-structured problems. Because many of the problems solved for a typical company are not always well structured, managers must also be familiar with the decision-centered approach to problem solving.

The analysis of bad debts in the accounts receivable department is a good illustration of the *decision-centered approach.* Essentially, it consists of structured elements, that is, the experience of the firm in the past regarding bad debts; and it consists of unstructured elements, that is, what impact the expanding or contracting economy will have on the company's customers' ability to pay. Based upon the integration of both structured and unstructured elements utilizing the decision-centered approach, the amount of the reserve for bad debts can be determined. Another illustration is the determination of what investments should be offered to clients by an investment counselor. Because each client has different investment objectives, and information about investments is semistructured in nature, it is advisable for the investment counselor to use a decision-centered approach to assist in the selection of appropriate investment opportunities for his or her clients.

CREATIVITY UNDERLIES THE PROBLEM-FINDING PROCESS

In the problem-finding process below, the focus is initially on information useful in getting at a company's future problems and opportunities. But more importantly, the focus then shifts to explore ideas that can be useful to solve future problems studied as well as new ideas that can enhance further important opportunities for a company. This new point of view displaces the prior belief that more information will solve a company's problems. There was a time when information was indeed the limiting factor and more information made for better decisions. Generally, this is no longer the case, that is, ideas are the limiting factor today since detailed analysis does not necessarily yield new ideas. The manager's mind can only see what it is prepared to see. The manager needs to start ideas on his or her own. Hence, the current emphasis on problem solving, even to the extent that all thinking is called "problem solving" in American psychological usage, needs to be changed so that it emphasizes the manager's creativity in terms of developing new ideas. Such is the approach found in the problem-centered and opportunity-centered approaches presented below.

USEFUL PROBLEM-FINDING TECHNIQUES

To assist in problem finding, it is helpful to employ one or more techniques that can help identify problems and/or opportunities. Among those useful in problem finding are: (1) creative process, (2) brainstorming, (3) synectics, (4) accurate problem definition, and (5) idea generators. All of these are explored below. Some of these techniques can assist managers and their support staffs in getting around the need to be right all of the time, which can be a significant barrier to developing new ideas. Thus, it is better to have some new ideas which may prove to be wrong. Or, to state it another way, managers and their support staffs will always be right without having any new ideas at all.

Creative Process. Many models have been formulated that relate to the creative process for problem solving by a decision maker working alone. In turn, many of these models are useful in problem finding. An early descriptive model of the creative process useful to an individual thinker was formulated by Graham Wallas in 1926. This process appeared in his book, *Art of Thought*.[7] He specified four phases of the creative process: (1) preparation, (2) incubation. (3) illumination, and (4) verification.

In the *first* phase, preparation consists of gathering facts, knowledge, and information that may be applicable to some problem under study. This phase can include standard and nonstandard approaches and methods that can bring the decision maker to the point where new alternatives can be devised. Typically, the *second* and *third* phases of this creative process involve, respectively: first, a pause (incubation) in which some unconscious sifting, sorting, and/or relating of information gathered during the first phase takes place; followed by a sudden awareness or recognition of a new relationship that has importance to the decision maker (illumination). Essentially, incubation is related to the search and identification of ideas and/or problem solution alternatives at a subconscious level, which means that this stage can be seen as the actual creative process itself. The illumination stage is the conscious awareness of new ideas and/or solutions to the problem under study by the decision maker. Finally, in the *fourth* phase, the insight gained from the illumination stage is tested and seen to be viable and acceptable or is not acceptable, or reworked until the insight becomes acceptable. In essence, the decision maker relates the initial notion to other concepts and places it into some logical context. The decision maker imposes closure, that is, accepting or rejecting the validity of the idea and/or solution for the problem under study.

Overall, the Wallas model provides a useful framework for describing what happens during the creative process for generating new ideas or solving problems. Also, this framework may be helpful not only to a decision maker working alone, but also helpful to a group of decision makers working together. As noted previously, this model (like other models to be presented in this chapter) do not prescribe how the creative-thinking process actually works.

Brainstorming. Probably the best known creativity technique is brainstorming, which was developed by Alex F. Osborn (confounder of BBD&O) to help solve advertising problems. It is used to improve problem analysis by providing more possible solutions and unusual approaches to the problem under study. A typical brainstorming group consists of six to twelve individuals who assemble to search for solutions to a problem. Most brainstorming experts recommend that the group members have a variety of backgrounds in order to facilitate the analysis of the problem from different points of view. Also, sessions lasting for about an hour are most effective.

Osborn suggests four rules necessary for the utilization of brainstorming. (1) Judgment is withheld; ideas may be criticized and evaluated later. (2) Wild ideas are encouraged; ideas are easier to modify than to originate. (3) Numerous ideas are desired; more ideas increase the possibility of obtaining an excellent idea. (4) The participants are encouraged to utilize the ideas of others to develop additional ideas. Other recommended procedures include: the sessions should be recorded because some ideas may be missed during a meeting; the problem must be manageable, even if it requires breaking large problems into smaller parts; and samples should be available if products are being discussed.

Based upon the foregoing rules, the following guidelines should be observed to provide the proper environment for a brainstorming session.

- Do not attempt to generate new ideas and to judge them at the same time.
- Do try to generate a large quantity of possible solutions.
- Seek a wide variety of solutions by using different approaches to the problem.
- Listen carefully to the input of the others as an opportunity to "hitchhike" onto an idea or ideas, as a combination or improvement.
- During the session, no idea, even the most seemingly impractical, should be discarded.
- "Ridiculous" is an unheard of word in brainstorming. It is both impolite and disastrous to the creative process.
- Before concluding the brainstorming exercise, some time should be allowed for *sub-conscious* thought about the problem, while *consciously* discussing other possible solutions. This incubation period can be extended to any appropriate time period—recycling and reorbiting as necessary.
- Recycling and backtracking are useful to a degree, but there should be an attempt to "lean" forward since this is where the solutions are to be found.

After the brainstorming session, the ground rules change radically, that is, the freewheeling, noncritical session ends. Now it is time to apply judgment to the flights of fancy. After brainstorming, the group must set up the criteria for evaluation. Then, all the ideas are evaluated based upon the criteria, and the best two or three possible solutions are chosen. An efficient way to begin the evaluation process is to scan the written list and group all ideas that are the same or, at least, very similar. Also, each group is considered as one idea.

Now that constructive criticism is being applied, there may be a need to modify any idea in order to make it more closely meet the desired criteria. In this way, a seemingly wild notion can be transformed into a workable solution. No problem-solving process is complete until the most promising solutions are placed into action. So, after working through the entire list of ideas, two or three solutions are selected that meet all or most of the desired criteria. The group may spend as much time on explaining and implementing the solutions as they did on their development. The final step is to evaluate regularly and revise the various solutions until one actually alleviates the problem.

After Alex Osborn devised brainstorming, one of his associates observed that when a group really gets going in a brainstorming session, a spark from one mind will light up a lot of important ideas in the others, just like a string of firecrackers. The manager and his or her group who seek a reputation for problem solving may find brainstorming to be a sure-fire way of reaching that goal.

Taking a fresh look by an uninhibited and unrestricted free assocation by group members can help solve problems where the proposed solutions are different from the existing ones.

Synectics. Although not as well known as brainstorming, synectics is based on the assumption that creativity can be described and taught. Its purpose is to improve the quality of creative output from those assigned to a synectics team. The people selected to participate determine the group's success. For this reason, team members are chosen only after very thorough testing and screening in order to ensure selection of the best combination needed to solve the problems of a specific company. The selection process results in a tailor-made synectics team composed of individuals best equipped, intellectually and psychologically, to deal with problems unique to their company. After selection, members are assigned to the synectics team and begin studying the creative process and learning the ways of synectics. A synectics team solves problems for the entire company, similar to operations research (management science) or systems analyst groups, and must be fully integrated into the company. For more detailed information on synectics, reference can be made to a book by W. Gordon.[8]

Essentially, the synectic process involves two steps: (1) making the strange familiar and (2) making the familiar strange. The first step requires that the problem be understood and that the ramifications be considered. The mind tends to emphasize one's own experiences and to force strange ideas into an acceptable pattern. Thus, it is necessary to reorient these strange ideas into familiar ones. The second step, making the familiar strange, involves distorting, inverting, and transposing the problem in an attempt to view the problem from an unfamiliar perspective.

To assist in viewing the problem from different angles (making the familiar strange), synectics uses the following mechanisms.

- *Personal analogy*—Members of the group try to identify, metaphorically, with elements of the problem. For example, when a synectics group attempted to develop a new constant-speed mechanism, each member of the group metaphorically entered the box and, using his or her body, tried to effect the speed consistency required. This eventually resulted in an efficient and economical model.

- *Direct analogy*—Parallel facts are compared. Bell used direct analogy by studying the human ear when he invented the telephone. Biology is an excellent source for direct analogies.

- *Symbolic analogy*—Objective and impersonal images are used to describe the problem. In one case, symbolic analogy was used in developing a jack to move heavy objects, such as houses or freight. The synectics group was making little progress until a member made a symbolic analogy with the Indian rope trick. This analogy proved to be the key and resulted in an innovative jacking mechanism.

- *Fantasy analogy*—Fantasies are used to solve the problem. For example, a vapor-proof closure for a space suit was developed using a fantasy analogy of little insects closing the opening. This analogy led to the development of a complex spring mechanism for closure.

Accurate Problem Definition. Many problem-solving failures occur since efforts are directed at solving the wrong problem or only parts of it. For one, an inability to identify accurately what is going on can lead to inaccurate problem identification. As an illustration, a company discovers that its sales have declined for the past three months. The vice president of marketing accepts the notion that sales volume is directly proportional to the number of calls made by company salespeople. He has heard from a number of sources that some of his salespeople have been overburdened with paperwork and have been spending more time on office matters and less time in the field. He might erroneously conclude that the problem of declining sales is caused by too much paperwork by all of his company's salespeople.

When identifying the causes of a problem, creative thinking is extremely helpful. Is it true that all salespeople are overburdened with paperwork? Has the number of sales calls really dropped off? Are sales falling off because of paperwork or for other reasons? Even if increased paperwork is causing the sales decline, is it causing the decline for all salespeople? Are all salespeople experiencing lower sales levels, or just those who are spending more time with paperwork? Specific questions can be asked to identify the real cause of declining sales.

Incorrect inferences can also lead to inaccurate problem identification. Inferences are conclusions based on observations and the facts at hand; if accurate, they are usually used as the basis for some kind of appropriate action. For example, smoke is seen pouring from a building. One might infer that there is a fire inside, and one might also, knowing that volatile or explosive substances are nearby, call the fire department and avoid going near the area until it is safe. Unfortunately, many decision makers cannot distinguish between their inferences and what they actually observe. There is no problem with this as long as their inferences are correct, but when they are not, there can be trouble. If people were aware of what they infer, they might be more cautious about taking actions based on their inferences. Decision makers, then, are advised to think through the probable consequences of their actions if their inferences are incorrect.

To assist in defining the real problem, a *cause and effect diagram* is recommended. Because problems cause other problems, a whole complex of symptoms and problems emerges in need of a solution. A problem-diagramming procedure can help to isolate root causes. First, list all the problems, symptoms, and related problems; and number each one. Next, write the numbers at random on a piece of a paper and draw a circle around each. Then draw arrows to show what causes what. For example, if problem 1 causes problem 2, draw an arrow from circle 1 to circle 2. Consider each circled number, asking, "Which of the other problems causes or helps cause this one?" After all the arrows have been drawn, the root problems become clear. They are represented by the circles with arrows leading only away from them.

In some cases, this procedure will reveal several unrelated problem complexes. As an example, a company is experiencing declining profits. Is the cause declining sales, lower prices, inadequate inventory turnover, lack of product line for changing times, inadequate warehousing of finished goods, lack of trained sales personnel, or something else? A wide range of symptoms and problems can be identified. Using a cause and effect diagram, the root or real problem can be identified.

Idea Generators. An important new direction in problem-finding techniques is idea generators. When making business decisions, it is more difficult for decision makers to visualize all possible options than it is to select the most attractive choice from the list. Research shows that decision makers tend to anchor their thoughts early in the process, using their first ideas as a starting point from which other ideas arise. Hence, solutions are often variations on a central theme rather than genuinely different options.

Although computers are unable to suggest new ideas on their own, they are free from a human's subjectivity and can aid the human decision maker exploring a broader range of possibilities in a systematic manner. Even though these programs are easy to learn, each demands that decision makers adapt their work styles to fit the program's interpretation of the idea-generation process. As such, idea generators can help organize random or related thoughts, but cannot create new ideas per se.

Typical packages include IdeaFisher, Idea Generator, Idea Tree, and Brainstorm. IdeaFisher (from Fisher Idea Systems Inc.) helps the user develop new ideas by providing a linked-idea database that fosters free association. For users who demand a more analytical or linear approach, the structured question-and-answer approach of Idea Generator (Experience in Software Inc.) may be more productive. Idea Generator's more analytical approach presents a series of questions designed to cultivate new perspectives. The questions can help users view problems from different points of view, but the program requires users to complete a problem analysis initially.

On the other hand, Idea Tree (Mountain House Publishing Inc.) structures the user's thinking through a hierarchical organizational chart to help define and document new plans. Idea Tree's graphical tree design is somewhat hard to use for conceptual brainstorming, though it can be helpful for project planning. For groups, Brainstorm (Mustang Software Inc.) improves the decision-making process by supporting group discussions on E-mail. However, it does not proactively help users evaluate new ideas or structure their creative thinking. Overall, these typical idea generators have their particular strengths and weaknesses. The decision makers must determine which software package meets their specific needs.

TWO APPROACHES TO THE PROBLEM-FINDING PROCESS

In the prior approaches to the problem-solving process, the accent has been on some type of analytical technique, which has been the main thrust of information systems. However, there is a need to go a step further by incorporating creativity in the form of "logical-analytical thinking." Logical-analytical thinking goes beyond analyzing present problems of an organization, typical of the problem-solving process. Its accent is on identifying *future problems* and their impact on the organization today and tomorrow. In addition, logical-analytical thinking is directed toward future problems that are actually *future opportunities* in disguise. In order to solve future problems and/or opportunities, it is helpful to employ one or more of the creativity techniques set forth in this chapter along with creative computer software. Generally, a manager who has identified future problems has also identified opportunities. As such, the problem-finding process can be separated into a problem-centered approach and an opportunity-centered approach.

For the *problem-centered approach*, logical-analytical thinking centers on examining the environment with the idea of looking out into the future and exploring problems that will have an impact on the organization now or at some time in the future. Essentially, the process is one of projecting into the future, determining important problems (i.e., problem finding), and bringing them back to the present to examine their cause-and-effect relationships. Likewise, logical-analytical thinking is needed in the *opportunity-centered approach*. However, the perspective is somewhat different in that the main focus is on identifying opportunities for the organization to pursue that generally comes from problems uncovered. In effect, managers do need to change an organizational liability into an asset, that is, identify problems that can result in important opportunities for the organization. Also, the opportunity-centered approach need not always be related to future problems. It can center on current opportunities that are identified by top management and/or the corporate planning staff. Specific opportunities can be addressed directly by organization members at the higher levels of management.

Problem-Centered Approach

The problem-centered approach set forth here is taken from one of the author's previous publications, with some modifications to include the generation of new ideas using creative computer software.[9] As shown in Figure 2.3, it consists of four steps plus the solution and implementation phases from the quantitative-centered approach or the decision-centered approach.

1. *Generation.* This first step is the most important one in problem search because it focuses on the probing of potential problems that might have a great

Figure 2.3

A Comparison of Steps in the *Problem-Finding Process*—The Problem-Centered Approach and the Opportunity-Centered Approach

Basic Phases	Problem-Centered Approach	Opportunity-Centered Approach
Search	Step 1 Generation - probe for potential problems that might exist in the future using a brainstorming approach	Step 1 Exploration - examine the environment for opportunities that come from problems uncovered using a brainstorming approach Use creative computer software (if appropriate) to explore new ideas to exploit these opportunities.
	Step 2 Evaluation - review problems uncovered for managerial concern, backed up by a cost-benefit analysis Use creative computer software (if appropriate) to generate new ways to evaluate future problems.	
Identification	Step 3 Validation - select actual problems for managerial concern	Step 2 Selection - determine that one or more opportunities should be explored by management, as related to the company's critical success factors
	Step 4 Establish Boundaries - define each potential problem within its boundaries so as to cover the whole area that the problem encompasses	Step 3 Examine Boundaries - survey the environment for each opportunity and determine the proper boundaries
Solution	Steps 5 and 6 Solution - use steps 3 and 4 of quantitative-centered approach or steps 2 and 3 of decision-centered approach	Steps 4 and 5 Solution - use steps 3 and 4 of quantitative-centered approach or steps 2 and 3 of decision-centered approach
Implementation	Steps 7 and 8 Implementation - use steps 5 and 6 of quantitative-centered approach or steps 4 and 5 of decision-centered approach	Steps 6 and 7 Implementation - use steps 5 and 6 of quantitative-centered approach or steps 4 and 5 of decision-centered approach

Note: There is *Feedback* from the Last Step of Both Approaches to the First Step.

impact on the organization. Initially, the analysis is "forward-looking" because this is a search for future problems. Once these problems are identified, the analysis becomes "backward-looking" since there is a need to evaluate the cause-and-effect relationships of each problem and its possible effects on the organization currently. Accent is placed on each problem, from the short range to the long range. It may also be necessary to look at each problem in different economic climates (good, average, and bad conditions).

To generate important problems, the best approach is to use *brainstorming*. Generally, top managers and their staff, along with members from the corporate-planning staff, meet periodically to brainstorm future organizational problems. In a typical session, all important problems uncovered are recorded; then analysis is performed to explore the important aspects of each problem. These steps are performed in a back-and-forth fashion. That is, the original question concerning the *problem as given* and the subsequent spontaneous ideas are all written down. When participants' minds have cleared, they concentrate on reformulations produced from the collected material, and a choice of one or more is made before continuing with questions in sequence concerning the *problem as understood*. (As noted, the initially forward-looking analysis becomes backward-looking.) This can be repeated until all aspects have been considered. Complex problems may require the application of other creativity techniques in order to uncover an unexpected, new angle.

2. *Evaluation.* After the problem-generation phase, the second step centers on examining problems in terms of their being worthy of managerial concern. Because many of these problems are found in the future—the next two to five or possibly ten years—the question can be asked, "Which problem or problems should be undertaken for solution?" To answer this question, there is need to evaluate the impact the solution to a problem has on the organization, as in terms of net profit and return on investment. In other cases, consideration might be given to other important areas of an organization, such as sales and customer service. Similarly, it may be necessary to relate the problem or problems back to the organization's critical success factors.

If a computerized mode is used, appropriate creative computer software can be used to generate new ways and ideas that are related to help in the evaluation of future problems. In this manner, a broader approach can be used to evaluate the problems uncovered in the first step. In this evaluation process, it is possible that more problems may be apparent. If this happens, it may be necessary to add these problems in this evaluation step.

Generally, there is a need to perform a *cost-benefit analysis* to determine the impact of the solution on the financial aspects of the organization today and tomorrow. This task, for example, can be relegated to managers at the appropriate levels and their staffs to determine which problems are of valid concern for managerial action. The problems generated, then, are evaluated in terms of benefits versus costs, thereby becoming the basis for validation in the next step.

3. *Validation.* Building on the prior step of problem evaluation, actual problems in this third step are selected as being worthy of managerial concern for today and tomorrow. The validation for solving these problems is generally backed up by a cost-benefit analysis. If such an analysis is not available or too difficult or costly to develop, it may be necessary to use alternative means, such as the consensus of the majority of this problem-finding group, to substantiate this selection as an important problem to be solved. For example, to determine what problems should be validated and solved, the problem-finding group meets again and reviews the recommendations of the managers and their staffs. For the most part, the staffs have prioritized the important problems to be solved. It is up to the problem-finding group to pass judgment on them. As noted, some of the problems cannot be resolved in terms of a cost-benefit analysis. Input from managers and their staffs is generally necessary to finalize the prioritized list for implementation.

4. *Establish Boundaries.* After the problems have been validated in step 3, it

is necessary to describe (define) each problem within its boundaries in this fourth step. This ensures that areas which the problem might touch or come into contact with will be included in the problem-finding process. The net result is that there is need for some fine tuning such that the appropriate boundaries of the problem will be considered in its solution. Typically, to establish realistic boundaries, the problem-finding group must have a good knowledge of the future (good, average, or poor economic conditions), a clear description of performance that a solution must fulfill, and a clear idea of what to expect from solving the problem. These areas must be as clear and as accurate as possible, because if the problem is badly defined, the solution is generally of no value to management.

5 and 6. *Solution.* Solution to the problem-centered approach can take one of two directions. One is the use of step 3 (development of alternative solutions) and step 4 (selection of optimum solution) of the quantitative-centered approach. The other is the use of step 2 (design) and step 3 (choice) of the decision-centered approach. The appropriate approach is dictated by the type of future problems being solved. In either case, the solution centers on solving future problems before they actually occur. The accent is on practicing management by perception, rather than the management by exception that is traditional in the problem-solving process.

7 and 8. *Implementation.* In these final steps for the problem-centered approach, the implementation steps for the problem-solving process are usable. Fundamentally, these steps for the quantitative-centered approach and the decision-centered approach are the same. In addition to implementation, it is necessary to establish control over the solution in order to detect how changing times are affecting it.

The foregoing eight steps are normally conducted in the order in which they were presented because of the uncertainty of the future. However, there may be circumstances that warrant changing the above sequence. As in the problem-solving process, there is need of *feedback* in the problem-centered approach.

Opportunity-Centered Approach

This second approach to the problem-finding process is also taken from a prior publication by the author.[10] As illustrated in Figure 2.3, three steps plus the solution and implementation phases from the quantitative-centered approach or the decision-centered approach are set forth. This opportunity-centered approach is related to managers and their staffs.

1. *Exploration.* This first step examines the internal and external environment for opportunities that come from problems uncovered. As in the problem-centered approach, *brainstorming* is generally used by managers and their staffs. The focus is directed away from the short range to the medium and long range, where every effort is used to determine what opportunities are presented by the problems discovered in the future. As in the prior approach, the analysis is initially forward-looking in that there is a search for future problems. Once the

problems have been identified, they are examined from the standpoint of identifying opportunities for improving the company's operations (from the standpoint of sales, profits, or whatever). From this perspective, the concept of opportunities has a "positive" connotation while the concept of problems has a "negative" meaning.

If a computerized mode is utilized, appropriate creative computer software can be gainfully employed to assist managers and their staffs in developing new ideas that exploit appropriate opportunities for a company to pursue. Generally, creative computer software results in the exploration of more new ideas than if performed manually. This will be apparent in the various examples given in Part III of this text. The selection of more opportunities helps to assure managers that this exploration step is performed in a most comprehensive manner.

2. *Selection.* Having identified appropriate opportunities, the second step is to determine what opportunities (one or more) should be explored by managers and their staffs. The selection process should focus on opportunities that relate to a company's *critical success factors*, that is, the factors that are critical to its success. Typically, these factors include price, sales promotion, customer service, product mix, inventory turnover, cost control, and quality dealers. In turn, the interrelationships of the critical success factors and the company's goals and objectives are discussed for further clarification. But more important, this discussion determines what opportunities should be pursued by the company, thereby identifying them in a clear and meaningful way. Moreover, it takes into consideration all the important facts that bear on important company opportunities. Where deemed necessary, a *cost-benefit analysis* can be used to determine what opportunities are more important than others in terms of how they affect the company's future profits.

3. *Examine Boundaries.* The third step centers on surveying the environment for the opportunities identified before pursuing an opportunity solution. Due to the nature of some opportunities, the boundaries may be quite wide, that is, they may extend beyond the company and may be related to emerging and established organizations and industries. Generally, greater opportunities are found when boundaries are extended. Thus, top management and the corporate planning staff need to examine the boundaries surrounding the opportunities from a narrow to a very wide perspective. The net result is that the proper boundaries are used in the solution and implementation of the opportunity.

4 and 5. *Solution.* As in the problem-centered approach, the solution to the opportunity-centered approach can take one of two directions: the quantitative-centered approach or the decision-centered approach. Current problem-solving approaches require that the decision maker pick the best solution from the set of feasible ones. An opportunity solution, then, requires that the decision maker pick the best opportunity from the set of feasible opportunities under study. As with the problem-centered approach, the main thrust is on practicing management by perception.

6 and 7. *Implementation.* For these last steps of the opportunity-centered ap-

proach, the implementation steps for the problem-solving process are used. The opportunity must be monitored and implemented, making the necessary adjustments to changing times.

As shown in Figure 2.3, the seven steps of the opportunity-centered approach are related to those for the problem-centered approach. Also, this approach provides for *feedback*.

Typical Applications of the Problem-Finding Process

To illustrate the *problem-centered approach*, a chemical products company is currently offering a line of chemical products which are sold to retail and industrial laundry and drycleaning plants. More recently, the president along with the vice-presidents (who assist the corporate-planning staff) are concerned about the direction the government is taking in terms of regulation and control of the drycleaning industry because of hazardous waste. This waste problem will force a decline of drycleaning chemical sales in favor of laundry products. Since drycleaning sales are 75 percent of the company's total sales, there is concern by the company's management. Upon brainstorming of the overall problem by the corporate-planning staff, a number of problems were generated (first step). One of these is the effect of shifting the manufacturing plants over to production of more laundry chemicals. An equally important problem is the need to change sales and marketing strategies toward the laundry market. Needless to say, other problems were identified. In turn, ideas related to overcoming these problems were evaluated using a creative computer software package. A cost-benefit analysis and compliance with organizational objectives and government regulations served as a final evaluation basis (second step).

At this point, the corporate-planning staff met with top management to validate the overall problem and the related problems (third step). After examining their impact on customers, production, and other concerns, a list of priorities was set forth for the specialized problem areas. Next, the scope of boundaries of each problem was addressed (fourth step). Changes in production and inventory levels were outlined for the manufacturing facility. The marketing efforts were defined in terms of advertising medias and markets to address. Other boundaries, like personnel, budgets, and time frames, were set for each problem.

Possible solutions to each of the problems were identified (fifth and sixth steps). Solutions for the manufacturing department include building a manufacturing facility exclusively for laundry products, contracting the additional work to other manufacturers, or having existing plants updated. After analysis of potential solutions, top management needs to decide which is the optimum solution for each problem after considering all of the factors. If updating the present manufacturing facility is identified as the best alternative, funds must be allocated to facilitate its completion. Next, the optimum solution for each problem must be implemented (seventh and eighth steps). In addition, there is a need to place proper controls over the implemented solutions.

To illustrate an *opportunity-centered approach* for the chemical products company (as set forth previously), managers and their staffs need to examine the environmental issues in more depth. That is, they need to identify future opportunities that may exist. If they feel that biodegradable products hold an edge in the future marketplace, then they need to examine such implications. This could include not only a more thorough exploration of the retail and industrial laundry market, but also the home products market (first step). Utilizing the same creative computer software package set forth previously, important ideas to exploit market opportunities were introduced by group members. The resulting opportunities in the home market centered on private labeling for an established firm, buying a firm for its distribution and marketing efforts in the home market, or breaking into the home market itself.

By looking at the tradeoffs of each alternative, one was selected for further review. Using a cost-benefit analysis, private labeling was determined to be the best alternative because of the company's contacts (second step). The boundaries of the private-labeling issue were examined (third step); that is, what companies would be interested in such a product line, what is the target home market, and what are the cost and pricing needs of offering such a product. These boundaries would lead to the best solution (fourth and fifth steps) and implementation of the best alternative (sixth and seventh steps). Additionally, controls need to be implemented to make sure that the solution is best for the times.

COMPARISON OF THE PROBLEM-SOLVING AND PROBLEM-FINDING PROCESSES

The major elements of the problem-solving and problem-finding processes were set forth previously in Figures 2.2 and 2.3, respectively. The accent of problem solving is on *management by exception* for solving all types of problems in the short range, and some in the medium range. This represents a *micro* or a *reactive* approach to problems. In contrast, the focus of problem finding is on *management by perception* for solving semistructured and unstructured problems covering the long range, and some in the short and medium range. This is representative of a *macro* or a *proactive* approach to problems.

Since the problem-finding process encourages the integration of the manager's capabilities with that of creative computer software if deemed appropriate, the quality of the final decision is enhanced. The human-machine interface allows the manager to retain control throughout the problem-finding process. From this view, creativity is an important part of these decision-making activities, just as intuition, judgment, and experience are helpful in understanding how the environmental factors react to the stimuli that decisions provide. Of equal importance is a systematic approach that forces the manager to evaluate the facts critically before reaching a final decision.

Typical problem areas that lend themselves to an OLAP environment are set forth in Part III of the text. More specifically, the areas of strategic planning, marketing, manufacturing, accounting and finance, and human resources are covered, along with representative OLAP applications to solve problems at hand or the development of new opportunities for goods and/or services. As such, the focus is on both problem solving and problem finding.

SUMMARY

The initial focus of the chapter was on the use of OLAP systems to help improve the decision maker's effectiveness. This discussion was supplemented by the capability of an OLAP system to improve an organization's effectiveness with an accent on an information focus and synergistic interaction between the manager and the computer. Next, the type of problems to be solved was discussed along with a planning and control framework for problems to be solved. Not only were the forerunners of the problem-solving and problem-finding processes presented, but so were their shortcomings for today's business world. In the problem-solving process, the quantitative-centered approach is useful in solving well-structured problems; and the decision-centered approach is helpful in solving semistructured and some unstructured problems. In the problem-finding process, the problem-centered approach pinpoints future problems that can be solved today to minimize their impact in the future. Related is the opportunity-centered approach, which searches the environment for opportunities that derive from problems uncovered. No matter which approach is used, the user-machine interface of an on-line analytical processing system allows managers and their staffs to retain control at the various stages of decision making.

NOTES

1. Charles T. Clark, "Synergy Is Key to Advanced Technologies," *Digital News & Review*, December 5, 1994, p. 19.

2. Robert N. Anthony, *Planning and Control Systems: A Framework for Analysis* (Boston: Harvard University Graduate School of Business Administration, 1965), pp. 15–18.

3. Robert A. Raitt, "Must We Revolutionize Our Methodology?" *Interfaces*, February 1974, p. 2.

4. James G. March and Herbert A. Simon, *Organizations* (New York: John Wiley & Sons, 1958).

5. Herbert A. Simon, *Models of Man: Social and Rational* (New York: John Wiley & Sons, 1957).

6. Herbert A. Simon, *The New Science of Management Decisions* (New York: Harper & Row, 1960), pp. 2–3.

7. Graham Wallas, *Art of Thought* (New York: Harcourt Brace, 1926).

8. W. Gordon, *Synectics: The Development of Creative Capacity* (New York: Harper & Row, 1961).

9. Robert J. Thierauf, *A Problem-Finding Approach to Effective Corporate Planning* (Westport, Conn.: Quorum Books, 1987), chapter 2, pp. 17–43.

10. Ibid.

Bibliography: Part I

Aihara, K., and R. Katayama. "Chaos Engineering in Japan." *Communications of the ACM*, November 1995.

Andrew, I., and S. Ellis. "Bringing Virtual Reality to Life." *AI Expert*, May 1994.

Anthony, R. N. *Planning and Control Systems: A Framework for Analysis*. Boston: Harvard University Graduate School of Business Administration, 1965.

Asch, T. "Designing Virtual Worlds." *AI Expert*, August 1992.

Baatz, E. B. "Making Brain Waves." *CIO*, January 15, 1996.

Badaracco, J. I., Jr. *The Knowledge Link: How Firms Compete Through Strategic Alliances*. Boston: Harvard Business School Press, 1991.

Bakos, J. Y., and P. deJager. "Are Computers Boosting Productivity?" *Computerworld*, March 27, 1995.

Barber, P. "OLAP Ready for Prime Time?" *Computing Canada*, February 15, 1995.

———. "Try the EIS/OLAP Alternative." *Computing Canada*, September 13, 1995.

Barker, Q. "Virtual Reality Market Analysis." *Virtual Reality World*, March/April 1994.

Birman, K. P. "The Process Group Approach to Reliable Distributed Computing." *Communications of the ACM*, December 1993.

Boiney, L. G. "When Efficient Is Insufficient: Fairness in Decisions Affecting a Group." *Management Science*, September 1995.

Buchanan, L. "The Knowledge Enterprise, Business Information: Scavenger Hunt." *CIO*, July 1995.

———. "The Knowledge Enterprise, The CIO Role: The Medium and the Message." *CIO*, July 1995.

Burger, D. "Sector Is Growing Like 'Wildfire': Executive Information Systems." *Computing Canada*, February 15, 1995.

Bylinsky, G. "The Marvels of 'Virtual Reality.' " *Fortune*, June 3, 1991.

———. "The Payoff from 3-D Computing." *Fortune*, Special Report, Autumn 1993.

Calloway, E. "Mind Meld." *PC Week*, April 15, 1996.

Carter, W. K. "To Invest in New Technology or Not? New Tools for Making the Decision." *Journal of Accountancy*, May 1992.

Chaib-draa, B. "Industrial Applications of Distributed AI." *Communications of the ACM*, November 1995.

Chesbrough, H. W., and D. J. Teece. "When Is Virtual Virtuous? Organizing for Innovation." *Harvard Business Review*, January–February 1996.

Clark, T. C. "Synergy Is Key to Advanced Technologies." *Digital News & Review*, December 5, 1994.

Codd, E. F., S. B. Codd, and C. T. Salley. "Beyond Decision Support." *Computerworld*, July 25, 1993.

Coleman, K. "The AI Marketplace in the Year 2000." *AI Expert*, January 1993.

Couger, J. D. *Creativity & Innovation in Information Systems Organizations*. Danvers, Mass.: Boyd & Fraser Publishing Company, 1996.

Coull, T., and P. Rothman. "Virtual Reality for Decision Support Systems." *AI Expert*, August 1993.

Crockett, F. "Revitalizing Executive Information Systems." *Sloan Management Review*, Summer 1992.

Davenport, T. "Think Tank: Finding the Information That Matters." *CIO*, June 1, 1996.

Davenport, T. H., S. L. Jarvenpaa, and M. C. Beers. "Improving Knowledge Work Processes." *Sloan Management Review*, Summer 1996.

Davidow, W. H., and M. S. Malone. *The Virtual Corporation: Structuring and Revitalizing the Corporation of the 21st Century*. New York: Harper Business, 1992.

Dayton, D. "Idea Generators Spark New Solutions." *PC Week*, March 18, 1991.

Ditto, W., and T. Munakata. "Principles of Applications of Chaotic Systems." *Communications of the ACM*, November 1995.

Dragoon, A. "The Knowledge Enterprise, Knowledge Management: Rx for Success." *CIO*, July 1995.

Drucker, P. F. "The Theory of Business." *Harvard Business Review*, September–October 1994.

———. *Managing in a Time of Great Change*. New York: Truman Talley Books/Dutton, 1995.

Dumaine, B. "Closing the Innovation Gap." *Fortune*, December 2, 1991.

Durlach, N. F., and A. S. Mavor, eds. *Virtual Reality Scientific and Technological Challenges*. Washington, D.C.: National Academy Press, 1995.

Edwards, J. "A Clear View." *CIO*, November 15, 1994.

Elam, J. J., and M. Mead. "Can Software Influence Creativity?" *Information Systems Research*, March 1990.

El-Najdawi, M. K., and A. C. Stylianou. "Expert Support Systems: Integrating AI Technologies." *Communications of the ACM*, December 1993.

Evans, J. R. *Creative Thinking In the Decision and Management Sciences*. Cincinnati, Ohio: South-Western Publishing Company, 1991.

———. "Creativity in MS/OR: Improving Problem Solving Through Creative Thinking." *Interfaces*, March–April 1992.

———. "Creativity in MS/OR: The Multiple Dimension of Creativity." *Interfaces*, March–April 1993.

Frank, M. "The Truth About OLAP." *DBMS*, August 1995.

Freedman, D. "Where Are We Now?" *CIO*, January 1993.

Froot, K. A., D. S. Scharfstein, and J. C. Stein. "A Framework for Risk Management." *Harvard Business Review*, November–December 1994.

Frye, C. "EIS Evolution: From Executive to *Everybody's* Information System." *Client/Server Computing*, August 1994.

———. "Business Problem Solving, Big Flap Over OLAP." *Client/Server Computing*, May 1995.

Garber, P. "Try the EIS/OLAP Alternative." *Computing Canada*, September 13, 1995.

Gigante, M., R. A. Earnshaw, and H. Jones, eds. *Virtual Reality Systems*. London, England: Academic Press, 1993.

Gill, P. J. "A Strategic Approach to Mission-Critical Applications." *Oracle Magazine*, September–October 1995.

Gordon, W. *Synectics: The Development of Creative Capacity*. New York: Harper & Row, 1961.

Gorry, G. A., and M. S. S. Morton. "A Framework for Management Information Systems." *Sloan Management Review*, Spring 1989.

Hamilton, J. O'C., E. T. Smith, G. McWilliams, E. I. Schwartz, and J. Carey. "Virtual Reality: How a Computer-Generated World Could Change the Real World." *Business Week*, October 5, 1992.

Hamit, F. *Virtual Reality and the Exploration of Cyberspace*. Carmel, Ind.: Sams Publishing, 1993.

Hamit, F., and W. Thomas. *Virtual Reality: Adventures in Cyberspace*. San Francisco, Calif.: Miller Freeman, 1991.

Harris, J. "Is Your EIS Too Stupid to Be Useful?" *Chief Information Officer Journal*, May/June 1993.

Helsel, S. K., and J. P. Roth, eds. *Virtual Reality: Theory, Practice, and Promise*. Westport, Conn.: Meckler Publishing, 1991.

Henkoff, R. "New Management Secrets from Japan—Really." *Fortune*, November 27, 1995.

Hildebrand, C. "The Knowledge Enterprise Information Mapping: Guiding Principles." *CIO*, July 1995.

Inmon, B. "Information Management: Charting the Course." *Data Management Review*, May 1996.

Keeney, R. L. "Creativity in Decision Making with Value-Focused Thinking." *Sloan Management Review*, Summer 1994.

Kiely, T. "The Creative Process." *CIO*, September 1, 1993.

Kleinschrod, W. A. "In Business, Knowledge Is Power." *Beyond Computing*, March/April 1995.

———. "Leveraging Technology." *Beyond Computing*, April 1996.

Krioda, C. D. "Booming Business Intelligence." *MIDRANGE Systems*, June 30, 1995.

———. "Laps Around Business Intelligence." *MIDRANGE Systems*, June 30, 1995.

Krugman, P. "Competitiveness: Does It Matter?" *Fortune*, March 7, 1994.

Langley, P., and H. A. Simon. "Applications of Machine Learning and Rule Indication." *Communications of the ACM*, November 1995.

Lawrence, J. *Introduction to Neural Networks: Design, Theory and Applications*. Los Angeles, Calif.: California Scientific Software Press, 1995.

Leavitt, H. J., and J. Lipman-Blumen. "Hot Groups." *Harvard Business Review*, July–August 1995.

Lenant, D. B. "CYC: A Large-Scale Investment in Knowledge Infrastructure." *Communications of the ACM*, November 1995.

Lim. L.-H., K. S. Raman, and K. K. Wei. "Interacting Effects of GDSS and Leadership." *Decision Support Systems*, December 1994.

Long, J., and B. M. Baker. "Distributed Computing." *Network Computing*, November 1, 1992.

MacCrimmon, K. R., and C. Wagner. "Stimulating Ideas Through Creativity Software." *Management Science*, November 1994.

Mackay, J. M., S. H. Bau, and M. G. Klitke. "An Empirical Investigation of the Effects of Decision Aids on Problem-Solving Processes." *Decision Sciences*, Vol. 23, 1992.

March, J. G., and H. A. Simon, *Organizations*. New York: John Wiley & Sons, 1958.

Marion, L. "For Better and for Worse." *Beyond Computing*, January/February 1995.

Martin, J. *The Great Transition: Using the Seven Disciplines of Enterprise Engineering to Align People, Technology and Strategy*. New York: AMACOM, 1995.

Maynard, H. B., Jr., and S. E. Mehrtens. *The Fourth Wave, Business in the 21st Century*. San Francisco, Calif.: Berrett-Koehler Publishers, 1993.

McKendrick, J. E. "Guaranteed to Make Your MIS Pop: Executive Information Systems Are Evolving Into Everyone's Information Systems." *MIDRANGE Systems*, October 26, 1993.

Newquist, H. P., III. "The State of the AI Business." *AI Expert*, February 1992.

———. "AI Burnout." *Computerworld*, April 18, 1994.

Nonaka, I., and H. Takeuchi. *The Knowledge-Creating Company*. New York: Oxford University Press, 1995.

Norton, R. "A New Tool to Help Managers." *Fortune*, May 30, 1994.

Nuernberger, P. *Increasing Executive Productivity: A Unique Program for Developing the Inner Skills of Vision, Leadership, and Performance*. Englewood Cliffs, N.J.: Prentice-Hall, 1992.

Parker, R. S. "Understanding Multidimensional Analysis: The 15 Keys." *Data Management Review*, May 1995.

Pimentel, K., and K. Teixeira. *Virtual Reality, Through the New Looking Glass*. New York: McGraw-Hill, 1993.

Prather, C. W. "Creation Theory." *CIO*, September 15, 1994.

Radding, A. "Is OLAP the Answer?" *Computerworld*, December 19, 1994.

———. "Users View the Same Data Differently with MDBMS." *Client/Server Computing*, February 1996.

Raitt, R. A. "Must We Revolutionize Our Methodology?" *Interfaces*, February 1974.

Rheingold, H. *Virtual Reality*. New York: Touchstone, 1991.

———. "Virtual Reality, Phase Two." *Virtual Reality Special Report*, published by the *AI Expert*. San Francisco, Calif.: Miller Freeman, 1993.

———. *The Virtual Community: Finding Connections in a Computerized World*. Reading, Mass.: Addison-Wesley, 1993.

Rothstein, L. R. "The Empowerment Effort That Came Undone." *Harvard Business Review*, January–February 1995.

Saaty, T. L. "Thoughts on Decision Making." *OR/MS Today*, April 1996.

Sabin, K. "Data Warehousing: From OLAP to OLTP." *Computing Canada*, June 21, 1995.

Sambamurthy, V., and W. W. Chin. "The Effects of Group Attitudes Toward Alternative GDSS Designs on the Decision-Making Performance of Computer-Supported Groups." *Decision Sciences*, March 1994.

Sandler, B-Z. *Computer-Aided Creativity: A Guide for Engineers, Managers, and Inventors.* New York: Van Nostrand Reinhold, 1994.

Shalley, C. E. "Effects of Coaction, Expected Evaluation, and Goal Setting on Creativity and Productivity." *Academy of Management Journal,* April 1995.

Simon, H. A. *Models of Man: Social and Rational.* New York: John Wiley & Sons, 1957.

———. *The New Science of Management Decisions.* New York: Harper & Row, 1960.

Simons, R. "Control in an Age of Empowerment." *Harvard Business Review,* March–April 1995.

Stipp, D. "2001 Is Just Around the Corner. Where's HAL?" *Fortune,* November 13, 1995.

Taylor, W. C. "Control in an Age of Chaos." *Harvard Business Review,* November–December 1994.

Thé, L. "OLAP Answers Tough Business Questions." *Datamation,* May 1, 1995.

Thierauf, R. J. *Systems Analysis and Design of Real-Time Management Information Systems.* Englewood Cliffs, N.J.: Prentice-Hall, 1975.

———. *Distributed Processing Systems.* Englewood Cliffs, N.J.: Prentice-Hall, 1978.

———. *Decision Support Systems for Effective Planning and Control, A Case Study Approach.* Englewood Cliffs, N.J.: Prentice-Hall, 1982.

———. *A Problem-Finding Approach to Effective Corporate Planning.* Westport, Conn.: Quorum Books, 1987.

———. *User-Oriented Decision Support Systems, Accent on Problem Finding.* Englewood Cliffs, N.J.: Prentice-Hall, 1988.

———. *Group Decision Support Systems for Effective Decision Making: A Guide for MIS Professionals and End Users.* Westport, Conn.: Quorum Books, 1989.

———. *Expert Systems in Finance and Accounting.* Westport, Conn.: Quorum Books, 1990.

———. *Electronic Data Interchange in Finance and Accounting.* Westport, Conn.: Quorum Books, 1990.

———. *Executive Information Systems: A Guide for Senior Management and MIS Professionals.* Westport, Conn.: Quorum Books, 1991.

———. *Image Processing Systems for Business: A Guide for MIS Professionals and End Users.* Westport, Conn.: Quorum Books, 1992.

———. *Creative Computer Software for Strategic Thinking and Decision Making: A Guide for Senior Management and MIS Professionals.* Westport, Conn.: Quorum Books, 1993.

———. *Virtual Reality Systems for Business.* Westport, Conn.: Quorum Books, 1995.

Tichy, N. M. "Revolutionize Your Company." *Fortune,* December 13, 1993.

Thornton, C., and E. Lockhart. "Groupware or Electronic Brainstorming." *Journal of Systems Management,* October 1994.

Thornton, E. "Japan's Struggle to Be Creative." *Fortune,* April 19, 1993.

Vaughan, J. "'Ludd, Blood, OLAP and Me." *Software Magazine,* September 1995.

Vince, J. *Virtual Reality Systems.* Reading, Mass.: Addison-Wesley, 1995.

Vitaliano, F. "Expert Systems and Neural Networks." *Digital Review,* June 10, 1991.

Wallas, G. *Art of Thought.* New York: Harcourt Brace, 1926.

PART II

The Essential Elements of OLAP Systems

3

Data Warehousing and Data Communications

ISSUES EXPLORED

- What is the basic framework that underlies data warehousing and data communications in an OLAP environment?
- What are the basic components found in a typical data warehouse?
- How are multidimensional databases different from relational databases for OLAP systems?
- What types of tools are needed in building effective data warehouses?
- What is the relationship of LANs and WANs to the development of OLAP systems?

OUTLINE

Data Warehousing and Data Communications in an OLAP Environment

A Basic Framework for Data Warehousing and Data Communications in an OLAP Environment

    Open-Systems Architecture

    Client/Server Architecture

    An Integrated and Flexible Approach Brings New Functionality to Users

On-Line Database-Management Systems

    Four Organization Models for Database-Management Systems

    Current Movement to Object-Oriented DBMS (OODBMS)

Multidimensional Databases Designed for OLAP Systems

Concurrent Movement to Data Warehousing

DATA WAREHOUSING AND DATA COMMUNICATIONS IN AN OLAP ENVIRONMENT

To place this chapter's material in its proper perspective, present developments of data warehousing and data communications are discussed in order to serve as a background for a rich discussion of OLAP development and applications later in the book. Within an OLAP environment, the essential goal of data warehousing, working in conjunction with data communications and networking, is to provide the *right information* to the *right people* at the *right time* so they can make the *right decisions*. From this broad view, much work needs to be done before OLAP systems can live up to their full potential.

It is highly recommended that new data warehousing and data communications operations be thoroughly planned since many of the products marketed in both areas do not work together at all or, at best, are somewhat compatible. Some consultants suggest that companies start with query and report writers linked to office suites while installing relatively straightforward OLAP applications. Once these applications are mastered along with appropriate OLAP products, the MIS department can move ahead to more challenging matters, like working with multidimensional databases and data mining. In effect, there is a learning curve to implementing successful OLAP systems. In all cases, consideration should be given to *scalability*, that is, the ability to add processors and disk drives incrementally as system demand grows, and *high availability*, including on-line backup and recovery.

A BASIC FRAMEWORK FOR DATA WAREHOUSING AND DATA COMMUNICATIONS IN AN OLAP ENVIRONMENT

In order to realize the full potential of OLAP (as discussed in this text), it is necessary to look beyond its technology and data requirements by establishing a fundamental framework that will facilitate the development of on-line analytical processing systems. Such a framework is found in an *open-systems* environment, which allows users to retrieve data locally that may be found halfway around the world. Complementary to this environment is *client/server technology*, which centers on the way that computers and networking technologies are applied. Because both are important, they are discussed separately below. In addition, it should be noted that the current movement to *object-oriented technology* provides a means for developing newer systems that operate within this basic framework. This technology will be discussed later in the chapter.

Open-Systems Architecture

Today, computer managers are being asked continually to manage more and more of the information technology, that is, hardware, software, and networks in their organizations. They must develop the ability to reach beyond the mainframe-oriented data center, into an end-user domain filled with a diversity of microcomputers, departmental systems, and networks as well as a mélange of software tools and applications. And they must be prepared to make the elements of this mixture work together. No longer can computer managers think in terms of a single vendor or hardware or a single operating system. Currently, they need to find ways to integrate an expanding assortment of computing products and services to meet the demands of enterprise*wide* and even *inter*enterprise information in a competitive environment that has expanded to a global scale. Such an approach is found in an open-systems environment.

Open systems implement specifications for interfaces, services, and supporting formats which enable properly engineered application software to be ported across systems, interoperate with other applications, and interact with users in a consistent manner. To place open systems in perspective, large retailers, such as Wal-Mart, Kmart, Dayton Hudson, and Sears, manage inventory by linking them to manufacturers as if in a single network. While this open-systems approach eliminates the advantages of a supplier's proprietary network, it also gives manufacturers valuable information. These retailers provide manufacturers with updated sales and inventory information electronically so they can plan production. With such data arriving in a standard format from so many customers, a manufacturer like Levi Strauss or Vanity Fair can easily estimate aggregate demand weeks in advance, and produce sales forecasts to help manufacturers plan production even further in advance. This capability can be very helpful to a company desiring to take the analysis one step further using OLAP technology.

From another perspective, system vendors previously dictated how the pieces were put together in a data-communications and networking structure. However, open systems is a change in the power relationship between the user and the vendor. Open systems is about users controlling their destinies, being in charge of what gets purchased and installed, and mandating that the vendors make sure it works together well. Thus, companies are more in the driver's seat in an open-systems environment.

Client/Server Architecture

A client/server is a computing architecture in which any device in a network can request information or processing services from any other. When a device is asking for data or processing power, it is a *client*. When it is supplying information or services, it is a *server*. As such, client/server architectures provide users transparent access to file servers, database servers, print servers, and other devices, thereby maximizing user options and network throughput while minimizing operating costs and response time over the network. The client/server model is a powerful method for writing applications that partition the program into pieces installed in two or more separate network stations. Tools built for implementing applications in this way allow program parts developed independently to interoperate over a network.

In reference to improving payoff for information and OLAP technology, client/server makes sense because it helps organizations maximize their extensive investments in processing power—from the desktop to the mainframe. Client/server architecture only makes sense if it is appropriate for all organizational applications. There are a number of factors for the shift to client/server computing. The most important ones are networks, standards, and the tremendous power and versatility of today's desktop devices. Currently, no single vendor can supply all the pieces to make client/server computing a reality. A good test of how well a vendor is positioned to meet an organization's client/server needs is to examine how open the company's product line is. Open computing, software, and network tools are the plug-and-play components that are the foundation of client/server architecture.

An Integrated and Flexible Approach Brings New Functionality to Users

The foundation of OLAP systems, as discussed above, should be built on an open-systems architecture, which promotes information sharing among all employees. Essentially, open systems are the key to harnessing the rising tide of technological innovation and preserving a company's investment in existing equipment. Related to an open-systems architecture is a client/server architecture where all company data are stored in a small number of computer systems or servers so that all employees have access to data as needed. Such an approach allows companies to *integrate* their operations in a cost-effective and orderly manner.

The cornerstone today of an effective information architecture for OLAP systems is an enterprise-wide information highway, that is, an intranet, specifically designed to facilitate communications among all company business systems as well as those outside the company. The goal of this highway is to make information easily accessible to all employees, thereby encouraging them to work together as a team. This important area of an intranet will be covered in more depth later in the chapter.

Generally, implementing effective OLAP systems today requires that they be built upon an open-systems architecture and client/server architecture. In turn, these architectures provide linkage to the information highway. This integrated approach provides the *flexibility* required in today's business environment. Companies using OLAP systems have improved the quality and timeliness of information retrieval, have been better able to evaluate new business opportunities, and have made more informed decisions about new-product development, pricing, and distribution, among others. Implementing OLAP applications on open-systems and client/server platforms that are linked to the information highway brings new functionality to users not possible before.

ON-LINE DATABASE-MANAGEMENT SYSTEMS

Because data is of great importance to a typical organization, there is need to provide on-line access to database elements for immediate processing using direct-access file-storage devices. One method of maintaining a large, complex database and managing relationships among the database elements is to employ a database-management system (DBMS). Thus, MIS managers should employ DBMSs to their fullest capacity to satisfy present and future needs of users, whether they are within or outside the MIS department.

Typically, the reach of a database-management system extends beyond the individual file management systems, such as inventory files and accounts receivable files of the past, to an entire database (or databases), consisting of corporate planning, marketing, manufacturing, accounting, personnel, and other data elements. Furthermore, a DBMS allows *procedure independence* of the database for a large number of data elements. This means that the programmer does not have to describe the data file in detail, as is the case with procedure-oriented languages like COBOL, but rather only specify what is to be done in a *data management language*.

Four Organization Models for Database-Management Systems

Vendors currently offer a variety of DBMSs that provide for the creation, access, and maintenance of data to aid companies in the effective management of databases. They fall into four categories: (1) hierarchical, (2) network, (3) relational, and (4) object. Generally, the first generation of database models is considered to be hierarchical and network, while the second generation is considered to be relational. Currently, the third generation of database models centers on object technology. All of these organizational models are discussed below.

A *hierarchical*-database system uses a tree structure to distinguish relationships between records in a file. Every data item or field is "owned" by a higher ranking item, and access to it must be routed through that hierarchy. In other words, items are arranged according to a parent/child relationship, whereby each parent may have many children, but each child may have only one parent. A fixed relationship between the data elements in the hierarchy is established, and data are retrieved by the database-management system moving along the hierarchy in a manner dependent on the request from the user.

A *network*-database system establishes individual files for each major element of data. "Pointers" in the records are used to link these elements together. Pointers are the disk addresses where each record in a file is stored. In effect, the network model allows "children" to be related to many "parents" and very general interdependencies can be expressed. As such, a network database tends to be more flexible than a hierarchical database.

A *relational*-database management system is simply a collection of two-dimensional tables (called relations) with no repeating group. In the tables, the rows constitute records and columns constitute fields. The term "relational" comes from the clearly defined relations that data within a field have, which orders the records in the database. For example, numeric fields can be ordered from least to greatest, alphabetic fields can be in alphabetical order, and so forth.

The relational model, which is found currently in DBMS models, offers many advantages over hierarchical and network models. It is based on a logical rather than a physical structure and shows the relationships between various items. Data are represented in tabular form and new relations can be created. Searching is generally faster than within the other schemes, modification is more straightforward, and the clarity and visibility of the database are improved. Because the relational-database-management system (RDBMS) is based on a flexible row-and-table format, this approach is appropriate for most business applications—from the simplest ones built by end users to high-volume applications involving millions of transactions per day built by computer personnel.

An RDBMS also processes records one set at a time. The computer will search for and identify all members of the sought-after set, for example, all past due accounts. By contrast, hierarchical DBMSs examine each record and identify whether it is past due. If it is not, the system goes to the next record. If overdue, the system sends out a notice. In addition, to these time-and money-saving attributes, the RDBMS has a formal theoretical foundation, which provides rules for structure, maintenance, and integrity (preserving the data against unauthorized changes). More important, organizations can add new data fields, build new access paths, and split tables without disturbing other programs or data stored in the database.

Current Movement to Object-Oriented DBMS (OODBMS)

Although relational DBMSs have been popular, they are being replaced or supplemented by object-oriented technology. Essentially, the simplicity of the relational model of data and the acceptance of the relational SQL (Structured Query Language) as an industry standard have contributed to its popularity. Even as the acceptance of relational database-management systems has spread, their limitations have been exposed by the emergence of various classes of new applications, including design, engineering, multimedia, geographic, scientific, and more recently OLAP systems. These highly complex applications do not always lend themselves to relational DBMS. However, object-oriented database-management systems (OODBMSs) are a more universal approach to a multitude of applications that extend beyond the business community.

Currently, object orientation is a term whose meaning changes in different situations. End users encounter *objects* in their graphical user interface in the form of icons or other graphical representations of parts of an application. Programmers use object-oriented programming (OOP) languages to write highly modular applications. In an object-oriented database-management system, developers use *objects* to store complex data, say, for CAD/CAM (computer-aided design/computer-aided manufacturing) or geographic information systems. Object-oriented analysis and design (OOAD) allows programmers to apply design methodologies and use CASE (computer-aided software engineering) tools to create object-oriented programs. In addition, Distributed Object Management provides a way for distributed, heterogeneous applications spread across a wide area network to communicate and share data. Typically, OODBMSs are interwined with computing activities throughout the organization.

The first users of OODBMSs tended to be engineers who found that relational databases were unable to handle the storage requirements of complex scientific data or CAD drawings. While RDBM systems can store straightforward, predefined alphanumeric data types, a system for storing scientific data might require the use of a variable-dimension array. A database for CAD drawings would need to preserve the relationships between the lines and angles of the vector graphics within each file.

In a somewhat similar manner, businesses have begun to consider OODBMS to centralize and simplify the storage of a wide range of complex data, such as text files and mapping data. Some of this information is stored in file systems with the applications that created them; much is still on paper. Business organizations are also expressing interest in OODBMS products for their capability to cut application-development backlogs by reducing development time through the reuse of code. As organizations move more toward a unified, organization-wide system, they will be able to take a lot of disjointed systems that have been built on an application-by-application basis, and create a single, local perspective on customers or products and services using object-oriented DBMS.

The leading OODBMS vendors include Object Design, Inc. (Burlington, Mass.), Gemstone Systems, Inc. (Beaverton, Ore.), O2 Technology, Inc. (Palo Alto, Calif.), Objectivity, Inc. (Mountain View, Calif.), Versant Object Technology Corporation (Menlo Park, Calif.), and Ontos, Inc. (Lowell, Mass.). Today, large relational DBMS vendors such as Informix Software, Inc., and Oracle Corporation are getting into the act by adding object-oriented DBMS features to their relational products. This usually takes the form of support for undifferentiated binary large objects (BLOBS). BLOBS, however, do not provide the performance of a true object-oriented database. Also, a group of hybrid relational/object-oriented DBMSs has emerged to bridge the gap between the two database worlds. It should be noted that until recently, object-oriented DBMSs have lacked many of the basic features considered necessary for business production use. These include locking (which prevents two users from changing the same data simultaneously) or rollback (which restores a database to its original state if a transaction is interrupted in midstream).

MULTIDIMENSIONAL DATABASES DESIGNED FOR OLAP SYSTEMS

Going beyond the above four organization models for database-management systems, there is a newer model that focuses on the use of *multidimensionality* in on-line analytical processing. Multidimensional databases (MDDs) logically store data in arrays rather than store information as keyed records in tables. Currently, there is no agreed upon multidimensional model, that is, MDDs have no standard data-access method, and range from narrow to broad in addressing user requirements for decision making. At the low end, there are single-user or small-scale LAN-based tools for viewing multidimensional data. Although the functionality and usability of these tools are high, they are limited in scale and lack broad OLAP features. Tools in this category include PowerPlay from Cognos, PaBlo from Andyne, and Mercury from Business Objects. At the high end, tools such as Acumate ES from Kenan Technologies, Express from Oracle, Gentium from Planning Sciences, and Holos from Holistic Systems have such diverse functionality that each tool could define a separate category. The pure multidimensional database engines are Essbase from Arbor Software, LightShip Server from Pilot Software, and TM/1 from Sinper. These latter multidimensional databases will be covered in more detail in the next chapter.

Basically, there are two approaches to multidimensionality: the hypercube and the multicube. The *hypercube*, exemplified by Essbase, is meant to describe a similar object of greater than three dimensions, also with flat sides and each dimension at right angles to all of the others. Designing a hypercube model is a top-down process, that is, start by selecting the aspect of the business to capture, such as sales activity or financial reporting. Next, identify the values to be captured, such as sales or account balances. This information is almost always numeric. Last, identify the dimensions or granularity of the data—the lowest level of detail at which analysis is feasible. Common dimensions are measure, time, scenario, geography, product, and customer. A single call in a cube, for example, could store the sales dollars in March, in the Southeast, and of a specific product.

Because MDDs store information in arrays, values in the arrays can be updated without affecting the index—the reason MDDs are so well suited for read-write applications. However, a drawback to this hypercube model is that even minor changes in the dimensional structure require a complete reorganization of the database. Another drawback is that every value shares the same dimensionality. For example, it is redundant to store customer discount repeatedly by geography if the same discount is used throughout the organization. Although some hypercube products get around this problem, a better approach is to employ the *multicube*. Inasmuch as implementations vary, multicubes dimension each variable separately and deal internally with the consequences. The drawback is that this approach is less straightforward and carries steeper learning curves. Hence, if multidimensionality can be handled with a hypercube, it is a much simpler approach.[1]

CONCURRENT MOVEMENT TO DATA WAREHOUSING

Along with the movement to object-oriented database-management systems from relational DBMSs and multidimensional databases designed specifically for OLAP systems, there is a concurrent movement to *data warehousing*. Essentially, the movement recognizes that the information requirements for managers and their staffs are just as important as those for the traditional legacy-processing systems. It is widely recognized that these legacy systems do not meet the real information requirements for managers and their staffs as well as for analysts. The inadequacies of the legacy environment are such that the question is no longer whether a company will move to the new information paradigm, but rather when. With this movement comes the very important question: What is a data-warehouse environment, and how does it work on a day-to-day basis?

Because the data warehouse is designed to serve the information needs of the entire company, there is the need to store data at different levels of granularity—from current detail data to highly summarized data. Generally, the more current the detail data is, the more immediate is its use. Current detail data supports day-to-day decisions while historical data supports trend analysis and long-term decisions. As such, a data warehouse combines various data sources into a single information resource for end-user access. As such, end users perform ad hoc query, analysis, and reporting against the warehoused information. Typically, data warehousing involves combining products from a variety of technology vendors into an integrated solution.

In the design of the data warehouse, one of the requirements is the ability to accumulate and manage large amounts of data. Thus, it is important to choose levels of granularity and summarization for the data in the warehouse. Other design considerations for managing large amounts of data in the warehouse are storing data on multiple-storage media, summarizing data when detail becomes obsolete, encoding and referencing data where appropriate, and partitioning data for independent management and indexing.

Common Applications for Data Warehouses

Typically, data warehouses are updated on a daily, weekly, or fortnightly basis. In this manner, the warehouse helps users make complex queries about a business without slowing the high input, frequently refreshed OLTP (on-line transactional processing) database. Users, that is, corporate executives, managers, and analysts, employ data warehouses to analyze historical and operational data. For example, a bank executive could use the data warehouse to interpret the profiles of credit-card applicants over the past years. Or a sales manager might need a history of sales orders to help launch a new marketing program. Or a corporate planner could analyze strategic information that provides the foundation for the company's five-year strategic plan. The data warehouse has even helped some companies downsize.

According to a survey of 250 information-systems professionals by the Meta Group, Inc. (Stamford, Conn.), the most common applications of data warehouses were : (1) customer information systems—26%, (2) marketing—24%, (3) finance—22%, (4) sales—12%, and (5) other—16%.[2] Some of the companies building and implementing data warehouses include insurance companies, telecommunications companies, financial services firms, pharmaceutical companies, and hospitals. Their common characteristic is the need to build better information systems about their customers to better track and direct their businesses.

Additionally, data warehousing has been helpful to companies wanting to improve their customer response times. Saving time in this area may be an important key to controlling short- to long-range costs. To achieve lower costs, data-warehouse architects should consider data-warehouse tools that link operational databases with the warehouse. In addition, they should consider using tools that extract, update, and replicate information as well as help users query databases. In this manner, a number of useful data-warehouse applications can be developed that do assist in making managers and their staffs more effective in their jobs.

Accessing Data-Warehousing Applications Using World Wide Web Browsers

An important goal of a data-warehousing strategy is to ensure that its information has value, and that the organization and its clients and suppliers can use it when and where it is needed. A good way to meet these needs is to deliver that information through a World Wide Web browser. For the typical data-warehousing manager, Web-based distribution reduces the complexity and delay associated with supporting remote users. New Web development tools automatically link Web pages to databases or warehouses. Among the key tools are those based on Sun Microsystems' JAVA language, which is embedded in the latest version of Netscape; Oracle's Web-enabled tools; and Web-enabled RO-LAP (relational on-line analytical processing) tools from Dimensional Insight, Information Advantage, and MicroStrategy.

Because both Webs and data warehouses have a common goal of data access, newer releases of query tools will be Web-enabled so that Web browser software is able to access data warehouses. In fact, innovative user companies, like MasterCard, are already building such interfaces between these applications. MasterCard now offers banks access to its customers' buying habits, for instance, based on their credit-card transactions. Hence, the Web allows a company to reach out to more of its clients and prospective clients by letting those

Figure 3.1
The Basic Components of a Data Warehouse

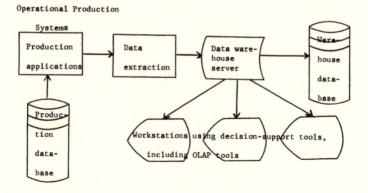

clients tap into data without waiting to receive specialized software from the data provider. Additional information will be given later in the chapter on the use of browsers for an intranet and for the Internet.

Components of a Data Warehouse

Today, there are many different data-warehouse architectures that are designed to meet the users' needs. Typically, data warehouses are composed of a distributed-data architecture with the bulk transfers of data occurring during off-hours and extensive interactive querying occurring at peak hours of the day. Thus, proper planning for warehouse operations is very important, especially in the area of a company's network infrastructure. To prevent performance disasters, networking professionals should be involved in each stage of warehouse planning and development, including implementation. Network analysis should consider a number of items, such as how often data updates should occur, how they should be scheduled, when they should occur, how much interactive querying to allow, how the front-end tools work, and what user query habits will be.

A typical data-warehouse architecture is illustrated in Figure 3.1. Essentially, there is data extraction of operational production data that is passed on to the warehouse database. A specialized data-warehouse server is used to host the warehouse database and decision-support tools, including OLAP tools. That is, this server is used to pass on extracted data to the warehouse database, and is employed by users to extract data from the data warehouse using some type of OLAP software or its equivalent to answer users' questions and meet their information-processing requirements. Although not shown in Figure 3.1, operational production databases are updated continuously via OLTP (on-line transactional processing) applications. In turn, a warehouse database is "refreshed" from operational production systems on a periodic basis, usually during off-hours when network and CPU utilization are low. Essentially, then, a data warehouse is a specialized database for supporting decision making taken from a variety of operational sources and then "scrubbed" to eliminate any inconsistencies or errors.

A common and simple type of data warehouse involves a *two-tiered, homogeneous architecture*. As an example, the IBM DB2 data on a mainframe computer might be periodically extracted and copied to a DB/2 database on a Microsoft Windows NT server. Then a data-access product, such as Information Builders Inc.'s FOCUS Reporter for Windows, can be used to read, analyze, and report on the warehouse data from a front-end graphical client on the Windows NT LAN. In contrast, more complex data warehouses are based on a *three-tiered architecture* that uses a separate middleware layer for data access and translation. The *first tier* is the host for production applications and is generally a mainframe computer or a midrange system, such as a Digital Equipment Corporation's VAX or an IBM's AS/400. The *second tier* is a departmental server, such as a Unix workstation or a Windows NT server, which resides in close proximity to warehouse users. The *third tier* is the desktop where IBM's PCs, Apple's Macintoshes, and X terminals are connected on a local area network. In this three-tiered architecture, the host (first level) is devoted to real-time, production-level data processing where the departmental server (second level) is optimized for query processing, analysis, and reporting. Also, the desktop (third level) handles reporting, analysis, and the graphical presentation of data.

Populating the Data Warehouse

Once the data-warehouse architecture has been established on the server, there are two primary methods for populating the data warehouse. The *first* method is called *change-based*, in which only the changes or differences are copied from the production database to the warehouse databases. The *second* method is called *batch copy*, in which the entire warehouse is periodically refreshed in a bulk upload or download of production data. Typically, bulk downloads can tax the network. Although transmitting only the changes puts less stress on the network, it requires more complex programming and maintenance. Which architecture is selected depends largely on the size of the warehouse and available resources. If there is limited network capacity, the change-based method is generally better. On the other hand, if the network can handle large data transfers, the batch-copy architecture will be simpler to set up and maintain.

Building an effective data warehouse, however, involves more than just copying data and letting users employ PC-based query and reporting tools. As the data warehouse is populated, it must be restructured, that is, tables must be denormalized, data must be cleansed of errors and redundancies, and new fields and keys must be added to reflect the needs of users for sorting, combining, and summarizing data. The more thought that is given to the design of the data model, the easier it will be to maintain, update, and retrieve warehouse data.

Overall, effective data modeling relieves network stress by rolling up or summarizing information into meaningful constructs so that users do not have to perform as many interactive queries to join tables in real time.[3]

Choosing the Proper Server Platform

A most important decision to be made when planning and constructing a data-warehouse architecture is the choice of server platform. Small databases with local-query activity can often be hosted by Pentium-based PCs or Unix workstations. However, for larger databases supporting a larger number of users, multiple network segments, and large queries, SMP (symmetric multiprocessing) computers are recommended. Where very large databases and very complex queries are required, companies usually use mainframe processors or sometimes turn to massively parallel database processors. In the final analysis, there is a need for careful planning and involvement of the networking staff in order to ensure a successful implementation. Many companies have found that data warehouses tend to create a lot more demand than originally anticipated. It is essential that extensive predictive analysis be undertaken so that network demand is estimated realistically.

To assist in choosing the proper server platform, there is a need to assess the work to be done by the client and the server. For example, to arrive at an answer to "Give me the top 20 customers by sales volume for the month of March," the system must add up all the business from all possible customers over that time period. There are two ways to determine the 20 customers. The *first* is to transfer all the customer and revenue data from that period across the network and process it on the *client*. The *second* is to place a query engine on the *server* to perform the query operation. In this second case, just the answer set—the information of the top 20 customers—gets sent back across the network to the client. The differences from the network perspective are quite substantial. The first scenario might involve a transmission of 200 MB, while the second might involve only 200 KB. Thus, depending upon the client/server situation, the demands on the company's networking can be quite different and must be considered by the networking staff.

Representative Data-Warehouse Software

Before focusing on representative data-warehouse products per se, it is helpful to state that most data-warehousing software products currently focus on one of three areas: (1) acquisition, (2) storage, and (3) access. Most software vendors that provide these products have a proven track record for performing one of these functions well. Generally, most have simply retrofitted existing products to meet warehousing requirements. In the *first* category, there are a number of vendors who have products designed to manage and automate the acquisition process. Some of the data-acquisition product vendors have begun to integrate

Figure 3.2
Popular Data Warehouses

Company	Product	Warehouse Management Features
Apertus Technologies Inc. New York, NY 800-310-4624 http://www.apertus.com	Enterprise/ Integrator	Graphical administration manager for configuration management
Hewlett-Packard Company Palo Alto, CA 800-737-7740 http://www.hp.com	Intelligent Warehouse	Summary management, usage reports, query blocking, partition management, security
IBM Corporation Armonk, NY 800-426-3333 http://www.ibm.com	Visual Warehouse	Access to heterogeneous data sources for population and updates, transformation and replication, management of technical and business meta data
Informatica Corporation Menlo Park, CA 800-653-3871 http://www.informatica.com	OpenBridge	Monitor and control of data transformation and loading, real-time reports
Information Builders Inc. New York, NY 800-969-4636 http://www.ibi.com	Enterprise Copy Manager	Management of queries, loading and updates, mapping and data transformation, log file and report generation
Intersolv Rockville, MD 800-547-4000 http://www.intersolv.com	DataDirect SmartData	Meta data management
Oracle Corporation Redwood Shores, CA 800-633-0596 http://www.oracle.com	Designer/2000, Open Gateways, Symmetric Repli- cation, Parallel Loader	Automatic replication of operational data, flat-file population to warehouse
Prism Solutions Inc. Sunnyvale, CA 800-995-2928 http://www.prismsolutions.com	Prism Warehouse Manager, Prism Directory Manager	Changed Data Capture modules for current or near-current data, captures only delta changes to source files
Red Brick Systems, Inc. Los Gatos, CA 800-777-2585 http://www.redbrick.com	Red Brick Warehouse	Company has partnerships with third parties providing data-extract tools
SAS Institute Inc. Cary, NC 919-677-8000 http://www.sas.com	SAS System for Data Warehousing	Menu-driven interface for managing building process, data extraction, transfor- mation, scheduling of updates
Software AG Reston,VA 800-843-9534 http:www.sagus.com	SourcePoint	Automated extraction, trans- port and population of a warehouse

several of their products into complete warehouse offerings. The largest vendors in this category include Prism Solutions Inc., Carleton Corporation, and Platinum Technology.

In the *second* category, there are a number of storage-software products. A representative listing is found in Figure 3.2. Currently, firms like Oracle, Sybase,

IBM, and Informix control the bulk of the market. When a typical Unix server or mainframe computer seems incapable of handling the envisioned workload, MIS executives look to SMP (symmetric multiprocessing) or MPP (massive parallel processing). For the truly large jobs, SMP may not be enough. In those cases, some companies are turning to MPP machines. Although SMP machines can handle up to 16 additional processors at a time, MPP systems incorporate the use of dozens or even hundreds of processors. The power of these machines cannot be approached by any other hardware on the market today.

For the *third* category, access-software products include the following. First, unlike the overly simplistic report-writers of the past, query-facilities tools turn a large, complex data-warehouse environment into a friendly, well-managed workstation. Second, access-software tools center on statistical analysis as found in products like SAS and SPSS. Third, a number of data-discovery products are getting a lot of attention. These include decision-support tools plus artificial-intelligence and expert systems. Using neural networks, fuzzy logic, decision trees, and other tools of advanced mathematics and statistics, these products allow users to sift through massive amounts of raw data to discover new, insightful and, in many cases, useful things about the company, its operations, and its markets. These data discovery products are widely used in data mining as covered later in the chapter. Fourth, data-visualization software products bring graphical representation to new heights. The most popular visualization tool falls under the heading of geographical information systems. Such systems turn data about stores, individuals, or anything else into easy-to-understand dynamic maps.

Fifth, the focus of on-line analytical processing is multidimensional software tools. As will be seen in the next chapter, these tools represent a whole new generation of high-powered user-friendly data investigation systems that allow users to look at information from numerous different perspectives. OLAP software products provide the capability to slice and dice reports dynamically, and to look at the same kinds of information from different perspectives. Numerous OLAP applications will be given in Part III of this text. As an example, at the press of a button, a product manager is able to view sales figures for a given product at the national level, view them broken down by division, drill down to view figures by territories within a division, check sales numbers for each store in a territory, and then compare them against sales of stores from a different territory. This last category of data-access products has a tremendous potential for enriching the manager's capability to ask and answer important questions facing him or her on a daily basis.

Starting with Data Marts

As recommended in the beginning of this chapter, there is a need to start small when developing OLAP systems for any functional area of a company. From this view, vendors, such as Sybase, Software AG, Red Brick Systems, and Microsoft, are marketing products and services that make it easier and much cheaper to deploy scaled-down data warehouses, known as *data marts*. Their sales pitch is that data marts put important business information into the hands of more decision makers. Rather than store all enterprise data in one large database, data marts contain a subset of the data for a single aspect of a company's business, such as finance, inventory, or human resources. Thus, the focus is on functional data warehouses.

Many experts feel that a data warehouse should be developed first. In turn, data marts can be built that are highly summarized subsets of the warehouse. The data must be filtered and cleaned to maintain its integrity, and the information must be updated regularly. On the other hand, not everyone can afford the enterprise-wide approach of a data warehouse; it may be best to build one or more data marts first. Such uses should keep a centralized orientation that focuses on the goal of an enterprise warehouse. Otherwise, the multiple data marts will not be able to coexist. In the final analysis, data marts are about speed because companies must make faster and better decisions.

Building an Effective Data Warehouse

To build an effective data warehouse means getting involved in identifying several different types of tools and related issues. A suggested list is as follows: (1) data-modeling tools; (2) a meta-data repository; (3) the core database; (4) data-transport tools; (5) data-extraction, scrubbing, and normalization tools; (6) middleware-connectivity tools; and (7) end-user data-access tools.[4] In addition, there is a need for tools to manage the data warehouse along with the means to handle replication and synchronization of multiple data warehouses. Based upon the data warehouse built, warehouse developers need to develop applications that use the data warehouse effectively.

In general, building a data warehouse can be costly (say, in the millions of dollars for a very large one) and time consuming (say, two years). This costly and time-consuming undertaking is evidence that the value of information is a strategic asset to a typical company. Getting there, however, is not simple since MIS managers must wrestle with the problem of moving various forms of data from legacy and OLAP systems. It requires preparing, conditioning, and staging data so business users armed with appropriate data-access tools can perform analyses that previously were either impossible, too expensive, or too time consuming.

DATA MINING VERSUS DATA WAREHOUSING

Today, data mining is considered to be a direct outgrowth of the data-warehouse concept. It allows data access and analysis that gives users unparalleled capabilities to extract hard-to-get-at data, spot trends, and recognize patterns in corporate databases. While many companies have built data warehouses to consolidate data located in disparate databases, they are implementing data mining to learn more about the data. While data warehouses are a part of the technology mainstream, available data-mining tools are now being marketed. Essentially, companies want to use data mining to improve their *knowledge* of their customers and markets. For example, retailers want to use it to target customers for sales promotions better or to manage inventory across various geographic locations. Similarly, telecommunications companies want to use data mining to forecast demand patterns, profile and segment customer groups, customize billing, and analyze profitability. In addition, financial-services companies are employing data mining to consolidate information from multiple sources, analyze customers' business patterns, and sell them more services.

Data-Mining Information

Because data mining reaches much deeper into databases, its tools provide users the capability to find patterns in the data and infer rules from them. Those patterns and rules can be used to guide decision making and forecast the effect of those decisions. In addition, data mining can speed analysis by focusing attention on the most important variables. Although users might find these patterns with a series of queries against the data, data mining lets the users explore a much wider range of possibilities than even the most sophisticated set of queries.

Typical types of information that can be obtained by data mining include forecasting, associations, sequences, classifications, and clusters. Essentially, all of these may involve predictions.[5] However, the *first* type (forecasting) is a different form of prediction in that it estimates the future value of continuous variables—like sales figures—based on patterns within the data. The *second* type of information centers on associations that happen when occurrences are linked in a single event. For example, a study of supermarket baskets might reveal that when potato chips are purchased, 60 percent of the time some type of cola is also purchased, unless there is a promotion, in which case cola is purchased 80 percent of the time. Knowing this fact, managers can evaluate the profitability of a promotion.

In the *third* type of information or sequences, events are linked over time. As an example, if a house is bought, then 60 percent of the time a new oven will be bought within one month, and 65 percent of the time a new refrigerator will be bought within three weeks. For the *fourth* type (classifications), patterns are recognized that describe the group to which an item belongs. It does this by examining existing items that already have been classified and inferring a set of rules. Because a common problem to many companies is the loss of steady customers, classification can help discover the characteristics of customers who are likely to leave, and provide a model that can be used to predict who they are. It can also help a company determine what kinds of promotions have been effective in keeping which types of customers. The *fifth* and last type of information is clustering. It is related to classification, but differs in that no groups have yet been defined. Using clustering, the data-mining tool discovers different groupings within the data. This can be applied to problems as diverse as detecting defects in manufacturing or finding affinity groups for bank cards.

Data-Mining Tools

To help users obtain the desired information as set forth above, vendors are offering neural networks, decision trees, rule induction, and data visualization. In addition, some tools are based on combinations of these methods.[6] It should be noted that some OLAP vendors are currently adding data-mining tools to their multidimensional engines.

The *first* type, that is, neural networks, are essentially collections of connected nodes with inputs, outputs, and processing at each node. Between the visible input layer and output layer may be a number of hidden processing layers. As such, the network is capable of learning since it has a training set of data for which the inputs produce a known set of outputs. Each case in the training set is compared with the known outcome; if it differs, a correction is calculated and applied to the processing in the nodes in the network. These steps are repeated until a stopping condition, such as corrections being less than a certain amount, is reached. Typically, neural network products are employed beyond the business information arena. Neural networks frequently are applied to more general pattern-recognition problems such as handwriting recognition and interpretation of electrocardiograms.

In the *second* type, decision trees divide the data into groups based on values of the variables. They use a methodology that resembles the game "20 Questions." The result is a hierarchy of "if–then" statements that classify the data. It should be noted that decision trees are not foolproof since some decision trees have problems handling continuous sets of data, like sales or usage, and require that data be grouped into ranges. The way in which a range is handled can inadvertently hide patterns.

The *third* type of data-mining tools is rule induction. Because a set of "if–then" statements can be every bit as obscure as a neural network, particularly if the condition list is long and complex, rule induction creates nonhierarchical sets of conditions, which may overlap.

The *fourth* and final type of data-mining tool is data visualization software, which presents a picture for users to see rather than automating the process. Since the visual representations of as many as four variables are shown in a single picture, it presents an enormous amount of information in a concise format. Essentially, there is a very wide range of information presented to the user that will often make peaks or valleys stand out.

RELATIONSHIP OF DATA REPLICATION TO OLAP

In the past, multiple-corporate databases were consistently synchronized and were, in essence, clones of one another. This task, frequently called "nightly refresh," has been practiced for years in the world of computer mainframes. When a few PCs were added, the job progressed into downloading and uploading data between the PCs and the mainframe. The situation was quite controllable. However, when there is a network with servers and users spread across multiple time zones along with groupware applications and reliance by users on real-time information, this chore becomes a network manager's problem, thereby requiring *replication*. Essentially, replication copies information from one database to another so that the contents of both databases are consistent. That can mean transferring data from a central mainframe to branch servers and then down to local workstations, from news feeds to reporting and analysis applications, between networked servers, or within almost any architecture. Data movement can be one-way or bidirectional. It can be event-driven which is triggered by data-value changes, or time dependent which is performed at regular intervals or nightly.

Typically, there are many benefits to replication. It is often implemented to offload processing onto a single server. Copies of corporate data are downloaded to branch offices where departmental users can access the local data more efficiently. Replication can also be an important part of a data-warehouse strategy, that is, consolidating data from multiple-operational databases to a single data store for analysis. Having multiple copies of data also sets the stage for quick disaster recovery and cost-efficient load balancing on busy networks.

Replicated DBMSs are recommended for applications such as backup and OLAP and DSS systems that do not require up-to-the-minute information. Most managers using OLAPs and DSSs to do number-crunching do not require up-to-the-minute information. Most companies doing backup do not require the up-to-date capabilities of two-phase commit. That is, many users would probably prefer working with a backup system that was slightly out of sync, rather than waiting for the main database-management system to be restored. Replication also allows companies to divide up a database and ship information closer to those users that work with it the most. Response time improves because the information is stored locally rather than at a central site. Wide-area network costs fall because users no longer need to access the network to work with the data they need.

EXTERNAL ON-LINE DATABASES

To assist company personnel in carrying out their duties, a new industry has emerged from vendors focusing on on-line databases. Large banks of information are processed, stored, and delivered electronically. What is provided is not so much additional information (most of it has been around in printed form for a long time), but an improvement in the ease with which information can be retrieved. From this perspective, timely external information is now available for a typical company to meet its daily needs, including its virtual reality needs.

The on-line industry had its roots in small, privately owned bulletin boards, which now number in the thousands. But it is evolving toward a more structured business with a few big mass-market services. Three leading commercial services alone account for over four million users. Both large and small services allow customers to communicate with friends or fellow hobbyists, join discussions, or download sample software programs. But the large networks, including America Online Inc., CompuServe Inc., and Prodigy Services Company, offer a variety of other services, from shopping to travel arrangements to stock trades. Additionally, there is the fast-growing Internet which is the largest computer network in the world, consisting of thousands of smaller regional networks that are *interconneted*—hence the name Internet. Every computer on the Internet has its own unique Internet address. This ad hoc group of private and public networks shares a common computer code and backbone network. More information on the Internet will be given later in the chapter.

Timely External Information for Business

For timely external information that is oriented toward business firms, the field is crowded with competing companies. Consider just the traditional publishers of financial data. Dow Jones & Company already has several offerings available via computer terminal, including a package that enables investors to learn the value of their portfolio every five minutes or so. Dun & Bradstreet sells on line some of the printed information that was formerly distributed by mail. McGraw-Hill owns Data Resources, Inc., probably the preeminent company in the on-line information field. Other companies with on-line database offerings include ABC, Boeing, Chase Manhattan, Citicorp, Control Data, General Electric, G.T.E., Mead, Time Inc., and Xerox.

A typical service is the Global Report which is Citibank's round-the-clock information service for executives and their staffs. It specializes in international news, rates, background information, and analysis. Global Report focuses on international business and carries world, country, and regional news; market, industry, and company news; and extensive market coverage, including bonds (corporate, Treasury, European and international, and mortgage-backed municipal), commodities, foreign exchange rates, funds and trusts, futures, money markets, options, and time-delayed stock prices.

Of all the on-line databases, one of the most widely used by business, as well as by government and education, is Dialog. The Dialog Information Retrieval Service gives users immediate access to the world's largest and most comprehensive computer storehouse of information. No matter what is needed, useful answers can be found among the more than 100 million references, abstracts, or statistical series from published material that can be searched on line with Dialog. With an inexpensive terminal or PC (connected via the telephone), users search quickly for the desired information, describing the topic in their own words and using simple English commands to get the results wanted. No programming knowledge is needed to access more than 150 Dialog databases that cover all major disciplines—science, chemistry, technology, medicine, law, business, finance, social sciences, humanities, the arts, public affairs, and general news. In turn, this information may be useful for typical OLAP business applications.

CURRENT APPROACH TO DATA COMMUNICATIONS AND NETWORKING

As information technology is moving in the direction of networks to support mission-critical as well as OLAP applications, it has raised the importance of managing data communications and networking. The complexity of tools, information, people, and processes needed to build, operate, and monitor networks has become visible to more and more users throughout the organization. The way an organization approaches the design, implementation, and operation of data communications and networking can make or break the quality of its network services. More than ever, networks of all types, whether they are LANs, MANs, or a combination of these (which are discussed below), are at the very heart of a company's operations. They must be managed with greater levels of reliability and service quality today as well as in the future.

LOCAL AREA NETWORKS (LANS)

Local area networks (LANs) meet the increasingly vital need to interconnect computers, terminals, word processors, facsimile, and other office machines within a building, campus, or a very small geographic area. A local area network may be designed to support only one vendor's terminal equipment, or it may be designed for multivendor support. Network logic may be embedded in the terminal equipment, in bus/network interface units, or in central controllers. Overall, LANs are flexible and cost-effective tools versus computer mainframes that greatly expand the variety of services that can be performed by microcomputers and workstations. A model based on the International Standards Organization's Open Systems Interconnection (OSI) helps explain the software and hardware characteristics of LANs. Fundamentally, the OSI model describes the seven layers of activity for typical LAN communications.

Wired LANs

Underlying any local area network is the physical wire connecting computing devices. Some LANs use either coaxial cable or twisted-pair wire. Each has advantages and disadvantages, depending on the particular application. A LAN that uses coaxial cable—Ethernet, for example—can link more than 1,000 devices in a single network. It can carry data transmission with a bandwidth of up to 100 megabits per second (Mbps). Generally, the greater the bandwidth, the more information that can be sent through a system in a given amount of time. The high bandwidth offered by coaxial cable, therefore, is a safe choice for a LAN that may be required to perform many transmission functions among many users. A high bandwidth is also needed to accommodate video signals or to transfer very large files, such as extensive spreadsheets.

Fiber-optic cable is a somewhat newer alternative to both coaxial and twisted pair. It offers higher bandwidth than both. Not only is fiber-optic cable used for LANs, but it is also often used to connect separate LANs that are located at some distance from each other. Also, fiber optics are useful for LAN situations where there are data security problems with electromagnetic interference. Compared with copper wire and coaxial cable, fiber cable is relatively immune from tampering and interference from electromagnetic radiation.

Fiber-optic networks are typically used as backbone links connecting islands of office networks, minicomputers, or shared peripherals. Fiber links are also employed as point-to-point data highways connecting computer mainframes to distributed systems or other LANs. In such applications, high bandwidth and distance—fiber links can stretch as far as four kilometers unrepeated—are the prime considerations. Even in office applications, fiber is preferable to copper wires because it suffers no bandwidth degradation due to signal reflection and is easier to maintain.

Wireless LANs

Today, wireless LANs are emerging as an important addition to present-day offerings of wired LANs because of cost, compatibility, and ease-of-use issues. Although wireless networks are unlikely to replace wire-based systems (as set forth above), they offer an attractive alternative for those looking to add new users to corporate LANs and support mobile workers who telecommute from far-flung locations. Within a wireless network operating mode, there are two kinds. Wide-area wireless networks, like cellular and public packet-switching wireless networks, cover relatively long distances (metropolitan areas) with modest data communications performance. On the other hand, local-area wireless networks cover a shorter distance (a floor of a building or a corporate campus), but offer a much higher bandwidth.

Virtual LANs

Another important direction in LANs today is virtual LANs. They are virtual in the sense that no physical wire or backplane necessarily defines the LAN. Because of the switching technology, a virtual LAN has many times the bandwidth of a regular LAN. Essentially, virtual LANs (VLANs) are logical group-ings of network addresses organized independently of the physical networks they reside on such that they have the ability to make the network configuration transparent so that users can communicate freely without knowledge of the net-work. The objectives of VLAN technology are threefold: (1) to provide and manage scarce bandwidth for the high-performance applications like graphics, CAD/CAM, and multimedia that are seen on current networks; (2) to separate the logical-network management from the physical-network infrastructure; and (3) to facilitate network node moves, adds, and changes. At their best, VLANs transcend both physical networks and geography, thereby allowing network ad-ministrators to change logical configurations and manage bandwidth as needs dictate.

METROPOLITAN AREA NETWORKS (MANS)

Going beyond the confines of a LAN existing within a building or several buildings in close proximity to one another, there are metropolitan area networks (MANs). A MAN is of limited geographic range, generally defined as within a 50-mile radius. In the past, a number of small companies have begun businesses by installing fiber-optic cable in metropolitan business areas. Their primary cus-tomers are all sizes of companies that need to communicate within the metro-politan area. The customer is usually responsible for providing equipment. The primary market is the customer that needs a lot of high-speed digital service. The MAN providers typically offer lower prices than the telephone companies, and offer diverse routing as well as provide backup in emergency conditions. Due to the pressing need to link a typical organization with other organizations locally, nationally, or internationally, the discussion below takes this important direction into account.

WIDE AREA NETWORKS (WANS)

Today, wide area networks (WANs) are generally considered to be those that cover a large geographic area, require the crossing of public right-of-ways, and use circuits provided by a common carrier. WANs may be made up of a com-bination of switched and leased, terrestrial and satellite, and private microwave circuits. The WAN for a large multinational company may be global, whereas the WAN for a small company may cover only several cities or counties. General Electric, for example, has a private global network to transmit voice, data, and video signals to GE offices in 25 countries.

Wired WANs

To overcome difficulties experienced by users in wide area networks, there is a need for a new approach, that is, the farther the computer is from the data, the harder it is for the user to get to it. This is especially true if it is found in another city or across the nation. Trading the security and relative speed of a LAN for the sluggishness and uncertainty of a wide area network creates unforeseen data bottlenecks and administrative headaches. A new universal network transport mechanism, called asynchronous transfer mode (ATM), gives the user easier access between a Token Ring or Ethernet local area network and wide-area mechanisms, such as T1 and X.25. By providing a common infrastructure that is suitable for everything from desktop and LAN applications to campus, metropolitan, and global networks, ATM offers a new direction in network technology.

Until recently, LAN and WAN technologies have approached data transmission differently. The driving force behind ATM is a new class of applications involving voice, video, multimedia, imaging, and client/server functions. These broadband applications demand much higher network capacity than the traditional personal productivity, on-line transaction processing, and database programs. The disparity between LAN and WAN transport protocols makes it difficult to create broadband enterprise networks. Regarded as a universal protocol for high-speed networking, ATM has been chosen by the CCITT (the international data communications standards organization) as the transport layer protocol for emerging broadband integrated services digital networks (BISDNs). Basic ISDN will be discussed later in the chapter.

Wireless WANs

Wireless WANs are being put to use in a variety of applications although current technology limitations make wireless WANs unsuitable for many applications now common on LANs and internetworks. That is, wireless services are well suited mainly for applications that involve short, bursty messages. Wireless data networks already have become a critical advantage in many industries. An example is the courier industry. In the late 1970s, Federal Express Corporation revolutionized the overnight delivery business by building a private wireless network to track its packages. The Federal Express network was not low in cost. It cost the courier hundreds of millions of dollars, but helped propel the company to the front of a very competitive industry.

Although wireless WAN services are found in organizations of varying sizes, the next few years will be critical in deciding how important they become in corporate networks. One of the most important issues that must be resolved is the matter of standards. Today's wireless WANs are based on proprietary technology even though several carriers have thrown open their systems to third-party developers. Until standards are in place, many organizations are reluctant to make major commitments to wireless WANs. As is the usual case with all standards, progress toward the development of standards for wireless WAN systems and equipment is slow.

INTEGRATED SERVICES DIGITAL NETWORKS (ISDNS)

One way of bringing together the preceding discussion on data communications and networking is to think in terms of total communications for a typical organization. Although this can take many directions, only one is discussed below due to space limitations. The focus is on integrated services digital networks (ISDNs) which can provide users with a total network in which compatible voice, data, and video configurations will be transported on a single pair of wires, eliminating leased line and digital circuits for data, voice lines for telecommunications, and cable services for video. It can offer users a multifaceted communications network to transmit and receive information worldwide. The concept of ISDN is that of a standard protocol that is used to link private and public networks to receive and transmit digital information. Compatibility stems from predetermined standards, allowing all types of equipment to interface, provided that they are manufactured to accepted standards.

The ultimate goal of ISDN is to combine all of the telecommunications services that are currently being provided by different networks into one large-scale network. Services to be offered through ISDN include telephony services (call forwarding, transferring, conference calling, automatic wake-up calling), data services (closed user groups, called and calling line identification, multiaddress calling), teletext services (delayed messages, multiple addressing, Telex access, and a graphic mode), facsimile services (delayed delivery and multiple designations), and video-text services (transactions, such as reservations and shopping, and special character sets). In preparing for ISDN, companies need to consider whether their current data communications decisions are compatible with an evolution to ISDN-based communications. In addition, companies should examine their internal structure for planning voice, data, and office facilities to ensure that internal conflicts between separate voice and data departments are minimized.

In summary, ISDN is an ideal technology for remote LAN access/work-at-home settings, satellite offices, Internet access for individuals, and computer-based videoconferencing. It is an international network architecture that offers a standard universal interface for voice, data, and video, thereby allowing highly efficient, interactive use of the public telephone network. In contrast, Open Network Architecture (ONA) is a regulatory development that will allow specialty information services, such as messaging, electronic mail, security, and answering services, to take place over a local telephone network. Although the implementation time of ISDN and ONA technologies is uncertain, it would depend in large part on public demand. But their impact on the microcomputer user throughout the 1990s and beyond will be felt. One probable effect of this implementation will be increasing numbers of at-home workers, including executives. Without immediate access to the workplace, *telecommunicating* on a widespread basis was not possible before now, but this will change as network communication from the home, without special cabling or transmission facilities, will enable it to function like the company-owned office. Thus, a home computer will begin to assume the importance of an essential storage and communications device, much like the telephone. The public telephone network will be asked to transport this information.

RELATED DATA COMMUNICATIONS AND NETWORKING TECHNOLOGIES

Complementary to the preceding discussion are electronic mail systems, voice messaging and speech recognition systems, and video conferencing, which are discussed below. For the first area of *electronic mail systems* (E-mail), if fast and accurate communications are needed and overnight couriers and telexes are too expensive in volume, there is need to consider electronic mail. Because E-mail distributes messages from one computer to another, transactions are very fast, are cost effective, and run 24 hours a day. This is especially helpful across time zones. Some E-mail systems even offer the ability to transfer entire desktop publishing programs, recalculable spreadsheets, revisable word-processing documents, and updatable databases—something a fax machine will never do. To use E-mail, the user enters the system and types a message. Tagged with an electronic address, the message is then transmitted to a ''mailbox''—a point in the main computer's memory where it is stored until called up. The message can be funneled into the PC of a specified system user or sent to a middle person who can print and deliver the message. Because a typical E-mail works through PCs, a user can work up a document on a PC and send it instantaneously without the hassles of couriers or post-office schedules.

Currently, there are over 6 million E-mail subscribers in the United States. Communication is increasingly available for companies with as few as six locations through public E-mail systems, such as Western Union's EasyLink, Dialcom, and MCI Mail. All of these firms are integrating E-mail with other telecommunications methods, enabling the computer to transmit via fax, telex, or cablegram—almost unlimited information and communications delivery capabilities. E-mail subscribers can often get access to a variety of public databases, financial reporting services, news clipping services, and news wires. Western Union, for instance, offers FYI News, a service that provides up-to-the-minute reports on business, finance, politics, entertainment, and more.

For company employees wishing to receive, use, and distribute calls and messages, *voice messaging* can be helpful for meeting that need and can dramatically speed up the communication process and make it more accurate. Essentially, voice messaging technology eliminates intervention between a caller and the intended message recipient. Messages incorrectly taken, lost, or forgotten are becoming a thing of the past. With a high-quality voice messaging system, company employees have to make only one telephone call to retrieve all their messages. In essence, voice messaging can be at the hub of all potential communication centers: business, home, car, pager, electronic mail, telephone answering service, facsimile machine, and push-button telephone. Voice messaging connects all of these spokes into one central message system, thereby saving the executive time, money, and energy.

A related area to voice messaging systems is *speech-recognition systems*. Speech-recognition software packages have two basic purposes: either accept voice commands to streamline the operation of the computer, or take verbal dictation that can be saved as a text document. The former class basically accepts verbal input to activate macros, many matching spoken words to a list of menu commands. For example, Voice Blaster from Covox, Inc. automatically creates a list of an application's menus items; the user trains the software to respond to his or her voice as commands are spoken. The program requires a sound card, yet supplies a microphone-and-earphone headset. All in all, it is expected that speech products in the coming years will be mature enough to warrant serious consideration for everyday business use.

Video conferencing, which is available for business units that are widely dispersed geographically, is designed to be used as a business tool to assist in overseeing dispersed operations. There are two distinct types of video conferencing. The first, "person-to-person," links one PC to another, thereby allowing two people to share moving pictures and some type of shared workspace. Usually these systems transmit postage-size images over ISDN, regular phone lines, or Switch-56 via a little video camera mounted on the monitor. The second type is "group-to-group" video conferencing that tries to merge two or more conference rooms. Large monitors, multiple microphones, and dedicated-transmission lines are usually required for this type of sharing, resulting in better picture and sound quality than person-to-person. Of course, the cost is much higher.

In group-to-group video conferencing, there can be an exchange of ideas that involves company personnel of distant operations. The accent may be on a free exchange of potential answers to specific questions that arise in the normal course of conversation. From this perspective, the interaction of participants at distant points from one another may signal the need to develop specific computer programs for answering the questions posed. At the next video-conferencing meeting, a presentation can be made that focuses on potential answers to the important business questions posed earlier.

Currently, several vendors are offering public rooms or sharing their private rooms with others. In a similar manner, many large corporations are currently making use of private broadcasts by satellite directly into their own facilities or into hotel meeting facilities to deliver corporate communications or training to employees. As they gained experience with the use of corporate video, companies have installed their own private networks of satellite-receiver dishes located at their corporate facilities that enable employees to watch regularly scheduled company programs.

There are many benefits from utilizing video conferencing. First, there is a reduction in travel costs. By eliminating many trips, a company cuts out the unproductive time people spend on traveling, thereby resulting in increased productivity. The ability to hold a meeting almost instantly in a relaxed atmosphere, with less time away from office and home, has removed a lot of stress often involved with meetings. In addition, video conferences enable the company to involve more people in meetings. These individuals might include experts or scientists, who would rather be at work in their labs than traveling to a meeting.

AN INTRANET

With the phenomenal popularity of the Internet (as discussed in the next section of this chapter) as a means of accessing information, companies are coming to view it as a messaging model. The result is an "intranet," a private-network version of the Internet. Often, the search methods are identical to those used on the Internet, thus maintaining a high comfort level for Internet users. It enables companies to make massive amounts of information available to their employees locally and remotely, and to improve their messaging strategies.

Typically, intranets are erected to support one or more publishing applications that, while not mission-critical, offer a real payback. For example, staff directories, product data sheets, employee handbooks, and other human resource materials fit into this category. Essentially, these are read-only data sets where user response is not required. These applications can be easily achieved at low cost. On the other hand, more ambitious applications use Web pages linked to back-end applications that retrieve or store data in databases. For example, many companies are building Web-based human resources applications that allow staff to check on vacation entitlements and other benefits. Overall, intranets change the way a company thinks about information access and distribution, as well as transform network infrastructures.

When a company designs and implements an Intranet, there is a need to decide whether the intranet will use an internal wide area network and local area network as the communication path between the employees and the intranet. If so, there is also a need to be aware of the possible traffic load that may be generated, and to determine if the WAN/LAN connection can handle the increased traffic. If a company decides to use an external network as the communication vehicle, such as the Internet, there are concerns about the security and privacy aspects of the intranet. With company information flowing around between the employees at their PCs and the Web server connected across the public Internet—perhaps information such as a company's policies and procedures—it is possible that outsiders could tap into the information and use it for their own purposes.

Essential Elements of an Intranet

The main building blocks of an intranet are shown in Figure 3.3 and are related to the Internet. More specifically, a typical intranet consists of servers,

Figure 3.3
The Building Blocks of an Intranet and Its Relationship to the Internet

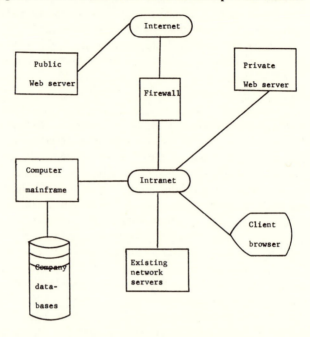

databases, browsers, firewalls, and dynamic HTML pages. At the heart of most intranet systems are *Web servers*. These simple but effective information distribution mechanisms are becoming increasingly sophisticated as vendors extend and enhance their basic functionality. Intranets can also involve the use of TCP/IP (transmission control protocol/internet protocol) as a transport and a number of TCP/IP applications that range from file transfer to audio and video distribution. As shown in the illustration, Web servers are integrated with *databases*, linked to mainframes and other legacy systems, and provide workflow services. Combined with the high bandwidth capacity of corporate-data networks, a company can capitalize on advanced features, such as real-time audio and video as well as collaborative applications and 3-D data representation.

A client *browser* is the means by which the user interfaces with the intranet. The most sophisticated browsers include Netscape's Navigator, Microsoft's Internet Explorer, Attachmate's Emissary, and Sun Microsystems' HotJava. These products will allow the user to support advanced presentation techniques and a whole range of add-on products. In contrast, a *firewall* is the main line of defense which is essentially a computer connected to both the corporate network and the Internet. Once companies create direct links between their private networks and the global Internet, their internal network is open to attack from anyone. As such, the need for a firewall is paramount for security reasons. Additionally, there is generally a need to convert the scanned documents into a text format suitable for Web access, that is, in a format known as HyperText Mark-up Language or *HTML*.

Beyond these basic building blocks, there are a number of specialized tools to help a company build an intranet. There are videoconferencing systems, such as the low-cost VideoPhone from Connectix Corporation (San Mateo, California), Web-based bulletin boards, such as the WebBoard product from O'Reilly & Associates, Inc. (Sebastapol, California), and conferencing systems, such as OpenMind from Attachmate Corporation (Bellevue, Washington). VideoPhone could be used for meetings, even over slow WAN links, while WebBoard could be used to maintain discussion areas for work groups or the entire company. While finding products is easy, deciding what is best for a company's intranet can be difficult. The key is to employ those products that address clearly identifiable needs, offer a quick payback, and are simple to implement.

The most important benefit of an intranet is in the area of new methods of information distribution and collection, new opportunities to involve staff in the process, and the cost benefits of recentralizing some of those functions that are difficult to manage in a distributed environment. Companies that build intranets will find that information publishing becomes a way of corporate life, and improved internal communications and a more effective community culture will be the result. Overall, intranets are here to stay and, as shown in Figure 3.3, can be linked directly to the Internet.

THE INTERNET

At this time, the Internet is the closest network that the United States has to a national information highway (i.e., the National Information Infrastructure), sometimes referred to as the electronic highway, the digital expressway, or just plain cyberspace. This ad hoc computer network was started in the late 1960s by the Defense Department. Fundamentally, two events converged to create the Internet: (1) technology and (2) necessity. The technology was the packet-switched networking. The necessity aspect was the perceived threat of thermo-nuclear war, that is, the U.S. Air Force was interested in building a computer network that stood a chance of surviving a major attack. Therefore, they built a network without a central control point so it could lose one, or several, computers and the computers remaining could still communicate with each other. This led to the creation of the ARPANET, the progenitor of today's Internet.

The Internet, which was briefly noted earlier in the chapter, has basically become the postal service, telephone system, and research library of the electronic age, thereby allowing millions of people to exchange information virtually anywhere in the world and at any time, usually in a matter of minutes, using available data communications and networking technology. The source of the Internet's appeal is that anyone on the Net can post and retrieve information; but the practical result, which is often frustrating to businesses accustomed to logical hierarchy and ordering, is that there is no defined or enforced structure for posting that information. As a result, experienced Internet users generally have difficulty when trying to receive information.

Doing Business on the Internet

Although establishing a direct connection to the Internet was difficult in the past, it is much easier as more commercial Internet-service providers have sprung up to meet the growing demand from businesses, and as increasingly powerful computers and software make it possible to hide the Internet's Unix command system behind graphical, point-and-shoot interfaces like Mosaic (a free software program developed with federal financing by the National Center for Supercomputing Applications) or even Microsoft Windows. Today, most of the Internet's traffic consists of people E-mailing, browsing the Web, reading and posting network news, or just languishing in artificial role-playing and interaction environments. Although the Internet's role as the new "global village" is not complete at this point, there is one thing that is clear: the Internet is linked to the need for communicating.

It should come as no surprise that the emphasis of most business use of the Internet is communicating with customers, potential customers, partners, distributors, and employees. The publishing industry is using the Internet, particularly that portion known as the World Wide Web, as an alternative distribution channel. The Web's allure is that it provides a relatively cheap, rapidly updatable, easy-to-distribute publication medium with a rich environment of text, graphics, sound, and video. However, the downside is the issue of how to make money from it. Nobody at this time has a good solution for charging for Web subscriptions. Hence, the current model is advertising support. Even that raises problems of metering and identifying the advertising readership, and of convincing advertising customers that on-line advertising is actually generating business. The relationship of OLAP with the Internet will be found in the next chapter, as well as in Chapter 9 to pursue and realize profits, and in Chapter 10 to find human resources.

Future Relationship of the Internet to EDI and VR

Going one step further in terms of the Internet in the twenty-first century and beyond, it is expected that most EDI transactions will take place on the Internet. Today, EDI managers do not seem ready to abandon EDI value-added networks (VANs) where they pay by the byte to transmit their EDI data to trading partners. But the lure of the Internet, with its flat-rate price, common network standards, and worldwide links to electronic mail and the Web, is becoming irresistible to many. Ten years from now, experts anticipate that most EDI will take place on the Internet, although sensitive EDI shipping data may not ride on the Internet.

Currently, some large banks are processing payment information over the

Internet. Still other banks plan to sell Web-based EDI software to their business customers for invoices as well as purchase and payment orders. Overall, Internet mail and the Web are increasingly viewed as easier, less expensive ways to carry EDI data. This means that smaller businesses do not have to invest in EDI translators or mapping software.

To further enhance the Internet in the future, it is expected that the synergy between VR and the Internet will create an entirely new kind of place with unique characteristics and exciting opportunities. Inasmuch as the Internet has already changed the way people work and play, it also has changed the way people meet and interact with each other. However, all communication on the Internet is still basically in the form of text, that is, words are sent across the Net, existing only in an otherwise empty void. While text is great, it is not really enough since people want to be able to interact with each other as done in the real world. Needless to say, this is where virtual reality shines.

In the future, collaborative work is one viable business VR application. If an architect has clients all over the world contracting for his services, he would be able to go through a design proposal with them interactively. That is, both could walk through a new building, make changes as needed, examine it at different times of day or in different locations, and agree on what the final result will be like. Once that is done, the client could go ahead and commit to building it. On the other hand, if a businessperson needs quick access to information without having to wade through mountains of text documents and on-line spreadsheets, then data visualization is a possible answer. Information in almost any form can be given a three-dimensional graphical representation; with multiparticipant virtual worlds, the user and coworkers can literally wander around in the data, seeing trends, and noticing connections that would not be apparent from text, numbers, or even bar charts.

At the current time, virtual reality on the Internet is centered around the Virtual Reality Modeling Language (VRML). VRML is a language for describing 3-D virtual worlds in the same way that HTML is a language for describing text. VRML worlds are explored using a VRML browser, a sort of 3-D Netscape or Mosaic. The browser lets the user navigate through the world and follow links to other worlds and different types of Net resources. Several VRML browsers are available today. However, they are typically in the beta-test stage, which means that they are not truly finished. Nevertheless, they show a tremendous amount of potential. They work well, run reasonably fast, and are easy to use. Because they are constrained by the VRML specification itself, VRML needs some features added to it before it can support real-time multiparticipant virtual worlds.

Although it is possible to design the architect's building using VRML, it is not possible to create objects with moving parts since that requires the use of "behavior" to be implemented in VRML. It is also not possible to share a virtual world with other users. However, it is expected that the next version of VRML will add behavior, although it is not clear what form it will take. In summary, bringing people together in cyberspace requires more than just behavior scripting. There is a need for networking standards that will allow for users to convey behavior efficiently to others and, in turn, their behavior back to users.

THE INFORMATION SUPERHIGHWAY

At this time, the Internet is not the final national information superhighway, but a forerunner or prototype of the futuristic superhighway that has been proposed by private industry and the federal government. The ultimate goal of the national information superhighway in the twenty-first century is to develop an information infrastructure that will enable all Americans to access information and communicate with each other, and to do so easily, reliably, securely, and cost-effectively in any medium whether it be voice, data, image, or video, at anytime and anywhere. The net result is that this capability will enhance the productivity of work and lead to significant improvements in education, social services, and entertainment. While Europe and Japan have government-subsidized programs to advance existing and future communications modernization, the United States has a long-standing course of marketplace-driven technology development by private industry. Current thinking is that there should be a cooperative relationship between private industry and the federal government to develop the national information highway of the next century.

Today, the technology exists to get started on this intended goal of the national information highway. Many of the enabling technologies for such a venture are emerging across a wide range of products and services. Fiber-optic systems, for example, are finding their way into millions of homes as cable operators and telecom providers race to upgrade their services. New technology ventures are realizing the power of multimedia data as well as cellular and wireless communication. The established hardware and software vendors along with information providers themselves, from entertainment and publishing firms to government agencies and universities, are encouraged with the possibilities of using the new technology to meet the challenges of the national information superhighway.

In the area of data communications and networking, the cable and telecommunications carriers' laying of fiber-optic cable coupled with the utilization of so-called broadband services such as asynchronous transfer mode (ATM), synchronous optical network (SONET), integrated services digital network (ISDN), and switched multi-megabit digital service (SMDS) will supply the infrastructure for a variety of new services, such as video-on-demand and on-line shopping. Also, a renewed interest in satellite transmission and the growing maturity of wireless technology will complement the terrestrial network. However, as important as all of the foregoing technology is, it is the whole that counts on the bottom line. Most of these providers are forming partnerships, alliances, agreements, and even large investments in the hope of creating industry *de facto* standards and locking out competition. Hence, the true bottom line is the issue of standards and not technology per se since the technology already exists.

SUMMARY

Because OLAP technology centers on multidimensional analysis rather than just information, there is a need for more than just hardware and software to effect viable applications for business. In this chapter, the fundamentals of data warehouses, data communications, and networking were discussed which are essential to developing an OLAP environment. In turn, this background will be helpful in gaining an understanding of how to build and implement OLAP applications as set forth in future chapters.

NOTES

1. Neil Raden, "Data, Data Everywhere," *InformationWeek*, October 30, 1995, pp. 60–65.

2. Katherine Bull, "Data Warehousing: The Ideal File Cabinet," *InformationWeek*, January 16, 1995, pp. 43–48.

3. David Baum, "Warehouse Mania," *LAN Times*, November 20, 1995, p. 70.

4. Alan Radding, "Warehouse Wake-Up Call," *InfoWorld*, November 20, 1995, pp. 1, 57–62.

5. Herb Edelstein, "Mining Data Warehouses," *InformationWeek*, January 8, 1996, p. 49.

6. Ibid., pp. 49–50.

4

OLAP Software

ISSUES EXPLORED

- How important is multidimensionality in an OLAP environment?
- What are the critical factors when evaluating software for an OLAP operating mode?
- What are the essentials of four widely used OLAP software packages?
- What other OLAP software is useful for decision making?
- What additional software may be useful in an on-line analytical processing mode?

OUTLINE

Successful OLAP Includes Selecting Appropriate Software
Focus of OLAP Is Multidimensional Analysis
 Multidimensional Cube Versus Relational-Flat Table
Critical Factors to Evaluate OLAP Software
Current Major OLAP Software Vendors
 Formation of OLAP Council
Arbor Software Corporation—Essbase Analysis
 Essbase Server
 Essbase Spreadsheet Client
 Essbase Application Manager
 Essbase Application Tools
Comshare, Inc.—Commander Decision and Commander OLAP
 Agent-Based Technology

Decision Server

Commander Decision

Commander OLAP with Detect and Alert

Oracle Corporation—Express

Product Offerings

OLAP Platform for Decision Support

Express Analyzer OLAP Tool for Reporting and Analysis

Pilot Software, Inc.—The Pilot Decision Support Suite

Pilot Desktop and Excel Add-In

Pilot Analysis Server

Pilot Designer

Pilot Sales and Marketing Analysis Library

Pilot Discovery Server

Pilot Internet Publisher

Other Current OLAP Software Vendors

Brio Technology, Inc.—BrioQuery Enterprise

Business Objects, Inc.—BusinessObjects

Dimensional Insight, Inc.—CrossTarget

Kenan Systems Corporation—Acumate Enterprise Solution

SAS Institute, Inc.—OLAP++ and MDDB

Additional Software Useful in an OLAP Environment

Natural-Language Query Systems

Electronic Spreadsheets

Financial-Planning Languages

Statistical-Analysis Packages

Business-Graphics Packages

Management-Software Packages

Selection of Appropriate Software for OLAP Is Situational

Summary

Notes

SUCCESSFUL OLAP INCLUDES SELECTING APPROPRIATE SOFTWARE

On-line analytical processing, as discussed in previous chapters, is a new business-intelligence technology that has become popular because it allows users to access and analyze large quantities of data. In addition, OLAP is attractive because it provides users with faster access to data that can be presented in new ways that do not require extensive custom programming. Its most appealing feature is that it is multidimensional. Typically, multidimensional-OLAP tools precalculate and aggregate values via extensively indexed arrays. As a result, end users can analyze data quickly using numerous keys. Since no one product can serve the full range of user-information needs, there is a host of products available today. Essentially, these products are the subject matter of this chapter.

For an on-line analytical processing system to succeed, it must be approached properly from the outset. Successful OLAP requires the cooperation of the vendors, the computer department, and the end users, that is, the company's decision makers and their staffs. Outside-vendor products can play an important part in a viable OLAP system. Most software packages have limitations and they will be reached the first time an end user says, "I need. . . ." What the user then finds is the package has provided what it thinks the user needs. The vendor can do little to adapt it. So instead of acquiring this type of package, there is the need to look for an OLAP package that provides capabilities to adapt to the personal needs of the company's decision makers at all levels—managers and nonmanagers.

This naturally leads to the next group that must be involved, that is, the computer department. Working with the computer department rather than treating it as an outsider will result in an on-line analytical processing system much better suited to the users' needs. These computer professionals, after all, have been providing much of the information that managers and their staffs now use. Hence, they understand what some of the managers' needs are already. They will also be the individuals who will build and install the OLAP system and adapt the chosen system to users' requirements.

Finally, the most important element in a successful OLAP system is the end users. It is necessary that they know what they need. Since it is important that end users get involved and support the effort behind getting the system up and running, there is a need to take time to sit down and discuss with the computer department what their real needs are. What information is used now and does it need to be improved to make the end users' jobs easier? What are their new information and knowledge requirements? Is there something they need that they have not asked for? End users can explore with computer professionals some of the reporting systems now in place and see how they can be improved using multidimensional analysis.

FOCUS OF OLAP IS MULTIDIMENSIONAL ANALYSIS

Inasmuch as OLAP software centers on multidimensional analysis (as noted previously in the text), it would be helpful to look at the essential components of this analysis for a final time. Essentially, multidimensional analysis is an architecture for performing computer analysis of different kinds from a business perspective. Within the multidimensional-analysis architecture, users are not required to know where or how the data is stored or the complexities of the databases. Rather, the focus is on analyzing the data in new and different ways.

Typically, multidimensional analysis divides data into the important dimensions used to manage the business. For example, dimensions for marketing applications might include products, market areas, distribution channels, and time periods. In turn, these dimensions can be used to describe each data point in the database, such as selling price, units sold, total revenue, and market share. Dimensions can be further described by attributes, such as location, size, or year. Attributes also can describe hierarchies within a dimension, even overlapping and inconsistent hierarchies.

From an end user's perspective, multidimensional analysis provides for the selection, analysis, summarization, and reporting by dimensions and attributes within dimensions. Multidimensional analysis can support virtually any time-series application. These include forecasting and budgeting. Current spreadsheet, database, and reporting-tool vendors are offering simplistic multidimensional tools. However, some of these vendors and others are offering more sophisticated tools. That is, all multidimensional engines are not created equal. There is a need to look for engines than can work with any data warehouse, use meta data, and can use any PC development tools for the user interface. Not only should the engine be robust to support an unlimited number of dimensions, custom groupings, and automatic and custom calculations, but also the engine needs to reside on a server large enough to support hundreds of users, large volumes of data, and intensive processing.

Multidimensional Cube Versus Relational-Flat Table

Since an OLAP system is primarily involved with reading and aggregating a large number of diverse data, it centers on data relationships to find any and all patterns and trends. To accomplish this analysis, a multidimensional database is an excellent way to meet a user's needs. As noted previously in the last chapter as well as the opening chapter, the old Rubik's Cube is a good way of visualizing a typical multidimensional database. That is, the structure is composed of cubes of data and, in turn, cubes within cubes of data. Each side of the cube is considered a dimension representing a category, such as product, region, sales, time. In addition, each cell within the multidimensional structure has aggregated data relating elements along each of the dimensions. For example, a single cell may contain the total sales for a given product in a region for a quarter. To better visualize a multidimensional cube, reference can be made to Figure 4.1, where a typical relational-flat table has been restated in the form of a multidimensional cube. In the (a) part, only the flat table for the first product is shown. Comparable tables need to be stated for the other four products. As can be seen, a multidimensional cube is a more efficient way to store data as well as retrieve data than from a relational-flat table, that is, file.

Typically, multidimensional databases provide users with consolidation, drill-down, and "slice-and-dice" capabilities. This consolidation allows users to combine data into ever-larger aggregations, such as rolling sales office data into

Figure 4.1
Two Data Models: (a) Relational-Flat Table (File) for One Product Only, and (b) Multidimensional Cube for Five Products

Product	Region	Quarter	Sales in Units
P1	R1	Q1	12,405
P1	R1	Q2	13,057
P1	R1	Q3	13,275
P1	R1	Q4	15,125
P1	R2	Q1	14,460
P1	R2	Q2	16,106
P1	R2	Q3	17,251
P1	R2	Q4	18,210
P1	R3	Q1	12,490
P1	R3	Q2	13,976
P1	R3	Q3	14,015
P1	R3	Q4	16,782

(a) appears to the left of the table.

Note: to be comparable to (b), flat files must be added for Products 2 through 5

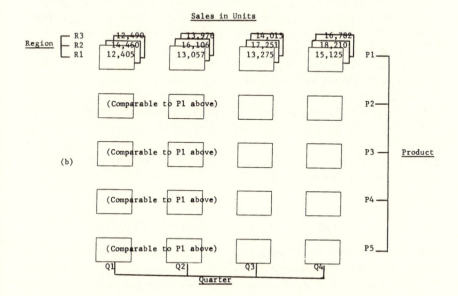

Figure 4.2
Summary of the Critical Factors to Evaluate OLAP-Software Packages

. Is the software easy to use?

. Does the software provide for multidimensional analysis?

. Does the software provide transparency?

. Does the software actually do what the users want?

. Does the software allow users to access and analyze large amounts of data?

. Does the software precalculate and aggregate values?

. Does the software provide consistent reporting performance?

. Is the software designed for the organization's size or will it be outgrown

  in a few years?

. How are changes and updates in the software handled?

. Is the software reasonably priced?

. Does the software provide flexible reporting?

. Will the vendor support the installation adequately?

. On what hardware does the software run?

. Is all documentation clear?

. Can the user visit at least one other user of the software?

district data into regional data. Drill down, which is the opposite of consolidation, allows users to seek increasingly detailed information on a particular topic. In addition, slice-and-dice provides the capability to look at the database from different viewpoints, such as showing sales of all products within a single region and sales of a single product across all regions. Going one step further, multidimensional databases are capable of storing data in compressed form, thereby making it possible to analyze large amounts of data while minimizing physical-storage requirements. The systems dynamically separate so-called dense data, where data exists for a large percentage of dimension cells, from sparse data, or dimensions where a significant portion of the cells is empty. Overall, multidimensional databases make it easier for users to obtain their desired information and knowledge within an OLAP mode.

CRITICAL FACTORS TO EVALUATE OLAP SOFTWARE

In order to acquire the appropriate OLAP software, it is necessary to evaluate their critical factors. A representative listing of these factors is given in Figure 4.2. As a starting point, the package should be easy to use such that it assists users in decision making. In other words, the software is designed to help users do their jobs naturally and not dictate their actions. Where the analytical capability that allows multidimensional analysis is located should be irrelevant to the users. The OLAP software should respond readily to the users' requests, that is, the users' current wants.

The OLAP software package should allow fast user access to data that can be presented in very sophisticated ways without custom programming. Similarly, it lets users access a very large amount of information in a format that allows them to find their own answers as questions arise. Because a multidimensional-OLAP tool precalculates and aggregates values, usually in extensively indexed arrays, users should be able to slice and dice quickly using a variety of keys. For example, users might want to look at contract enrollment by product and by market over a period of time—a question with four dimensions. Related to the foregoing is consistent reporting performance, that is, performance should not be affected by an increased number of dimensions the user selects.

Additionally, the software must be able to handle the organization's size or it will be outgrown in a few years. Users must be satisfied that the software allows for changes and updates as deemed necessary. The OLAP software should be reasonably priced and flexible to meet users' needs. It should be flexible to allow changes of different types of analysis in order to manipulate the data in whatever form is most useful. As specific capabilities are required, they can be added without losing other functions or requiring changes in the basic software. Other factors come into play that can be asked as questions: "Will the vendor support the installation adequately?" "Will the software run on the organization's hardware?" and "Is the documentation clear?" Needless to say, these questions must be answered to evaluate critically the decision of whether to proceed with a specific software vendor. It should be noted that it is helpful to visit one other user of OLAP software to get a first-hand look.

It is highly recommended that the above factors be investigated fully to the users' satisfaction before signing a contract for purchase or lease of the software operating in a PC or mainframe environment. The computer department, working with end users, should resist the temptation to sign the vendor's standard agreement. If possible, the matter should be referred to the company's lawyer rather than trying to handle the matter alone. In the final analysis, the key to longevity of OLAP software is its flexibility to meet the changing needs of users.

CURRENT MAJOR OLAP SOFTWARE VENDORS

Because multidimensionality is the core of on-line analytical processing, major vendors have developed specific software to focus on this feature. These vendors recognize that users need to look at different slices of data trending by time periods and by types of transactions. Their needs go beyond the traditional spreadsheets. Typically, users would enter numbers into spreadsheets and work them through until they thought they had it right. There was no inherent integrity to the results. However, with many OLAP products, users can perform such analyses quickly and simply since all the required calculations and aggregations have been already executed and validated.

The major OLAP software products include Arbor Software, Inc.'s Essbase; Comshare, Inc.'s Commander; Oracle Corporation's Express; and Pilot Software, Inc.'s LightShip Suite. These products are explored in the next sections of the chapter. As will be seen in this exposition of OLAP vendors, their products exhibit some interesting and helpful features to users. However, they have a few weaknesses. For one, some software is limited to so many elements along a single dimension. Some handle up to six dimensions with ease, but more than that requires conjoint dimensions which entails extra work. Another weakness is sparsity, which refers to a condition where an array is populated with many null values. This can occur when a particular product may not be offered in all the markets served by the company, thereby resulting in null values for many of those markets. Still another is that only numerical data can be stored and not textual material.

From another perspective, some users are still turning to alternative products because they are considered easier and faster to implement. For example, Business Objects from Business Objects, Inc. is such a product since it gives managers the ability to perform complex multidimensional analysis, thereby allowing them to follow lines of questioning on their own. As another example, SAS Institute's SAS/EIS uses fourth-generation language-based packages that are designed to provide multidimensional views and analyses. Due to the diversity of ways to perform multidimensional analysis, there will be an exposition of other software useful in an OLAP operating mode later in the chapter.

Formation of OLAP Council

Vendors of OLAP software have formed a council to address current OLAP problems. Currently, the group has a twofold objective. The *first* is to develop standard client-to-server OLAP links, that is, to iron out interoperability standards. The *second* is to promote multidimensional-OLAP technology such that the current complaints of its difficulty to use are overcome. The four vendors that established the OLAP Council are Arbor Software Corporation, Comshare Inc., IRI Software (which is now part of the Oracle Corporation), and Pilot Software Inc. They plan to recruit more vendors to their cause.

To meet the first objective, they will develop a standard-object specification for multidimensional navigation through data stored on OLAP servers. Such a specification and associated APIs (application programming interfaces) allow any OLAP-vendor's client software to access any vendor's multidimensional database. The lack of such interoperability has led to the products being labeled proprietary. Regarding the second objective, the council maintains that multidimensional OLAP is better suited for data-analysis tasks than are relational databases. As noted in the prior chapter, relational databases are designed for on-line transactional processing (OLTP). Relational tables basically flatten out multidimensional data. The basic issue is whether a user can do real OLAP with that kind of configuration. Retrieving relational data for analysis generally requires writing queries using structured-query language (SQL) or using applications based on Microsoft Corporation's Open Database Connectivity (ODBC) technology.

ARBOR SOFTWARE CORPORATION—ESSBASE ANALYSIS

The Arbor Software Corporation markets the Essbase product family which is a flexible and comprehensive multidimensional-analysis solution to business problems. It includes Essbase Server, Essbase Spreadsheet Client, Essbase Application Manager, and Essbase Application Tools. Essbase is useful for a wide range of on-line analytical-processing applications, including: budgeting, forecasting/planning, financial consolidations, customer and product profitability analysis, sales and marketing analysis, and manufacturing-mix analysis. It allows the user to see the big picture as well as analyze the details, providing a strategic view of many different business scenarios. And with Essbase, this information is immediately available to managers and analysts closest to the business and market conditions.

Essbase Server

Essbase Server is a multidimensional database that lets the user simultaneously share, analyze, and update data using an unlimited number of dimensions, such as time, account, region, channel, or product. Based on a client/server architecture, Essbase Server manages the user's analytical data model, data storage, calculations, and data security. With data residing on the server, the user maintains data integrity, reduces network traffic, and eliminates the need for costly upgrades on each client computer. Essbase Server operates on Windows NT, OS/2, and UNIX operating systems over all leading networks.

Essbase Spreadsheet Client

Essbase Spreadsheet Client is desktop software that merges seamlessly with Microsoft Excel (Windows and Macintosh) or Lotus 1-2-3 for Windows spreadsheets. This client software turns a standard spreadsheet into a tightly integrated client for Essbase Server. A user requires little training to become proficient with Essbase. And the user can still use a spreadsheet's computation, graphics, and charting capabilities so as to leverage a user's existing skills and software investment.

With Essbase, the user has access to powerful analytical capabilities by simply clicking a mouse or using basic menu commands. For example, to connect to the Essbase database, the user chooses the "Connect" command, enters a password, and clicks OK. A simple right-mouse click or "Pivot" lets the user view relationships between data by instantly changing columns to rows, or rows to columns. A double-click or "zoom" is used to navigate up and down through levels of detailed data. And the user can select "Lock" and "Send" to update data on the server.

Essbase Application Manager

By using the Windows-based Application Manager, the user can easily build, modify, and manage analytical models, calculations, data-access security, data-loading rules, and dimension-building functions. Essbase's powerful data loading and dimension building features ensure that applications are built rapidly with tight links to OLTP or data-warehouse repositories. Essentially, the Application Manager provides the user with an intuitive outline format for defining the analytical model. The individual creates the model using an outline representation of dimensions (Time, Products, Markets), hierarchical structures within dimensions (Weeks, Months, Quarters), and embedded dimensional calculations (Gross Margin = Sales − Cost of Goods Sold). By storing the outline separately from the actual data, Essbase lets the user revise the analytical model at any time without having to reload the data.

The Essbase-calculation engine gives the user flexibility and power for defining and running large-scale analytical calculations. For example, the user can express essential analytical calculations such as allocations, percent market share, ratios, variance and percent variance without programming. Also, Essbase includes a wide range of predefined functions, such as net-present value, standard deviation, and depreciation, which ensures accuracy and saves time when creating applications.

The Application Manager provides the user with essential functions for automatically loading data into Essbase applications from multiple sources, such as legacy systems, relational DBMSs, data warehouses, and spreadsheets. The user can specify data-loading rules that can select, manipulate, concatenate, or substitute incoming data values. Essbase stores these rules on the server so that they can be reused for future-data loads. Essbase dimension-building capabilities save time and allow the user to keep an analytical application in sync with transaction systems. The user can automatically define new data dimensions, add new dimension members (a new product, for example), or change the hierarchy within a dimension when data is loaded.

Essbase Application Tools

The user can extend and enhance Essbase applications with the following options. Currency Conversion converts financial data using any currency exchange-rate scenario. This module lets the user model the impact of exchange rates and performs ad hoc conversion directly from a spreadsheet or custom application. The SQL Interface provides access to more than 20 PC and SQL relational databases by making the Essbase Server operate as an ODBC client. The Extended Spreadsheet Toolkit includes more than 20 macros and VBA functions, thereby letting the user build custom Microsoft or Lotus 1-2-3 applications that integrate with Essbase. The Application Programming Interface (API) lets the user employ standard tools to create custom Essbase applications that take advantage of the robust data storage, retrieval, and analytical capabilities of Essbase. The Web Gateway provides all essential OLAP features including drill up/shown/across, pivot, slice and dice, and full read/write capabilities from standard Web browsers. Essbase Web Gateway allows a company to deliver applications, like management reporting and budgeting, to users. Last, the SQL Drill-Through provides tight links between the summary data in Essbase and the detail data in OLTP and data-warehouse relational databases. This module automatically creates the SQL query which corresponds to the Essbase data in the spreadsheet, executes the query, and returns the detail data to the spreadsheet.

COMSHARE, INC.—COMMANDER DECISION AND COMMANDER OLAP

Currently, Comshare is marketing two decision-making products that are helpful to decision makers. They are Commander Decision and Commander OLAP for EIS with Detect and Alert. These tools are helpful to managers and their staffs in solving information analysis and reporting issues for applications like executive information systems, customer and product profitability, sales analysis, financial consolidation and analysis, enterprise budgeting, business unit analysis, and other mission-critical DSS applications. Both are discussed below. However, agent-based technology and the Decision Server are set forth first.

Agent-Based Technology

Comshare added software-agent technology to its product line in early 1995. The agents, dubbed Detect and Alert, scan both text and numeric databases for changes. Detect and Alert can monitor Comshare's Commander OLAP database, Notes, and on-line information from the Dow Jones and Reuters information services. Essentially, agent software acts on a user's behalf to perform repetitive or time-consuming tasks across networks, such as monitoring stock prices for changes or checking news trends for keywords. Scanning can look for complex conditions based on multiple factors within the data. The software creates alerts when it finds changes that meet user-specified criteria, and forwards automatically the information to users via E-mail.

Decision Server

Basically, the Decision Server has three functions that range from data loading to data analysis. The *first* of these functions is data integration. If the data for user's applications reside in a single location, is already "clean," and can be mapped directly from the source into multidimensional form, then Commander Decision's SQL load module is the fastest and easiest way to load a decision-support database. On the other hand, if the situation is not that straightforward, Decision's Data Integrator is designed to extract data from many different sources and prepare it for multidimensional databases. With over 200 processes designed for data manipulation, the Data Integrator is an industrial-strength data-manipulation language for any data problem.

The *second* function centers on the database itself. Multidimensionality makes all aspects of a user's information—accounts, time, product, geography, customers, business units—equally available for exploration, rotation, and side-by-side comparison. Decision Server is built around a multidimensional database that is concurrent multiuser read and write, multitasking, multithreaded, and symmetrical multiprocessor enabled (Arbor Software's Essbase). It has the dynamic sparsity control that is required in virtually all analytical applications, and turns a base-level business transaction data into end-user information by adding business rules for data aggregations, allocations, alternative roll-ups, and more. It has the ability to handle large data volumes and still provides rapid, predictable response times.

The *third* and final function is data interpretation. The Decision Access Model is a calculating engine that sits on the server and handles the interaction between the clients and the database. It has two primary roles. The first is to handle the requests of the users and efficiently process them. Functions such as sorting, calculation of ratios and variances, and personalized monitoring are handled by the engine. High-powered servers do the compute-intensive work, right next to the database where it should be done. The results of the calculation, which are often just a couple of data points, are sent back to the client. This optimizes the client, the server, and the network traffic. The second role for the engine is to off-load the database of unnecessary processing and storage. Calculations, ratios, variances, alternate hierarchies, and other calculations are evaluated "on the fly." There is no need to store this data if it can be calculated quickly. This results is much smaller databases on the server while preserving rapid response for the users.

Commander Decision

Commander Decision is a client/server-based planning, analysis, and reporting system which promotes innovative thinking as well as identifies alternatives and monitors progress. With fully integrated components for legacy and modern database access, software agent-based Detect and Alert (covered above under "Agent-Based Technology"), a high-performance multidimensional engine, and a Windows-based end-user interface, Comshare customers use Commander Decision applications to support executives, managers, and analysts across the organization. Commander Decision includes a Commander Server, a multidimensional database analysis facility, a high performance, high capacity, multidimensional engine (Essbase from Arbor Software), a data refining and shaping-analysis capabilities, decision support for ad hoc visualization, and application-administration facilities. In addition, Commander Decision includes Excel and Lotus 1-2-3 as fully integrated desktop clients; Windows 95–based, plug-and-play applications for end-user analysis, like Execu-View for point-and-click slicing and dicing of multidimensional information; and intelligent software agents or ''robots'' which perform routine surveillance of massive amounts of numerical and textual data and deliver personalized alerts to users' desktops.

Commander OLAP with Detect and Alert

Commander's Detect and Alert integrates information from countless sources across the organization and around the world so that the user can see competitive news, stock-market trends, legislative plans, and other external news prioritized and integrated with the company's internal performance information. Detect and Alert keeps the user up to date with results, unexpected events, trends, and troublesome patterns, without spending time searching through numerous reports and data sources to piece together special analysis. In effect, Detect and Alert makes it possible for the user to allocate scarce staff resources in more productive ways.

Because management is demanding easy access to more and more detail for decision making, the logical end can be databases and data warehouses so large and complex that users, that is, executives, managers, and analysts, cannot possibly deduce within the massive volumes of data the important milestones toward goals, unexpected events, emerging patterns, and trends they need to see. Commander OLAP with Detect and Alert represents a whole new way of thinking about reporting business information: personalized automatic surveillance of business data, immediate-desktop alerts, and instant links to the underlying context information. It is an important means to solve information overload and ends one-size-fits-all reporting by putting the most advanced agent technology to work for the user.

When a user wants to understand more about the stories reported in a particular newspaper, Detect and Alert offers a range of exploratory tools accessible at the touch of a button. Commander's point-and-click Execu-View is one way a user can investigate the underlying context of a story. One can drill down to more detail, compare the out-of-range results to those of other products or units, create a quick trend chart, or calculate ratios to get a better understanding of the problem and communicate one's understanding to generate effective action. In summary, Commander OLAP with Detect and Alert lets the user put a tireless personal assistant to work in order to find significant exceptions, hot trends, and subtle patterns in an organization's performance. Detect and Alert replaces masses of standard reports with *proactive* personalized reports that alert the user to the most significant issues related to the company's key objectives, goals, and strategies.

ORACLE CORPORATION—EXPRESS

To extend its lead in the data-warehousing market, the Oracle Corporation acquired in 1995 from Information Resources, Inc., IRI Software's on-line analytical processing business. Oracle thereby complements its information management software with Express multidimensional products used for decision support. The portion of IRI Software purchased by Oracle becomes the OLAP Products Division. Oracle Express technology allows users to access, analyze, model, and share data stored in data warehouses, relational databases, and legacy systems. Oracle OLAP applications for sales, marketing, and finance easily support strategic decisions in data-intensive industries. These include pharmaceuticals, manufacturing, retail, insurance, banking, utilities, telecommunications, and government.

Product Offerings

Oracle Express is a server that is optimized for the query and analysis of corporate data. It is known as an OLAP server because it is based on a multi-dimensional-data model. The model ensures that end users can analyze data in a structured or ad hoc fashion without requesting special programs from computer personnel. Oracle Express complements relational systems used for on-line transactional processing. It comes in two versions: the Personal Express is a local server on a PC, and the Oracle Express Server can be remote. Both server products support a complex OLAP architecture: data cache, application-development environment, and applications. The multidimensional arrays of the cache are optimized for query and analysis and complement the relational data-structures supporting on-line transactional processing.

In addition, there is the Oracle Express EIS which is a point-and-click application environment that combines the analytic power of the Oracle Express cache with GUI (graphical user interface)-application generator tools. It supports the rapid implementation of sophisticated EIS/DSS systems. An object-oriented desktop-reporting tool for analyzing multidimensional data is the Oracle Express Analyzer which accesses relational data. Without burdening computer personnel, users of the Oracle Express Analyzer can create comprehensive management briefings and share them on a LAN or through E-mail.

Oracle Express is the foundation for the following applications. The Oracle Financial Analyzer is an enterprise solution for financial reporting, budgeting, and planning that complements the General Ledger. It manages all of a company's financial information in one central server within a distributed environment. It helps meet financial objectives, which include simplifying the budgeting and forecasting process, answering ad hoc requests efficiently, improving cost control and performance measurement, and identifying areas for profit improvement. Also, there is the Oracle Sales Analyzer. An Oracle Express cache is customized for sales and marketing analysis, such as market-share calculations, ranking reports, and 80/20 analysis. Oracle Sales Analyzer presents this information through a set of user-defined reporting templates. The product's analytical engine, user interface, documentation, and support are all targeted to sales and marketing users.

OLAP Platform for Decision Support

An Oracle Express architecture integrates the data sources of an enterprise, supports a variety of front ends, and offers application servers and data-smart objects to speed custom development. Underlying this architecture is the Oracle Express multidimensional-data model that is optimized for analysis because it implicitly builds relationships between measures, such as Sales or Units, and the business dimensions, such as Product, Market, and Time, that structure a measure. To meet the various requirements of corporate departments, Oracle Express supports measures of different dimensionality in one database. For example, the measure Unit Cost, which is dimensioned only by Product and Time, can coexist with Sales, which is dimensioned by Market, Product, and Time. Oracle Express measures resemble objects. Each object has a different shape. Each edge of an object represents a dimension of the data that is important to the end user.

For example, managers often manipulate sales data as if it were a cube, where the edges represent the dimensions Market, Product, and Time. A product manager may want to analyze one product's sales across all markets for all time periods. Regional sales managers, in contrast, may want to see sales for several products, only in their markets, across all time periods. The Oracle Express is designed for this type of end-user data retrieval and analysis. Queries, such as period-to-period comparisons of sales within a market, have consistently fast response times as they slice the cube. Oracle Express excels at trend analysis, such as the calculation of moving averages and internal rates of return.

To provide a choice of development platforms, Oracle Express is *scalable*. Developers can create Express-based applications on a PC and then scale them up to run on a server or a mainframe. Conversely, applications can be created on large machines and then scaled down to run on smaller ones. This scalability helps to extend OLAP across the enterprise and reduces the cost of development. No matter the choice of development platform, Oracle Express has built-in functions for mathematical, financial, statistical, logical, and string-manipulation data model. The server supports procedural constructs and user-defined functions. Oracle Express tools enable modeling, simulation, forecasting, and ''what-if'' analysis.

Express Analyzer OLAP Tool for Reporting and Analysis

The Oracle Express Analyzer, as noted previously, is a reporting and analysis tool that meets the needs of users in the Windows environment. Being a complete set of visual desktop tools for selecting, viewing, analyzing, annotating, and sharing corporate data, the Express Analyzer delivers the power of on-line analytical processing to users in any discipline: marketing, operations, sales, manufacturing, or finance. It leverages the multidimensional Oracle Express Server, which is open to the corporate data that users need to make informed decisions. Oracle Express provides access to relational systems, legacy systems, and data warehouses. The Oracle Express Analyzer presents intuitive displays of such data through three "data-smart" objects: Table, Graph, and Selector. Because these data-smart objects understand multidimensional-data structures, users can concentrate on performing analyses instead of on accessing the data. If an Oracle Express Analyzer user wants to investigate sales data, the Table object automatically organizes that data in report format. The Graph object automatically creates configurable charts or graphs of sales with axes and legends. The Selector object has point-and-click tools for creating simple or complex queries about sales. The result is users who can independently create timely, accurate, and complete briefings for management review.

The Oracle Express Analyzer users publish their analyses through briefings. *Briefings* are subject-oriented analyses built with reusable objects. Arranged on a briefing page, these objects are interactive. Users can rotate, drill-down, and query data in any Table or Graph on a briefing page to perform their own ad hoc analysis. The scope of briefings is limitless. They can contain information from any application that meets the Microsoft standard of Object Linking and Embedding (OLE 2). Yet briefings are easy to use and create with point-and-click tools. Casual users, who usually read briefings, page through them with pulldown menus or navigation buttons. Power users, who often create briefings, do not need to program. They do not have to leave the briefing to extend its analysis with an OLE-enabled application. Because the Oracle Express Analyzer supports communication across the enterprise, users can access the same briefing simultaneously when it is stored on a LAN. This accessibility establishes a collaborative workspace. Briefings can be saved and appear as icons on the Windows desktop. The Oracle Express Analyzer users can also send briefings to other users via E-mail.

PILOT SOFTWARE, INC.—THE PILOT DECISION SUPPORT SUITE

The Pilot Decision Support Suite offers a comprehensive system with predictive data mining, high-performance OLAP, and flexible visualization in an open, plug-and-play architecture, which is fast to implement, easy to modify, and supports analysis anywhere. It includes: Pilot Desktop and Excel Add-Inn, Pilot Analysis Server, Pilot Designer, Pilot Sales and Marketing Analysis Library, Pilot Discovery Server, and Pilot Internet Publisher, all of which are discussed below.

Pilot Desktop and Excel Add-In

The Pilot Desktop provides a complete OLAP environment that can be used stand-alone or as a client in a network application for interactive business analysis. It offers a complete set of dimensional tools that allow users to drill down, rotate, and pivot through consolidated data. Using the system's colorful and intuitive tables, charts, and maps, business professionals can graphically navigate through and understand data. The development of powerful, renewable multidimensional business models is also enabled with Pilot Desktop.

Pilot Excel Add-In advances the client capabilities of the Pilot Decision Support Suite. This optional component allows Excel users to seamlessly integrate the capabilities of the Pilot environment into their Excel solutions. Users can access information in several-dimensional Excel models with Pilot Excel Add-In's dimensional selection object, drill-down, and rotate facilities.

Pilot Analysis Server

Pilot Analysis Server, a scalable multiuser OLAP server with a rich array of analytical-modeling capabilities, features a library of built-in functions for dozens of forecasting techniques, correlation methods, and regression analysis. Its time intelligence capability automatically comprehends how data changes over time, collects data from predefined time frames, and automatically reconciles them without programming or maintenance. While it supports standard calendars, the Pilot Analysis Server also handles a wide range of nonstandard fiscal-year calendars.

With the Pilot Analysis Server's time-based analysis and dynamic dimensions, users can easily analyze large amounts of data without data preconsolidation. And the Server's data-driven architecture automatically adapts to new data. So, whether rebuilding an entire analysis model or simply adding new data, all activities are completely automated. Users access a dynamic multidimensional model within days instead of months, and automatic refresh and maintenance facilities create a virtually maintenance-free system. And the Pilot Analysis Server's scalable architecture provides analysis anywhere to meet the evolving requirements of laptop, work group, and distributed environments.

Pilot Designer

Pilot Designer, which is an application design environment, is used for rapid customization, data access, and flexible visualization. Supporting Windows 95 graphical-user-interface standards and a Visual Basic scripting language, the Pilot Designer delivers a complete suite of dimensional objects for customizing the desktop and applications, building libraries, and extending existing analyses. Its tool set helps create a variety of decision-support applications ranging from simple executive information system front ends to complex OLAP applications.

With Pilot Designer, decision makers at all levels of an organization have unparalleled access to data, wherever it resides. And they obtain that information through a wide variety of powerful graphic formats, which combine tabular, geographical and graphical data, text, images, audio, and video. Compliant with OLE 2.0 standards, including automation of OLE Custom Controls (OCX), the Pilot Designer can help users enrich their environments with additional visualization of multimedia objects. Additionally, the Pilot Designer incorporates Pilot Desktop, which allows application test and validation, and a Software Developer Kit for designers who want to integrate the Pilot Suite into their applications created with other client/server development tools.

Pilot Sales and Marketing Analysis Library

The Pilot Sales and Marketing Analysis Library is an optional prebuilt library of advanced analysis tools. This library performs detailed business reporting in an environment that can be tailored to the needs of sales and marketing professionals. It features modules for 80/20 Pareto analysis, time-based ranking, BCG quadrant analysis, trendline, and statistical forecasting. With instant access to key information, business professionals can easily conduct flexible analyses, such as rank product performance, perform exceptions analysis to identify channels above or below plan, and forecast unit shipments of costs of goods. These prebuilt functions can be customized or extended with Pilot Designer. Leveraging the Pilot Decision Support Suite of products, the Pilot Sales and Marketing Analysis Library provides flexible information to the desktop every day. Running on the Pilot Desktop, the Pilot Sales and Marketing Analysis Library also works within a multiuser environment with the Pilot Analysis Server.

Pilot Discovery Server

Pilot Discovery Server is the industry's first data-mining product designed for sales and marketing professionals. Using vital customer metrics such as profitability, life-time value, or new product return on investment, Pilot Discovery Server drives a focused market segmentation and proactive analysis of customer behavior or evaluates the profitability of future marketing efforts. Working directly with and residing in a relational data warehouse, Pilot Discovery Server issues standard SQL queries for database analysis. This patent-pending relational database integration delivers highly visual and easily understood results. Combining the strength of data mining and OLAP technology with visually oriented analyses, Pilot Discovery Server enables applications to span the entire customer life cycle.

Pilot Internet Publisher

The Pilot Decision Support Suite facilitates the distribution of meaningful information by incorporating Internet/Intranet capabilities. Combining the communication power of the internet or a corporate intranet with OLAP's analysis capabilities delivers maximum business performance information with minimum effort. Pilot's initiatives in these areas will include enhancing the interactive capabilities of Internet browser-based OLAP applications, as well as using the Internet to support distribution of multidimensional information to dedicated analysis users. As web technology matures, Pilot will deliver value-added technologies, complementing evolving Web technologies (e.g., HTTP and FTP servers, browsers, Java applets, ActiveX controls), to deliver decision-support applications over the Internet.

OTHER CURRENT OLAP SOFTWARE VENDORS

Besides those discussed above, there is a growing number of software vendors that are offering multidimensionality as a part of their product line. Some multidimensional-desktop tools, such as PowerPlay (from Cognos Inc.) and Business Objects (from Business Objects, Inc.), already provide some measure of multidimensional analysis capability for relational data without the need for a multidimensional database. For example, the Cognos approach assumes that relational databases are the foundation of most data architectures, and that most users do not want to add a second special-purpose server.

In addition, other products on the market, such as DSS Agent (from MicroStrategy Inc.), MetaCube (from Stanford Technology Group Inc.), and IA Decision Support Suite (from Information Advantage Inc.), provide true multidimensional analysis capabilities for relational data. By providing a data dictionary that resides on relational database systems, these software products provide users with a multidimensional view of relational data. Other vendors offering multidimensionality in their products are set forth below. They include Brio Technology, Inc. (BrioQuery Enterprise, Version 4.0), Business Objects, Inc. (Mercury, Version 4.0), Dimensional Insight, Inc. (CrossTarget, Version 5.0), Kenan Technologies (Acumate Enterprise Solution, Version 1.2), and SAS Institute, Inc. (OLAP++ and MDDB).

Brio Technology, Inc.—BrioQuery Enterprise

BrioQuery Enterprise, Version 4.0, is an all-in-one query and desktop OLAP tool from Brio Technology, Inc. It supports both managed and ad hoc query capabilities to allow both an easy entry point for new users, while clearly defining a growth path for more experienced users who will outgrow predefined structures. BrioQuery Enterprise goes beyond simple data access, combining visual query building, multidimensional cross-tab analysis, charting, and report writing in one easy-to-use and easy-to-administer package. It is released simultaneously on Windows, Macintosh, and Unix, and supports a variety of RDBMSs.

BrioQuery Enterprise competes directly with products such as PowerPlay from the Cognos Corporation and Andyne Computing Ltd.'s Pablo. Unlike PowerPlay and Pablo which require that administrators set up, distribute, and maintain hypercubes, BrioQuery Enterprise uses its Desktop OLAP engine to create local datacubes on the fly to analyze the user's relevant subset of data. This software stores data retrieved from the database in a Desktop Database Cache, which the reporting tabs access to populate datacubes. In addition to allowing users to create multiple reports from a single query, the Desktop Database Cache allows users to work independently from the database server, thereby liberating mobile users and decreasing database server and network congestion. Overall, BrioQuery Enterprise, Version 4.0, is a multidimensional analysis tool that provides strong query and reporting capabilities for users in multiplatform environments who need to work off-line, eliminating excessive database usage.

Business Objects, Inc.—BusinessObjects

Business Objects, Inc. is marketing an integrated query, reporting, and OLAP tool called BusinessObjects 4.0 (previously called by its code name, Mercury). It is available for Windows 95, Windows NT, Windows 3.1, Unix, and Macintosh clients. Essentially, BusinessObjects 4.0 integrates OLAP-style multidimensional query capabilities into Business Objects' existing data-query and reporting tools without requiring users to invest in specialized multidimensional databases. It works by automatically generating small ad hoc multidimensional databases or "cubes" on the client's PC rather than on the network servers, pulling that data from a variety of popular relational databases, OLAP servers, or personal data on the client. The tool requires information system users to assign dedicated server and relational databases to store a repository of metadata that describes whatever data is available for queries in all the connected legacy and relational databases. BusinessObjects 4.0 uses this data to generate dynamic cubes and build queries, shielding end users from the complexities of the underlying database schema.

By contrast, competitive OLAP tools from vendors such as Arbor Software, Comshare, and Pilot use specialized, static cubes that reside on network servers and must be built in advance by corporate developers. Typically, such cubes can grow very quickly to many gigabytes in size. As such, BusinessObjects 4.0 is countering some of the complaints about the complexity and size of these kinds of OLAP solutions.

Dimensional Insight, Inc.—Cross Target

Dimensional Insight, Inc. currently markets CrossTarget which now features a scaled-up version of its graphical user interface, called the Diver. Release 5.0 uniquely integrates reporting and analysis functions for faster and more efficient decision making. In addition, Diver 5.0 offers enhanced reporting capabilities, including geographic maps and cataloging functionality. Essentially, Cross-Target is a data-mart solution that enables Fortune 1000 companies to transform very large volumes of raw data into multidimensional data models that can be navigated with point-and-click ease. These models or data marts are ideally suited for the specialized needs of work groups, departments, of functional areas. Users can analyze and view data at any level, from highly summarized views down to the most minute details.

With Release 5.0 of the Diver, users can create customized, callable reports that may be saved. Upon request, the reports are populated with "live" data, allowing full drill-down to underlying detail. Another feature, called the DiveBook, provides an easy way to save, categorize, and select frequently used reports, thereby providing EIS functionality. Newly added geographic maps, based on state, zip code, longitude, or latitude, provide a new data presentation option. Fully integrated with the Diver, the maps also provide full drill-down and are based on "live" data. Users may toggle between maps and other formats with the click of a mouse.

Kenan Systems Corporation—Acumate Enterprise Solution

Kenan Systems Corporation offers Acumate Enterprise Solution (ES), a customer-centric OLAP solution. Acumate is a high-end high-performance OLAP toolkit that allows application developers to address the most complex marketing and customer-analysis requirements. Product components include the following. The Acumate Server is a powerful multidimensional database and application development environment, featuring a multidimensional stored procedural language (MSPL), advanced analysis tools, and powerful data-loading tools for accessing heterogeneous transaction data stores and data warehouses. In contrast, the Acumate Client is a standard API to access the database functionality and a set of Visual Basic Extensions (VBXs). The Acumate Client also includes a powerful spreadsheet interface to the Acumate Server for analysts who want to access subsets of multidimensional data in a spreadsheet environment.

Acutrieve is a customizable decision-support application optimized for analysts and other data-intensive end users, thereby providing a powerful OLAP environment for turning data into information. The Acumate Workbench is a graphical front end to Acumate's multidimensional stored procedure language. Workbench enables OLAP application developers to take advantage of the Windows environment to build graphical front ends as well as sophisticated OLAP application logic—all from the client. The Acumate Web is a CGI parsing engine and HTML generator which can be used to enable static and ad hoc reporting using Web-browser technology. Acumate Web's toolkit allows users to build HTML-based customized Web applications.

SAS Institute, Inc.—OLAP++ and MDDB

SAS Institute's OLAP++, which enables the development of executive information system applications, has the capability to analyze large amounts of data on any type of server. This is a combined software and service offering that includes installation and customized object libraries. OLAP++ is an extension of the company's OLAP architecture which organizes data in multiple-dimension hierarchies and enables users to create, calculate, and analyze complex relationships relatively fast. The dimensions can include time, products, sales channels, or geographic regions. OLAP++ includes two class libraries—one containing display objects that are typically employed in EIS applications, the other a multidimensional engine. Although the system is designed for end users, some assistance may be needed for information systems personnel. Currently, the software is available for Windows, Windows NT, OS/2, and UNIX clients. On the server side, there are Windows NT, OS/2, UNIX, HVS, CHS, OpenVHS versions. Basically, OLAP++ uses an object-oriented approach to multidimensional analysis which eliminates the need for multidimensional database-management systems.

More recently, this software house has enhanced the SAS System's data-warehousing capabilities by adding a multidimensional database (MDDB) to its family of business-intelligence tools. As an integrated part of the Institute's decision-management architecture, this model for on-line analytical processing enables better decision making by giving business users quick, unlimited views of multiple relationships in large quantities of summarized data. The Web-enabled MDDB offers fast, flexible data summarizations, analyses, and reporting capabilities so business users throughout an organization can identify and track trends for strategic decision making. The MDDB speeds the process of building a data warehouse. In addition, this multidimensional feature underlies the architecture of SAS Institute's recently announced Business Solutions line of packaged software solutions, which are designed to ease decision making for specific end users within corporate departments, such as finance and human resources. Overall, adding an MDDB structure to SAS's architecture offers companies increased speed and performance of their data-warehouse exploitation and analysis. No matter where data exists—internally or externally on the Web—users can effectively access, organize, and analyze it. This saves time and money and leads to faster, more accurate business decisions.

A summary of the foregoing OLAP software vendors is set forth in Figure 4.3. The question can now be asked about OLAP technology versus executive-information-system technology, that is, "How does OLAP stack up against traditional EIS technology?" EIS is not for the typical end user because the focus is on assisting the typical power user. On the other hand, OLAP allows most decision makers to build applications as necessary. The aim is to allow the

Figure 4.3
Popular OLAP-Software Packages

Company	Product	OLAP Software Features
Arbor Software Corporation Sunnyvale, CA 800-858-1666 http://www.arborsoft.com	Essbase Analysis	Essbase Server, Essbase Spreadsheet Client, Essbase Application Manager, Essbase Application Tools
Brio Technology, Inc. Mt. View, CA 415-961-4110 http://www.brio.com	BrioQuery Enterprise Version 4.0	An ad-hoc query tool designed for data-warehouse-based decision support
Business Objects, Inc. San Jose, CA 408-953-6000 http://www.businessobjects.com	Business Objects 4.0	Adds OLAP-style multidimensional query capabilities to Business Objects' existing data query and reporting tool
Comshare, Inc. Ann Arbor, MI 800-922-7979 http://www.comshare.com	Commander Decision and Commander OLAP	Agent-based technology, Decision Server, Commander Decision, Commander OLAP with Detect and Alert
Dimensional Insight, Inc. Burlington, MA 617-229-9111 http://www.dimins.com	CrossTarget, Version 5.0	An upgrade to its multidimen- sional analysis tool that con- tinues to provide financial- analysis options
Kenan Systems Corporation Cambridge, MA 800-775-3626 http://www.kenan.com	Acumate Enter- prise Solution, Version 1.2	Analysis copilots which guide users step-by-step through complex analyses
Oracle Corporation Redwood Shores, CA 415-506-7000 http://www.oracle.com	Express	OLAP Platform for Decision Support, Express Analyzer OLAP Tool for Reporting and Analysis
Pilot Software, Inc. Cambridge, MA 800-944-0094 http://www.pilotsw.com	The Pilot Decision Support Suite	Pilot Analysis Server, Pilot Designer, Pilot Sales & Marketing Analysis Library, Pilot Discovery Server, Pilot Internet Publisher
SAS Institute, Inc. Cary, NC 919-677-8200 http://www.sas.com	OLAP++ and MDDB	An extension of the company's OLAP architecture which organi- zes data in multiple-dimension hierarchies

desktop to have interactive analysis in making decisions, which is typically not the case with EIS.

ADDITIONAL SOFTWARE USEFUL IN AN OLAP ENVIRONMENT

Additionally, there are a number of software packages that can be utilized by themselves or in conjunction with OLAP software (as presented above) to provide users with some type of multidimensional analysis. They are: (1) natural-language query systems, (2) electronic spreadsheets, (3) financial-planning languages, (4) statistical-analysis packages, (5) business-graphics packages, and (6) management-software packages. All of these are discussed below.

Natural-Language Query Systems

Although not as popular as they were a few years ago, there are a number of natural-language query systems that can be useful in limited analysis. These systems include INTELLECT (marketed by the Artificial Intelligence Corporation), Q&A (marketed by the Symantic Corporation), and DOSTALK (marketed by SAK Technologies). INTELLECT employs the technology of artificial intelligence to understand even the complex pronoun references and incomplete sentences that one uses in conversational English. Managers and their staffs can access data themselves—more easily than ever before—without learning any jargon or "computerese." INTELLECT is not just for simple "what-if" questions. The system can combine information from several files to respond to a query, so a request does not have to be confined to a single file. Users can compare different sets of data with one question, as when comparing actual sales figures with projections. If INTELLECT/DB2 is used, users can employ DB2 databases or other databases and file structures in many ways. With INTELLECT's PC Link, they can ask questions in English on a PC, have the results from DB2 reformatted into a Lotus 1-2-3 worksheet, and sent down to a PC.

INTELLECT can handle questions such as: "Give me the sales managers with salary plus commissions, plus bonuses, minus deductions greater than $40,000," or "I wonder how actual sales for last month compared to the forecasts for people under quota in New England." By defining words and phrases in a *lexicon*, the query system understands each user's vocabulary, linguistic style, and external view of the database. The lexicon can be expanded easily; it takes literally seconds to add new words, definitions, or synonyms. For new users, "lexicon managers" receive four days of training on developing and maintaining the dictionary. Defining the lexicon for specific applications is something users do themselves.

INTELLECT handles pronoun references and partial or ungrammatical sentences. When faced with overly complex, ambiguous phrases or words not found in its lexicon, INTELLECT asks for clarification. The following dialogue demonstrates how the same question may be phrased differently but understood by INTELLECT: "How many clerical people work for the company?" "Count the clerical people." "How many employees are clerical?" "Give me the number of employees in clerical." "Clerical count." INTELLECT interprets all these requests as "Count the employees within the group 'clerical.' " INTELLECT's ability to understand English is so unique that IBM and leading software companies have arranged to integrate it into their product lines.

Electronic Spreadsheets

A popular software approach that has prompted the development of OLAP technology is electronic spreadsheets on PCs. Why have business people embraced electronic spreadsheets? The reason is that ledger-sheet analysis is a singularly tedious, repetitive, and error-prone task. Consider the following scenario: a group of managers of a somewhat large company must submit a report that projects income for the next five years. The managers must assume values for sales revenues, overhead costs, interest rates, repeat business, and cost of materials. The managers' support staff makes a ledger sheet containing all the information and submits it to the company's controller, who asks that the repeat business be assumed at 85 percent instead of 80 percent. The staff must then recalculate all ledger values affected by this change in the repeat business category. Manually recalculating the effects of this single change is so arduous and time consuming that very few managers allow their staff to make more than two assumptions per category.

A spreadsheet program, however, transforms a microcomputer screen into a large ledger sheet. By simulating the rows and columns of a ledger sheet, the program lets a user work with a large number of interrelated values. When a user changes a given value on the spreadsheet, the program automatically recalculates any affected values in seconds. The program not only makes manager's projections less time consuming and more accurate, but it also encourages them to ask more "what-if" questions and to make more complex assumptions.

Although originally intended for accountants, spreadsheet programs are now widely used by managers and their staffs who need to recalculate figures. Spreadsheet programs are used to produce budgets, action-and-profit plans, and sales forecasts. They also help to produce income statements, cash-flow projections, currency conversions, expense reports, and job-cost analyses. The more popular electronic spreadsheets, such as Excel (from the Microsoft Corporation) and Lotus 1-2-3 (from the IBM Corporation), have sold in the millions.

Financial-Planning Languages

When managers and their staffs find that their models are too large for electronic spreadsheets and have need of advanced features such as risk analysis, linear optimization, and goal seeking, financial-planning languages that operate in conjunction with micros or mainframes are used. They are high-level financial generators designed to excel in a certain class of applications that includes financial planning and analysis, strategic planning, budgeting, modeling, and business simulations. Actually, they are quite useful in handling any problem whose answer is likely to end up on a row-and-column format or whose complex nature reflects logic and data manipulation rather than support for managers; their statements must resemble a typical person's vocabulary and must track unstructured and continually changing thought processes. Furthermore, these generators must react in sufficient time to allow a person's attention to remain focused on the problem. Decision-making support is further promoted by permitting the language statements to appear in any order.

Financial-planning languages, such as Comshare's Commander and Information Builders, Inc.'s Focus, enable managers and their staffs to become competent in building and solving models in an interactive, exploratory manner. The largest users of financial models were found to be in the manufacturing industry, followed by banking and finance. In addition, the larger the sales of the corporation, the more likely it was the company would be using a financial model. Corporate planning is the single largest user group, followed by finance. The modeling application most frequently used in cash-flow analysis is in such areas as cash from operations, short-term investments and debt structure, accounts payable, and inventories. Other typical uses include pro-forma financial reports and financial forecasts, investment analysis, profit planning, sales forecasts, budgeting, merger-and-acquisition planning, and project models. The most important modeling techniques identified by users include "what-if" analysis, financial-ratio analysis, sensitivity analysis, ROI analysis, and forecasting and regression analyses.[1]

Statistical-Analysis Packages

Although many of the financial-planning languages have statistical-analysis capabilities, there are software packages that are designed primarily as statistical-analysis systems. Although most were designed initially for use on computer mainframes, they are widely usable today on microcomputers or minicomputers. For a business situation in which a series of data is used to see what the results are with a certain set of conditions, its output can be plotted. Interactively, the set of conditions can be changed and new output plotted. Needless to say, there is a whole series of business problems that benefit from graphic solutions: project planning, breakeven analysis, learning curves, and so forth. A picture is often worth a thousand words, a thousand lines of printout, or ten minutes of discussion. Because the eye is able to discern patterns better than it sees individual numbers on a computer printout, managers are able to absorb a tremendous amount of information as it is shown graphically. Because OLAP systems make great use of computer graphics, they allow organization personnel to build models and speculate with their computers using graphic output on how hypothetical decisions might translate into reality.

As with financial-planning languages, a number of statistical-analysis packages are available currently. Among these are SAS (Statistical Analysis System) from the SAS Institute, Inc., SAM (Strategic Analysis Model) from Decision Sciences Corporation, SPSS from SPSS, Inc., STATII from CompuServe, and DISSPLA and Tell-A-Graf from Integrated Software Systems Corporation. SAS is used for most statistical applications that are widely found in business today. SAM has been used for expediting strategic planning by generating alternative future scenarios. SPSS is useful in market-research studies; STATII centers on business statistics, forcasting, and econometric modeling. DISSPLA is a graphics-software system with a high-level subrouting plotting language for producing graphs, surfaces, and maps. Tell-A-Graf enables users to call up graphs, charts, and plots using simple English-like statements.

Business-Graphics Packages

As discussed previously in the text, business graphics cut right to the heart of an issue, generating an impact that is not easily forgotten. But the real benefit of graphics is their ability to simplify complex-data relationships in a way that captures attention. For managers and their staffs operating in an OLAP environment, graphics are an exciting and viable means of communicating numerical and financial data. Because statistics and graphics go hand in hand, it is no wonder that graphics packages are essentially extensions of statistical-analysis software. For example, SAS Institute's SAS/GRAPH, while also a stand-alone product, is especially designed to be tightly linked with the SAS system for statistical analysis and data management and retrieval. At the core of the system is Base SAS, a fundamental management and reporting library of modular components that users can pick and choose from. One characteristic that sets SAS/GRAPH apart from many of the typical business-graphics packages is its mapping feature.

Somewhat recent announcements from the five market leaders herald a surge in 3-D on the desktop. For example, Digital Equipment Corporation introduced graphics processing that it claims makes its products the most powerful computers available on the desktop. IBM and Sun Microsystems have brought down the price of 3-D graphics, thereby making it afforable to a much larger group of users. Silicon Graphics Inc. and Hewlett-Packard have begun offering graphics capabilities never before available on the desktop. Taken together, these announcements will change the way workstations are used, not only in high-end applications, such as animation and imaging, but also in more traditional workstation markets, such as business processing, scientific processing, and computer-aided design (CAD). In effect, graphics capabilities are becoming standard, including 3-D capabilities.[2] Going one step further, Autodesk Inc. has formed a new multimedia unit and launched tools for authoring and viewing 3-D graphic files on the Internet. The new unit, called Kinetix, unveiled both a Windows NT version of 3D Studio Max and Hyperwire, a tool for creating Java applets from two-dimensional and 3-D graphics.[3]

Management-Software Packages

Although not labeled as OLAP software per se, there a number of management-software (sometimes called MBA-ware) packages that can be useful to managers and their staffs. Typical ones are set forth as follows. Performance Now! by KnowledgePoint (Petaluma, California) asks users to rate employees on a scale of one to five for skills ranging from "takes responsibility for own actions" to "keeps abreast of current developments in the field." Then it develops descriptive text that supports the rating. Typically, Performance Now! has improved employee reviews by making them more consistent and direct. Employee Appraiser by Austin-Hayne (Redwood, California) takes a slightly different approach. Instead of using a numerical rating, it provides sample text that the user can adjust to be more positive or negative using a "writing turner" function. Also, this software package includes extensive coaching that gives managers ideas on how to improve employee performance between reviews. Many software experts think that programs like Performance Now! and Employee Appraiser will be the first MBA-ware widely adopted across different industries. In contrast, Negotiator Pro from Negotiator Pro Company (Brookline, Massachusetts) provides users with formal negotiation training. Essentially, this software package helps prepare a psychological profile of an individual and his or her opponent as well as a detailed negotiation plan.

Inasmuch as not all MBA-ware is designed for specific tasks, Business Insight by Business Resource Software (Austin, Texas) helps managers brainstorm about larger issues such as strategic planning. It is helpful to managers and their staffs to figure out the best way to introduce new products and services. Forecast Pro from Business Forecast Systems (Belmont, Massachusetts) analyzes data and enables managers who do not have a degree in statistics to run simple forecasts. Finally, ManagePro from Avantos Performance Systems (Emeryville, California) is useful in creating a dynamic database that links goals with the people assigned to meet them, and reminds the manager to give adequate coaching and feedback.[4]

SELECTION OF APPROPRIATE SOFTWARE FOR OLAP IS SITUATIONAL

The foregoing exposition of OLAP software using relational or multidimensional databases plus additional software useful in an OLAP environment shows the diversity of approaches to the subject matter of this book. Typically, most companies are likely to end up with more than one software package where the situation dictates which software is judged best by the users. That is, the focus is *situational* to solve business problems. Typically, multidimensional databases are used when there are larger volumes of data and detailed analysis is required to solve problems. When the queries are simpler and the data is smaller, simple and easy-to-use software will do the job to answer questions surrounding the problems. However, more and more companies today find themselves in situations where users demand multidimensional analysis for a wider range of decision support, EIS, and OLAP problems.

SUMMARY

Initially, the chapter explored multidimensional analysis (the focus of on-line analytical processing), followed by the critical factors in evaluating software for

OLAP systems. Emphasizing a very practical approach, the use of typical OLAP-software packages to assist managers and their staffs in decision making was presented. Additional software, that is, natural-language query systems, electronic spreadsheets, financial-planning languages, statistical-analysis packages, business-graphics packages, and management-software packages, useful in an OLAP operating mode was discussed. Lastly, a brief discussion on the selection of the appropriate OLAP software centered on a situational approach. Overall, the software as set forth in this chapter, along with the appropriate data warehousing and data communications from the prior chapter, provide the means for users to undertake decision making as needed on a day-by-day basis.

NOTES

1. Jürgen Hahn, "Management Warms Up to Modeling Languages," *Infosystems*, July 1980, p. 46.

2. Jerry Lazar, "Workstations, Graphic Content," *InformationWeek*, August 28, 1995, pp. 43–45.

3. Chris Jones, "Autodesk Plans 3-D Web Authoring," *InfoWorld*, April 15, 1996, p. 12.

4. Alison L. Sprout, "Surprise! Software to Help You Manage," *Fortune*, April 17, 1995, pp. 197–203.

5

Implementing a Successful OLAP System

ISSUES EXPLORED

- How does one justify the implementation of on-line analytical processing systems?
- What is the relationship of rapid application development to successful OLAP implementation?
- What software tools can be used to implement an effective on-line analytical processing system?
- What are the key steps to implement a successful OLAP system?
- What are the newer considerations in implementing OLAP successfully?

OUTLINE

Getting Started on Implementing OLAP Systems
    Cost Justification for OLAP Systems
Current Environment of Rapid Application Development (RAD)
    Prototyping and Iterative Development
Software Tools to Implement OLAP Successfully
    Proprietary-OLAP Packages
    In-House Development
    Graphical-User-Interface (GUI) Development Tools
    Fourth-Generation Languages
    Presentation-Graphics Software
    Natural-Language Systems

GETTING STARTED ON IMPLEMENTING OLAP SYSTEMS

Typically, OLAP systems go beyond executive information systems (EIS) by informing more than executives. Whereas classic EIS was electronic briefing books of predigested data for senior executives who were computer illiterate, OLAP systems reach managers and analysts throughout the organization. Basic characteristics of OLAP systems, like ease of use and consolidated data, derive from classic EIS systems. However, OLAP systems have a goal of giving company personnel, often overwhelmed with data, actionable information and knowledge about their operations no matter where these operations are located. It is from this perspective that implementing OLAP systems successfully is set forth in this chapter.

Implementing an on-line analytical processing system, generally, is not too much different from developing any other major system or application. They all involve the familiar process of planning, development, programming, program maintenance, and training. What makes an OLAP system a special case is the relatively high visibility of the project since there is a tie-in with a company's critical success factors and their measurement via key performance indicators over time. Often, the OLAP undertaking enjoys the special interest of one or more senior managers. The on-line analytical processing system may extend information links to far-flung corners of the organization. Although the risks inherent in developing OLAP can be indeed high at times, so can the rewards. Hence, there is the need to take a look at the diverse elements found in its implementation. They include cost verification, current environment of rapid application development (RAD), software tools to implement OLAP successfully, key factors to implement a successful OLAP system, plus implementation and support of OLAP systems on a daily basis. Other important considerations, that is, OLAP-Web integration for distant users and OLAP-virtual-reality integration for business users, are also covered in the chapter. Lastly, several OLAP case studies are presented that have been implemented successfully.

Cost Justification for OLAP Systems

An often-asked question by corporate sponsors of OLAP systems is, "How do you justify the expense of one in terms of a traditional cost-benefit analysis?" The answer given by most managers, within or outside the computer department, who have tried is that one does not. For the most part, the payoffs from an OLAP are different from other types of information systems in that they are often less tangible, less quantifiable. For example, in implementing a new accounting system, an information systems manager is able to estimate specific savings from tracking accounts receivable more closely. With OLAP, the focus is on providing managers and analysts with improved information and knowledge via multidimensional analysis on a timely basis. The real payoff is in giving managers and their staffs at all levels quick access to analytical information and knowledge that can be used in new combinations and may lead to new ways of thinking and better decisions. Hence, the typical company manager can do a more effective job in performing his or her duties in the organization.

On the other hand, there can be instances where savings or gains can be tied directly to an OLAP system. For the most part, however, no one has been able to come up with a model or system for cost justifying an OLAP system. Typically, managers do not try to do a cost-benefit structure. They use the system, and they know the value of it. It is not even that easy to predict the total cost of a system. The largest expense generally comes from ongoing applications development and data acquisition as managers become more familiar with the system and seek more multidimensional analysis of pertinent information.

Because of the difficulty to cost justify an OLAP system, many computer departments keep from proposing such systems in the first place. If the managers who are pushing for OLAP have enough clout, the cost-justification issue usually fades into the background. Usually, an OLAP system gets cost justified by one or more managers high up in the organization saying, "Give me this new analysis tool or I may look elsewhere for employment." Overall, cost justifying an on-line analytical processing system tends to be an evasive one versus that found in traditional mission-critical systems.

CURRENT ENVIRONMENT OF RAPID APPLICATION DEVELOPMENT (RAD)

The current environment of rapid application development (RAD) was first popularized in the 1970s by James Martin, a recognized authority on information technology. Martin created RAD as a trademarked methodology that is still sold today. Essentially, it has been generalized to represent the development of applications by small teams of highly skilled specialists working very closely with end users over a several-month time span. This is in contrast with the more traditional approach of a large group of IS professionals coordinating their activities over a longer period of time, say two years or more, along with less contact with end users. The net result is that RAD eliminates exhaustive and rigorous project design and review before coding begins. An application's summary description should be no more than a page or two long, not counting JAD deliverables, such as screen, report, and data designs.

Because there are fewer formal, ongoing reviews of the project, progress on the project should be monitored closely and daily by the team members who work side by side as the system is developed. This should not mean that little or no design or review is done. But rather, the effort is compressed into the development phase with more frequent reviews of less material. Rather than everything being reviewed before the project begins, each component is reviewed as it is added, modified, or enhanced. To assist RAD developers, a wide range of advanced technologies, such as Windows and graphical-user-interface (GUI) tools, are used to allow truly rapid development of easily modified components. With older technologies, developing program components took longer, and programs were typically harder to implement in such a way that they were easily modified later. However, since windows, programs, and reports can be easily developed in hours or days as opposed to weeks, true rapid application development is possible.

Prototyping and Iterative Development

Two techniques that are central to rapid application development are prototyping and iterative development. *Prototyping* can be defined as the development of a subset of a potential system to demonstrate the feasibility of such a system. This technique is a useful approach for developing an OLAP system. Its goal is to provide users, that is, managers, with programs that feature multidimensional analysis such that they are of the highest quality at the lowest cost in the minimum amount of time practical, given the need to keep quality high and cost low. Prototyping has a definite advantage over traditional design specifications, owing to the speed with which the program can be developed and the user's ease in understanding what is being proposed. The old phrase "a picture is worth a thousand words" really holds true here. Within an OLAP environment, prototyping serves as a substitute for more formal, detailed-design specifications.

Not only is it used to drive out the design for the system the user really needs, but it also serves as a way to refine the initial requirements. The result is a higher-quality product that is better suited to the user's needs. Because of prototyping, managers are able to see the product earlier in the process (in easily digested, incremental steps) than would have been possible using traditional-design techniques.

Since the focus of prototyping is on computerization, typical prototyping tools for IS professionals and end users include the following:

	Sample tools
CASE tools	LMBS-System Engineer, Popkin-System Architect, Bachman Analyst, JAMM
Advanced GUI development tools	PowerBuilder, SQL Windows, Visual Basic, Visual APPBuilder, ObjectView, Enterprise Developer
PC-based DBMS tools	MS-Access, Paradox for Windows, dBASE for Windows
Spreadsheets	Excel and Lotus 1-2-3
Presentation tools	PowerPoint, Persuasion, Freelance

Some of these tools are for prototyping only, while others are robust enough to support the actual development of the application. The considerations for picking the appropriate tool are impacted not only by the particular requirements of a specific application, but also should address functionality, learning curve, stability, reusability, availability of trained resources, and vendor support. Thus, consideration should be given to the following. First, the prototyping tool should be easy to learn and use. Second, the tool should have a degree of functional richness such that a user-interface prototype is capable of showing screens in a default sequence. Third, if a prototype is to be extensive, it is helpful that the prototype tool accept design or implementation documentation, such as screen layouts and special-key assignments, which is typically provided by CASE tools. If CASE tools are not used, object-oriented tools that support the reuse of objects can be another effective approach. Fourth and last, prototyping tools should work on the same operating systems as the intended application. Depending on the application requirements, availability under other operating systems may also be important.

In contrast to prototyping, *iterative development* refers to an approach in which a RAD team goes through the development cycle (i.e., system requirements, design, code, and review) quickly several times for small portions of the entire system. As opposed to developing a complete program or area of the system, only a small, functional portion is completed. In turn, this is reviewed immediately by end users to get sign-off or additional input. If sign-off is not given, the process iterates a number of times until sign-off is received. The name iterative development, then, is appropriate to this method of development. Typically, end users remain involved because very little time goes by between being promised something and seeing it delivered.

Although the tools used in prototyping and iterative development are often the same, these two RAD approaches are not the same because prototyping is often developed with the idea of throwing away the prototype and starting from the beginning. However, it should be noted that as the technology improves, tools which can be employed for prototyping plus development are more desirable. With proper planning, some of the prototype components can be used in the actual application. In fact, CASE tools allow user-interface prototyping, screen, and database designs to be reused. On the other hand, iterative development consists of delivery components of an application in small increments at frequent intervals (say, days or weeks). As such, end users can start realizing some improvements before the entire application is completed.

SOFTWARE TOOLS TO IMPLEMENT OLAP SUCCESSFULLY

There are a number of software tools currently available for implementing an on-line analytical processing system. Typically, there are two basic approaches to developing an OLAP system. These approaches break down in terms of installing a proprietary-OLAP package (refer to Chapter 4) or developing the system in-house. Although it comes down to *buy or build* which is common to virtually every development effort, the author has added four other viable approaches that can be useful in developing OLAP systems. They are GUI-development tools, fourth-generation languages, presentation-graphics software, and natural-language systems. These approaches, which focus mostly on two-dimensional analysis, can be complementary to multidimensional analysis.

Proprietary-OLAP Packages

Currently, most organizations today are using proprietary-OLAP packages as the basis for their own efforts to provide multidimensional analysis. There are a number of systems on the market, each with its own strengths and limitations. As noted in the previous chapter, four major software packages are: (1) Essbase Analysis, (2) Commander OLAP, (3) Express, and (4) LightShip Suite. For the most part, they are designed for *rapid prototyping*. Essentially, great flexibility is built into the commercial OLAP application software. By their nature, OLAP systems are capable of interfacing with many kinds of computer platforms (PC, minicomputer, and computer mainframe) and information sources (internal and external databases, computer networks, and the like). Some of these packages offer underlying DSS and EIS capabilities which can be used to perform consolidations, projections, comparisons, as well as to generate reports and three-dimensional graphs.

An important function of a proprietary-OLAP package is to permit managers and their staffs to use the monitoring method which serves up data on an exception basis. This can take the form of variance reporting, in which the OLAP system produces only exceptions that are based on a periodic review of the data. For a non-periodic review of operations, the monitoring method can also be used, in which case the OLAP system makes all of the technical decisions and provides input for the tactical ones as well.

Because the information and knowledge generated by an OLAP system is communicated increasingly to third parties, such as to board members for overview purposes or to outside banks for loaning money, it is important that the quality of the graphics output be high. The use of colors and windows enhances the output. Most managers will also require a high-resolution bit-mapped display screen. The advantage of this technology is that it offers managers and their staffs a way of displaying the multidimensional information. If an OLAP system is to be successful, it must offer a better approach to the traditional paper-based methods. If a manager can save ten minutes here and there, make communication with peers and subordinates more effective, and give the manager more timely access to focused information and knowledge, it will help ensure the success of implementing a proprietary-OLAP package.

Currently, OLAP and database query-tool vendors are tuning their tools to give end users a better grip on corporate data. For example, Oracle Corporation's OLAP division is marketing its Express Objects as a tool designed to create OLAP applications tied to the company's multidimensional database. Although the tool is designed for corporate developers, Oracle expects end users to be able to use the tool to create applications by visually tying together prebuilt components. Essentially, Oracle Express Objects can be used with Oracle's Express Analyzer front-end OLAP tool to meet a wide range of needs, from simple end-user ad hoc querying to complex custom applications.

In the data-querying and report-writing market, Information Builders Inc. is taking the same approach as Oracle by bringing tools closer to end users. It is marketing Focus Six Visual Business Information Suite, a Windows 3.1 and Windows NT upgrade, to its report and querying tool that introduces a report writer for end users, called Managed Reporter. With Managed Reporter, users can create reports by using prebuilt templates. The tool employs a three-tier architecture, in which most processing is done on the server and a minimum of data is sent over the network, to improve performance.

In-House Development

From the viewpoint of in-house development, there are two alternative starting points in implementing an on-line analytical processing system. One is to deliver a basic OLAP to as wide a management group as possible. The other is a more evolutionary approach, starting with one or two OLAP applications and gradually enlarging the system with other related functions. In the *first* approach, the OLAP's ready capability to define and capture historical data goes a long way toward meeting basic analysis and reporting needs for a wide user base. The chief benefit of starting with these basic capabilities is that a usable system can often be delivered in several weeks—and even in a complex situation, in less than six months. This reduces the risk of implementing an OLAP system as usable results can be delivered quickly to meet a broad segment of managerial and staff needs. But the number of people who have to be trained, and the amount of technical support needed, can be somewhat high.

In contrast, the *second* or evolutionary method of implementation targets and addresses one or two specific application areas. This approach generally results in a high-value solution for a specific management group. After implementation of that capability, additional areas can be addressed, and over time an integrated OLAP can be developed. Because it is targeted at a more specific audience, this approach requires less comprehensive support and training. It can be every bit as useful as the other, although care should be taken in the design to ensure easy integration of future applications.

For both situations, the in-house development approach centers on the use of the latest techniques in application development. Currently, these include those discussed in the next sections of the chapter (i.e., GUI development tools, fourth-generation languages, presentation-graphics software, and natural-language systems) plus object-oriented programming (OOP) and visual programming. The essence of object development is the idea that once objects are built, they can be reused, speeding up future application development. On the other hand, visual programming centers on the construction of software programs by selecting and arranging programming objects rather than by writing program code.

Typically, it is unlikely that an organization can determine its requirements beforehand that solves most problems facing its managers and analysts. However, for some straightforward OLAP applications, an in-house development effort may be appropriate. Also, in-house development may be effective for general data management. However, it is typically weak in the areas of data modeling, consolidation, and analysis, as well as decision support. Generally, in-house development is not undertaken since the cost is somewhat high. Currently, efforts have shifted from finding the best tool that will let users build an application from scratch to finding an existing OLAP package that will provide the best fit and then customizing it.

Graphical-User-Interface (GUI) Development Tools

When users interact with a PC or a computer mainframe, the interaction is controlled by an operating system. The user interface is part of an information system with which users interact. Users communicate with an operating system through the user interface of that operating system. Early PC operating systems were command driven, such as DOS, requiring the user to type in text-based commands using a keyboard. For example, to perform a task such as deleting a file named DATAFILE, the user must type in a command such as DELETE C:\DATAFILE. Users need to remember these commands and their syntax to work with the computer effectively. On the other hand, a graphical user interface (GUI) makes use of icons, buttons, bars, and boxes to perform the same tasks. It has become the dominant model today for the user interface of PC operating systems. Commands can be activated by rolling a mouse to move a cursor about the screen and clicking a button on the mouse to make selections. Icons are symbolic pictures and they are also used in GUIs to represent programs and files. For example, a file could be deleted by moving the cursor to a "Trash" icon. Many graphical user interfaces use a system of pull-down menus to help users select commands, and pop-up boxes to help users select among various command options. As such, some graphical analyses can be produced by using GUIs.

It should be noted that the availability of robust, GUI development tools today is an important factor for developing successful prototypes. These advanced tools are typically interpreted rather than compiled, which makes them well-suited for prototyping. Advanced GUI features can be implemented with the click of a mouse, rather than by writing many lines of code. With these tools, system developers can sit with users and develop running prototypes before the users' eyes. As the one or more users provide input, the developer can modify the program. The net result is that there is instant feedback that allows the users' requirements to be captured more accurately and quickly. As such, developers can focus on user requirements rather than on more technical issues.

Fourth-Generation Languages

Fourth-generation-language (4GL) development systems are tools that permit rapid application development and easy interface prototyping. In many respects, OLAP-proprietary packages are an outgrowth of fourth-generation languages. Hence, these languages can represent another approach to developing on-line analytical processing systems without focusing on multidimensional analysis per se. They are designed to let managers, including their staffs, develop appropriate analyses on a PC or a mainframe. The focus is on letting users have as much control as possible over the access and manipulation of relevant information.

An important advantage of fourth-generation languages is the facility to generate customized reports or graphs to summarize key statistics and highlight trends. Although the current software products differ considerably in this respect, especially in the quality of their graphics, all are a big improvement over doing the same thing by hand. Many hours can be spent preparing charts or graphs manually for a presentation that can be produced by 4GL software products in a matter of minutes. Although many benefits can be attributed to using fourth-generation languages, they are not as successful as the proprietary-OLAP packages mentioned previously. That is, 4GLs are excellent for data management but are not as good at data analysis and consolidation. From this perspective, proprietary-OLAP packages are generally preferred over 4GLs by managers since OLAP-software packages do more of the basic functions that are found in a manager's job no matter the level.

Currently, fourth-generation languages range from simple screen painters to fully integrated programming environments that have CASE features, open-networking facilities, and powerful front-end object-oriented code generators. Typical 4GLs for their ease of application development include PowerBuilder, Uniface, Focus, and SmartStar Vision. These tools provide some of the earliest uses of object-oriented technology. The best tools use object orientation to create GUIs easily and provide sufficient flexibility for multiple platforms—a big plus in client/server environments. However, the bottom line for any 4GL is the ability to produce a quality, maintainable application that meets current user needs.

Presentation-Graphics Software

Another approach that can be complementary to OLAP systems is presentation graphics software using a current windows approach, such as Windows 95. Typical programs are: (1) Lotus Development Corporation's Freelance Graphics 96, (2) Software Publishing Corporation's Harvard Graphics 4.0, and (3) Microsoft Corporation's PowerPoint. They are 32-bit products with preemptive multitasking capabilities and support the Universal Naming Convention or long-file names (as many as 256 characters). In addition, these software packages support workgroup capabilities, thereby allowing multiple people to work on the same project. Because Windows 95 contains a lot of 16-bit code for backward compatibility, and because these programs were not written from scratch as true 32-bit applications, basically they are in some ways no better than their 16-bit counterparts in operating performance. Nevertheless, the new versions of Freelance Graphics, Harvard Graphics, and PowerPoint all provide enhanced features for delivery of slide shows, group editing, and presentations over a network. Lotus, for example, promotes its TeamReview concept as a major feature for both presentations and other document types in its SmartSuite 96 package. It is a strong networking delivery program in its class and its Publish to Internet feature breaks new ground in deliverying presentations over the Internet and companywide networks. PowerPoint is not far behind with its intelligent Presentation Conference Wizard. Whether it is a LAN, a WAN, or the Internet, these presenters can reach audiences in ways they never could before.

Another typical presentation-graphics software package is Corel Corporation's Presents. This latest version is a 32-bit application designed to run on Microsoft's Windows 95 although it does not support workgroup capabilities or the capability to conduct presentations on the Internet or through videoconferencing. However, Presents is comparable to PowerPoint and Harvard Graphics in its scope and complexity, but the interface is a bit harder to master for those users who do not know CorelDraw. Counteracting that problem are Present's connections to the rest of the CorelDraw suite, giving it a full array of content-creation and editing features that are not found in most presentation-graphics packages.

Natural-Language Systems

Currently, a seldom-used approach to developing OLAP systems centers on natural languages, that is, the native language of users or English. Today, there are natural-language systems on the market that transcend natural language-to-language translation and, indeed, have mastered natural language-to-computerese translation to an admirable degree. Commercial natural-language processing is finally a reality. Many of the words that the natural-language processor encounters are generic, that is, they are relevant to a wide variety of applications. These words are usually built into the dictionaries of commercial natural-language systems prior to delivery. However, other words tend to be application-specific. For example, words like tenure or residence might be part of a personnel staffer's everyday vocabulary, but are foreign to an engineer. Words such as these might not appear in the system's preprogrammed vocabulary, but can be added to the dictionary by users in accordance with their individual needs.

Natural-language processing has emerged in computing at the computer mainframe and the PC level. Perhaps the difference in sophistication and functionality of these systems is most readily evidenced by the price tags they carry. Whereas micro-based systems like Lotus HAL and EQL can be purchased for less than $200, a mainframe system like INTELLECT from the AI Corporation costs many thousands of dollars. The primary difference is in the sophistication of the data to which they can interface. Computer-mainframe databases are far larger than their PC counterparts and are also much more complex. The fact that many users are sharing the same information on a mainframe means that there are different perspectives of that same data. For example, financial users might want to compare profit and loss, marketing users might want to look at things by product line, salespeople might want to know how they are doing by region, and engineers might want to look at data from a technological viewpoint. In effect, the database must be structured to accommodate these various views, and the data has to be more complex in order to deal with inherent relationships. An INTELLECT system on the mainframe will be dealing with much larger and much more complex multifile databases.

As discussed, natural-language system packages are easy to use since they incorporate the English language. However, they are limited in that they are not capable of undertaking the detailed analysis and consolidating of data plus multidimensional analysis that is typically found in an on-line analytical processing system without extensive programming. From this perspective, a proprietary-OLAP package is generally recommended over a natural-language package. In certain cases, a natural-language system package might be used initially to get the manager used to the computer. The next step up would be an OLAP package.

KEY STEPS TO IMPLEMENT A SUCCESSFUL OLAP SYSTEM

There are a number of key steps that should be undertaken for a successful on-line analytical processing system. Essentially, there is an order that should be followed in undertaking these steps, as follows:

1. get support for OLAP by starting at the top of the organization

2. select a project team to assist in implementing OLAP

3. choose an emphasis for developing OLAP applications

4. select OLAP software tools that meet users' needs

5. determine the proper organization of data for OLAP

6. develop initial application(s) that relate to a company's CSFs.

Due to the importance of each step, they are individually covered below.

Get Support for OLAP by Starting at the Top of the Organization

The first step in implementing any type of OLAP system is to identify the *corporate sponsor* of the system. No OLAP system will succeed without a strong advocate at the very highest level. Ideally, it should be the number one or two executive in the organization. If top management support is not there, the on-line analytical processing system is not going to go very far. This is like trying to undertake OLAP from a grass-roots effort. Overall, getting started centers on obtaining the support of the president of a company or, at least, the support of the company's executive vice president.

Additionally, sponsorship must go beyond a corporate executive sponsor and include an *operating sponsor*. As indicated, the corporate sponsor will be the most senior executive who makes the initial request for the system and oversees its development. But sponsorship means more than sitting back and saying, "I'm for this project and will be its champion throughout the development process," and then delegating all of the work to others. A successful OLAP implementation requires a commitment from a corporate sponsor who will personally spend time on the project. Because the corporate sponsor delegates some of the work, that is where the operating sponsor comes in. The operating sponsor (or sponsors) is a manager or a well-respected staff person below the corporate sponsor who knows both the business and something about OLAP technology. The person is capable of operating comfortably in either the business or technological areas of an organization.

Select a Project Team to Assist in Implementing OLAP

After the appropriate operating sponsor has been recruited, there is the need for the corporate sponsor to establish a project team to carry out the implementation of the OLAP system. Because the corporate sponsor would normally be the individual for whom the OLAP is being developed, it helps if the individual is knowledgeable and amenable to newer technology. Since such a senior executive seldom has the time on a day-to-day basis necessary to develop the OLAP system, generally an operating sponsor is appointed. Ideally, the corporate sponsor's representative should be available at least two days per week, have an excellent understanding of both the organization's and management's needs, and have priority access to the corporate sponsor. Hence, the operating sponsor should have the proper credentials to head the OLAP project team.

To get a better idea of the composition of the OLAP project team, a balanced mix of technology specialists and business/financial analysts is needed. The technical specialists from the information systems department are responsible for database administration, network management, capacity planning, and security. The business analysts are responsible for identifying, locating, and formatting the information required by the company's management at all levels. Ideally, the analysts representing the business/financial area should be providing information currently to the company's managers or the information originates from a new area that will be contributing to the objectives, goals, and strategies of the company.

Choose an Emphasis for Developing OLAP Applications

One of the major keys to a successful system is deciding what the company's managers want from the OLAP applications to be developed. Many managers want to avoid having to sift through internal reports for the page that contains the information they need, or would like to see all relevant information in terms of multidimensional analysis. For this type of system, there is a need for ease of access to the information. Menus with fixed choices of reports based on distilled information from internal or external systems might be a good alternative. It would make information access easy and not require that users become skilled programmers to use the OLAP system.

On the other hand, there might be an emphasis on developing OLAP applications that give users the ability to analyze the information that they see, that is, look behind the numbers and apply their own assumptions to the data. Such an emphasis may well include statistical-analysis software, decision-support capabilities, and expert systems. Although it would be easy to use, it would require that the user have a bit more computer expertise to move around in the OLAP system. From this IS perspective, it might have to be based on some form of a natural-language interface, a DBMS with a sophisticated query-language, and a contextual-search capability. Also, the new OLAP system could be used as a tool for motivating the members of a company and speeding up the way the business is run.

Select OLAP Software Tools That Meet Users' Needs

Based upon the chosen emphasis for developing applications (as set forth above), the next step is to select appropriate OLAP-software tools that will allow this emphasis to be realized. More specifically, if the emphasis is on ease of access to information with fixed choices of output, the OLAP software could be one of those tools described in the prior chapter. These tools should utilize a simple interface and be easy to use. As time goes on, users will ask for more multidimensional analyses that generally require an enlargement of the fixed choice of output. Generally, IS professionals will develop the additional OLAP output that will meet users' needs. Hence, it is prudent to choose those OLAP-software tools that will give the ability to build flexibility into the OLAP system as users' needs multiply over time.

From another perspective, choosing an emphasis where the user can see behind the analyses centers on selecting OLAP-software tools which can lead in many directions. For one, establish the OLAP systems as a prototype in one area and expand it in increments over time. In turn, the expansion can be extended to include other areas where related computer technologies may complement OLAP software. From another viewpoint, the software could allow users to develop OLAP programs that focus on a company's critical success factors and their measurement using key performance indicators and financial ratios. Within this framework, users could add new programs for a more in-depth analysis. Still another direction might focus on improving the exchange of critical information among users at the same level or various levels in a company. No matter the orientation, the goal of the selected OLAP-software tools is to expand the user's understanding of vital company information and its related knowledge plus tying-in with newer computer technologies, such as virtual reality where the user can experience what is transpiring—good, bad, or indifferent.

In addition, selecting appropriate OLAP-software tools should be evaluated regarding their contribution to assist managers and analysts. Obviously, the OLAP system will not solve all problems nor should it attempt to be a total solution because people are the problem solvers. The system is simply a tool to assist in supporting company personnel. Ultimately, the manager and analyst will have to ask "why?" and they will have to come up with the solution. Overall, not only do OLAP-software tools need to be selected that give users *flexibility* in building these type systems, but also the output from these tools should provide the capability to improve the *effectiveness* of the company managers, analysts, and their staffs.

Determine the Proper Organization of Data for OLAP

Once the appropriate OLAP-software tools have been selected for a chosen emphasis, it cannot be assumed that the data exists. If it does, it cannot be assumed that the data is compatible with the OLAP environment. Because multidimensional analysis represents a key tool for leveraging the contents of an organization's production data and other data stored in the data warehouse, there is a need for the proper organization to the data for this type of analysis. At this stage of the OLAP-development process, the problems of timeliness and issues such as the political implications of data ownership and data acquisition must be addressed. Most data will probably exist within the organization. However, some of it may only be available from a combination of internal and external sources.

In working through these problems, OLAP developers must give users the capability of storing and retrieving data in new and different ways. Although each aspect of typical company information—product, pricing, cost, region, and time period—represents a dimension, business people often think in terms of multiple dimensions. A product manager might want to know how many products were sold in the Southeast region in March, how that compares to the previous month and the previous March, and how it compares to the sales forecasts or correlates to the advertising and promotion expenditure. To get these answers from a relational database requires numerous, complex SQL-queries.

In contrast, a multidimensional tool can handle such queries with ease by preaggregating and indexing the data. Summaries and subtotals are preprocessed, time-series calculations are built in, and OLAP developers define the dimensions once. Users, in turn, can use queries by specifying the dimensions they want to see, which typically requires only a click of the mouse. Each query returns a different dimension of the data. As an example, a finance manager might want to analyze performance by factory, product, and time period in light of several different cost factors, such as materials and labor. A marketing manager at the same company might want to view the same data by product, sales or region, over time in light of special promotions and advertising spending. Thus, a multidimensional database can go a long way toward meeting the diverse needs of users. As such, multidimensional analysis represents a method for leveraging the contents of the organization's production data in a company database and other data stored in the data warehouse.

Develop Initial Application(s) That Relate to a Company's CSFs

The project team should start with one (or two) important application(s) that can be prototyped. The prototype should demonstrate what an OLAP system can do for the company. Very often, a prototype can serve to arouse a manager's interest in the project so that the individual becomes a sponsor of the company's OLAP system. As noted earlier in the chapter, in-depth interviewing is usually not important when prototyping because the manager's specifications are not based on how well the builder interprets the spoken requirements. Instead, the specifications are based on the demonstrated working prototype. Furthermore, the OLAP builder does not need to uncover the requirements at the beginning because each version of the prototype helps refine the essential requirements and identify missing ones. Each version of the prototype performs more of the desired functions in an increasingly efficient manner. When a prototype has been completed, the manager should be able to describe what he or she likes and dislikes about the OLAP application and what other analyses he or she would like to see as output.

No matter how the new OLAP application is developed using prototyping or some other method, there is a need for managers to relate this application to a company's critical success factors. (Critical success factors which were noted briefly earlier in the text will be expanded upon in the next chapter.) Identifying the CSFs does not by itself make the OLAP implementation successful. It is necessary to decide how to monitor and measure them using key performance indicators and financial ratios. If, for example, quality or customer satisfaction are two critical success factors, what information, especially in the form of multidimensional analysis, should be displayed for managers to evaluate these areas? Determining the measurements requires both familiarity with the company's business and intimate knowledge of the types of data and information available to the OLAP. Quality might be measured by the volume of product defects; the level of complaints or new sales to existing customers might be the measures of customer satisfaction. Overall, the final OLAP system and its many applications should allow managers and analysts to view important analyses that are not found in traditional EIS or DSS.

OTHER IMPORTANT CONSIDERATIONS TO IMPLEMENT A SUCCESSFUL OLAP SYSTEM

As noted so far in this text, there is an intense interest in building effective information systems that go to the heart of the organization's objectives, goals, and strategies. Whether the objective is improving product quality, getting new products to market faster, or serving customers better, astute managers and their staffs grasp the connection between information systems and their success. Amid talk of mission-critical or strategic applications, today's managers are confronted with the need for comprehensive information and knowledge. In order to do this successfully, there is a need to go a step further and integrate the Internet and newer IS directions, such as virtual reality, with current considerations for implementing a successful OLAP system. Both OLAP-Web integration for distant users and OLAP-VR integration for business users are covered below.

Also related to these newer considerations that affect implementing OLAP technology is the need to improve interfaces between the user and the computer. Currently, the computer industry seems to be stuck in the graphical paradigm of menu bars, dialog boxes, multiple windows, and icons. It is not that there is something wrong with the graphical user interface—but it should not be the end. A number of vendors are working on *human-centric interfaces* which are aimed at making computers easier and more pleasant to use. As such, these interfaces take a number of forms, but they are all designed to incorporate the gestures and biometric tools—hands, voice, eyes, and ears—that humans bring to their interactions with machines. A key advantage of these interfaces is that they are intuitive and familiar, thereby injecting a reassuring element of competence and control in what can be an unfamiliar experience. Human-centric interfaces allow multiple senses to be engaged simultaneously, thereby making users more productive and applications more interesting. In effect, these interfaces actually make the user want to engage in an ongoing dialogue with the computer.[1]

OLAP-Web Integration for Distant Users

Building upon selecting the appropriate software tools to implement OLAP successfully, an important trend that has recently emerged is integrating OLAP client and server software with World Wide Web technology. Such an arrangement makes it possible to access an OLAP database from the Web or a corporate intranet. For example, Fidelity Investments (Boston, Massachusetts), a mutual funds company, uses OLAP software from Arbor Software, Hyperion, Pilot, and Oracle's IRI subsidiary. It has tested a Web gateway to its Essbase database from Arbor Software. The gateway functions as a translation layer between a Web server and an Essbase database, converting Essbase data into HTML pages that can be viewed from a Web browser. This means that the mutual funds company has found a cost-effective means of delivering OLAP across the enterprise.

The number of OLAP vendors with Web-enabled products is growing. Information Advantage (Minneapolis, Minnesota) is marketing WebOLAP, a Web-ready version of its DecisionSuite Server. Currently, Information Advantage has a partnership with Unisys to deliver an integrated OLAP package aimed at retailers. Also, Management Sciences Associates (Pittsburgh, Pennsylvania) is marketing BusinessWeb 2.0, a client/server package that uses a Web browser to access an OLAP server. Release 2.0 includes a toolkit that makes it easier to create custom data-analysis applets. Essentially, these new software packages make it possible for OLAP databases to become enterprisewide, thereby serving hundreds and potentially thousands of users. From this view, OLAP has broken out of its niche as a departmental product to one that can be used globally wherever it is needed.[2]

It should be noted that knowledge-based systems also can be tied-in with the Web. An expert system's ability to answer specific well-defined problems makes it ideal as a Web-resident technology for product selection, technical support, help-desks, and regulations. That is, any area that requires specific decision-making knowledge is a logical candidate for the Web. Accessing an expert system on the Web as opposed to a Frequently Asked Question list is like talking to an expert instead of reading a technical manual.

OLAP-VR Integration for Business Users

As will be seen in Part III of this text, there can be a tie-in of virtual reality with OLAP systems. This has been made possible by the availability of powerful PCs based on such computing workhorses as Intel's Pentium Pro and Digital's Alpha processors. Also, the emergence of reasonably priced OpenGL-based 3-D accelerator cards contributes to the ability of these computers to process and display 3-D simulations in real time. While a standard 486 PC with as little as 8 MB of RAM can provide enough processing power for a basic VR simulation, the more powerful the computer, the more satisfying is the VR experience. That is, a Pentium-based PC with 32 MB of RAM can transport users to a convincing virtual environment, while a dual Pentium configuration with OpenGL acceleration and 24 MB of VRAM (virtual RAM) running Windows NT rivals the horsepower of a graphics workstation.

In terms of software products that fall under the category of "desktop VR," these range from high-end authoring toolkits that require significant programming experience to packages for which familiarity with the computer's operating system is the only prerequisite. Despite the differences in the types of virtual worlds these software packages can deliver, the various tools are based on the same VR-development model: they allow users to create or import 3-D objects, to apply behavioral attributes such as weight and gravity to the objects, and to program the objects to respond to the user via visual and/or audio events. Programming toolkits include those from Superscape, Sense8, and Division. While Superscape's product was designed specifically for the PC, both Sense8 and Division have ported their workstation-based products to this platform. While some of these packages, such as Sense8's WorldToolKit, rely exclusively on C or C++ programming to build a virtual world (the WorldToolKit consists of a libary of C functions), others offer simpler point-and-click operations to develop a simulation. Sense8's World Up, for example, utilizes the WorldToolKit paradigm, but relies on a GUI-based interactive development environment. Similarly, with Superscape's icon-based VRT product and Division's dVISE, building basic worlds requires minimal programming.

In addition to VR toolkits, there are a number of software packages that enable the user to create and display virtual worlds on a PC, called VR modeling/simulation software. They are often limited in what they can offer professionals in many of the target application areas. For example, they provide little if any support for importing objects created with other packages; so an architect hoping to develop an interactive walkthrough of a 3-D studio-generated design could be out of luck, as might be an engineer who wants to create a virtual prototype. Although less flexible than the toolkits, the lower-end modeling/simulation tools offer a number of advantages. They do not require programming, they have a short learning curve, and they are relatively inexpensive. For example, VRCreator from VREAM offers a rich set of tools for creating 3-D objects and the ability to assign actions, reactions, and connections to them via a point-and-click interface.

In summary, virtual reality has a lot more credibility today compared to the past. The real driving force is that users are able to interact in real time on a standard PC and get the kind of performance and resolution that they used to get only from a $100,000 SGI (Silicon Graphics Inc.) machine. The smoothness of performance has been the key to the current demand for VR products of all types. In turn, the low cost of VR will result in a natural integration with OLAP systems.[3]

IMPLEMENTATION AND SUPPORT OF OLAP SYSTEMS ON A DAILY BASIS

If the OLAP system is developed and implemented correctly, there should be little need for formal training of managers and their staffs. Essentially, managers and their staffs need to know how to use the applications displayed on their screens. If this approach is taken, the OLAP system stands a much better chance of being accepted because a manager or an analyst will not bother with a user's manual or even a user's pamphlet.

During the prototyping process, many companies supplement the project team with outside consultants. The use of consultants during development does not relieve the company from acquiring expertise in the OLAP system. Usually, the consultants have a broader perspective that may help avoid pitfalls and may speed up the learning curve. Outside consultants can give the OLAP effort an extra boost and ensure the final success of on-line analytical processing.

After the initial prototypes have been developed for the corporate sponsor and other managers, a cycle of implementation and support begins. In essence, the OLAP-project team becomes an OLAP-support team. The rationale is that it usually takes fewer people to support the OLAP system than to develop it initially. The support-team members can be taken from the OLAP project team and should have a continuing interest in the success of the OLAP system.

Once an OLAP system is implemented, it can cause a major change throughout the organization because it alters the flow of information and knowledge to and from the top of the company. An OLAP system allows managers to spend more time analyzing the company's strategic-business direction. Whereas approximately 80 percent of a manager's time was previously spent gathering data, now data collection requires less than 20 percent of the manager's effort. Thus, time savings allow more time for intensive analysis. As the world-renowned management consultant Peter Drucker has said in the past: that which is measured ultimately improves.

FINAL CONSIDERATIONS TO IMPLEMENT A SUCCESSFUL OLAP SYSTEM

This chapter has centered on the basic factors in implementing an OLAP system successfully. In addition, there are several other considerations that should be taken into account. *First*, the OLAP system should focus on the business first, not on technology. Nothing can throw an OLAP project off its tracks faster than forgetting that the investment is centered on better service of specific business objectives, goals, and strategies. In effect, OLAP must not become an end unto itself. *Second*, the system should be visually attractive, that is, it should make use of creative graphics, colors, windows, and other devices. If the company does not have the expertise in these areas, it should be obtained before starting the project. *Third*, there is the need to reduce the physical interaction between user and the keyboard or mouse. That means, if the system does not use common input devices, the system's chances for success are generally reduced.

Fourth, given the truism that "knowledge is power," organizations have evolved specific mechanisms for routing information to the top. As such, an OLAP system can threaten those information providers. The best way to reduce the threat is to make sure that the staff people who "own" the data are brought into the process, that is, let them know what is being sent up the pipeline and include their participation in the whole development and implementation process. *Fifth*, and last, when an OLAP system starts being used, most of the managers and their staffs will clamor to be on it. After all, who does not want to see the information and knowledge that the president and chief executive officer gets? While there are political as well as technical implications, the system and its infrastructure should be robust enough to deal with reasonable expansion. From this perspective, an OLAP system should be considered to be an ongoing project. Once one major milestone is reached in terms of specific OLAP applications, the corporate sponsor or operating sponsor will move the OLAP target for more applications to a higher level of actionable information and knowledge.

OLAP CASE STUDIES

Before looking at typical OLAP case studies, it would be helpful to take a look at a company using a combined approach, that is, drill into data with OLAP and ad hoc query tool combination. Because OLAP uses terms like dimensions, drill down, and roll up, it allows users to gather summary information or aggregates. In comparison, ad hoc query and report-writing tools make use of relational databases, thereby helping users access detailed information, such as lists of names and addresses. For example, users at Moen Inc. (Cleveland, Ohio) are making use of their data warehouses by employing the tools in tandem. Being a plumbing and faucet manufacturer, the company has designed a sales system using Cognos Corporation's PowerPlay OLAP front-end and an Oracle Corporation's database, while tapping Cognos' Impromptu for ad hoc query and report writing. With the OLAP software, Moen's managers can identify sales trends and other summary information for particular product types, customer types, and regions. Using Impromptu, their assistants capture details such as customer names, phone numbers, and the specific products they buy. Overall, both software products provide users with access to corporate data that is typically stored on a server, both greatly ease the user's access to corporate data, and both eliminate the need for the IS department to produce reports. In addition, both technologies use the term ad hoc because they can respond to queries made on the fly.[4]

Land o'Lakes Inc.

At Land o'Lakes Inc., the company's first OLAP application was developed in just 12 weeks. The IT group developed a tool that would cut the job of creating analytical sales reports for customers from three days to three hours. The project leader chose a specialized relational-OLAP system that allowed him to capitalize on resources already in place. He found that 90 to 95 percent of what had to be done could be accomplished with a desktop suite. At first, the sales-force automation project started out to be a rewrite of software on the mainframe. Instead, he chose to merge the company's current Red Brick Systems specialized relational database to a Microsoft Excel front-end. The addition of Visual Basic put the finishing touches on the application.

Not only was quick turnaround one benefit of this approach, but also training and implementation costs were kept to a minimum because he already had the Microsoft Office Suite, and the 100 users were familiar with Excel. As a result of his part experience with OLAP, he advocates picking the appropriate software and then "just do it." This can-do attitude will go a long way to getting the job done, especially when confronted with a number of OLAP approaches.[5]

Tri Valley Growers

Tri Valley Growers, which has a streamlined order-processing system, found that its workers were struggling to fill orders on time. Unpredictable growing seasons, label availability, transportation, and customer credit, among other factors, were the prime problem areas. To address these problems, Tri Valley users and its IT group teamed up to create an OLAP application using Planning Science Inc.'s Gentium. Although the company was not thinking of OLAP when it went looking for a solution, it knew the task called for a more state-of-the-art tool that could handle multiple dimensions of data. Gentium, which uses a multidimensional database and comes with its own client-side front-end, was selected.

Armed with the OLAP application, Tri Valley's director of forward warehousing can now get a handle on trends from poor customer credit to low inventory in one hour. In contrast, this same task used to take days. During the development process, he helped define the dimensions for the application and designed its screens. Much of the work was accomplished during the two-day training session on Gentium. However, prepping the data was a difficult task

for IT because it took four to six months to "scrub" all the overlapping information into a standardized format.[6]

PepsiCola International

Headquartered in Boca Raton, Florida, PepsiCola International's (PCI) Latin
American Division (LAD) sets strategy, coordinates activities, and tracks sales
performance for Pepsi in 35 Latin American countries. Planning and forecasting
is the job of LAD's Planning group. All 35 countries report to the Planning
group, consolidating volume, price, cost, marketing data, and other financial
information for franchise operations through separate profit-and-loss statements
and balance sheets. It is a lot of data and everyone plans and forecasts a bit
differently. Because the software business turns on a dime, targets and planned
numbers are the name of the game. That means planning and forecasting must
be nimble too. However, the company's planning environment was not keeping
up. Its planning models were cumbersome and slow. In an effort to combine
accounting, forecasting, planning, and consolidation into a single system, 10–
12 spreadsheets were linked together. However, data handling became slow, the
model required endless debugging, formulas were calculated differently, and the
whole thing was difficult to maintain. In effect, Pepsi had reached the limitations
of its spreadsheet platform and really needed a major shift in how planning
functioned.

At the time, Pepsi knew that the ideal planning platform would have to allow
for flexible multidimensional-data management, combine powerful planning and
modeling capabilities, and be easy to use. LAD worked with Andersen Consulting of Miami and Kefal Sistemas of Mexico to develop PCI's Financial
Planning System Project. The company chose Essbase from Arbor Software
Corporation as the software solution that met its rigorous criteria. Not only did
Essbase have multidimensional-data management and analysis features needed
as well as powerful reporting capabilities, but also it gave access to data from
the company's legacy databases and even linked with some of the older models.
The new planning system also had to fit with PCI's long-term MIS strategy and
be easy to use by financial users.

Currently, PCI's Essbase Financial Planning System application tremendously
simplifies planning and forecasting. Not only does it receive data from almost
all other Pepsi systems and applications, but it also adjusts different data formats.
Data is consolidated from everywhere, that is, from accounting systems, product-
case sales data, marketing-expense data, invoicing system, product-pricing system, and a myriad of data formats. Data from all sources is loaded into the
Essbase model. The model itself contains 354 data elements spread across seven
data dimensions—time, geography, products, packages, legal entities, accounts,
and categories. Analysts can now calculate sales to specific markets by product
and by container (12-oz. Pepsi can, 26-oz. Diet Pepsi bottle, etc.). They can
simulate specific price-volume scenarios. They can assess the effect of a pro-

motion on a given container size. And they can quickly and easily receive profit-and-loss statements, balance sheets, and reports that incorporate various pricing, marketing, and cost-fluctuation assumptions.

In addition, Essbase has brought even more fundamental changes to data analysis at PCI since multidimensional analysis brings new ways of thinking about real-world markets and a better understanding of the business. This is especially important when revenue is spread over so many elements. For example, being able to view the lowest levels of data gives the planning team lots of information that was not available before. And with Essbase, the necessary data is available instantly. This speed and flexibility enables Pepsi to better advise management about attainable targets, accurately plan market strategies, and implement specific percentage sales increases. Essbase allows Pepsi to fine tune the company's business objectives without a nightmare of numercial detail.[7]

SUMMARY

Because managers at all levels are driven by competitive forces and more sophisticated information technology, they are turning to on-line analytical processing systems to provide on-line access to their transactional processing databases and data warehouses, as well as to access to outside sources of information to make them more competitive. OLAP gives them access to critical-multidimensional analyses that are timely for solving problems. In light of these happenings at the managerial level, the chapter looked at the factors necessary for installing an OLAP system. Among the important factors treated were getting started on implementing OLAP systems, current environment of rapid application development, software tools to implement OLAP successfully, key steps to implement a successful OLAP system, and other important considerations to implement a successful OLAP system. In addition, cost justification was examined initially in the chapter for a typical on-line analytical processing system. Although cost justification is somewhat elusive, an OLAP system basically makes a company's managers more *effective* as opposed to being more *efficient*. Lastly, several OLAP case studies were presented to demonstrate the wide range of these newer-type systems.

NOTES

1. Amy D. Wohl, "Humanizing Computers," *Beyond Computing*, May 1996, p. 10.
2. John Foley, "Analysis Goes to Next Level," *InformationWeek*, April 8, 1996, pp. 76–77.
3. Robert J. Thierauf, *Virtual Reality Systems for Business* (Westport, Conn.: Quorum Books, 1995), chapters 1–10.
4. Erin Callaway, "The Flavors of OLAP," *PC Week*, July 17, 1995, p. 15.

5. Ibid., pp. 14–15.

6. Ibid., p. 15.

7. Essbase in Action, "PepsiCola International" (Sunnyvale, Calif.: Arbor Software Corporation, 1995).

Bibliography: Part II

Adhikari, R. "Migrating Legacy Data: How to Get There From Here." *Software Magazine*, January 1996.

———. "Taking Care of Business." *Software Magazine*, June 1996.

Alexander, S. "Hospital Takes Its Own Pulse with Elastic OLAP System." *InfoWorld*, July 8, 1996.

Anderson, D. "OLAP Debate." *Computerworld*, February 27, 1995.

Anonymous. "The 12 Rules." *Computerworld*, July 26, 1993.

———. "New OLAP Industry Advocacy Group Found." *The OSINetter Newsletter*, January 1995.

———. "Quartet of Developers Defines OLAP Technology, Draws Fire." *PC Week*, January 30, 1995.

———. "OLAP Council Outlines Guidelines for Expanded Membership." *The OSINetter Newsletter*, February 1995.

———. "OLAP Council States Objectives." *MIDRANGE Systems*, February 10, 1995.

Appleton, E. L. "Use Your Data Warehouse to Compete!" *Datamation*, May 15, 1996.

Armstrong, A., and J. Hagel, III. "The Real Value of On-Line Communities." *Harvard Business Review*, May–June 1996.

Armstrong, D. "How Rockwell Launched Its EIS." *Datamation*, March 1, 1990.

———. "The People Factor in EIS Success." *Datamation*, April 1, 1990.

Baker, D., and S. Klein. *Data Warehousing & Decision Support Systems in Telecommunications: A Worldwide Survey & Market Analysis of Telecom Buyer Demand & Requirements.* New York: Technology Research Institute, December 1995.

Barenstein, N. S. et al. "Perils and Pitfalls of Practical Cybercommerce." *Communications of the ACM*, June 1996.

Barquin, R., and A. Paller. "10 Data Warehouse Mistakes to Avoid." *Application Development Trends*, July 1995.

Bart, J. "Product Comparison: Videoconferencing Systems, Pipe Dreams Discovered." *InfoWorld*, October 16, 1995.

————. "Data Mining's Midas Touch." *InfoWorld*, April 29, 1996.

Basu, A., and R. W. Blanning. "Metagraphs: A Tool for Modeling Decision Support Systems." *Management Science*, December 1994.

Baum, D. "Application Development: Visual Tools Exploit Cheap, Powerful Desktops." *InfoWorld*, May 1, 1995.

————. "Warehouse Mania." *LAN Times*, November 20, 1995.

————. "Data Warehouse: Building Blocks for the Next Millennium." *Oracle Magazine*, March/April 1996.

Beckman, M. "ISDN Survival Kit." *InfoWorld*, April 1, 1996.

————. "The Web Goes Interactive." *MacWorld*, July 1996.

Berg, A. "Security: How Safe Is Your LAN?" *LAN Times*, June 17, 1996.

Bishop, D. S., and P. S. Bishop. "Object-Oriented Enterprise Modeling." *Data Management Review*, July 1993.

Bolt, R. C. "Essbase to the Rescue." *DBMS*, March 1995.

Bowen, B. "Application Development: What's the Right Tool." *Information Week*, January 8, 1996.

Bowen, B. D. "IT and Business Analysts Cooperate in Effective Data Warehouse Endeavors." *Client/Server Computing*, December 1995.

Brackett, M. H. *The Data Warehouse Challenge: Taming Data Chaos*. New York: John Wiley & Sons, 1996.

Breidenbach, S. "The Changing Role of the LAN Manager." *LAN Times*, January 8, 1996.

Bridges, L., and B. Proffit. "Open Systems to Fuel Industrial Automation." *PC Week Special Report*, March 29, 1993.

Bull, K. "Data Warehousing: The Ideal File Cabinet." *InformationWeek*, January 16, 1995.

Bylinsky, G. "At Last! Computers You Can Talk To." *Fortune*, May 3, 1993.

Byron, D. "What If?: OLAP Tools on the Move." *Application Development Trends*, June 1995.

Cafasso, R. "OLAP: Who Needs It?" *Computerworld*, February 20, 1995.

Caldwell, B. "Farming Out Client-Server." *InformationWeek*, December 12, 1994.

————. "Client Server, Can It Be Saved?" *InformationWeek*, April 8, 1996.

Callaway, E. "The Flavors of OLAP." *PC Week*, July 17, 1995.

Cassidy, P. "The Next Best Thing to Being There." *LAN Times*, December 4, 1995.

Champy, J., R. Buday, and N. Nohria. "Creating the Electronic Community." *InformationWeek*, June 10, 1996.

Cheek, M. "Holiday Inn Builds Profits with Client/Server." *Communications News*, April 1996.

Chepetsky, S. "4GLs Offer Less Code, Reduced Development Complexity." *Digital News & Review*, December 19, 1994.

Coffee, O. "SPSS More Than a Pretty Face." *PC Week*, February 12, 1996.

Crockett, F. "Revitalizing Executive Information Systems." *Sloan Management Review*, Summer 1992.

Darling, C. B. "How to Integrate Your Data Warehouse." *Datamation*, May 15, 1996.

————. "Want Fast Internet Access? Go ISDN." *Datamation*, June 1, 1996.

DePompa, B. "There's Gold in Databases." *InformationWeek*, January 8, 1996.

Dewitz, S. D. *Systems Analysis and Design and the Transition to Objects*. New York: McGraw-Hill, 1996.

Dieckmann, M. "Business on the Internet: Is This the Right Time?" *Managing Office Technology*, April 1996.

Dippert, J. P. "Exploring ISDN." *LAN Times*, September 25, 1995.

Douglas, M. "Hidden Traps in Client/Server Development." *Data Management Review*, May 1996.

Earls, A. R. "Has Replication Arrived?" *Client/Server Computing*, January 1996.

Eckerson, W. "Data Warehousing: Turning Data Into Decisions." *Computerworld*, September 4, 1995.

Edelstein, H. "Faster Data Warehouses." *InformationWeek*, December 4, 1995.

———. "Mining Data Warehouses." *InformationWeek*, January 8, 1996.

Eldred, E. "Entering the Realm of Complex Data." *Client/Server Today*, May 1994.

Eldred, E., and T. Sylvester. "Two Databases for Modeling Complex Data Without the Oh-Ohs." *Client/Server Today*, May 1994.

Essbase in Action. "PepsiCola International." Sunnyvale, Calif.: Arbor Software Corporation, 1995.

Ettle, R., P. Fingar, and D. Read. "Shared Objectives." *CIO*, March 1, 1995.

Fayad, M. E., W. T. Tsai, and M. L. Fulghum. "Transition to Object-Oriented Software Development." *Communications of the ACM*, February 1996.

Finkelstein, R. "MDD: Database Reaches the Next Dimension." *Database Programming & Design*, April 1995.

Fogarty, K. "Data Mining Can Help to Extract Jewels of Data." *Network World*, June 6, 1994.

Foley, J. "Analysis Goes to Next Level." *InformationWeek*, April 8, 1996.

Foley, J., and B. DePompa. "Data Marts: Low Cost, High Appeal." *InformationWeek*, March 18, 1996.

Foss, W. B. "Fast, Faster, Fastest Development." *Computerworld*, May 31, 1993.

Francett, B. "Decisions, Decisions: Users Take Stock of Data Warehouse Shelves." *Software Magazine*, August 1994.

Frank, M. "The Truth About OLAP." *DBMS*, August 1995.

———. "Object Relational Hybrids: A Look at Technology and Products That Blend Object and Relational Features." *DBMS*, July 1995.

Frye, C. "Business Problem Solving, Big Flap Over OLAP." *Client/Server Computing*, May 1995.

———. "Business Problem Solving: EIS/DSS." *Client/Server Computing*, May 1995.

———. "Outsiders Clear Client/Server Migration Path." *Software Magazine*, September 1995.

———. "EDI Users Explore Internet as Tool of Trade." *Software Magazine*, December 1995.

Gambon, J. "Local Area Networks: The Price of Freedom." *InformationWeek*, February 26, 1996.

Gareiss, R. "ISDN, Stop Singing Those Blues." *Data Communications*, March 1996.

———. "Mobile Data Networks: The Business Case." *Data Communications*, May 21, 1996.

———. "Wireless Data: The Pepsi Challenge." *Data Communications*, May 21, 1996.

Garry, G. C. "How the Object-Oriented World Translates Into Reality." *Client/Server Today*, May 1994.

———. "No Matter the Translation, ISDN Spells Speed." *Client/Server Computing*, January 1996.

Gibbs, M. "Managing Web Madness." *Network World*, May 6, 1996.

Gill, P. J. "A Strategic Approach to Mission-Critical Applications." *Oracle Magazine*, September/October 1995.

Gillot, I. "Wireless Nets Come of Age." *Network World*, February 19, 1996.

Graham, S. "The Financial Impact of Data Warehousing." *Data Management Review*, June 1996.

Greenberg, I. "OLAP Hits Client/Server Suites." *InfoWorld*, October 16, 1995.

Greenfield, D. "A Realistic Approach to Virtual LANs." *Data Communications*, February 1996.

———. "ISDN Routing at Remote Sites: Now It's Personal." *Data Communications*, July 1996.

Griffin, J. "The Role of the Repository in the Data Warehouse." *Data Management Review*, May 1995.

Grygo, E. M. "Mobile Computing Becomes a Necessity." *Client/Server Computing*, June 1995.

———. "Data Mining Takes on a New Look." *Client/Server Computing*, December 1995.

———. "OLAP Stakes Rise for Arbor." *Client/Server Computing*, March 1996.

———. "Intranet Reality Check." *Client/Server Computing*, May 1996.

Guthrie, L., J. Pustejovsky, Y. Wilks, and B. M. Slator. "The Role of Lexicons in Natural Language Processing." *Communications of the ACM*, January 1996.

Haag, S., M. K. Raja, and L. L. Schkade. "Quality Function Development." *Communications of the ACM*, January 1996.

Hackathorn, R. "Data Warehousing Energizes Your Enterprise." *Datamation*, February 1, 1995.

Hahn, J. "Management Warms Up to Modeling Languages." *Infosystems*, July 1980.

Haight, T. "Client-Server SQL Databases: Building Access to Corporate Data." *Network Computing*, March 1992.

Haley, B. J., and H. J. Watson. "Using Lotus Notes in Executive Information Systems." *Information Strategy: The Executive's Journal*, Spring 1996.

Hall, C. L. "Distributed Transaction Processing: A Three-Tiered Architecture." *Data Management Review*, February 1996.

Hanna, M. "Seeding the Intranet." *Software Magazine*, June 1996.

Harmon, P. "Object-Oriented AI: A Commercial Perspective." *Communications of the ACM*, November 1995.

Henderson, D. "A New Advantage for Market Intelligence." *Computing Canada*, October 25, 1995.

Hildebrand, C. "Form Follows Functions." *CIO*, November 1, 1995.

Hoffman, T., and K. S. Nash. "Data Mining Unearths Customers." *Computerworld*, July 10, 1995.

Horwitt, E. "Client/Server Standards: No Easy Task." *Computerworld*, March 21, 1994.

Huckzermeier, J. "System Development: Objects in Business." *PC AI*, July/August 1996.

Hufford, D. "Data Warehouse Quality: Part I." *Data Management Review*, January 1996.

———. "Data Warehouse Quality: Part II." *Data Management Review*, March 1996.

Huntington, D. "Knowledge-Based Systems: Yesterday, Today, and Tomorrow." *PC AI*, July/August 1996.

Hurwitz, J. "Navigating Around the Client/Server Iceberg: Business Requirements for Corporate-Wide Client/Server Applications." *Computerworld*, August 7, 1995.

Inmon, W. H. "The Data Warehouse: Managing the Infrastructure." *Data Management Review*, December 1994.

———. "Data Warehouse Success Requires Development Automation." *Application Development Trends*, March 1995.

Inmon, W. H., and R. D. Hackathorn. *Using the Data Warehouse*. New York: John Wiley & Sons, 1994.

Inmon, W. H., and C. Kelley. *Rdb-VMS: Developing a Data Warehouse*. New York: John Wiley & Sons, 1993.

Jacobs, P. "Value-Added Networks Look to LANs." *LAN Times*, February 19, 1996.

Jerram, P. "Videoconferencing Gets in Sync." *New Media*, July 1995.

Johnson, J. T. "Client-Server's Magic Bullet?" *Data Communications*, August 1995.

Jonah, M. "Data Lessons Learned." *InfoWorld*, July 31, 1995.

Jones, B. "Branch-Office ISDN: Five Difficult Pieces." *Data Communications*, February 1996.

Jones, C. "Autodesk Plans 3-D Web Authoring." *InfoWorld*, April 15, 1996.

Joslow, S. "Case Study: Building an EIS." *Information Center Quarterly*, Winter 1991.

Juck, W. *The Standard Catalog of Data Warehousing & Decision Support*. New York: Spiral Communications, Inc., February 1995.

Kara, D. "Client/Server Tool Taxonomy Update: Visual Basic Effect." *Application Development Trends*, November 1995.

Kay, D. "Object Technologies: Code That's Ready to Go." *InformationWeek*, August 22, 1994.

Kelly, S. *Data Warehousing: The Route to Mass Customization*. New York: John Wiley & Sons, 1994.

King, M. "Evaluating Natural Language Processing Systems." *Communications of the ACM*, January 1996.

Kinlan, J. "EIS Moves to the Desktop." *Byte*, June 1992.

Kirkpatrick, D. "Here Comes the Payoff from PCs." *Fortune*, March 23, 1992.

———. "Riding the Real Trends in Technology." *Fortune*, February 19, 1996.

———. "The Internet Saga Continues . . . IBM and Lotus: Not So Dumb After All." *Fortune*, July 8, 1996.

Korzeniowski, P. "Are You Tired of Drilling for Data?" *InformationWeek*, September 19, 1994.

Krivda, C. D. "Booming Business Intelligence." *MIDRANGE Systems*, June 30, 1995.

Kuehn, R., and R. A. Flick, Jr. "Implementing an EIS in a Large Insurance Corporation." *Journal of Systems Management*, January 1996.

Kupfer, A. "Look, Ma! No Wires!" *Fortune*, December 13, 1996.

———. "Craig McCaw Sees an Internet in the Sky." *Fortune*, May 27, 1996.

Laberis, B. "10 Trends That Will Reshape Your Network." *Network World*, April 29, 1996.

Lambert, B. "Data Modeling for Data Warehouse Development." *Data Management Review*, February 1996.

Larribeau, B. "Two Routes to ISDN Access." *Network World*, January 15, 1996.

Lazar, J. "Workstations, Graphic Content." *InformationWeek*, August 28, 1995.

Leinfuss, E. "Managing Data Diversity Poses Challenges in Corporate Data Warehouse." *Client/Server Computing*, November 1994.

Levey, R. "OOPS: Building a World Without Programmers." *Chief Information Officer Journal*, July/August 1993.

Levin, R. "Checking Up on Software." *InformationWeek*, May 20, 1996.

Lewis, D. D., and K. S. Jones. "Natural Language Processing for Information Retrieval." *Communications of the ACM*, January 1996.

Liebmann, L. "Network Access: ISDN Unplugged." *InformationWeek*, April 22, 1996.

Lindgaard, G. *Using the Data Warehouse: A Guide for Designing Useful Computer Systems*. New York: Chapman & Hall, 1994.

Linn, M. C. "Key to the Information Highway." *Communications of the ACM*, April 1996.

Loney, K. "All I Really Need to Know I Learned from My DBA: Seven Basic Rules for Managing a Busy Database." *Oracle Magazine*, May/June 1996.

Mayor, T. "Mining the Possibilities." *CIO*, June 1, 1996.

McCarthy, V. "Desktop Videoconferencing: Still a Rough Cut." *Datamation*, May 15, 1995.

————. "Are Virtual LANs Still Virtual Reality?" *Datamation*, July 1, 1995.

McClelland, D. "The Video Connection: Videoconferencing—Desktop Fact or Science Fiction?" *MacWorld*, May 1996.

McKendrick, J. E. "Guaranteed to Make Your EIS Pop: Executive Information Systems Are Evolving into Everyone's Information Systems." *MIDRANGE Systems*, October 26, 1993.

Meador, C. L. "Planning for Data Replication." *InformationWeek*, December 18, 1995.

Menninger, D. "Bringing Business Intelligence to Knowledge Workers." *Data Management Review*, December 1994.

Merenbloom, P. "Client/Server Applications in a MAN or WAN Environment." *InfoWorld*, March 14, 1994.

Moad, J. "On-Line Transactional Processing." *Datamation*, May 15, 1992.

————. "Client/Server Costs: Don't Get Taken for a Ride." *Datamation*, February 15, 1994.

Mohan, S. "What, Really, Is Client/Server Computing?" *LAN Times*, September 6, 1993.

Molta, D. "Videoconferencing: The Better to See You With." *Network Computing*, March 15, 1996.

Monarchi, D. E., and G. I. Puhr. "A Research Typology for Object-Oriented Analysis and Design." *Communications of the ACM*, September 1992.

Moore, A. "Application Development." *Imaging World*, March 1, 1996.

Mullins, C. S. "Dealing with Data Outhouses." *Data Management Review*, March 1996.

Nash, K. S. "Data Warehouses Tax Administrators, Staff." *Computerworld*, August 21, 1995.

Nerson, J. M. "Applying Object-Oriented Analysis and Design." *Communications of the ACM*, September 1992.

Oliva, D., and J. Shifrin. "Connecting the Web to Corporate Databases." *InformationWeek*, May 6, 1996.

Olson, J. "Building a Database Topology Strategy." *Database Programming and Design*, June 1995.

O'Reilly, T. "Publishing Models for Internet Commerce." *Communications of the ACM*, June 1996.

Owen, D. E. "Building an Executive Support System Is Not a Rocket Science." *Chief Information Officer Journal*, Spring 1990.

Parker, R. S. "Enterprise Decision Support for Client/Server." *Data Management Review*, December 1994.

———. "Understanding Multidimensional Analysis: The 15 Keys." *Data Management Review*, May 1995.

Perey, C. "Desktop Videoconferencing and Collaboration Systems." *Virtual Workgroups*, March–April 1996.

———. "Using ISDN Connections for Multiple Purposes." *Virtual Workgroups*, May–June 1996.

Pihlman, M. "Desktop Videoconferencing Challenge." *New Media*, November 1995.

Pinella, P. "PowerBuilding Enterprise Applications." *Datamation*, July 15, 1993.

Pleva, J., and S. Pliskin. "Client Server Everything." *CIO*, July 1995.

Poe, V., Contribution by L. Reeves. *Building a Data Warehouse for Decision Support*. Englewood Cliffs, N.J.: Prentice-Hall, 1995.

Potter, C. D. "What Do CAD Users Want?" *Computer Graphics World*, June 1996.

Press, L. "Windows NT as a Personal or Intranet Server." *Communications of the ACM*, May 1996.

Radding, A. "Is OLAP the Answer?" *Computerworld*, December 19, 1994.

———. "4GL Developers Finding Scalability Has Multiple Meanings." *Client/Server Computing*, May 1995.

———. "Warehouse Wake-Up Call." *InfoWorld*, November 20, 1995.

———. "Users View the Same Data Differently with MDBMS." *Client/Server Computing*, February 1996.

Raden, N. "Data, Data Everywhere." *InformationWeek*, October 30, 1995.

———. "Warehouse, Wake-Up Call." *InformationWeek*, November 20, 1995.

———. "Modeling a Data Warehouse." *InformationWeek*, January 29, 1996.

———. "Warehouses and the Web." *InformationWeek*, May 13, 1996.

Radosevich, L. "Internet Plumbing Comes to Groupware." *Datamation*, May 15, 1996.

Ray, G. "CASE Tools Up Productivity 50%." *Computerworld*, February 1, 1993.

Ricciuti, M. "OLAP Council to Set Interoperability Standards." *InfoWorld*, January 16, 1995.

———. "New Council Scorned in Flap Over OLAP." *InfoWorld*, January 23, 1995.

Rice, R. "The Challenge of Delivering Quality Client/Server Systems." *Client/Server Computing*, March 1995.

Rist, R. "Building a Data Warehousing Infrastructure." *Data Management Review*, February 1995.

Robinson, T. "Who's Running This Intranet, Anyway?" *LAN Times*, June 17, 1996.

Roehl, B. "VRML: A Standard for Virtual Worlds." *Virtual Reality Special Report*, March/April 1996.

———. "VR and the Future of the Net." *Virtual Reality Special Report*, March/April 1996.

Rogers, A. "OLAP Council Responds to Criticism." *Communications Week*, January 23, 1995.

———. "Pilot Enhances Client/Server Tool." *Communications Week*, March 27, 1995.

Roman, B. "Managing the Cost of Complexity." *Internetwork*, February 1996.

Roth, P., and W. Juch, eds. *Data Warehousing & Decision Support: The State of the Art*. New York: Spiral Communications, Inc., April 1995.

Rowe, G. J., and D. J. Blum. "The Great Replication Debate." *Network World Collaboration*, March/April 1996.

Rubin, K. S., and A. Goldberg. "Object Behavior Analysis." *Communications of the ACM*, September 1992.

Rumbaugh, J., M. Blaha, W. Primerlani, F. Eddy, and W. Lorensen. *Object-Oriented Modeling and Design.* Englewood Cliffs, N.J.: Prentice-Hall, 1991.

Rysavy, P. "Wireless Data Made to Order." *Network Computing*, March 15, 1996.

Sabin, K. "Data Warehousing: From OLAP to OLTP." *Computing Canada*, June 21, 1995.

Schaffer, R. H., and H. A. Thomson. "Successful Change Programs Begin with Results." *Harvard Business Review*, January–February 1992.

Schultz, B. "Drilling Down into an Intranet." *Intranet Magazine*, June 1996.

Schultheis, R. A., and D. B. Bock. "Benefits and Barriers to Client/Server Computing." *Journal of Systems Management*, February 1994.

Semich, J. W. "Here's How to Quantify IT Investment Benefits." *Datamation*, January 7, 1994.

———. "What's the Next Step After Client/Server?" *Datamation*, March 15, 1994.

Seybold, P. B. "Beware the Warehouse Hype." *Computerworld*, September 11, 1995.

Shimberg, D. "Client/Server Development: Roles and Infrastructure." *Data Management Review*, May 1995.

Shumate, J. "Doing OLAP in a Snap." *PC Week*, April 8, 1996.

Sinka, A. "Client-Server Computing." *Communications of the ACM*, July 1992.

Smith, W. M. "A Client/Server Approach to Enterprise Information Access." *Data Management Review*, March 1995.

Spar, D., and J. J. Bussgang. "Ruling the Net." *Harvard Business Review*, May–June 1996.

Sprout, A. L. "Surprise! Software to Help You Manage." *Fortune*, April 17, 1995.

———. "The Internet Inside Your Company." *Fortune*, November 27, 1995.

Stearns, T. "Visual-Programming Tools for Database Front Ends." *LAN Times*, June 19, 1995.

Stevens, R. T. *Object-Oriented Graphics Programming in C++.* Boston: Academic Press, 1994.

Stewart, T. A. "Managing in a Wired Company." *Fortune*, July 11, 1994.

Tanler, R. "Data Warehouses & Data Marts: Choose Your Weapon." *Data Management Review*, February 1996.

Taylor, K., and K. Tolly. "Desktop Videoconferencing: Not Ready for Prime Time." *Data Communications*, April 1995.

Thé, L. "OLAP Answers Tough Business Questions." *Datamation*, May 1, 1995.

Thierauf, R. J. *Group Decision Support Systems for Effective Decision Making.* Westport, Conn.: Quorum Books, 1989.

———. *Executive Information Systems: A Guide for Senior Management and MIS Professionals.* Westport, Conn.: Quorum Books, 1991.

———. *Image Processing Systems in Business: A Guide for MIS Professionals and End Users.* Westport, Conn.: Quorum Books, 1992.

———. *Virtual Reality Systems for Business.* Westport, Conn.: Quorum Books, 1995.

Tristam, C. "People Power." *PC Week*, January 15, 1996.

Tyo, J. "Viewing Data Your Way." *InformationWeek*, July 8, 1996.

———. "Slicing Data on the Desktop." *InformationWeek*, July 15, 1996.

Vacca, J. R. "3D World on the Web." *Computer Graphics World*, May 1996.

Varhol, P. D. "Three Routes to OLAP." *Datamation*, August 15, 1995.

Varney, S. E. "Datamarts: Coming to an IT Mall Near You." *Datamation*, June 1996.

Vaughan, J. "OLAP Adapts." *Software Magazine*, June 1995.

Velasquez, S. "The Wireless Enterprise." *ENT*, April 1996.

Vogel, P. "Know Your Business: Build a Knowledgebase!" *Datamation*, July 1996.

Watson, H. "Avoiding Hidden EIS Pitfalls." *Computerworld*, June 25, 1990.

Weil, W. "Data Warehouse: Data Integrity Impact." *Data Management Review*, March 1995.

Weissman, S. "Buyer's Guide: Path to Your Development Tools." *Network World*, April 24, 1995.

Whiting, R. "A New Push in the OLAP Software Arena." *Client/Server Today*, March 1995.

Willis, D. "State of the WAN!" *Network Computing*, April 15, 1996.

Winston, P. "GUI Development Time Traps." *Data Management Review*, January 1996.

Wohl, A. "Humanizing Computers." *Beyond Computing*, May 1996.

Wreden, N. "Data, Data, Who's Got the Data." *Beyond Computing*, November 1995.

PART III

Typical Applications of OLAP Systems

6

Strategic Planning in an OLAP Environment

ISSUES EXPLORED

- How can problem finding be used within an OLAP-operating mode?
- What newer directions in strategic planning should be considered when developing an on-line analytical processing system?
- What is the relationship of executive visioning to long-range strategic planning?
- How can a typical company benefit from OLAP in the area of short-term to long-term strategic planning?
- What areas of planning are logical candidates for an OLAP-VR integration?

OUTLINE

Strategic Planning in an OLAP Environment
   Short-Range to Long-Range Strategic Planning in a Changing World
Newer Directions in Strategic Planning That Underlie OLAP
   A Problem-Finding Approach to Strategic Planning
   Undertaking Executive Visioning
   Need for Knowledge in Strategic Planning
   Utilization of Critical Success Factors (CSFs) and Their Measurement
   Benchmarking the Company Against the Best
   Business-Planning Software to Develop Strategic Plans
Strategic-Planning Areas That Lend Themselves to an OLAP Environment
   Linkage of Visioning to Lower Levels by Corporate-Planning Staff

STRATEGIC PLANNING IN AN OLAP ENVIRONMENT

A number of leading futurists have predicted that today and into the twenty-first century will be times of great change. Many of the anticipated changes are not minor perturbations, but major adjustments in business and social environments. Several of the driving forces behind these changes are global competition, the restructuring of business organizations, the aging of the U.S. population, continued variations in the inflation rate and the stock market, periodic energy shortages, and accelerating technological changes of all types. Top-level managers are going to be hard-pressed to deal with this new environment without changing the process of solving problems. Future decisions will involve more complex ideas and data than in the past and, to be effective, must merge together both quantitative and qualitative analyses. Solving the problems of the near future and beyond centers on on-line analytical processing systems for providing top-level managers and their staffs with timely strategic-planning information they need to make quality decisions.

To assist the typical manager in getting a handle on this important area relative to OLAP, the first part of the chapter examines the need for top-level managers and their staffs to have a real feel for the newer directions in strategic planning. For example, strategic-planning needs for top-level managers and their staffs need to be tied-in with executive visioning and to problem finding where deemed appropriate. All of these newer directions set the stage for strategic-planning areas that lend themselves to an OLAP-operating mode, in particular, short-range to long-range strategic planning. Finally, the integration of OLAP with virtual reality provides a means for extending the capabilities of both system approaches to strategic planning—each of which is not capable of providing individually.

Short-Range to Long-Range Strategic Planning in a Changing World

As a starting point for effective strategic planning, every organization should recognize that *change is the engine of growth*. The challenge lies not in embracing this business tenet, but in anticipating, adapting to, and generating fresh ideas that exploit change. Because strategic planning is a logical means for adapting to change, it centers on setting or changing organization objectives and goals as deemed appropriate, obtaining the resources to meet these objectives and goals, and determining the strategies and programs to govern the use and disposition of these resources. Because it occurs at the highest level and is related directly to top-level executives and their corporate-planning staff, strategic planning merges the appropriate external and internal factors that are critical to setting the proper present and future direction for the organization. In turn, it provides input for lower- and middle-level managers.

Strategy considerations relative to future market opportunities and products to fill them are basic to *long-range strategic planning*. A distinctive characteristic of this highest-planning level is the use of marketing facts to discover opportunities, and then develop effective strategies and programs to capitalize on these opportunities. Similarly, the focus is on bringing future problems back to the present time for solution. The long-range strategic plans which embrace all aspects of the organization and its environment provide a basis for more detailed medium-range strategic planning.

Medium-range strategic planning, sometimes called *tactical planning*, is concerned primarily with financial planning to place the organization in the best financial position for the next several years. This fiscal planning involves developing the operating programs and associated budgets for the next several years. On the other hand, *short-range strategic planning* (or detailed operating planning) is related to the financial plans of the current year only. For an organization that has practiced formal planning on a regular basis, it is normal for every major functional area to prepare annual plans for the coming year. Essentially, these financial plans are brought together from a detailed examination of the key measures of the business, such as product-line profitability, variable and fixed costs, inventory turnover, manufacturing capacity, and financial ratios, for the coming year.

NEWER DIRECTIONS IN STRATEGIC PLANNING THAT UNDERLIE OLAP

Today, the changing world that impacts the typical company should be regarded as a *constant*. Corporate-planning experts state that fundamental changes take years (at least ten), while superficial changes can be achieved in a shorter time frame. To assist corporate management in adapting to all types of changes, including changing IT technology, newer directions in strategic planning that underlie OLAP are set forth below. These center on the following: (1) a problem-finding approach to strategic planning, (2) undertaking executive visioning, (3) need for knowledge in strategic planning, (4) utilization of critical success factors (CSFs) and their measurement, (5) benchmarking the company against the best, and (6) business-planning software to develop strategic plans.

A Problem-Finding Approach to Strategic Planning

For effective problem finding, there is the need initially to obtain strategic-planning information. Strategic-planning information involves both external- and internal-environmental factors that affect the organization, from the short range to the long range. Many times, such information is found in the company's data warehouses. The most important *external-environmental factors* focus on customers, suppliers, the government, investors, the public, financial institutions, and competition. The most important *internal-environmental factors* center on organization strengths, organization objectives, functional areas of the organization, organization personnel, and organization problems. Obtaining and using this information is an integral part of the strategic-planning process. Overall, strategic-planning information is the raw material needed by top management and their corporate-planning staff to initiate problem finding. Likewise, it is the means by which strategic decisions are made to further organization objectives.

To have an effective planning process, top-level managers with the assistance of their corporate-planning staff need to *identify potential problems* in the future and bring them back to the present time for resolution. This same group needs to *identify opportunities* that are related to future problems. As in the past, top-level managers and their corporate-planning staff must also be involved in problem solving. Strategic planning, then, needs to go beyond problem solving and be actively involved in problem finding to do an effective job of allocating and using the organization's resources.

To assist this highest-level group in problem finding, appropriate analysts along with mathematical and statistical models can be employed. Because the highest-level problems tend to be semistructured and unstructured, a series of "what-if" questions using these analyses and models can be asked to get a feeling for future problems that are poorly defined. Hence, the needs of top-level decision makers where they are oriented toward the near future usually center on using multidimensional analysis as a means to answer pressing problems. However, as the time frame is extended further into the future, the problems become even more unstructured and may need to utilize heuristics in conjunction with mathematical and statistical models. Due to the vast number of uncertainties over time, the reliability of answers to these "what-if" questions are, needless to say, less accurate. Nevertheless, top-level executive needs are being met in the best way possible based on a magnitude of unknowns. For more information on problem finding, reference can be made to Chapter 2 and a number of publications by the author.[1]

An important benefit from problem finding is that if a manager is warned early enough to take corrective action, a manager can prevent a molehill from becoming a mountain. What is it worth to a manager to be warned of a business problem sometime sooner? What is the avoidance of a crisis worth to the manager and to the company? Many times, it is too late to react to problems that are already out of control. This strategic advantage from using problem finding, while difficult to quantify, is very significant and real for the typical company today.

Undertaking Executive Visioning

An important element underlying strategic planning for a typical company is *executive visioning*. Many times, executive visioning is tied-in with problem finding. An executive view entails farsightedness along with an eagerness to look ahead, but, at the same time, to be of a practical sort. Effective executive visionaries are not necessarily those who can predict beyond the turn of the twenty-first century; rather, they are decision makers who can draw a conceptual road map from where the company is now to some imagined future—those who can say, "This is how we get there." Visioning implies a chance from the status quo, which helps explain why visionaries are overrepresented in the ranks of entrepreneurs. It is also why they come in handy to an organization in deep trouble—think of Mr. Lee Iacocca saving Chrysler. Vision is not for the complacent. While the executive visionary sees things a bit differently, the individual is no mystic. The person's sources of information are down to earth—customers and suppliers, for example—and extend beyond his or her gut-level feelings. The most visionary executive can take in large amounts of information, and not just from inside himself or herself.

Typically, a broad grounding in a particular industry is almost always a prerequisite to successful direction setting. It is helpful to look at the early career of an executive who comes to be regarded as a visionary. Usually, the individual finds an assignment or a series of assignments that enabled the person to see the company from many different perspectives, that is, the individual served as vice president of marketing, then production, then finance; or had a tour as executive assistant to the president. As examples, Jan Carlzon held all sorts of positions in the travel business before becoming head of SAS, and Louis Gerstner studied the financial services industry as a McKinsey consultant before taking over American Express's credit card and traveler's check businesses.

From another view, there can be situations where the executive does not need to be steeped in an industry to conceive a vision of its future. Upstarts like Steve Jobs dwell on the dangers of falling prey to the "standard world view," thereby missing opportunities that arise when that standard world begins to show a few cracks. The skeptics concede, however, that someone who has grown up in the business stands a better chance to realize his or her vision.

Executives with vision typically share a couple of other characteristics. They have a high degree of self-confidence. It takes a lot of inner strength to imagine a future at variance with the common expectation, and to sustain that imagining in the face of responses ranging from incredulity to derision. The visionary may also be a bit of a loner. Ego strength can mean that the individual has less need of other people. But executive vision has a way to excite others somehow. An executive visionary has an appeal to the emotions and aspirations of people that goes beyond the usual carrot-and-stick approach.

Most corporate visions come out looking like tarted-up strategies. William Hewlett and David Packard established a company which is dedicated to producing the best instruments for the world's scientists—that surely counts. Ray Kroc, who built McDonald's, and Kemmons Wilson of the Holiday Inn chain, are both visionary achievements of twentieth-century American capitalism. Vision by itself is not enough for the executive to possess. The executive visionary must be able to communicate what he or she has dreamed, and the company must have the required skills needed to execute it. The leaders of the organization must act consistently with the vision in everything they do.

As noted previously in the text, and to be emphasized in this chapter, the execution of visioning can be facilitated by use of an on-line analytical processing system. Too often in the past, top-management teams work up a statement of corporate vision, promulgate it, and then think their work is done. What they overlook, and what dooms this kind of superficial effort, is the need to plan and control this vision over time. An on-line analytical processing system is an excellent vehicle for assisting in the fulfillment of carrying out the executive vision.

Need for Knowledge in Strategic Planning

To help managers translate the executive vision such that it involves around a company's strategies, and express it in terms that guides action at the local level, it is helpful that this executive vision be based on knowledge of a company's operations. To assist a company in getting a grip on its knowledge base, companies are designating a new executive position, that is, a chief knowledge officer, to harvest and distribute professional expertise via information technology. Unlike a chief information officer (CIO) who is typically interested in how to manage data, the chief knowledge officer—also called the chief learning officer or VP of information strategies—identifies what corporate knowledge needs to be developed and retained, as well as what knowledge is useful in strategic planning. As noted in Chapter 1, knowledge was defined as that which is obtained from experts based on actual experience. As such, the focus is on seeing patterns and trends that enable decision makers to make the transition to insight and prediction.

A number of companies, such as Coca-Cola and Coopers & Lybrand, have named executives to chief knowledge officer or similar posts. These companies are identifying not only what professional knowledge needs to be captured, but also how to disseminate it. Because companies like professional services firms do not want to reinvent the wheel with every client, the ability to tap and reuse this knowledge is what will differentiate competitors. A person who can help his or her company do this is very valuable.

For example, Andersen Consulting has developed the Knowledge Xchange, an in-house version of the kind of consulting help it sells to clients. Knowledge Xchange creates *virtual communities of practice*: Lotus Notes groupware and Microsoft Office Suite run on a Novell NetWare-based LAN; the LAN is connected to a proprietary client/server-based WAN. Because the value of this consulting firm is in its knowledge capital, Knowledge Xchange makes all of the firm's accumulated knowledge and skills immediately available to each of its consultants, and, therefore, to every client. It is a virtual place where all of the firm's 27,000 consultants can share their knowledge and expertise in global communities of practice. The Knowledge Xchange is available to each consultant on desktop and laptop computers, and affects the work done on a daily basis. In fact, it lets a consultant find out who has skills out there that he or she does not have, so the consultant can quickly put together an on-line team to help solve the client's problem.

Utilization of Critical Success Factors (CSFs) and Their Measurement

For any business, critical success factors (CSFs) are the limited number of areas in which results, if they are satisfactory, will ensure successful competitive performance. They are the key areas where things must go right if the organization is to flourish. If results in these key areas are not adequate, the organization's efforts for the period will be less than desired. As a result, the critical success factors are areas of activity that should receive constant and careful attention from management. The current status of performance in each area should be continually measured, and that information should be made available to the higher levels of management.

Typically, critical success factors support the attainment of measureable organizational goals. These goals represent the endpoints that an organization hopes to reach. Critical success factors are the few areas in which good performance is necessary to ensure attainment of those goals. For example, the automobile industry has four industry-based CSFs: having the right styling for the times, having a good-quality dealer system, having effective cost control over selling and manufacturing operations, and having the capability to meet current energy standards in terms of average mileage per gallon for all cars produced. Although the automobile manufacturers must pay attention to many other factors, these four areas represent the underpinnings of successful operations.

Figure 6.1
From Executive Visioning to Corporate Objectives and Goals to Critical Success Factors (CSFs) to Key Performance Indicators (KPIs) and Financial Ratios

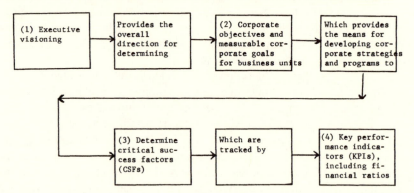

From a broad viewpoint, the principal sources of critical success factors have been identified by John F. Rockhart at MIT's Sloan School of Management. They are as follows.[2]

- *Structure of a particular industry.* Each industry by its very nature has a set of CSFs that are determined by the characteristics of the industry itself.

- *Competitive strategy, industry position, and geographic location.* For smaller organizations in an industry that is dominated by one or two large companies, the actions of the major companies will often produce new problems for the small companies. The competitive strategy for the latter may mean establishing a new market niche, getting out of a product line completely, or redistributing resources among various product lines.

- *Environmental factors.* As the economy changes, potential factors change, energy problems become more acute, and the like; critical success factors can change for an organization.

- *Temporal factors.* Internal organization considerations often lead to temporal critical success factors. Inventory, for example, which is rarely a CSF for top management, might become a high-level CSF if there is far too much or too little stock.

Although these four sources for identifying CSFs are determinable, critical success factors are different for an individual industry and even for companies within that industry.

Going one step further, the concept of *key performance indicators* (KPIs) is a way of formalizing and describing critical success factors. Fundamentally, a comprehensive CSF system has four basic components which are shown in Figure 6.1. *First*, executive visioning sets the overall direction for a company and is linked to corporate objectives and goals. *Second*, general company objectives are related to overall corporate goals, which are then broken down into appropriate measurable goals for divisions and business units. These goals provide the means for developing appropriate corporate strategies and programs. *Third*, each business unit identifies a number of critical success factors that must be performed well to achieve its goals and strategies as well as carry out its programs. These activities are then assigned to the people responsible for their completion, *Fourth*, each business unit establishes a measurement system to quantify success. These measures are the key performance indicators which normally include a number of financial ratios.

For example, a company has decided that one of its corporate goals is to improve customer satisfaction by 10 percent this year. At the corporate level, a periodic survey of customers would be a key performance indicator, since corporate managers are responsible for the overall corporation effort. Measurable activities that contribute to improvements might be: improved product quality, improved customer service and support, improved delivery times, and more customer-suggested product improvements. Each of these activities suggests its own set of key performance indicators. The most important part of this process is that the KPIs are measures that the people responsible for them can actually control and be held accountable for. And because of this combination of responsibility, control, and accountability, these KPIs, including financial ratios, are certain to be relevant and important to the managers assigned to them. A further exposition on the utilization of CSFs and KPIs is found later in this chapter and in Chapter 9.

Benchmarking the Company Against the Best

An important way to judge the performance of a company is not only to compare it to other units within the company, but also to outsiders that represent the best industry practices. Commonly, this technique is called *benchmarking*. When the Xerox Corporation started using benchmarking not too long ago, management's aim was to analyze unit production costs in an manufacturing operations. Uncomfortably aware of the extremely low prices of Japanese plain-paper copiers, the manufacturing staff at Xerox wanted to determine whether their Japanese counterparts' relative costs were as low as their relative prices. The staff compared the operating capabilities and features of the Japanese machines, including those made by Fuji-Xerox, and tore down their mechanical components for examination.

As somewhat expected, the investigation revealed that production costs in the United States were much higher. Discarding their standard budgeting processes, U.S. manufacturing operations thereby adopted the lower Japanese costs as targets for driving their own business plans. Top management, gratified with the results, directed that all units and cost centers in the corporation use benchmarking.

In contrast, distribution, administration, service, and other support functions of Xerox found it difficult to arrive at a convenient analog to a product. These nonmanufacturing units began to make internal comparisons, including worker productivity at different regional distribution centers, and per pound transportation costs between regions. Next, they looked at competitors' processes. In logistics, that meant comparing the transportation, warehousing, and inventory management of Xerox's distribution function to those of the competition.

The initial step in the process is to identify what will be benchmarked, that is, measured, expense-to-revenue ratios, inventory turns, service calls, customer satisfaction—whatever the "product" of the particular function is. Then it is necessary to pinpoint the areas that need improvement. In Xerox's experience, managers tend to concentrate first on comparative costs. But as they become more knowledgeable about benchmarking, managers discover that understanding practices, processes, and methods is more important because these define the changes necessary to reach the benchmark costs. Moreover, as managers become more confident about benchmarking, they can readily extend it beyond cost reduction to profit-producing factors, like service levels and customer satisfaction.[3]

An important source for the purpose of comparison are annual reports and other easily available publications. They can uncover gross indicators of efficient operation. Universally recognized measures like return on assets, revenue per employee, inventory turns, and general and administrative expenses will help identify the well-managed companies. To identify superior performance in specific functions, a company can utilize trade journals, consultants, annual reports, and other company publications in which "statements of pride" appear, and presentations at professional and other forums. The same well-run organizations keep turning up.

Business-Planning Software to Develop Strategic Plans

To assist small businesses in enhancing their planning efforts, software packages provide an effective starting point and can lead the planner through the process of generating an effective business plan. The software-planning packages not only are easy to install in standard hardware, but they are also easy to use and provide some capabilities to carry out "what-if" analysis. In addition, they offer an effective alternative to programming a business-planning model from scratch.

While there are variations of business-planning software, typically a formal business plan consists of several typical elements: Executive Summary, Company Overview, Products/Services, Market Analysis, Marketing Plan, and Financial Plan.[4] A snapshot of the whole plan is represented by the *Executive Summary* which highlights the company's mission, measurable objectives and goals, product and marketing strategies, and the financial plan. When preparing the Executive Summary, a rule of thumb is to keep it short and simple—from one to several pages is ideal.

Following the Executive Summary is the rest of the business plan. The *Com-*

pany Overview sets the stage for the venture and provides details of its history and ownership, operating structure, management team, and business purpose. *Products/Services* describes what the company sells, how it develops, produces, and distributes it; an analysis of competition; and future plans. This is followed by the *Market Analysis* which describes current and potential customers and the demographics of the marketplace. In addition, the *Marketing Plan* reveals the company's strategy for reaching its markets through advertising, alliances, distribution channels, promotions, and a sales force. Finally, the *Financial Plan* sets the words to numbers and shows the recent operating history. It projects the next three to five years' worth of cash flow, profits, and asset and liability balances. It also typically contains a break-even analysis, financial ratios, capital requirements, and the timing and amount of the return on investment.

For the most part, preparing an accurate and effective business plan is a challenging task that requires a thorough understanding of all aspects of a business as well as the marketplace in which it operates. No software program can replace the *wisdom* and *knowledge* necessary to be successful. However, the business planner who has those prerequisites can speed the process of producing a presentable plan by taking advantage of the computer's capabilities. By providing the tools needed to generate tables, charts, and text efficiently in a complete document, business plan programs remove a lot of drudgery.

Typical business-planning software include the following. *Business Plan Pro* produces a complete, integrated, and good-looking plan with an appropriate mix of text, tables, and colorful charts. *BizPlanBuilder* provides a wealth of background information and advice, along with comprehensive templates that the user can readily work with using familiar word-processing and spreadsheet programs. *Plan Write* incorporates substantial formatting and editing capabilities into its expansive outline function.

STRATEGIC-PLANNING AREAS THAT LEND THEMSELVES TO AN OLAP ENVIRONMENT

In order to visualize the application of OLAP to corporate strategic planning, marketing, manufacturing, accounting and finance, and human resources in this chapter and the following ones, reference can be made to either a manufacturing-oriented company or a service-oriented company. In either company, the strategic-planning system is linked directly with other systems, that is, planning activities are related to external-environmental factors through the organization's objectives and goals. In turn, they are related to a company's internal-environmental factors, that is, marketing, manufacturing, accounting and finance, and human resources. Both external- and internal-environmental factors form the basis for short- to long-range database elements. These data elements, when used in conjunction with the appropriate strategic-planning program, provide the necessary planning output for the various time periods. The capability to extract on-line data *now* makes this system a forward-looking one. Information can be obtained to answer questions about the future. From this viewpoint, the strategic-planning system makes great use of multidimensional analysis. In many cases, mathematical and statistical models are useful to answer tomorrow's questions in view of today's projections.

Linkage of Visioning to Lower Levels by Corporate-Planning Staff

In view of the newer directions on strategic planning that underlie OLAP, there is a need for a new planning model that translates visioning down to a practical level. That is, *executive visioning* can be used to help managers build a consensus around its strategies and programs such that it guides action at the lower or local levels. This necessitates letting managers *communicate* these strategies and programs up and down the organization and, at the same time, linking them to each business unit and individual objectives and goals. This planning model enables the company to integrate its *business and financial plans* at the lower levels. Also, this model allows for *feedback* since it gives the company the capability to study alternatives for strategic improvement. Strategic improvement consists of continuous feedback that is testing the environment on which the strategies are built, and making the necessary adjustments where deemed necessary.

Since analyses needed for short- to long-range strategic planning in a typical company are found in OLAP systems, generally these planning analyses are undertaken by the corporate-planning staff. This group is responsible directly to the president or chief executive officer (CEO), has relatively few members, exists at the corporate level, and operates on a full-time basis. This corporate-planning staff operates in an environment characterized by product and technological change. Also, the character of a company's departmentalization seems to influence the organization structure for strategic planning. An important part of the corporate-planning staff's time is spent on analyzing the company's critical sucesss factors plus related key performance indicators, including financial ratios. For example, this staff has determined CSFs to be: (1) prices (responsiveness to competitive pricing), (2) cost control (reducing the cost of plant and office operations), (3) inventory turnover (improving the times the inventory turns over yearly), and (4) product mix (having the right products for the times). These CSFs are in line with those set forth earlier for other industries, and can be related to key performance indicators and financial ratios.

Five-Year Strategic Planning

Generally, long-range strategic planning, that is, five-year strategic plans, begins with a realistic understanding of existing products, divisions, margins, profits, return on investment, cash flow, availability of capital, research and development capabilities, skills and capacities of personnel, and so forth. For a manufacturing-oriented company, this understanding needs to be extended to an analysis of manufacturing operations that is tied-in with centralized operations at the corporate level. There is a need to examine the past few years' plus the current year's performance as part of a beginning overall review process. Evaluating significant aspects of past and current operations is the basis for determining how well the organization objectives and goals are being met. In like manner, plans for the coming five years, based on short- to medium-range plans for improving operations, become an essential part of getting started on long-range strategic planning.

A typical five-year plan for a manufacturing-oriented company includes the *external-environmental factors* shown in Figure 6.2 that are generally not controllable, such as customers, government, public, competitors, suppliers, investors, and financial institutions. On the other hand, four *internal-environmental factors* that are controllable by the company center on the following.

- *Marketing planning* focuses on expanding the present product lines and entering new product markets; it also means increasing use of selling outlets and/or distribution to sell the company's products, changes in pricing policy and pricing practices to effect higher sales, and consideration of new advertising media for more effective penetration of the company's markets.

- *Manufacturing planning* centers on major facilities contemplated and improvements in processing efficiency, including the percent of capacity that is now and will be employed with present facilities and machinery, as well as the steps that are being undertaken to use any excess capacity.

- *Financial planning* relates to projected sales by product lines, contribution (sales less direct manufacturing costs) by product lines, indirect manufacturing costs plus sales and general-and-administrative expenses, net profits before federal income taxes by product lines, fixed and working capital needs, return on investment by product lines, and comparable financial ratios and analyses.

- *Human resources planning* centers on projected requirements for key management personnel and production labor when considering turnover and future growth.

To develop projected strategic plans, the corporate-planning staff employs the company's corporate databases and data warehouses to analyze meaningful long-range information. In turn, this output from the various functional areas (marketing, manufacturing, finance, and human resources) is used to finalize its five-year strategies and programs.

AN OLAP APPROACH TO LONG-RANGE STRATEGIC PLANNING

In reference to the above planning model, an OLAP approach to strategic planning views decision making as a *continuous decision process* since it centers

Figure 6.2
Relationship of External- to Internal-Environmental Factors for Short-Range to Long-Range Strategic Planning for a Typical Company (Operating at the Corporate Level)

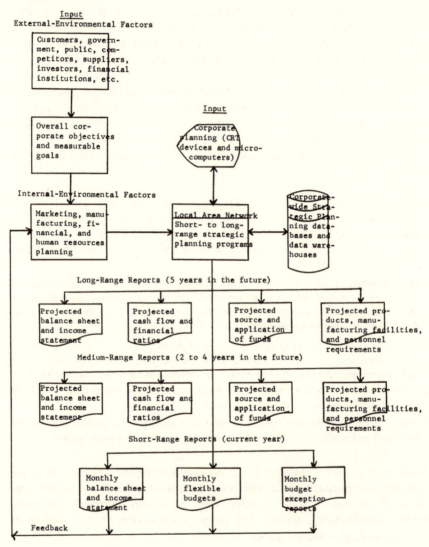

on setting appropriate corporate objectives and measurable goals, employing strategies and programs to achieve these desired objectives and goals, allocating a company's resources in an optimum manner, specifying the critical success factors, and determining the key performance indicators and financial ratios to measure the CSFs. As shown previously in Figure 6.1, all of these planning and related activities are influenced by executive visioning. The implemented plans are then monitored to keep them on course and to correct any deviations from the original or revised plans. Revisions are usually necessary. In fact, *change* (as noted previously) is integral to the nature of corporate planning and its decision process. When a company decides to hire 30 employees at a certain plant with certain skills—and two months later decides to increase the number to 50 employees because it appears that an increased workload is likely to be constant for the future—it is revising its plan as it relates to human resources.

Since there is a need to evaluate planning alternatives continuously for achieving stated objectives and measurable goals, the capability to study various aspects of the long-range strategic plans in its various stages becomes critical. In practical terms, this means producing many runs or variations of the same plan, using different sets of assumptions and perhaps different logic. In *evaluating resources*, for example, varying combinations of resources can be applied, and numerous questions concerning their nature and size can be posed. Do we have the necessary resources to achieve our objectives, or must they be acquired? If resources are to be acquired, at what cost and in what time span? Will they be operational in time to achieve the corporation's objectives within a given schedule? What are the optimum mixes of resources to satisfy different objectives under different sets of conditions? What are the likely effects of miscalculating availability and cost of equipment, personnel, or funds to acquire the needed resources? What can happen for every 1 percent of error in the forecast and, therefore, how critical is it that we hold strictly to the plan? Similarly, in *evaluating strategies*, for example, various questions can be asked concerning improved revenues, lower costs, higher reliability, meeting customer requirements, relationship to other products, enhanced image in customer eyes, better information, and relationship to organizational plans and derivative programs.

The anticipation of consequences of given assumptions and the evaluation of alternatives is a major activity of a company's managers at the highest level and the corporate-planning staff. The utilization of multidimensional analysis in this planning model is helpful because it provides the means whereby the final strategic plan mirrors the real world as closely as possible. Multidimensional analysis can help corporate planners evaluate alternatives and (usually) choose the best one. Such evaluation has come to be known as: "what" is likely to happen "if" the company takes or does not take a certain course of action. As will be seen in the following, OLAP can prove to be extremely useful for a company's highest-level decision makers.

Integrate Changing Times with Long-Range Plans and Strategies

An integral part of the continuous decision process (as set forth above) is the integration of changing times with long-range strategic plans. A Labor Department study, for example, forecasts a slowdown in future economic growth. It

Figure 6.3
Relationship of Company Long-Range Strategies to Allocation of Company Resources and Their Measurement Using Key Perfomance Indicators and Financial Ratios

Company Long-Range Strategies	Allocation of Company Resources	Key Performance Indicators and Financial Ratios
Grow	Improve market share	Market share
	Develop new products	Sales volume growth
	Increase manufacturing capacity	Capitalized ROI
	Expand sales force	Relative quality
Protect	Maintain market share	Marketing expenses/sales
	Optimize margins	R&D expenses/sales
	Differentiate products	Investment/sales
	Increase efficiency	Capacity utilization
Divest	Forego market share for profits	ROI
	Hold prices and margins	Net cash flow/investment
	Prune product lines	Pretax profit/sales
	Shrink sales force	Sales/assets

estimates that the country's gross domestic product, adjusted for price change, will grow at annual rates of just over 3 percent. That would be about 25 percent below the average growth rate of about 4 percent that has prevailed during much of the time since World War II. In addition to the external long-range factors, a typical company's executives and their corporate-planning staff should consider the internal factors that affect the long run. Essentially, they include the factors mentioned above (marketing, manufacturing, financial, and human resources). The interplay of these internal-environmental factors with the external-environmental factors can have a dramatic impact on the company's strategic plans. In fact, incorrect information concerning the internal- and external-environmental factors may lead a typical company down the wrong planning-path.

To get a better idea of how to adapt to changing times as reflected in a company's long-range strategies, reference can be made to Figure 6.3, for three typical situations. First, a company can invest available resources in order for the business to *grow* and thereby strengthen its profitable position. Second, it can *protect* business strengths in order to maintain a strong position in a moderately attractive and mature market. Third, it can *divest* the business in order to exit from a weak position in a relatively unattractive market. Based on these three typical situations, allocation of a company's resources differs as noted in Figure 6.3. Similarly, measurement and analysis using KPIs and financial ratios also differs based upon the situation. In all three situations, multidimensional analysis can be useful to management trying to get a complete understanding of a grow, protect, or divest long-range strategy. From another view, the projected results of the three situations versus one another over a five-year period lend themselves to on-line analytical processing.

Once a company defines its current state and its long-range strategy, it can and should match its people to that strategy. These three typical strategies require distinct sets of managerial characteristics and management styles. Broadly speaking, an entrepreneur is needed for the *grow* situation, a competent manager for the *protect* situation, and a critical manager for the *divest* situation. Not only do these three types of organizations differ in the optimum management style of their executives, but also in the way they are organized and the climate that exists within each organization, as well as the current economic climate. For example, in the *grow* situation, corporate planning for problem solving and problem finding is longer term in its outlook and there is a great deal of delegation of authority, while there is considerably less freedom to act independently in the *protect* organization and planning is mostly medium-term in nature. The successful manager in either situation is one who thrives in the company's culture and feels most comfortable within its organizational structure.

Integrate an Organization's CSFs and KPIs with Long-Range Strategic Plans

To get an idea of the relationship of an organization's CSFs and KPIs to long-range strategic plans, reference can be made to the RT Manufacturing Company. Currently, the company is a textile firm with annual sales of approximately $300 million; it manufactures towels, bath mats, drapes, and tablecloths, and sells its cloth at intermediate stages in the production process. Production is handled at a number of plants; there are three cloth mills, a yarn mill, a dye house, and a finishing plant. The company's management reviewed its corporate strategic plans. To avoid competition from foreign imports, the company chose to focus on being the low-cost producer in the market niches selected. Because the company values employee satisfaction as much as profitability, the company's mission is twofold: first, to be the dominant supplier of textile products for the most profitable segments of the domestic textile market; and second, to provide a high-quality work life for its employees. Senior corporate management has determined its corporate objectives to be: (1) compete in profitable markets, (2) operate as a low-cost producer, and (3) offer high-quality products. In Figure 6.4, the first of these three objectives is broken down into the goals and strategies needed to accomplish these corporate objectives. It should be noted that the company's goals are very specific, and target dates are identified and, in turn, are related to specific corporate strategies.

Next, the critical success factors were selected. CSFs important to the company for achieving the first objective included effective market intelligence, new product development, and dominance in chosen market segments. For the second

Figure 6.4
Relationship of Corporate Objectives, Goals, and Strategies with Critical Success Factors and Key Performance Indicators for the First Objective of the RT Manufacturing Company (Compete in Profitable Market Segments)

Corporate Objective	Corporate Goals	Corporate Strategies	Critical Success Factors	Key Performance Indicators
Compete in profitable market segments	Identify and enter five new market segments with high-profit potential next year	Upgrade market research to identify high-profit potential market segments	Effective market intelligence	Market research data
	Increase market share 15 percent in high-profit market segments in which the company is the dominant supplier within two years	Develop a product line that fits the requirements and needs of the high-potential market segments	New product development	Evaluation of new products and market share
	Increase product distribution by 5 percent next year	Expand product distribution network	Dominance in chosen market segments	Percent of product distribution

corporate objective set forth previously (operate as a low-cost producer), the critical success factors are high-labor productivity and low-material cost. Similarly, the CSFs related to the third corporate objective (offer high-quality products) center on updating the production process with new methods so as to improve or at least maintain product quality, and installing new equipment that can improve final product quality. Finally, it was necessary to determine and communicate the key performance indicators to appropriate company personnel. Key performance indicators related to CSFs are shown in Figure 6.4. In Chapter 9, there will be a further elaboration that includes financial ratios.

At this point, the question can be asked: what does all this have to do with OLAP? Simply this, OLAP has shown its ability to deliver focused information and knowledge along with the analysis required for CSFs and KPIs far better than traditional management information systems. The greatest potential value of an OLAP system is its ability to focus attention on key business issues by the company's managers at all levels. It is important to remember that CSFs and KPIs relate to the activities of specific executive levels or groups. A KPI which is very important to one area (for example, a sales executive who is measured on revenue generation) may be irrelevant to another (such as an operations executive who is measured by a return-on-investment figure). An OLAP's ability to draw information together from throughout the company and to compare that information in dozens of ways adds to its suitability for KPI applications that are related to the company's critical success factors.

Although the above focus is more on the short term, there is a need to go a step further and relate critical success factors to long-range strategic plans. As a starting point, company managers need to identify the CSFs affecting the overall direction of the company that can be tied with long-range strategic plans. In other words, the company's managers must determine what the company must do to reach its stated goals. Identifying the strategic determinants by which each manager measures performance does not by itself make an OLAP implementation successful. There must be agreement on how to monitor and measure them along with key performance indicators over time, such that knowledge can be obtained about the company's long-term performance. For example, if quality and customer satisfaction are important critical success factors, what information should be displayed for the company's managers? Determining the measurements requires both familiarity with the company's business and intimate knowledge of the types of data and information available to the OLAP system. Quality, then, might be measured by the volume of product defects and the level of complaints. Or new sales to existing customers might be measures of customer satisfaction.

Once the measures are selected, it cannot be assumed that the data exists or, if it does, that it is easily compatible with any OLAP system. At this stage, the problems of timeliness must be examined, and issues such as the political implications of data ownership and data-acquisition technology must be addressed. Most data will probably exist within the company, although some of it may be only available from external sources. In working through these issues, alternate measures of critical success factors may have to be developed. Hence, there is a need to analyze thoroughly the requirements for measuring a typical company's performance that can be related to long-range strategic plans. In this manner, the company is developing appropriate long-term strategies that are critical to its success over the long term.

A Problem-Centered Approach to Long-Range Strategic Plans

Once the company's objectives, goals, strategies, CSFs, and KPIs, including financial ratios, have been clearly defined and integrated with executive visioning, they provide the stepping stones for corporate management to undertake problem finding. As discussed previously, company executives and their corporate-planning staff must combine knowledge of today's marketplace, including economic and political analysis, with a vision of the future. To planners, economic and financial forecasting is a multidirectional effort. Planning involves not a forecasting of the future in the conventional sense, but rather a projection of a variety of possible scenarios under good, average, and poor economic conditions. Against these scenarios, the planners will analyze the strengths and weaknesses of the organization and evaluate its resources. This will include a rigorous study of the finances. Market forecasts and financial modeling are thus the foundation of any strategic plans. To illustrate the problem-finding process (as set forth in Chapter 2), the problem-centered approach is applied to strategic marketing plans in the discussion to follow. In turn, the opportunity-centered approach is set forth in the next chapter to highlight the need to develop a new line of products. This comprehensive example is undertaken to demonstrate the viability of an OLAP operating mode.

The president of this corporation engaged in selling products to the home market recognizes that its future markets may well change drastically over time. In fact, the president is convinced that about half of the present products will not be sold five years hence. In view of this potential major upheaval in the marketplace, he has contracted the services of a national consulting firm. These consultants, who were assigned to this marketing project, formed a group of high-level management personnel, consisting of the executive vice president, the marketing vice president, four regional sales managers, and themselves.

As a starting point, the group met for two days at corporate headquarters and initially centered on *problem generation* (first step) regarding present and future products using decision conferencing. The group, under the direction of a senior consultant, examined marketing problems by using a brainstorming approach. The major discussion focused not on the products being marketed under good, average, and poor economic conditions, but on the changing nature of customer buying habits. Due to the continuing trend toward smaller living quarters and smaller families caused by inflationary times and other factors, the corporation is faced with developing new products to reflect the changes as they affect the home market. The group also brainstormed the trend toward more people living alone.

Based on the information displayed on a public screen, *evaluation* (second step) consisted of reviewing the marketing areas of the future and their related problems. As it turned out, all of the above areas displayed on the public screen were determined to be valid for managerial concern in the *validation* stage (third step). The trend toward smaller living quarters represents a major problem for the corporation. In contrast, its present products are oriented toward medium-sized to large-sized homes where space is ample to accommodate them. In light of this major problem and its related problems in the future, the group spent some time *establishing boundaries* (fourth step). Although the home market in foreign countries was considered to be a viable one, it was decided to put first things first by channeling the corporation's resources into the development of new products for the domestic market.

Although a number of problems needed to be solved, the major one was the first one solved, that is, developing over the next five years a wide range of new products that would be more compact and, at the same time, capable of performing a wide range of services to meet homeowner needs. The *solution* took the form of having the group pass judgment on the profitability of the proposed products and comparing one to another for implementation. The profitability of the products, that is, net profit on sales and return on investment, were determined by utilizing OLAP software in terms of modeling the anticipated revenues and costs over their life. Overall, the employment of the problem-centered approach resulted in identifying future product problems. In turn, these problems were brought back to the present time for solution. As a result, management by perception was put into practice by this high-level executive task force for determining future strategic-marketing plans.

AN OLAP APPROACH TO SHORT-RANGE AND MEDIUM-RANGE STRATEGIC PLANNING

Short-range strategic planning, sometimes called operational planning, is a derivative of medium-range strategic planning which, in turn, comes from long-range strategic planning. For a typical company, short-range strategic planning is concerned with the efficient use of available capacities. It is a detailed quantitative plan that specifies both how the company's objectives and goals for the coming year will be attained and the procedures for managing daily operations. As such, the short-range plans outline the specific steps to accomplishing the long-range plans. They thus play a major role in implementing business strategies by translating long-range plans into action.

Additionally, short-range plans center on detailed objectives and specific measurable goals and strategies of the company and a means for achieving them, usually in the form of flexible budgets, or profit plans by product groups. Management needs cost and revenue margin information so that it can identify areas of strength and weakness. Product margin or contribution information is also needed to measure the profit impact of alternative courses of action. Hence, approved short-range strategic plans become budgets such that actual results can be measured and compared to them monthly for more effective control.

Review of Quarterly Financial Forecasts to Finance an Expansion

To assist in short-range strategic-planning activities, OLAP software can be helpful in the review of quarterly financial forecasts. For example, top-level managers can apply for a loan to finance an expansion although it actually lacks the historical-financial data necessary for a statistical analysis of earnings. The solution is to construct a four-quarter earnings forecast combining present market conditions with their best guesses about the future. The data-gathering process is started by polling the managers for number estimates and market assumptions. For the modeling process, there is almost complete consensus among managers on all assumptions other than unit sales and selling price. The importance of unit sales and selling-price growth, coupled with the range of estimates received, makes the use of multiple projections prudent. Consequently, the model provides the best-case and worst-case scenario forecasts for review by top-level managers and their staffs.

Basically, the model incorporates assumptions for several variables, including growth factors for unit sales and selling prices for the next four quarters. Also, current sales along with the actual cost of goods sold, sales commissions, administrative expenses, and federal income taxes are needed for the current quarters. Using the estimates based on assumptions, projected quarterly income over four periods can be displayed for high-growth and low-growth projections in unit sales, and selling prices along with income can be used in the model since they represent the best-case and worst-case forecasts. Additionally, sensitivity analysis allows the company's managers to examine the impact of a change in one variable. A more rigorous multidimensional analysis can be performed by varying a number of variables to see what impact each change has on net profit on sales. In this way, managers can evaluate how sensitive the model is to changes in given variables.

Another forecasting approach is to utilize one of the popular software packages available today. For example, Forecast Pro for Windows allows users to have the package—via its expert system—determine the best forecasting model based on the software's observation of the data. As such, the software package not only recommends a forecasting model, but also the software will even explain why a particular model was selected. This feature provides an accurate model as well as teaches the user what to look for when analyzing a data series.

Preparation of Short-Range and Medium-Range Profit Plans

For a typical company's products, an annual profit plan is an integral part of corporation-wide strategic planning. In a similar manner, overall profit plans are determined for two, three, and four years hence. Reference can be made to Figure 6.2 for typical output. As information becomes available that is reflective of changing times, profit plans for the coming year must be revised to reflect the changes and expected changes in the business environment. Effective profit planning, therefore, must be a *continuous* effort rather than a periodic one. Although budgets for profit planning are generally prepared by the accounting department, the responsibility rests with the corporate-planning staff, who must not only select the appropriate financial data for specific planning decisions, but must also combine these data from corporate databases and data warehouses in useful and meaningful ways. Staff members must also review and coordinate the estimates provided by the functional managers involved in a particular decision. They must provide a measure of the profit impact of alternative courses of action, and advice on the meaning and significance of financial analysis. Overall, the long-range strategic plans are translated into medium-range plans for the next several years and finally into short-range strategic plans, that is, annual profit plans (including budgets) for the coming year (refer to Figure 6.2).

Flexible budgets or detailed profit plans for the coming year are developed that take into account planning for marketing, manufacturing, human resources, and finance that have an impact on the current year. Similarly, overall profit plans for medium-range strategic plans can be developed. To assist the corporate-planning staff, an OLAP-software package is useful to answer a series of "what-if" questions about planning, and to use sensitivity analysis to determine the impact the change of one or more variables might have on the final profit

Figure 6.5
**Typical Short-Range Planning Analysis (Forthcoming Six Months) to Answer
"What-If" Questions During the Budgetary Process About the Profitability of
New Products**

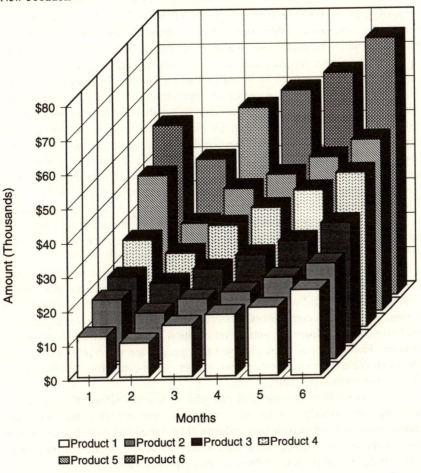

plans. As shown in Figure 6.5, managers and their staffs interact with the company's data to answer "what-if" questions and to undertake sensitivity analysis.
In this case, there is a six-month analysis of six new products in terms of
profitability. As shown, profits increase over the months due to a number of
factors, including a reduction in production times, larger sales volumes due to
the acceptance of the product, and a reduction in scrap as the learning curve
improves. Hence, a wide variety of answers can be obtained to assist in the
development of profit plans—the corporate strategic plans for current and future
operations.

Comparison of Company Against Competitors and Non-Competitors

Going beyond assistance in the preparation of final flexible budgets and review of quarterly financial forecasts, an OLAP approach is also helpful in measuring a company's operations against other competitors as well as non-competitors. To enable corporation executives to accomplish such analysis, there may be a need for pertinent data from external databases. That is, specific data for such analysis must be stored on-line for later use by executives. When executives develop plans that center on improving productivity for manufacturing operations, adequate data is available to set the wheels in motion for developing short- to long-range strategic plans for beating or, at least, meeting competition. Similarly, external financial data on competition can be stored on-line that allows executives to measure their own corporation's performance against competition. In this manner, executives can see where the corporation is experiencing good, average, or poor performance in its major areas of operation against the best of its competitors. Comparison of a corporation by its executives against competitors using an on-line analytical processing system can provide essential information in the short run to benefit a corporation in the long run.

It should be noted that benchmarking against the competition poses problems. For one thing, comparisons to competitors may uncover practices that are unworthy of emulation. For another, while competitive benchmarking may help a corporation meet its competitors' performance, it is unlikely to reveal practices for beating them. Moreover, getting information about competitors is obviously difficult. Finally, it has been observed that people are more receptive to new ideas that come from outside their own industry. Non-competitor benchmarking, then, is the method of choice.

A non-competitive investigation can give executives information about the best functional practices in any industry. These may include technological advances unrecognized in their own industry (like bar coding, which originated in the grocery industry but has since been widely applied). Adoption of these practices can help a corporation achieve a competitive advantage.

Referring to the prior discussion on "Measurement Against the Best," the Xerox Corporation was cited. One of Xerox's most valuable benchmarking experiences was with L.L. Bean, Inc., the outdoor sporting goods retailer and mail-order house. It was carried out by the Xerox Logistics and Distribution (L&D), which is responsible for inventory management, warehousing, and transport of machines, parts, and supplies. Historically, Xerox's L&D's productivity increases had been 3 to 5 percent per year. Recently, it was clear that improvement was necessary to maintain profit margins in the face of industry price cuts.

The inventory-control area had recently installed a new planning system, and the transportation function was capitalizing on opportunities presented by deregulation. Warehousing was next in line for improvement, and the distribution-center managers wanted a change. They identified the picking area as the worst bottleneck in the receiving-through-shipping sequence. A new technology—automated storage and retrieval systems (ASRS) for materials handling—had appeared on the scene and was the subject of hot debate in Xerox's distribution function. The corporation had just erected a high-rise ASRS warehouse for raw materials and assembly parts in Webster, New York, in the same complex as a large finished-goods distribution center. Internal benchmarking evaluations by L&D showed that heavy investment in capital equipment for ASRS could not be cost-justified for finished goods. They needed a different way to boost warehousing and materials handling productivity—but what?

The L&D unit assigned a staff member half-time to come up with a suitable non-competitor to benchmark in the warehousing and materials handling areas. The staff member combed trade journals and conferred with professional associations and consultants to find the companies with the best reputations in the distribution business. He then targeted those companies with generic product characteristics and service levels similar to Xerox reprographic parts and supplies. The staff member had singled out L.L. Bean as the best candidate for benchmarking in terms of their warehouse operations.

The staff member was particularly struck with the L.L. Bean warehouse system design. Although extremely manual in nature, the design minimized the labor content, among other benefits. The operation also did not lend itself to automation of handling and picking. The design therefore relied on very basic handling techniques, but it was carefully thought out and implemented. In addition, the design was selected with the full participation of the hourly workforce. It was the first warehouse operations designed by quality circles.

To the layperson, L.L. Bean products may bear no resemblence to Xerox parts and supplies. To the distribution professional, however, the analysis was striking; both companies had to develop warehousing and distribution systems to handle products diverse in size, shape, and weight. This diversity precluded the use of ASRS. Later, a Xerox team visited Bean's operations in Freeport, Maine. Besides the person in charge of benchmarking in L&D, the team consisted of a headquarters operations executive and a field distribution-center manager. These two people represented the line employees who would ultimately make any changes.

The findings resulted in L&D incorporating some of L.L. Bean's practices in a program to modernize Xerox's warehouses. These practices included materials location arranged by velocity, to speed the flow of materials and minimize picker travel distance, as well as enhancing computer involvement in the picking operation. Xerox plans to put together a totally computer-managed warehouse.[5]

A TYPICAL REAL-WORLD OLAP APPLICATION RELATED TO PLANNING FOR PROFITS

The supermarket industry has operated on historical information taken from a data warehouse and not from current information coming from the now ubiquitous in-store scanners. This means supermarket managers do not have a handle on what merchandise sells in what particular store. The end result is that they treat all stores as if they had the same exact customer, which is far from true. Also, there can be too much inventory or too little inventory. Either scenario is far from optimum. But if stores could stabilize inventory and distribute it better, it is estimated that the U.S. supermarket industry could save $40 billion annually. Because the industry does not have the information infrastructure, they have need of OLAP and Efficient Market Services (Deerfield, Illinois) which places a RISC box in a store's headquarters. Then every retail outlet gets a PC which is attached to the customer in-store controller. This computer essentially houses the software that runs all the cash registers and pricing data for scanner references, item descriptions, and more. All in-store controllers are polled daily for point-of-sale data.

Due to pricing fluctuations, most of the data that occurs during the course of the day is contaminated. However, the Efficient Market Services cleans up the data and prepares a forecast for the next-day's sales for each item. OLAP technology comes in to help determine items that are over or under forecast. After the in-store editing of data is done, it is sent to the corporate headquarters computer, which runs Red Brick's decision-support software. OLAP databases are then created for buyers, merchandising managers, and advertising managers at headquarters to reference and query. The data has a greater level of detail and is preprocessed to be fed directly into OLAP end-user systems.

Because of the richness of this data set, the buyer at headquarters can track exactly what happened at each store, identify problems, and fix them. And the system is available for a fraction of what other retailers have invested in older technologies. (Costs range from $100,000 to $400,000.) An important item is cleaning up the supermarket industry which has a minimum of 25,000 items. If the inventory cannot be controlled, customers have to pay with higher prices. The stores themselves suffer since, by operating at higher costs, they are in danger of losing customers to discount stores. By controlling inventory with appropriate forecast information, the supermarket industry can get the goods to the customer faster and cheaper. OLAP coupled with clean data is the key to turning plans into profits.[6]

APPLICATIONS THAT CAN BENEFIT FROM OLAP-VR INTEGRATION

In all of the preceding strategic-planning OLAP applications, a reader should have come away with a very important message. That is, if a person reads, he or she tends to forget. If a person sees, he or she tends to remember. In contrast, if a person experiences virtual reality, he or she is undergoing a learning experience which is far superior to a reading or seeing experience. The ability to travel to places which most people regard as too remote, too complex, or simply too costly allows users to visualize the results of incorrect decisions in ways not possible previously. This capability alone may justify the utilization of simulated virtual worlds being joined with OLAP systems not only in strategic planning (as found in this chapter), but also in marketing, manufacturing, accounting and finance, and human resources (as found in future chapters). More specifically, an OLAP-VR integration for strategic planning explored below centers on urban planning, planning for a company's future operations, and other planning areas.

Urban Planning

In the area of urban planning, Virtual Environment Theater technology is quite at home. This technology gives users a virtual-reality tour of the port of Seattle's long-term plans for the area's central waterfront development project. The tour lets users examine proposed buildings and waterfront expansion without stretching their imaginations. The potential of being able to see the impact of the architecture on the landscape and the environmental impact of things, such as the wind on a building, is tremendous.

Typically, architectural visualization is done the traditional way, that is, with scale models and drawings, or with somewhat higher-tech methods, such as videotaped animation and computer-rendered still pictures. In contrast, a virtual-reality approach allows viewers in the theater to find themselves seated inside a sort of "vehicle"—a structure with a roof, windows in front and on the sides, and a dashboard equipped with a computer keyboard. The windows are rear-projection screens. The operator uses the keyboard to give the "passengers" a tour of the Seattle waterfront area from any vantage point. They can "fly by" buildings that have not yet been constructed, drive down streets to see the impact of urban canyons yet to be created, or sail past the waterfront on a boat in Puget Sound. In essence, the theater is a space vehicle that one can drive, fly, float, and go backward in time.[7]

Planning for a Company's Future Operations

To help companies plan their future operations, virtual reality is quite at home in this important area. EDS, a very large applied-IT company, has opened its Detroit Virtual Reality Center which is believed to be the first commercial VR center in the world. Thousands of business people from hundreds of companies have seen VR demonstrations. The company has a VR theater and a VR "cave" where clients can use the facilities, consult with companies that want to set up their own operations, and work with partners to improve hardware and software. Thus, simulation software for manufacturers plus companies using it for designing and the architectural area are typical applications. The center has more than 50 business partners co-developing various VR-commercial applications. Clients include the General Motors R&D Center and Albert Kahn Associates Inc.

Other Areas Related to Planning

Other areas that are related to planning include functional areas by well-known corporations. These include McDonnell Douglas Aerospace, which is using VR design analysis in early product development. General Motors is applying VR in the design of its upcoming models. Similarly, the Ford Motor Company and the Chrysler Corporation are wasting no time either. Bechtel Corporation is using virtual reality in every phase of architecture and engineering. Electrolux (a Belgian appliances maker) uses a VR showroom to test-market new appliances. The Gulfstream Corporation uses VR to let clients choose comforts for corporate jets. If secrecy is any indication, then VR has arrived. Although these VR applications are not linked directly with OLAP, they can be extended to include the integration of these two important information technologies. Future chapters will also focus on other important areas where there is a natural tie-in between the two.

SUMMARY

The main thrust of this chapter was on strategic planning to assist managers and their corporate-planning staffs in the proper acquisition, use, and disposition of an organization's resources. Because corporate strategic planning is an important focal point of on-line analytical processing systems, its purpose is to decide *what to do* in terms of strategic plans based on organization objectives and goals, *how to* implement specific strategies and programs, and *when to* perform them in terms of short-, medium-, and long-range plans to accomplish organization objectives and goals. Important relationships and feedback that exist among these basic elements were explored throughout the chapter. As a means of giving direction to strategic planning, the chapter examined initially newer directions in strategic planning within an OLAP environment. Next, an OLAP approach to strategic planning for a typical company was presented in the long run and then the short run. In addition, the chapter presented a real-world strategic-planning application to demonstrate the effectiveness of OLAP to support managerial decisions. Finally, applications that can benefit from integrating OLAP with virtual reality were set forth.

NOTES

1. Robert J. Thierauf, *A Problem Finding Approach to Effective Corporate Planning* (Westport, Conn.: Quorum Books, 1987); *User-Oriented Decision Support Systems—A Problem-Finding Approach* (Englewood Cliffs, N.J.: Prentice-Hall, Inc., 1988); *Group Decision Support Systems for Effective Decision Making* (Westport, Conn.: Quorum Books, 1989); and *Creative Computer Software for Strategic Thinking and Decision Making: A Guide for Senior Management and MIS Professionals* (Westport, Conn.: Quorum Books, 1993).

2. John E. Rockhart, "Chief Executives Define Their Own Data Needs," *Harvard Business Review*, March–April 1979, pp. 86–87.

3. Frances Gaither Tucker, Seymour M. Zivan, and Robert C. Camp, "How to Measure Yourself Against the Best," *Harvard Business Review*, January–February 1987, pp. 8–9.

4. Gerald Herter, "Business Planning Boosts Your Chances," *Accounting Technology*, April/May 1995, pp. 21–30.

5. Tucker, Zivan, and Camp, *op. cit.*, p. 9.

6. Christine Comaford, "OLAP Can Transform Your Plans Into Profits," *PC Week*, July 17, 1995, p. 15.

7. Stuart J. Johnson, "Virtual Reality Takes Architectural Leap," *Computerworld*, June 20, 1994, p. 72.

7

Marketing in an OLAP
Environment

ISSUES EXPLORED

- Why is it important to rethink the marketing mix in an OLAP environment?
- How can sales and marketing organizations utilize OLAP tools to identify market changes?
- How important is the problem-finding process to marketing managers and their staffs in on-line analytical processing?
- What real-world OLAP applications are a natural to help manage marketing activities better?
- What marketing areas can benefit from an integration of OLAP with virtual reality?

OUTLINE

Marketing in an OLAP Environment
   Rethinking the Entire Marketing Mix
Newer Directions in Marketing That Underlie OLAP
   A Problem-Finding Approach to Marketing
   Enlarged View of Core Competence to Develop New Opportunities
   Venture-Analysis Model
   Expanded View of Market Research
   Database Marketing Useful to Develop Knowledge About Customers
   Utilization of Principles from Profit Impact of Marketing Strategies (PIMS)
Marketing Areas That Lend Themselves to an OLAP Environment

MARKETING IN AN OLAP ENVIRONMENT

To gain a better understanding of a company's marketing efforts, it is extremely helpful to evaluate these efforts within an OLAP environment. In turn, this analysis can be helpful to marketing managers in giving direction to a company's future marketing efforts. Typically, past marketing approaches have all concentrated on "what is" in a stable environment. There is the need to refocus on "what can be" such that marketing managers can generate creative and constructive new products and services for customers. But even that change of mind-set apparently may not be enough. For example, Raytheon, which developed the Patriot missile but also invented the microwave oven years ago, did nothing with it. Japanese firms turned it into a huge market success. United States corporations continue to spend millions and millions of dollars on research and development projects in hopes of inventing creative new products and services. But if these corporations are run by stodgy chief executives "uncomfortable" with unproven new concepts, creative products and services will not go anywhere. Besides, new ideas should be a companywide effort. In light of these current problems in the United States, the whole marketing function needs to be rethought.

Initial discussion in the chapter centers on newer directions in marketing that underlies OLAP. This background serves as a means of exploring typical OLAP applications from an enlarged perspective. OLAP approaches to product and sales information as well as product pricing are illustrated. Also, a typical real-world on-line analytical processing application is set forth. Finally, the relationship of OLAP to virtual reality and their application to marketing are high-lighted.

Rethinking the Entire Marketing Mix

Before exploring newer directions that underlie OLAP in marketing, it would be advisable to take a look at the marketing mix today and tomorrow. That is, the focus is on rethinking how the typical marketing manager views the marketing mix, that is, product, price, place, and promotion. For a company to be successful in the future, it is necessary that it offer the *right products* at the *right price* in the *right place* along with the *right promotion*. Needless to say, a successful company must change with the times since there are fundamental changes in demographics and consumer preferences ahead for the end of this decade that will force companies to rethink their marketing mix. In addition, there are dramatic changes to take place in the twenty-first century.

In the retailing field, marketing executives must be responsive to the changing demographics and preferences (as mentioned above) in order to succeed. Altering *product offerings* is one way retailers can respond. Traditionally, retailers selected their merchandise assortments for breadth and depth. To meet ever-changing consumer preferences, however, retailers need to change their thinking. For example, retailers such as The Limited Stores and The Gap have stuck with their original formulas of offering a small focused assortment in great depth. A stroll through any of the regional malls reveals many similar specialty merchants—stores that sell exclusively sunglasses, nuts, brushes, bathing suits, and so forth. These specialty stores represent the traditional department in a department store.

Regarding *pricing strategy* and *promotion*, retailers have a method to carve out a niche for themselves. The meteoric rise of discounters in the 1970s and the early 1980s has reached its peak, primarily because of heavy competition in that market. Currently, growth appears greatest among those firms that dominate their categories. The reason is that they are specialists who are able to create their own customers and become market leaders within a chosen segment. The ability of these super specialists to offer both broader and deeper assortments within a limited category ensures them steady traffic without promotional price-cutting.

Currently, pricing trends focus on everyday low prices and high/low promotional pricing. Although promotions encourage comparison shopping to obtain the best price, many people with demands on their time refuse to do that and instead will trade potential savings for time. This partially explains the success of Walmart. From a management perspective, everyday low pricing means labor savings because of reduced marking and remarking of price tags, and fewer stock shortages on the promotional items. In addition, rather than ticketing an item as an expected selling price, the retailer sets an artificially high ticket price. Markdowns or promotions then bring the item down to the expected selling price. Retailers that choose this pricing and promotion strategy will have to be good merchants, combining fresh merchandising with crisper visual presentations and perhaps adding store attractions to keep the traffic flowing. The promotions of the department stores will most likely continue since they depend more heavily than others on selling quickly changing fashions.

The changing demographics are best illustrated in the emergence of *new channels of distribution* and the resurgence of some old channels of distribution. The demand for convenience, not just price, has allowed nonstore retailers to flourish. Since the technology is changing so rapidly, it is impossible to guess what the end of the next decade will bring, but here are some of the important trends: electronic shopping, mail-order catalog/direct mail, manufacturer's outlets, and hypermarkets.

NEWER DIRECTIONS IN MARKETING THAT UNDERLIE OLAP

To have global success today and tomorrow, companies need to go beyond the "me-too" product attitude. The focus should be on corporate visioning, which is the starting point for corporate strategic thinking (refer to the prior chapter). *Visioning* of the marketing function is envisioning markets for products and services that do not exist today. In other words, a typical U.S. company should generate new products and services such that the company is out there ahead all on its own, as Raytheon could have been with the microwave oven. In this century, as well as into the twenty-first century, marketing battles will be won by companies that can build and dominate fundamentally new markets.

Creative new products, such as micro robots, speech-activated appliances, and self-parking cars not only make the inconceivable conceivable, but also allow a company to influence the direction of the market. In the years to come, more and more companies will close the gap with their rivals on costs, quality, and delivery. But without the capacity to stake out new territories with products and services, many U.S. companies will find themselves faced with traditional and shrinking markets for products and services. Hence, there is a need for a new direction that is tied-in with the ability to analyze where the company has been as well as where it should be headed.

Some of the newer directions in marketing that are related directly or indirectly to an OLAP environment are given below. They are: (1) a problem-finding approach to marketing, (2) enlarged view of core competence to develop new opportunities, (3) venture-analysis model, (4) expanded view of market research, (5) database marketing useful to develop knowledge about customers, and (6) utilization of principles from Profit Impact of Marketing Strategies.

A Problem-Finding Approach to Marketing

Inasmuch as marketing planning and control are related directly to on-line analytical processing systems, the obtainment of this information often involves the employment of computerized mathematical models that enable marketing managers to retain control over problem solving. These models are also useful in problem finding in that marketing managers can solve nonprogrammable problems. Since marketing managers are leaders who communicate with work groups, motivate employees, and supervise ongoing organization activities, the computer is an extremely important tool that can assist them in decision making. From this view, marketing managers are able to increase their effectiveness. In an OLAP environment, marketing managers need a knowledge of surrounding environmental factors, a vision of their responsibilities, and an initiative to cope with change. A human-computer interface, then, assists them in the analyses of problem solving and problem finding as well as resolving problems and identifying future opportunities.

The use of the problem-finding process for a typical manufacturing company centers on marketing managers seeking satisfactory solutions to their problems. In a similar manner, production and financial managers seek good answers to their problems. Unfortunately, each has a different and possibly narrow perspective. To manage the marketing area (as well as other areas) effectively, the company needs to utilize problem finding for future problems so that the marketing-manufacturing interface clearly produces the best results for the company. Seasonal sales can be forecast, and slack periods can receive the benefit of promotional efforts in order to smooth sales and reduce variations in production and inventory levels. In addition, production savings can be compared to promotional costs, and a coordinated budget can be developed to reduce overall costs. Problems of conflicting objectives, underutilization of resources, overreaction to changing economic indicators, and rigid budgetary constraints that prohibit the company from optimizing its overall objectives can be overcome. The solution, then, is to implement planning of the marketing function with the company's other functional areas through a problem-finding approach. In effect, the company needs to look out into the future and to bring its problems back to the present time for solution in terms of relating its marketing area to other functional areas.

Enlarged View of Core Competence to Develop New Opportunities

In order to create new markets for products and services, early and consistent investment in what is called "core competencies" is one important factor. In turn, corporate imagination and expeditionary marketing are the keys that unlock these new markets. A company that underinvests in its core competencies, or inadvertently surrenders them through alliances and outsourcing, generally robs its own future. But to realize the potential that core competencies create, a company must also have the imagination to envision markets that do not yet exist and the ability to stake them out ahead of the competition. In a few words, a company must anticipate what the customers want before they are aware of what they want.[1]

A company will strive to create new competitive space only if it possesses an opportunity perspective that goes far beyond the boundaries of its present businesses. This perspective identifies, in broad terms, the marketing territory top management hopes to stake out over the coming years, a terrain that is unlikely to be captured in anything as precise as a five-year marketing plan. The initial enthusiasm that several Japanese companies brought to developing high-definition television (HDTV) grew out of just such a vision. Creative considerations of the many new opportunities that might emerge if HDTV could be made a reality led them beyond the traditional boundaries of color television business to identify potential markets in cinema production, video photography, video magazines, electronic museums, product demonstrations, and training simulations, among others.

As this example demonstrates, a company's opportunity perspective represents its collective imagination of the ways in which an important new benefit might be harnessed to create new competitive space or reshape existing space. Commitment to an opportunity perspective does not rest on ROI (return on investment) calculations but on an almost visceral sense of the benefits that customers will finally derive should pioneering work prove successful. The more fundamental the envisioned benefits and the more widely shared the enthusiasm for the opportunity, the greater the company's perseverance will be.[2]

Although there is a need for core competencies to create new markets, there is also a need for an enlarged view of these competencies. Conceiving a company as a group of core competencies rather than as a group of products and services is one way to extend the opportunity perspective considerably. Because Motorola sees itself as a leader in wireless communications, it is not just a producer of paging devices and mobile telephones. Rather, the company's charter permits it to explore markets as diverse as wireless local area computer networks and global-positioning satellite receivers. Ajinomoto, a giant grocery-products company, is not only in the food business, but also applies the skills it has mastered in fermentation technology to produce an elastic paper for Sony's top-end headphones. The point to be made from these examples is that if company managers are not able to think outside current business boundaries, they will miss important new opportunities that depend on the combination of skills from several divisions.[3]

Venture-Analysis Model

One of the most extensive and sophisticated marketing mathematical models is venture analysis. It is an investment-planning system for analyzing new opportunities and encompasses such techniques as probability, decision theory, and the time value of money as well as mathematical modeling. Because it is a massive system of gathering, relating, appraising, and projecting all data pertinent to a complete business venture over its life cycle, this mathematical technique stores many kinds of information. All costs involved in the product project are developed. Manufacturing costs include raw materials, direct labor, depreciation, and overhead. These data are modeled for each step of the production process. For the pricing and promotional effort, product prices are estimated at various desired levels to determine an optimum price. All promotional costs involved in marketing the product are broken down by media selected and projected. Research-and-development costs plus general-and-administrative costs are scheduled to make the data complete.

Because venture analysis is very comprehensive in nature, other members of the marketing chain—suppliers and retailers—are included in the model. In a similar manner, key decisions that would affect sales of the product, such as the introduction of similar products by competitors, are defined, related, and programmed. Also, the consumer's awareness and reaction are taken into account to make the model complete. All of the marketing factors, then, are modeled according to cause and effect. For any reaction on the part of a company competing in the field, the corporation estimates the reaction and effects on the other competitors. The total of all marketing interactions described above results in a sales forecast and a profitability picture. A computer-simulation program provides for analyzing and summarizing in a logical manner all the available information about markets, investments, costs, customers, and competitors in venture analysis.

Currently, variations of venture analysis are offered by a few software vendors. For example, Cincom Systems Inc. (Cincinnati, Ohio) is marketing a suite of software products, called Control:Acquire, to automate and support the tasks required to bid on new business. This software package manages an entire sales cycle from prospecting for business to estimating costs and developing proposals. One feature of the software is called Workbench Configuration. It can process product requests from customers so sales staff and customers have a complete picture of the components needed to meet a customer's needs. The Workbench feature can lead a customer through the selection of product parts and tasks. The software then can compare those choices to a knowledge bank of product information to make sure that the customer has selected a buildable product.

A second feature is called Estimating, designed to give timely and accurate cost estimates when developing proposals. A third feature is Proposal Management, which automates the job of maintaining information on sales proposals and can also send sales orders. A fourth feature, Work Breakdown Structure Planner, automates the task of scheduling and monitoring the implementation of a customer's order. Essentially, this product is designed to reduce sales overhead costs, order-to-shipment cycle times, and expensive order revisions.

Expanded View of Market Research

An important part of market research is to lead a company's customers where they want to go before they know it themselves. For example, NEC pursues a telephone that interprets between callers speaking in different languages. Similarly, Motorola envisions a world where telephone numbers are attached to people rather than places, and where a personal communicator allows millions of out-of-touch business travelers to be reached anywhere. Market research and segmentation analysts are unlikely to reveal such opportunities because deep insight into the customers' needs, lifestyles, and aspirations is required.

There are many ways such insights may be garnered, all of which go beyond methods of market research. For example, Toshiba has a Lifestyle Research Institute and Sony explores human science as vigorously as it pursues the leading edge of audio-visual technology. Yamaha gains insights into unarticulated needs and potentially new functionalities through a "listening post" it established some years ago in London. Stocked with leading-edge electronic hardware, the facility offers some of Europe's most talented musicians a chance to experiment with the future of music making. The feedback helps Yamaha continually extend competitive boundaries it has staked out in the music business. In effect, Yamaha's approach illustrates a basic point. To gain the most profound insights into its customers, the company must observe, up close, the coming needs of its most demanding customers.

Companies that succeed in educating customers as to what is possible develop both marketers with technological imagination and technologists with marketing imagination. As an example, in one Japanese company, senior technical officers spend as many as 30 days a year outside Japan talking to customers. The aim is not to solve technical problems nor to close a sale, but to listen and observe customers and absorb their thinking. In another example, a Japanese chief engineer of a major new business-development program lived for a time with an American family thought to be representative of the customers his company hoped to win. In each case, the goal was not to improve the flow of information between marketers and engineers nor to manage the balance of power between the two groups, but rather to blur organizational and career boundaries by ensuring that both communities had a large base of shared experiences. The net result was a good mixture of market and technical imagination.[4]

Database Marketing Useful to Develop Knowledge About Customers

As markets grow more competitive and companies focus on competitive advantage, it becomes increasingly clear that marketing management needs to keep existing customers happy while trying to find new ones. Since giving customers what they want is more essential than ever, database marketing is becoming a key to reaching that goal. Recent studies have shown that approximately 80 percent of recurring revenues come from 20 percent of a client base. As such, database marketing provides the tools to discover who makes up that 20 percent so that marketing management can target campaigns to those customers or look for replacements.

As noted in Chapter 3, a typical data warehouse contains key business-intelligence data in a highly logical and integrated view. It has a historical perspective so that trending can be accomplished, and is used for decision making in the business. Although it is not a dump per se of all company data into one place, it is a highly architected environment containing a lot of useful data. With this in mind, database marketing is an extension of the data-warehouse concept. In a broad sense, database marketing is a set of activities ranging from promotional selling to strategic market analysis. It is definable as a collection, analysis, and use of individual customer attributes and behavior patterns. In the past, marketing databases were built on mainframes or midrange systems. The trend is to distribute query analysis functions through client/server architectures. Client/server configurations provide flexibility, high speeds, and user-friendly interfaces. Additionally, they can easily be linked to PC-based applications for additional analysis and presentation, all at a fraction of mainframe computer costs.

The features of an effective database-marketing system includes marketing, advertising, product management, direct mail, and promotion along with query capabilities to study customer data, and tracking mechanisms to measure the success of promotional campaigns. They also should be capable of segmented lists to target parts of the database with promotional messages or campaigns. The capability to ask "what-if" questions is another major component within an OLAP-operating mode. "What-if" capabilities not only suggest ways to improve the performance of existing marketplace efforts, but also they can suggest complementary new products or business ventures.

Some companies develop marketing databases strictly as analytical tools to maintain, consolidate, and analyze information captured by other transactional-processing systems, while others use them to automate both transaction and analysis functions. Typically, companies gather large amounts of data on customers and their buying habits. In turn, marketing-database software helps companies merge data from separate files, thereby yielding new information about customer attitudes and preferences, while computers and analytical tools help marketers use that information to develop a deeper understanding of trends in consumer behavior. In this process, raw data is transformed into useful information and, through the use of sophisticated tools, converted into useful knowledge.

Utilization of Principles from Profit Impact of Marketing Strategies (PIMS)

Profit Impact of Marketing Strategies (PIMS) is a computerized approach for planning market strategy that is run by the Strategic Planning Institute. It is a data pool of information on the marketing experiences of its members.[5] Several hundred corporations submit data annually on a total of about 3,000 of their business units, each of which is a distinct product-market unit. Each member provides PIMS with the most intimate details on matters such as its market share, investment intensity, product quality, and total marketing and R&D expenditures. Through computer simulation, the company can then test its own market strategies against the real experiences of hundreds of comparable companies, including competitors. What it receives are answers to questions, such as these: What is the normal profit rate for a business or a product line given its combination of circumstances, and why? If the business continues on its current track, what will its future operating results be? What will happen to short- and long-term performance if certain strategic moves are made? What changes will create the best profits or cash returns?

Typically, what a member company wants from PIMS is to find out what it will cost to make a particular strategic move, and how much better off the business will be afterward. For example, consider return on investment, which PIMS considers one of the best measures of how a business is doing. The PIMS models can forecast how much ROI for a business line will change because of a strategic move involving more marketing, R&D, capital equipment buildup, or whatever—both what the ROI will be immediately following the move and what it will be several years in the future. Some new as well as traditional principles which have emerged from PIMS-computer models of the real-life experiences of its corporate members are set forth as follows.

- There is a set of operating rules that govern all business. Some 37 factors—including market share, capital intensity, and vertical integration—jointly explain 80 percent of the successes or failures of any business; only 20 percent of a business's return-on-investment can be attributed to factors that are unique or special, such as the quality of working relations.

- Anything more than a minimal R&D program does not make sense for a company with a weak market position. Copying competitors' products rather than inventing them is probably its best bet. This can be a very profitable strategy.

- High-marketing expenditures for low-quality products can have a devastating effect on profits.

- High product quality can offset a weak market position.

- Weak companies should not become vertically integrated, whereas strong ones should.

- High costs in more than one area, such as capital investment, R&D, or marketing, can ruin any business.

When extrapolating from the PIMS database, it is recommended that companies should not automatically compare themselves to competitors in the same industry or business category to find out how well they are doing. According to PIMS, industry breakdowns are not all-important. A better yardstick may be the performance of companies in other industries whose total situation is comparable. A tire company, for example, may have even more in common and more to learn from the market strategies of a small appliance manufacturer than from those of another tire company.

Currently, there is a PIMS personal computer (PC) approach. What makes PIMS/PC different from electronic spreadsheets is that it goes beyond simply calculating, storing, and displaying a strategic plan. It allows the user to test the plan's viability by comparing it to the actual experience of similar businesses. Until recently, executives of member firms who wanted to use the PIMS program had to get on-line to the mainframe in Cambridge, Massachusetts, to do so. However, PIMS/PC is a personal computer version that now makes telecommunications unnecessary.

MARKETING AREAS THAT LEND THEMSELVES TO AN OLAP ENVIRONMENT

In the preceding sections on newer directions in marketing that underlie OLAP, the focus was on being *proactive* to the needs of customers versus being *reactive*, as so often is the case today. For example, I have experienced the following situation that, in turn, can be multiplied by many thousands of customers. I had phoned to reserve a room at a hotel for an eagerly awaited out-of-town vacation. After the dates and rates were agreed upon, the reservations operator began to ask the usual questions. I responded that I am a member of their frequent hotel guest program. This is my number. After a brief delay, the operator came back and informed me that my frequent hotel guest number has been terminated because of inactivity. Although I had an urgent impulse to tell the operator that I had suddenly decided to stay inactive, my good judgment prevailed. However, in retrospect, I am appalled at the chain's lack of marketing savvy to collect information on my preferences that it could have used to lure me back relatively easily with targeted marketing. Instead, the hotel chain felt it was better to ignore people like myself who have the time and money to take advantage of special offers. In essence, the lack of creative thinking caused this hotel chain to focus its sales attention on serving and expanding their relationships with active customers, thereby bypassing a hugh potential market of inactive customers.

Currently, it is common for companies to purge their databases of inactive customers so that they do not waste magnetic storage. But reducing costs this way is not a creative way to expand a customer base. In effect, these companies are throwing away customer names while their advertising and marketing departments are spending many thousands, even millions, of dollars to identify and entice prospective customers. The cost of storing the data describing an inactive customer is generally much less than a penny, while the cost of identifying a new prospect can range from tens to hundreds of dollars. Moreover, every company knows more about the preferences and buying habits of the inactive customer than of the prospective customers. Why not, then, design a marketing program to induce inactive customers to do business again? A company that undertakes a creative approach that is proactive to inactive customers can utilize OLAP to help get a better handle on this past customer base.

Marketing areas that lend themselves to an OLAP environment are varied, as will be seen in this second half of the chapter. The capability of sales and marketing personnel to evaluate marketplaces in real time will be apparent in the following discussion. For the most part, the capability to analyze key aspects of the changing marketing landscapes, and the capability of marketing managers to make key decisions about the present and future directions of markets, will make a very important difference between being somewhat successful to being extremely successful. Equally important is the pricing of a company's products to meet changing times. Typical other areas that lend themselves to an OLAP operating mode include advertising, market research, and sales forecasting. In addition, sales-order processing and physical distribution are potential candidates for on-line analytical processing. Due to space limitations, only the areas of marketing analysis and product pricing are treated below.

AN OLAP APPROACH TO MARKETING ANALYSIS

In a business environment characterized by shrinking profit margins, global markets, and faster product cycles, companies are spending millions of dollars annually on their marketing efforts, including product promotions. The demand to produce maximum results from these promotions is phenomenal. Success means that companies must focus constantly on identifying market changes. Their mission is to search the vast amounts of corporate data for answers that enable their company to make intelligent marketing decisions. Sales and marketing managers have need of a system that delivers a wide range of marketing information to their desks every day, which allows them to rank products, analyze channel performance, or create quickly ad hoc views of sales by account or region. To be useful to the manager, the system must be flexible, timely, and intuitive. Such an approach is possible within an OLAP environment.

In the areas of forecasting and pricing, for example, marketing managers have great impact on the needed input for these areas. However, they should go a step further by maintaining control over these forecasts and prices. The forecasted sales on the corporate database or data warehouse allow marketing managers to compare projected product sales to actual sales activity (updated on a daily basis) for some specific time period. To make comparisons of actual to forecasted sales on a periodic basis (say daily, weekly, or monthly), it is helpful for marketing managers to utilize a multidimensional-analysis approach to sales analysis. It should be noted that analysis of marketing activities goes beyond just sales analysis. It also involves marketing analysis to develop a specific marketing strategy as well as assistance in the development of an overall marketing strategy. Essentially, the foregoing areas which are covered below are related directly to the important elements of the marketing mix (as set forth earlier in the chapter).

Sales Analysis by Geographical Areas to Identify Market Changes

The use of a typical OLAP software package (refer to Chapter 4) is quite useful to analyze sales by geographical areas in order to identify market changes. As such, a three-part level of inquiry formats can be utilized, that is, (1) total geographical sales, (2) detailed geographical sales, and (3) exception geographical sales. In the process of doing so, marketing managers can manipulate the data by looking for trends; performing audits of the sales data; and calculating totals, averages, changes, variances, or ratios.

The highest level of marketing analysis, *total geographical sales*, is the overall sales performance for the current year as well as past years. This level of marketing inquiry can be extended to include an overall performance summary that describes the sales budget and actual month-to-date, last month-to-date, year-to-date, and last year-to-date sales by geographical areas. If a given geographical-sales performance is deficient compared to the budgeted figures, control can then be transferred to successive levels of detailed reports relative to the area of interest.

The second level of inquiry, *detailed geographical sales*, allows for optional levels of detail to be obtained. Normally, the inquiries requested of this structure are triggered for further analysis by the total sales inquiry. As with the first level, data are available for the same time periods and by the same sales categories at the detailed level. Also, this inquiry format is programmed to enable the sales managers to format report structures because they might be interested in certain sales ratios or sales-to-expense ratios. An example of detailed geographical sales is found in Figure 7.1, where the total sales history for one geographical area of the United States over the last five years is shown by months. Comparable analyses can be developed for the other geographical areas of the United States plus other geographical areas of the world. In all cases, the focus of the analysis is on the highest six-month sales periods for one geographical area versus other geographical areas. Such an analysis might help determine where goods could be shipped from one part of the world to another to smooth out production flows in the many manufacturing facilities of the world.

Lastly, the third level of inquiry, *exception geographical sales*, is generally more complex and flexible than the first two. The exception inquiry is structured to highlight a certain condition or conditions. A typical inquiry might be: "Which products in a certain geographical area of the United States are above

Figure 7.1
Total Sales History by Months for One Geographical Area of the United States Over the Last Five Years

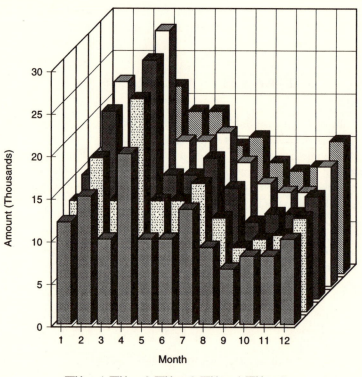

110 percent of forecast sales and below 90 percent of forecast sales for the current month?'' or ''Which salespersons in a certain geographical area of the United States are below their sales quotas for the current month?'' This inquiry level provides not only information to individual sales managers about the effectiveness or lack of it in terms of the company's marketing effort, but also provides a forum for a group discussion by marketing managers such that each geographical-sales area of the United States can be compared to other areas.

Customer Analysis to Select a Specific Market Strategy

Using multidimensional analysis, marketing managers of a typical company can create a marketing strategy for next year. As a beginning point in this example, there are comparable data to work with: surveys, market tests, and market audits performed by the market research department. But none of them answers the important questions. What would happen to contribution to fixed costs and profit if the number of users increased next year for the company's products, that is, the "proportion usage" increased over the current year? Similarly, what would happen to contribution to fixed costs and profit if the "rate of usage per year" for the present number of users increased next year over the present year?

To answer these two questions, there is the need to analyze the past and future possible demand for the company's products and to develop a specific market strategy based on this analysis. Several reasons and methods exist for analyzing demand. If the sales manager wants to look at cash flow or set inventory levels, the individual might analyze and forecast various elements of demand—predictable cycles, seasonal fluctuations, and so forth—and thus come up with a sales forecast. Because a new market strategy must be devised, OLAP can be used to analyze demand in order to understand why a given level of sales took place.

Once the "why" of the demand is undertaken, a specific marketing strategy can be developed to change certain events and thus increase sales. For example, a most important element is the market segment of newly formed families who are concerned about using the product. As noted above, there are two possible strategies for increasing demand: (1) increase the proportion of buyers in this market segment, or (2) increase the usage rate of those who presently buy such a product. In addition, these strategies can be developed under optimistic, average, and pessimistic conditions.

Multidimensional analysis within an OLAP environment can be used to analyze the components of the problem in order to answer the preceding questions. Generally, historical data on the number of persons, proportion buying, and rate of buying per year are given, along with the unit price, variable costs percentage, and the number of buyers expected. To increase the proportion-using category, say from 60 percent to 65 percent under *pessimistic* conditions (first case), 70 percent under *average* conditions (second case), and 75 percent under *optimistic* conditions (third case), appropriate multidimensional analysis can be undertaken in terms of contribution to fixed costs and profit by products and cases. An alternative is to accept, say, the 60 percent proportion, and find a way to increase the usage rate, say from 1.95 to 2.15 people under *pessimistic* conditions (fourth case), 2.25 people under *average* conditions (fifth case), and 2.35 people under *optimistic* conditions (sixth case) next year by products and cases.

The number of possible marketing strategies is limited only by the manager's creativity. An OLAP-multidimensional approach stimulates creativity by allowing a marketing manager to spell out alternative strategies and assumptions in a precise form. Each strategy can be translated into an estimated contribution to fixed costs and profit by products and time periods. Based upon the data, the best marketing strategy is selected, such as: an increase in buyer usage gives the greatest return for the company's products under study for future time periods.

Assistance in Developing an Overall Marketing Strategy

In the development of an overall marketing strategy, multidimensional analysis can be helpful in getting a handle initially on who the customer really is. Marketing managers need not only bring insights and expertise to determine who the customer is, but also must recognize that the customer is the most important entity in the distribution channel. As such, marketing managers need to consider the present needs and future wants of their customers in every step of the distribution channel. They need to spend a typical day in the life of their small-, medium-, and large-size customers from the standpoint of meeting their needs today and their wants tomorrow. For example, even though the company ships all of its orders 95 percent on the average, the customer views it differently since the order must be 100 percent complete before they can introduce the item into production. This is where OLAP comes into play since multidimensional analysis can be used to understand fully the customer's viewpoint. In the example given, multidimensional analysis of three important variables (percent of shipments received on time, percent of shipments received late, and days late for remaining items) may give marketing managers a better perception of its operations through the eyes of a typical customers. The results may not be very positive. However, OLAP is capable of presenting the true picture to marketing managers—good, bad, or indifferent.

From another perspective, on-line analytical processing can be of assistance to marketing managers in developing an overall marketing strategy by concentrating on customer satisfaction. It is a generally known fact that retaining existing customers is usually much more profitable than focusing on acquiring new customers. Even though many companies state that customers are important, often company employees do not rate customer satisfaction as a top priority of their company. Many times, there is a large gap between what a company says it does and what its customers perceive it as doing. Hence, multidimensional analysis can be used to get a handle on customer satisfaction or lack thereof.

Still other ways to employ OLAP can be found in the marketing efforts of well-known companies. For example, the Procter & Gamble Company has undertaken a global initiative to make its marketing efforts more efficient. In its Market Breakthrough 2000 plan, the effects of P&G's effort to find more efficient ways of marketing its wide array of products can already be seen in the Cincinnati-based company's United States operations. In the United States, P&G is building closer ties to a reduced number of outside companies that do everything from art to package design to printing materials for promotional campaigns.

Procter & Gamble is looking at its whole system of developing and executing its marketing programs with its suppliers to find ways to improve flexibility, save time, and get the results it seeks at a lower cost. Additionally, P&G is leveraging its size as the nation's largest advertiser in terms of spending by using one agency to make all of its media purchases. When the agency, TEL-

Vest, part of DMB&B, negotiates with media companies for time and space, it can use its position to win the best prices for P&G.

AN OLAP APPROACH TO PRODUCT PRICING

Pricing of a company's products, as noted previously in the chapter, is one of the four elements comprising the marketing mix. Because of the complexity of the marketing environment, there is a great need for setting correct prices. Pricing is a problem when a new product is being introduced, when a price change is contemplated in the face of uncertain customer and competitor reactions, or when a company must react to a competitor who has just changed its price. Pricing is also a problem when sealed bids must be submitted. And it is a problem when the company's product line is characterized by substantial demand and cost interdependencies. In view of these problems, new product pricing can best be determined by applying appropriate statistical or mathematical models to proposed selling prices and estimated demand. Such an approach can be an integral part of *venture analysis*. In addition, there is a need to evaluate pricing as related to competition along with the relationship of product quality with price charged. All of these approaches can be related to those presented below.

Pricing Over Life Cycle of Product

Of paramount importance for venture analysis (per the previous discussion) is the definition and evaluation of specific variables, assumptions, constraints, and like items to be considered for inclusion in the model. For example, in terms of variables, an itemization of all candidate variables based on the subjective judgments of marketing executives is necessary. Knowledge of the marketing environment and the relative importance of various factors is necessary. It is imperative to build a data warehouse of historical data covering not only this company's new products, but also all new products introduced in the industry over the past few years for which adequate source data are available. It is from these data that the statistical and/or mathematical relationships subsequently expressed in the model are derived. Thus, it is apparent that considerable pertinent data are needed before a new product can be effectively evaluated.

Utilizing the venture-analysis model for a new product or service, a marketing-research facilitator can meet with marketing managers who will supply various estimates as they are called for by the model, including the estimated size of the target group, recent product trial data, repeat purchases, the promotional budget, size of investment, target rate of return, product price, and gross profit margin for each product under study. The model will analyze this information under computer control and display a forecast for price along with the total number of customers, company's market share, windfall profits (if applicable), period profits, and discounted cumulative profits. The marketing managers can alter various input estimates and readily ascertain the effect of the altered data on sales and profits. Additionally, prices can be varied over the life cycle of the product. That is, the first year(s) allows a company to charge higher prices due to the newness of the product. As competition moves in, prices are generally lowered and profits tend to fall per unit. When the product is removed from the market or changed to meet emerging customer needs, there can be a change in the pricing structure of the product or service to meet changed conditions in the venture-analysis model.

Although the foregoing analysis has centered on one product or service, in actuality there are generally a number of products or services that undergo the venture-analysis model. After all analyses have been performed that are deemed appropriate for the new products or services under study, there is a comparison of alternative product or service ventures by marketing managers to determine the most viable one to be accepted. For example, as shown in Figure 7.2, for five different products, the proposed product "2" gives the highest return on investment over the next five years for upgrading the company's product line.

Review of Pricing as Related to Competition

An important part of the venture-analysis model, as previously noted, is a determination of prices at various stages over the life cycle of the product. Utilizing a pricing approach within venture analysis, the model relates a myriad of price, advertising, personal selling, and sales promotion combinations for the product under study, and pertinent facts about competing products. Essentially, the venture-analysis model hypothesizes about the degree to which competitors will react to a price change, and in what form this reaction will occur. It analyzes, using an appropriate statistical and/or mathematical model, what blend of marketing decisions will go best with a given price. In turn, it determines what effect the given price will have on the sales of other products in the product line. The pricing aspects of a new product, then, are included in the venture-analysis model along with the prices charged by competition. However, it is up to the marketing managers to review these prices and make appropriate adjustments if deemed necessary for reasonableness based upon their experience and judgment. Otherwise, unrealistic prices will be used to evaluate a product over its life cycle. In turn, the product will be priced unrealistically in terms of its competition.

Currently, Procter & Gamble is slowing the growth of its marketing budgets in order to try to lower prices on some of its brands. It has cut its spending on coupons in half over the last several years because the low-redemption rate makes them an inefficient marketing tool. In its core-suppliers program, P&G is working closely with several key suppliers to study processes and save money. That partnership has led to improved results and reduced expenditures. In essence, Procter & Gamble is trying "to do more with less," that is, it is cutting

Figure 7.2
Proposed Product "2" Out of Five Products Gives the Highest Return on Investment Over the Next Five Years

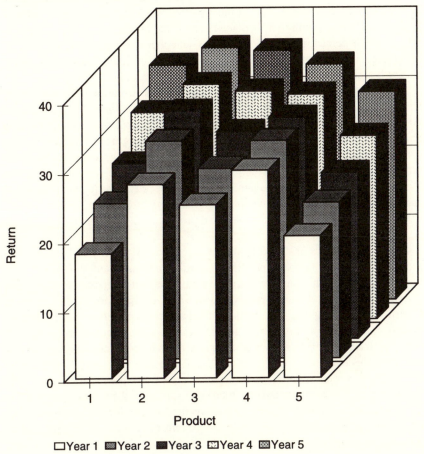

□Year 1 ▨Year 2 ■Year 3 ▧Year 4 ▨Year 5

selling prices and finding ways to cut costs even more than the corresponding drop in prices.

Relationship of Product Quality to Pricing

The Profit Impact of Market Strategy (PIMS), as discussed previously in the chapter, is an extremely important research study. This research yields solid evidence as to what works, what does not, and why. Although PIMS principles are clearly explicated by Robert Buzzell and Bradley Gale in their book, the most important single factor affecting a business unit's performance in the long run is *the quality of its products and services*, relative to those of competitors.

Buzzell and Gale clearly illustrate the linkage between relative quality and business performance in their Perdue chicken example.[6] Chickens have as strong a claim to commodity status as pork bellies or crude oil. The performance of each competitor was the same as each product and service attribute. (This was actually ranked by the PIMS study.) This placed Perdue and his representative competitor at the fiftieth percentile on relative quality—neither ahead nor behind. With no differences in performance on product and service attributes, the customer basically bought on price.

After Frank Perdue took over the chicken business from his father, he pulled ahead on almost every non-price attribute that counts on the purchase decision. His research showed that customers in his served market prefer their chickens plump and yellow. Careful breeding and the judicious use of food additives enabled Frank to produce meatier, yellower chickens than competitors. Over time, Perdue initiated capital investments to improve the real and perceived quality of his chickens. Needless to say, Perdue executed an effective advertising campaign dedicated to communicate the quality of its chickens. Although such analyses were not called on-line analytical processing at the time, today it would be construed as such.

Essentially, Perdue invested heavily to create a real quality difference in its product. According to extensive PIMS research and as noted above, the most important factor in the long run affecting a business unit's performance is quality of its products and services relative to those of competitors. Perdue built its advertising around a big idea, namely, Perdue chickens were superior. In turn, Perdue charged a premium price for its chickens. Major advertising research indicates the price of a product or a service must be consistent with the image it is trying to build.

In the short run, superior quality yields profits via premium prices. PIMS businesses (3,000 business units in total) that ranked in the top third on relative quality sold their products or service, on average, at prices 5 to 6 percent higher relative to competition than those in the bottom third. In the long run, on the other hand, superior quality is the most effective way to grow. Quality leads to both market expansion and gains in market share. The resulting growth in volume means that a superior-quality competitor gains economies of scale advantages over competition.

A TYPICAL REAL-WORLD OLAP APPLICATION RELATED TO MARKETING

To demonstrate further the application of OLAP in marketing, reference can be made to the British drug firm Wellcome Foundation. Recently, Wellcome merged with London-based Glaxo, best-known for its Zantac drug, to form Glaxo Wellcome. The combined entity is now the world's top revenue-producing pharmaceuticals firm. However, growing global competition prompted the company to install an executive information system with OLAP features that helps senior managers track product and sales information. Since its implementation, the system has proven helpful in addressing the company's productivity woes. In its move to allow end users to perform on-line-analytical-processing tasks, Wellcome acquired a multidimensional database design based on LightShip Server from Pilot Software.

Basically, the LightShip system has enabled senior managers in various locales to access important data from their desktops, that is, corporate sales and marketing statistics to industry news to prices and exchange rates. The new system runs on local Compaq servers running Novell NetWare. Client machines are 486s or laptops, networked on the X.25 Wellcome Group Network, the corporate WAN. The system is linked to Lotus Notes for internal communications, so that managers using the LightShip GUI can access relevant Notes data.

In the past, Wellcome had trouble disseminating decision support data to end users. Senior managers wasted valuable time trying to access information that should have been available at their fingertips. The company had numerous information sources but none was coordinated. With information coming from both internal and external sources, and no structured guidelines for dealing with it, inconsistency and duplicated efforts were common. Managers needed a way to identify trends and easily manipulate data. For example, they wanted to be able to discover not only which Wellcome products were selling well in each country, but how quickly sales of drugs were rising or falling, and what portion of revenue could be attributed to each drug.

To assist in getting a handle on important and timely information, the data-warehousing concept was enlarged. To get an idea of what information would be needed in their decision-making process, the project leader for the implementation talked to more than 40 senior executives in the United Kingdom and the United States. According to these managers, the firm's performance hinged on the availability of eight data types: (1) registration dates and forecasts for new drugs, (2) competitor and industry news, (3) sales and finance, (4) market performance, (5) share prices, (6) exchange rates, (7) research-and-development project information, and (8) human resources data. As an example, registration dates are important to pharmaceutical concerns because they signal salespersons to start selling products. Companies want to start selling as soon as possible so they can maximize profits during the period of time the product is covered by a patent. Unfortunately, Wellcome's sales staff were typically neither aware of registration dates nor were they usually warned about a patent when it was about to expire. Hence, there was no coherent database for product registration; it was essentially done ad hoc.

This new system was not Wellcome's first foray into decision support systems. They had previously run Pilot's Command Center Plus on a mainframe in their U.K. operations to monitor various R&D programs. However, end users were reluctant to use the system due to steep chargeback costs. Because the firm's IS group also found it difficult and costly to get new applications up and running in the mainframe-based environment, they decided to migrate to a client/

server system. Through its experience in the EIS realm, it was determined that Wellcome's new system was an application that demanded a multidimensional-database approach. The rationale was that relational-database systems cannot easily cope with the complex queries required for sales analysis. Also, a relational DBMS's response time for such queries is another problem. Thus, multidimensional functionality was inherent in the system desired by the company's decision makers. It should be noted that LightShip's future at Wellcome may be in doubt since the merger with Glaxo. As is often the case following large mergers, Glaxo Wellcome is planning a large-scale reorganization. Plans to roll out the LightShip EIS in the United States, Italy, and Belgium are not clear at this time.[7]

APPLICATIONS THAT CAN BENEFIT FROM OLAP-VR INTEGRATION

There are a number of marketing applications that can benefit from an OLAP-VR integration. Typical ones are market research, merchandising, and advertising which are covered below. Other marketing applications that lend themselves to an OLAP-VR integration are also given below.

Market Research

Market research, for example, could go beyond its traditional role of analyzing the size of new emerging markets for products and services by getting actively involved in ongoing market-research activities. Market researchers, if necessary, could simulate in real time a topographic map of the United States that includes detailed demographic data of the major and minor metropolitan areas. Maps of these areas show the same data at different intervals in the past. There could be simulated comparison of the past versus the possible future. These data could represent gross-statistical information about representative population samples, their total income, for example; being scaled to their median age. There could be a further elaboration which could become much richer to explore the demographics. Different variations could represent educational differences or the breakdown of data by sex.

In such a simulated environment where the past is compared to the future, market researchers could fly over this synthesized landscape, and could look down and notice certain patterns of growth or decline. One particular area might show tremendous growth potential. Given the information available in this cyberspace system, the market researcher could note both prevailing patterns of change and new growth areas. The market researcher might see new patterns not evident in the traditional method of analysis. The individual could then zoom in for a closer look, and might, while walking among the major and minor metropolitan areas, see that the higher levels of income are related to certain age groups, educational backgrounds, and residential patterns. These variables, then, would all be taken into account in further statistical-analysis models on metropolitan areas.

The focus of this VR-exploratory process is that this investigation proceeds by actions which market researchers do most frequently and most intuitively. Market researchers view things and, when curious, move in a bit closer to see more of the detail. On the other hand, to gain a broader perspective, they move back a few steps. In this VR market-research application, the created virtual reality distills multiple layers of what are typically varied and dissociated data. Because the VR variable is no longer mere abstractions or tabular representation, the data have become immediately more accessible and more alive to those in market research who have need of such data.

Merchandising

In the area of merchandising, a marketing manager may want to analyze in detail some aspects of a new type of store that is envisioned by his or her company. This analysis goes beyond that shown by some type of financial summaries for the present and the future. The VR-modeling process can be used for a new store before construction. The ways in which products are displayed within a department store or a supermarket are critical to its ultimate success. To get a feel for the store's layout, a cross section of customers can be invited to try out the new store in a virtual world and get their reactions. Although this approach is somewhat subjective, it can point out important problems before the actual store is built. Too often in the past, stores had to be redesigned after the store was built because some important considerations were ignored or not contemplated originally. This VR modeling of a store before the fact can save a typical company many millions over the long run because shoppers like to shop in "your store" versus the "competition."

Just as new stores can be designed using virtual worlds, the same can be done for remodeling a store. Layouts, including aisle-displays, can be tested by customers to get their reactions to redesigned stores. As with a new store, there is no need to undergo the changes until there is sufficient testing from the customer's viewpoint to cost-justify the changes. There is no need to make changes for the sake of change when there will be little or no impact on the store's profits.

Going beyond the modeling of a new store using virtual reality, the same can be done on a larger scale, such as for a proposed new city or town. From this perspective, VR allows city planners to develop a whole new world from scratch where people can live, work, and play. Or city planners can redo present cities or towns that are noted for specific products and/or services, and marry the best of the old with proposed new facilities, highways, and waterways. Hence, VR worlds can be beneficial to city planners since they allow the planners to interact with the ever-changing landscape.

Advertising

When referencing the area of advertising, an OLAP approach typically centers on traditional methods of measuring advertising's effectiveness which can be flawed by several assumptions. For one, advertisers assume that if a potential customer remembers a radio or television commercial, the individual is more likely to buy the product or service. This leads to overreliance on advertising which may be unique but may not influence buyers in a positive way. Or the same commercial may be repeated continuously such that the potential customer is turned off by the repetition. Such approaches miss the point because the influence of an ad campaign is revealed in many different and subtle ways. To come reasonably close to understanding how effective the advertising is doing, an advertiser must collect and analyze as much information about as many different factors as possible, from as many different sources. In turn, the advertiser considers this information in light of the complete advertising program, and not simply as it related to a specific advertisement.

Newer technologies in use can be found at The Arbitron Ratings Company, Nielsen, Information Resources, Inc., and other research companies. Nielsen, for example, installs UPC (universal product code) scanners, cousins of the holographic scanners used in supermarket checkout counters, in the same homes where its "people meters" track the television programs each family member watches. After a shopping trip, family members scan the UPC codes on products they have purchased so Nielsen can correlate what its surveyed families buy with the TV programming they watch. Analyzed along with records of total purchases (Nielsen and others buy from the supermarkets records collected by the checkout scanners), this information can reveal key correlations between an advertiser's share of the "ad space" and its market share, even at a very local level. In the latest technology upgrade, Nielsen is using a new kind of people meter that knows who is in the room. The meter compares this information to the database of images it has stored on the system, so it can say exactly who was in the room watching TV. The ultimate goal of this technology is to provide advertisers with more information which is less influenced by biases. In effect, what is now available is better information about what is actually going on.[8]

Without computerized tools, however, advertising managers cannot accurately assess all the information. Emerging are computerized-software systems intended to help advertisers analyze research data from various sources along with their own data. Systems to analyze market data have been around for some time, but the new ones stress ease-of-use, broad access to multisource data, and graphical-modeling tools. For example, Metaphor Computer Systems (Mountain View, California) markets what it calls its data-interpretation system, consisting of a workstation that features a Macintosh-style interface and software that accesses and combines data from many different sources, including Nielsen and corporate-mainframe databases. Another example is the New York-based Interactive Market Systems, Inc. (IMS). IMS sells a range of marketing-analysis software products that summarize and combine data from more than 400 databases, including Nielsen, Gallup, Simmons, and others. The MixMastr is an intermedia-planning system that evaluates total campaign reach and frequency based on all media used—print, broadcast, or whatever. Another IMS product, Link, combines information from an ad-expenditure database with audience information from several different databases to help advertisers assess audience delivery per dollar for print advertising.

Although these present computerized systems have made great strides in assisting advertising managers, there is need to reassess the direction currently being undertaken. More specifically, this centers around virtual reality. Cyberevent Group, Inc. (Brooklyn, New York) is offering a VR-software package called Experiential Advertising. It has the capability to be one of the most innovative applications for virtual-reality technology. Consumers will be able to enter and, more importantly, interact with marketing messages of all types. Consumers will be able to experience almost any marketing world. Virtual reality offers advertisers an excellent sampling opportunity that will draw attention to any product as well as provide important information about a company's products and services. Also, information could be given about discounts along with the actual issuance of the discount coupons. Hence, advertising within a VR environment is an unusual opportunity for a company to influence the buying decisions of today's consumers where buying possibilities are varied and numerous.

Other Marketing Areas

Although OLAP systems can be used to develop interesting multidimensional analysis, its impact at trade shows is not as effective as virtual reality. Today, millions of dollars are spent on trade shows for the purpose of putting a company's products in the best possible light, emphasizing whatever advantages it may have over its competition. Virtual reality is ideal for this use since it can double both as a "fly-paper" for trade show exhibits and as an educational tool. Since companies pay hundreds of thousands of dollars for video creation and rental of video walls and custom fabrication of exhibits for the trade-show floor, the resultant attractiveness of these exhibits is sometimes questionable and is difficult to quantity. However, a company that uses virtual reality in the trade-show environment can ride on the wave of enthusiasm for VR and benefit from the resulting free publicity. Virtual reality offers a proven means of attracting attendees to a booth as well as provides a unique educational experience. Typically, attendees will wait a long time to try virtual reality versus video walls or traditional interactive-computer programs and video discs.[9]

Sales and marketing departments can benefit greatly from being able to utilize interactive VR-presentations rather than relying on prerecorded audio-visual material or brochures. Products that are in the preliminary design stage can be visualized in three dimensions, thereby highlighting quite effectively their benefits. Concepts and features, including motion, can be easily portrayed. For example, a company in the distribution and warehousing sector uses a desktop VR system to win new business via an interactive-sales presentation that focuses on the visualization of the latest techniques in warehousing systems. The company is in the rapidly developing area of computerized warehousing where space optimization is the key criterion. Currently in use by the presentation department, the Virtual Reality Toolkit (VRT) is used in conjunction with other design packages to provide the company with a complete range of presentation media. Because interaction and movement are the most important elements, virtual reality is used to show how an automated warehouse will operate in real life.

In this example, virtual reality provides a sales medium for showing customers how their goods will be stored and transported. Using the VRT, objects are endowed with characteristics of friction, gravity, and movement, such that the complete working of the warehouse can be displayed realistically. In the early stages of development, the company's designers used the VRT to create sections of a warehouse and to show pallet arrival, identification, and subsequent transportation to a user-defined destination. Stored pallets can also be retrieved from the system and transported to loading bays. In essence, a virtual-reality approach provides the needed assistance to the sales department to close a sale for a new warehouse.[10]

SUMMARY

This chapter emphasized the need to rethink the entire marketing mix in order to make the most effective use of on-line analytical processing. Marketing areas that need to be addressed that underlie OLAP included a problem-finding approach to marketing, an enlarged view of core competence to develop new opportunities, a venture-analysis model, an expanded view of market research, database marketing useful to develop knowledge about customers, and the utilization of principles from Profit Impact of Marketing Strategies. Essentially, these newer directions focused on market leaders who know what customers want when developing a company's products and services. Or to state it another way, revamped marketing thinking stresses the fact that the company knows what its customers want before they know themselves, and influences the direction that the market will take today and tomorrow. For the most part, creating a new way of thinking about OLAP systems must come initially from the higher levels of marketing management. In the second half of the chapter, applications that showed the relationship of rethinking the marketing function to OLAP were presented. Additionally, marketing applications that can benefit from an OLAP-VR integration were highlighted. Overall, these applications demonstrate the wide diversity of OLAP, including VR, to the marketing function.

NOTES

1. Gary Hamel and C. K. Prahalad, "The Core Competence of the Corporation," *Harvard Business Review*, May–June 1990, p. 79.

2. Gary Hamel and C. K. Prahalad, "Corporate Imagination and Expeditionary Marketing," *Harvard Business Review*, July–August 1991, pp. 81–82.

3. Ibid., p. 83.

4. Ibid., pp. 85–86.

5. Paula Smith, "Unique Tool for Marketers: PIMS," *Management Review*, January 1977, pp. 32–34.

6. Robert D. Buzzell and Bradley T. Gale, *The PIMS Principles: Linking Strategy to Performance* (New York: The Free Press, 1988).

7. George Black, "Wellcome Prescribes OLAP for Decision Support," *Software Magazine*, December 1995, pp. 94–95.

8. Ned Snell, "How Hard Is Our Advertising Working?" *EDGE*, January/February 1990, pp. 44–46.

9. Jonathan R. Merril, "VR for Medical Training and Trade Show 'Fly-Paper,' " *Virtual Reality World*, May/June 1994, pp. 56–57.

10. Andy Tait, "Authoring Virtual Worlds on the Desktop," *Virtual Reality Special Report*, published by *AI Expert* (San Francisco, Calif.: Miller Freeman, 1993), p. 12.

8

Manufacturing in an OLAP
Environment

ISSUES EXPLORED

- How important is a broad-based view of manufacturing in an OLAP-operating mode?
- What are the typical newer directions that underlie an effective OLAP-operating environment for manufacturing?
- What important manufacturing areas lend themselves to on-line analytical processing?
- How can multidimensional analysis assist managers in the areas of purchasing plus production planning and control for a typical manufacturer?
- What areas of manufacturing benefit from an OLAP-VR integration?

OUTLINE

Manufacturing in an OLAP Environment
  A Broad-Based View: Computer Integrated Manufacturing
Newer Directions in Manufacturing That Underlie OLAP
  A Problem-Finding Approach to Manufacturing
  Reengineering to Improve Productivity
  Focus on Total Quality Management (TQM)
  Utilization of Purchase-Performance Models
  Value Analysis to Reduce Product Costs
  ERP Systems Provide Unprecedented Levels of Functionality and Integration
  Computer-Aided Simulation of Manufacturing Activities
Manufacturing Areas That Lend Themselves to an OLAP Environment

MANUFACTURING IN AN OLAP ENVIRONMENT

The marketplace, as highlighted in Chapter 7, is rapidly changing in new ways that are different from the past. Worldwide competition demands a renewed emphasis on product and service quality. Typically, in a Japanese company, a product is examined in great detail before it is made, that is, in the design stage. In turn, the manufacturing process is engineered to be stable and reliable. If the design is good, as well as the process, quality is inherent. In the United States, companies have now realized that quality improvement is essential. It is not just good business but is essential to a company's success. It is necessary not only to build a product faster and cheaper, but also to make that product better. This approach to quality emphasizes the cost-effectiveness of productivity in all areas of a company—from design to the assembly line. It is easy to forget that improvement in the office is as important as improvement in manufacturing or elsewhere in a company.

It is from this perspective that there is a need to rethink the manufacturing function from a broader perspective—the subject matter of the first part of this chapter. Next, appropriate OLAP applications in purchasing and manufacturing are presented wherein total quality management is assumed. The concept of total quality control centers on applying quality principles not only in the factory, but also to every operation, including dealings with suppliers. At the end of the chapter, the integration of on-line analytical processing with virtual reality is set forth and illustrated. All in all, an OLAP approach to manufacturing allows for improving quality up and down the supply chain to the ultimate customer. In addition, it gives managers and their staffs access to multidimensional analyses along the way that is not found in prior information systems.

A Broad-Based View: Computer Integrated Manufacturing

As a starting point, it is helpful to look at the total framework that underlies all manufacturing activities in a typical company. Such a framework today and in the future centers on a broad-based view that can be called computer integrated manufacturing (CIM). For the most part, CIM means blending manufacturing with marketing, finance, accounting, personnel, as well as other functional areas where deemed necessary. CIM is currently crucial to the survival of manufacturers because it provides the levels of planning and control for manufacturing along with the flexibility to change with the times. The basic objective of CIM is to change management's thinking by establishing a framework within which manufacturing operations are defined, funded, managed, and coordinated. This framework requires specific mechanisms for production planning, cost control, projection selection and justification, project management, and project performance monitoring. The role of the enterprise view of CIM is to ensure that the appropriate levels and types of integration are appropriate.

Related to the CIM concept is the whole idea of *flexibility*. Flexibility at the plant level refers to the ability to adapt or change. However, there are many ways to characterize such an ability. That is, one plant manager might be talking about the cost of changing from one product to the next, or another plant manager might be talking about the ability to increase or decrease production volumes to fit the market demand. Yet another might be talking about the ability to increase the range of available products. All these abilities refer to flexibility but they require different courses of action to develop. Essentially, the type of flexibility a given company should employ is determined by its competitive environment. Whether one is referring to products, production volumes, or manufacturing processes, flexibility is about increasing or decreasing output, or achieving a uniform output. As such, the CIM concept not only depends on the technical factors to make the appropriate changes, but also on the people factor to achieve desired results.

Updating the flexibility concept, there is a current trend that centers on *agile manufacturing*. Agile manufacturing is currently defined as the ability to respond quickly to rapidly changing markets driven by customer-based valuing of products and services. It says that agile companies have the ability to reconfigure operations, processes, and business relationships swiftly. Thus, the agile concept emphasizes ultraflexible production facilities; constantly shifting alliances among suppliers, producers, and customers; and direct feedback of sales data into the factories.

Using state-of-the-art design and manufacturing technologies, many companies have gotten better at meeting customers' needs, responding to changing markets, and producing higher-quality products. They have reduced paper flow, prototyped products quickly, shortened cycle times, linked supply lines electronically, created virtual inventory and companies, and given customers more choices. Some results have been widely reported, such as Motorola's customized pagers and Levi Strauss's customer-tailored jeans. Others not as widely reported include the Big Three automakers, the aerospace industry, semiconductor makers, the computer industry, and pharmaceutical companies. All have been able to speed up design, manufacturing, and customization using the agile concept to meet changing customer needs.

Today, when rethinking the design and manufacturing activities of a company, the CIM concept needs to be expanded to include virtual worlds. More to the point, expanded CIM virtual worlds have the potential to assist management in reengineering their operations, whether they are manufacturing or otherwise, to improve the productivity of the company. As discussed in the next sections, reengineering focuses on doing more with less such that the productivity of personnel and equipment are improved. As an example, an experimental assembly modeling system at the Northrop Corporation has been tested that radically changes the way aircraft are produced. The prototype system makes use of 3-D stereo display and input devices to simulate the assembly process. The system could save money in development costs by eliminating the need for full-scale mockups. Thus, Northrop's assembly modeler is a good example of the benefits of stereo viewing and desktop VR in manufacturing.[1]

NEWER DIRECTIONS IN MANUFACTURING THAT UNDERLIE OLAP

In manufacturing, newer directions that are related to OLAP systems are generally complex because there is a need to relate manufacturing activities to many other functional areas of the organization. To produce meaningful and operational information for planning and controlling manufacturing operations, changes must be made in the decision processes. In addition, appropriate mathematical and statistical models, which allow manufacturing managers to control their activities on a "now" basis, need to be introduced to assist them and their support personnel in performing their daily tasks. In the material to follow, a number of important newer directions that impact OLAP for assisting manufacturing managers and their staffs are given. More specifically, they relate to the following: (1) a problem-finding approach to manufacturing, (2) reengineering to improve productivity, (3) focus on total quality management, (4) utilization of purchase-performance models, (5) value analysis to reduce product costs, (6)

ERP systems provide unprecented levels of functionality and integration, and (7) computer-aided simulation of manufacturing activities.

A Problem-Finding Approach to Manufacturing

The major emphasis of a problem-finding approach is to provide manufacturing executives with a broad view of production planning and a wide span of control over manufacturing activities. In an environment of rapid change, this is accomplished by forward information integration. External-environmental information must be integrated with forecasting information. This, in turn, feeds the material-requirements plan, the output of which goes into the purchasing and production planning and control systems. New data are captured at all points, thereby providing information for inventory and accounts payable. Although much of the thrust for information integration comes from the increased integration required of manufacturing, a large portion is generated by the need for effective management of the production processes. Better production planning and more effective material acquisition policies demand more accurate and timely information to support their operations. Overall, the integration of information from other related systems with a manufacturing planning and control system is a must for effective day-to-day operations.

For the typical manufacturing-oriented organization, the preceding integration process starts with the five-year strategic plan. More specifically, in terms of the manufacturing area, it is related to product-line planning, facilities planning, and personnel planning as developed by the corporate-planning staff for top management. Next, these manufacturing-oriented long-range plans are translated into medium-range plans, and finally into short-range plans as the current-year plans. In effect, the long-term strategic plan that locates future marketing problems and solves them in terms of future opportunities is eventually refined into integrated plans for this year's manufacturing operations. From that view, it is easy to understand why timely planning and control of manufacturing resources through problem finding and the resulting information integration can be a vital factor in the long-term success of an organization.

To assist in the information integration process for effective problem finding and problem solving, the manufacturing planning and control system utilizes appropriate mathematical and statistical models that assist in planning and control of its resources. It is a logical approach for overcoming common management problems encountered in manufacturing operations, such as the misuse of available productive capacity. *Productivity* sometimes is far less than it should be or could be. Techniques to plan and control manufacturing resources are readily available, but only a few organizations have learned to use this combination of mathematical models, computerized systems, and company personnel effectively. Many industrial-oriented organizations, ranging from small to large ones, have recently implemented these proven techniques. Now they effectively utilize their productive capacity even in a world of persistent uncertainty and growing complexity.

Reengineering to Improve Productivity

Reengineering is currently one of the most important directions for business because the most successful and promising companies must develop new techniques that will allow them to survive in an increasingly competitive climate. To reengineer, that is, reinvent their companies, managers need to abandon past organizational and operational principles and procedures and create entirely new ones. No matter what industry companies are in, how technologically sophisticated their products or services are, or what their national origin is, basically they trace their work styles and organizational roots back to the prototypical pin factory that economist Adam Smith described in *The Wealth of Nations* (published in 1776). Smith's principle of the division of labor embodied his observation that some number of *specialists*, each performing a single step in the manufacture of a pin, could make far more pins in a day than the same number of *generalists*, each engaged in making whole pins. Today's airlines, car manufacturers, accounting firms, and computer manufacturers, to name a few, have all been built around Smith's central idea. Typically, the larger the organization, the more specialized is the work, and the more separate steps into which work is divided, whether manufacturing or non-manufacturing firms.

Business reengineering means starting from scratch, that is, it centers on forgetting how work was done in the past and deciding how it can best be done now. Old job titles and old organizational arrangements—divisions, departments, groups, and so forth—cease to matter. What matters, however, is how work is organized given the demands of today's markets and the power of today's technologies. At the center of business reengineering is the concept of discontinuous thinking, that is identifying and abandoning the outdated rules and fundamental assumptions that underlie current business operations. Every company is replete with implicit rules of the past, for example, local warehouses are necessary for good customer service, or local marketing decisions are made at headquarters. These rules are based on assumptions about technology, people, and organizational goals that no longer hold.

To reengineer a company's business procedures, it is necessary to rethink these procedures and redesign the *business processes* to achieve improvements, so that the company's employees go from being specialists to generalists to improve productivity. A business process is a collection of activities that takes one or more kinds of input and creates an output that is of value to the customer. For example, when filling an order, the delivery of finished products is the value that the process creates. However, Adam Smith's notion of breaking work into its simplest tasks and assigning each of these to a specialist tends to lose sight of the larger objective, which is to get the goods into the hands of the customer who ordered them.

As an example of reengineering, where employees go from specialists to generalists, consider the accounts-payable department of the Ford Motor Company. Previously, 500 accounts-payable clerks (specialists) spent the majority of their time straightening out the problems whereby purchase orders, invoices, and receiving documents did not match. However, with the new system, the clerk at the receiving dock takes in the goods and depresses a button on the terminal keyboard that tells the company's database that the goods have arrived. Receipt of the goods is now recorded in the database, and the computer automatically issues and sends a check to the supplier at the appropriate time. On the other hand, if the goods do not correspond to an outstanding purchase order in the database, the clerk on the dock will refuse the shipment and send it back to the supplier. Thus, payment authorization, which used to be performed by the accounts-payable specialist, is now accomplished by the receiving dock generalist. The old process fostered enough complexity to keep 500 clerks busy. The new process comes close to eliminating the need for an accounts-payable department altogether. Ford now has just 125 people involved in supplier payment. In some parts of Ford, the head count in accounts payable is a small fraction of its former size.[2]

Focus on Total Quality Management (TQM)

After being viewed as a manufacturing problem in the past, quality has become a service issue—not just for service-sector businesses like communications, health care, and finance but for the service side of manufacturing companies as well. The focus is on *total quality management* (TQM), that is, quality in the offering itself and in all the services that come with it. If product quality is essentially the same across the industry, service becomes the distinguishing factor. Overall, TQM has become a prerequisite for survival today and tomorrow.

With TQM, the postwar quality movement has moved into its third stage. When the growing popularity of Japanese automobiles, televisions, and radios forced U.S. manufacturers to take another look at themselves in the late 1970s, most companies were still in what quality experts call the first or inspection phase, relying on sampling techniques to get rid of defective items. Too often, however, they did not. In 1980—the year an NBC White Paper introduced audiences to W. Edwards Deming, the American statistician who had shown the Japanese how to use process controls to catch defects at the source—manufacturers who took the issue seriously started moving into the second, or quality-control, phase. Now, with TQM, quality is no longer solely in the quality-control department. It is sponsored by top management and diffused throughout the company.[3]

Essentially, employees see a gap between what the company says is important in regard to quality and the company's follow-through. Needless to say, this is less than a rousing vote of confidence in the quality performance of American businesses. Employees want to see better results. Substantial proportions of survey respondents said the quality programs in their companies have had either no effect or a negative effect in specific areas (ranging from 22 percent negative on communications to 42 percent negative on their pay and benefits). Workers stated that the two most important ways the company can make it easier for them to do high-quality work are, first, to provide more training in job skills and, second, to offer job security. Other things, in order of importance, that workers would like to see their companies do are the following: have a more supportive attitude from top management, train workers in interpersonal working skills, respond faster to employee ideas, offer more up-to-date tools and technology, have a more supportive attitude from middle management, and offer better access to available information.

As an example, take the case of Federal Express, which handles 1.5 million packages per day. The reason that customers can rely on such a complex organization is that Federal Express has made a 100-percent service level and a 100-percent customer satisfaction level as its key goals. Every employee has the right, the authority, or backing to do whatever is necessary to satisfy the customer. Essentially, Federal Express has put a lot into mechanisms to feed information back to the people who are doing the job so, if they have a quality problem or an error, they know it and can fix it. The company has spent a lot of time training its people in quality methods. Company employees are educated on how important good quality is to the company's future viability. In each of the preceding points, monetary issues play a role, but they are consistently ranked by the survey respondents below other concerns. The points are a road map to quality by the people who work with the company's customers.[4]

Utilization of Purchase-Performance Models

Before meaningful purchasing reports and evaluation can be obtained by manufacturing executives, mathematical formulas that reference the corporation's database must be employed. These models are generally based on *price, quality,* and *delivery,* which are weighted according to their relative importance. The weights selected represent the judgment of the purchasing department as well as that of manufacturing executives. No matter what weights are agreed upon, they form the basis for evaluating vendor and buyer performance. Due to the importance of the weighting factors, they are discussed below.

Price. To measure the price variable, past costs provide the best available standard for the present. Current costs that are considerably above those of the previous period is a signal that the purchasing function might be performing poorly. Of course, it is possible that an increase in price is due to a general rise of prices in the economy. But such an all-encompassing movement would tend to affect all prices; in such situations, management should be able to filter out the impact of this general increase. More typically, variation of prices is due to a variety of causes. It is this type of variation that management wants isolated and remedied, if possible.

Quality. Price is not the sole determinant of a "good buy." The firm must also consider the quality of goods it needs before it is possible to evaluate whether it really did get a good buy. The receiving department must examine the goods to determine whether or not incoming shipments contain defective items. Although the typical corporation does not employ extensive statistical sampling of incoming parts and materials, many other firms have an extensive and organized inspection procedure. No matter what procedure is employed, a measure of the proportion of deliveries that actually are accepted is useful for measuring the effectiveness of purchasing.

Delivery. Late deliveries, like poor-quality materials and purchased parts, can negate a seemingly good buy. At their worst, late deliveries may result in closing down a production line or even in the loss of future sales. From this viewpoint, it is easy to visualize why a measure of how well vendors meet their specified delivery dates is essential for evaluation purposes. Also, such a measure is useful in evaluating the delivery dependability of particular vendors, and in evaluating the buyers who choose to purchase regularly from such vendors.

Purchase-Performance Index. The aggregate of the price, quality, and delivery indices is a purchase-performance index, sometimes called PPI. The purchase performance index (a single value) summarizes the actual performance against expected performance, stated on a quarterly basis or some other time period. It is a composite index, requiring some kind of averaging or weighting process in order to combine these three indices into one. The weights depend on purchasing management's judgment as to the relative importance of each index factor. Common weighting factors are to assign a weight of 50 to the price index, and 25 to each of the quality and delivery indices. Such an assignment of weights indicates that the organization places twice the emphasis on price when compared to the remaining two factors.

The purchase-performance index, based on the foregoing weighting factors, is 105; its price, quality, and delivery indices are 94, 107, and 125, respectively.

Index	Index Value	Weight	Index Value × Weight
Price	94	50	4,700
Quality	107	25	2,675
Delivery	125	25	3,125
		100	10,500

PPI = 10,500/100 = 105

The above PPI, which is over 100, represents an improvement over the prior period. A value of less than 100 indicates just the reverse.

Value Analysis to Reduce Product Costs

Because expanded computer integrated manufacturing centers on a very broad approach to manufacturing, it also includes the final product design by engineering. To assist a manufacturer in designing products that are profitable, *value analysis* or *value engineering* is needed. This approach requires that the engineer adopt a broader point of view and consider whether the parts contained in the finished product perform their required functions both as efficiently and as inexpensively as possible. The appraisal focuses on the function that the part—or the larger assembly containing the part—performs. In an inspection-oriented plant, for example, more than half of all workers are somehow involved in finding and reworking rejects. The total investment in this process can account for 20 percent to 40 percent of production costs, and in extreme cases, 50 percent. In contrast, the Japanese inspect a product before it is made, that is, in the design stage, and they engineer the manufacturing process to be stable and reliable.

To illustrate a practical value-analysis approach within a TQM environment, the product is dismantled and each part is mounted adjacent to its mating part on a table. The point is to demonstrate visually the functional relationships of the various parts. Each component is studied as it relates to the performance of the complete unit, rather than as an isolated element. A value-analysis checklist contains literally hundreds of questions and key ideas for reducing overall costs, as well as maintaining the same level of product performance.

Typical questions that can be used are set forth as follows.

- Can the part be eliminated?
- If the part is not standard, can a standard part be used?
- If it is a standard part, does it complement the finished product or is it a misfit?
- Can the weight be reduced with lower-priced materials?
- Are closer tolerances specified than are necessary?
- Is unnecessary machining performed on the item?
- Are unnecessary finishes required?
- Can one produce the part less expensively in the plant, or should one buy from the outside?
- Is the product properly classified for shipping purposes to obtain lowest transportation costs?
- Can the cost of packaging be reduced?
- Do certain parts, such as precision motors and parts, exceed the expected life of the finished product?

When using value engineering to appraise overall costs, possibilities for making component-part design simplifications are frequently more apparent than is possible under the conventional design conditions. This in no way reflects unfavorably on the work done by the design engineer; the discovery of such potential improvements is the result of an analysis with a substantially broader orientation than that possessed by the original designer. A value-analysis study undertaken by a typical company utilizes the background and skills of several people, because it is not possible to find the multiplicity of skills and experiences of that group in a single designer. Resulting design changes often permit the substitution of standardized production operations for more expensive operations requiring special setup work. In other cases, an entirely different material or production process turns out to be more efficient than the one originally specified. In the final analysis, value analysis, operating within a TQM environment, contributes to the profitability of new products for a typical manufacturing-oriented company.

ERP Systems Provide Unprecedented Levels of Functionality and Integration

Oliver Wight, a key proponent of manufacturing-process automation many years ago, used the term "MRP-II" (manufacturing resource planning) to distinguish this discipline from the narrower field of MRP (material requirements planning). In effect, Wight was peering into the manufacturing side of the enterprise from a business view: from accounting, purchasing, marketing, customer service, sales, operations, and information systems. Today, however, a major problem is the lack of integration with non-manufacturing systems. Most of today's MRP and MRP-II packages fail to allow an employee to look into the computer and get a snapshot of the status of any customer order, whether it is a production, marketing, or a finance view. Yet this is exactly what a company needs to do today. The reason for this problem is that most MRP and MRP-II packages on the market work off large computer mainframes and cumbersome languages. Writing links to corporate accounting or marketing databases is possible, but fraught with expense and frustration. The primary goal of manufacturing software today should be customer service: getting the right product to the right place at the right time at the right price.

Because traditional MRP and MRP-II systems, even in client/server environments, are too rigid for some users, some developers are already reslanting their products to newer manufacturing models: Enterprise Resource Planning (ERP) and Customer-Oriented Manufacturing Management Software (COMMS). Typically, MRP-II is host-based, proprietary, and hard to modify, while ERP systems are open systems, based on RDBMS software in 4GL client/server environments.

Fundamentally, enterprise resource planning is real-time manufacturing software that incorporates the entire supply chain from sales and order to production, inventory, and distribution. It comes under the umbrella of the CIM concept set forth previously. Since companies are implementing client/server systems that manage the entire supply chain (from the time a product order comes in to the moment it is delivered), ERP systems represent an integrated set of applications modules that ties together a host of functions. As such, they are highly integrated application suites that support many processes, including sales forecasting, order management, purchasing, production scheduling, inventory management, distribution, scheduling, engineering, maintenance, and accounting. These systems become the nerve center of a manufacturer. Overall, enterprise resource planning systems have the capability to provide competitive advantage through lower costs and faster response time.

While many vendors sell systems that manage different parts of a manufacturer's business, only a few actually offer client/server software that spans most of a manufacturer's needs. It should be noted that the skills necessary to create ERP systems for client/server operations are expensive and not readily available today. Hence, some organizations that previously generated their own core applications are now outsourcing software development to package vendors.

In contrast, some developers are proponents of COMMS, which unites a manufacturer's departments and suppliers around its customers. COMMS, allows a company to be more responsive to customers in terms of quality and ability in order to meet their needs on a timely basis. Because the entire manufacturing order is organized with the customer at the hub, managers can tell at a glance which plant has excess capacity, and can provide an accurate price and delivery cost if a product is not in stock.

Computer-Aided Simulation of Manufacturing Activities

Simulations in the area of manufacturing are hardly new, although the ability to watch the simulations run as animated images is. To illustrate the simulation's results using this approach, a simulation programming language from Systems Modeling Corporation (Sewickley, Pennsylvania) is currently available, called Siman. Siman's animation feature shows how a company's products move through an assembly line. Typically what one gets out of the simulation is just numbers with stacks of computer printouts. The utilization of Siman allows the user to see what is actually going on.

For the most part, simulations provide more information than just the start-to-end response time. They can graph how much traffic is in various queues and how much delay and productive time there is in different places. For example, if it turned out that the biggest bottleneck occurred in the lathe department, the company could assign more people to that department. The move turned out to be the most efficient way of evening out the production flow as opposed to adding personnel to other production departments, like small assembly or major assembly operations. Overall, computer-aided simulation takes advantage of all the information available; and by performing the simulation in a structured way, it ensures consistency and traceability of its output.

Running an assembly line is just one kind of business process that simulation software can help streamline. With emphasis today on business-process reengineering (BPR), the Continuum Company (an Austin, Texas-based supplier of software and services to the financial industry) uses simulation to help insurance companies reconfigure the flow of paperwork. Queuing problems turn out to be a most important issue in business workflows. Needless to say, it helps to have a simulation tool actually calculate queuing problems. As an example, by re-training employees to perform more than one function at a time, an insurance company reduced the time it took a document to pass through this business-process from between seven and ten days to less than one day with the same skill set. Without the simulation, recommendations would have been based on the intuition born of experience. Simulating the renovated process reduced the risk that intuition might prove them wrong.

Where experience is lacking, simulation can often take its place. One such area is in the design of client/server applications where software engineers decide what part of the application should run on the client and what should be on the server. Typically, businesses are somewhat unsure about client/server technology because there are a tremendous number of unknowns. Although mainframe systems have comparably few variables and can be handled somewhat easily, the same cannot be said for non-mainframe environments. Continuum developers, for example, simulated the performance of its workflow-management product, Business Process Manager, which incorporates an object-oriented database and a rules-based knowledge system. It expected to find a bottleneck at the computer's central processor where reasoning was taking place. Instead, the simulation revealed that the real problem lay with the capacity of a small utility used to move data around in the system. Hence, more attention was paid to how the utility was used.[5]

MANUFACTURING AREAS THAT LEND THEMSELVES TO AN OLAP ENVIRONMENT

To better understand implementation efforts that are related to an OLAP environment, it should be recognized that there is a great deal of complexity involved in this area of manufacturing. For this reason, outside consultants may be useful. While supportive consulting may improve the chances for success of an OLAP system, there is a lot of risk involved. The possibility always exists that manufacturing managers for whom the system is intended will find it cumbersome, too slow, or not intuitive or informative enough. Despite the time and potential risks involved in development, a successful OLAP system can have far-reaching positive effects since a well-designed system allows managers to respond immediately to timely manufacturing issues. In addition, manufacturing managers can use the operational policies of successful manufacturing areas to examine troubled operational areas. An OLAP system can break down a successful operation into specific elements. In light of these comments, two common OLAP-manufacturing applications which are related to purchasing and production planning and control are set forth below.

As expected, on-line analytical processing is quite useful in a number of other manufacturing operations. More specifically, engineering efforts prior to daily manufacturing operations are a natural since their management can analyze the ins and outs of engineering projects over time and determine appropriate rules-of-thumb that can be applied to future engineering projects. Similarly, an OLAP system can assist manufacturing managers in analyzing manufacturing operations and quality control problems plus those related to inventories, from the raw-materials stage to the finished-goods stage. In fact, OLAP systems are useful to most manufacturing managers in their analyses for most situations, starting with incoming materials at the initial stage of the manufacturing process to those physical distribution activities after the manufacturing process.

AN OLAP APPROACH TO PURCHASING

Typically, the major functions of a manufacturing-oriented company consist of buying, maintenance, and follow-up. In these fast-changing times, there is a need to go one step further by getting a broader perspective of these functions. This can be accomplished by having manufacturing managers oversee and review purchasing operations. The purchasing areas to be investigated include reengineering the purchasing process, vendor and buyer evaluation, as well as purchased materials and parts evaluation. In addition, product review using value analysis and analysis of critical purchasing areas are found below. Fundamentally, all of these areas are explored within an OLAP-operating mode.

Reengineering the Purchasing Process

A starting point for a newer direction in the purchasing process centers around reengineering in terms of its relationships between the purchasing department and its internal customers, its outside suppliers, and the IS department. Reengineering offers many companies the opportunity to broaden and satisfy their relationships with suppliers and to understand their own internal relationships better. Once they dissect their own business practices, many companies find that purchasing is not an island unto itself, but a complex web of interactions that takes a purchase from request to reality. From this broadened perspective, there is a movement toward improved productivity for not only purchasing, but also for others involved in the total procurement process.

There are several examples. Pacific Bell has created a purchasing process from scratch as part of its overall reengineering efforts, shifting the focus from processing purchase orders to managing relationships with clients. At TRW's High Reliability Electronics Product Group, the procurement department became a reengineering project for an entire business division looking for a quick success. The experience highlighted the difficulties of implementing new ideas through

Figure 8.1(a)
A Monthly Buyer-Performance Report for a Typical Manufacturing-Oriented Company

Monthly Buyer-Performance Report					For Month Ending 6/30/9-	
					Date of Report 7/2/9-	
Buyer Name	Total Amount Purchased Last Month	Index Price	Quality	Delivery	PPI	Total Amount Purchased This Month
R. Breyer	$475,200.75	105.15	100.50	98.25	102.26	$481,275.75
J. Cosgrove	445,988.22	120.25	75.15	78.15	98.45	450,978.12
J. Fox	501,657.67	99.50	102.50	105.15	101.66	471,981.68
.	.	.	.	.	.	.
.	.	.	.	.	.	.

IS. And the State of Oregon used reengineering technology to put the responsibility for researching and initiating bids into the hands of the bidders and to make the process more competitive.[6]

Analysis of Vendor and Buyer Performance

Related to a typical company's reengineering efforts is the assurance that purchasing management has the ability to evaluate its vendors' and buyers' performance. As an example, a typical monthly vendor-performance report is an evaluation of outside vendors who have supplied raw materials, supplies, and parts to a typical manufacturing-oriented company. A comparison of the total amount purchased last month and this month using a PPI index (as set forth earlier in the chapter) gives an indication as to whether buyers have been shifting business to or from certain vendors. Normally, it would be expected that vendors with indices below 100 (expected PPI is 100) would be currently used less than they had been in the past.

Just as vendors can be evaluated, so can the company's buyers. From a managerial-purchasing viewpoint, monthly buyer-performance reports have great meaning. Purchasing managers generally have little direct control over vendors, but they exercise considerable control over their buyers. By having buyers evaluated on a comparable basis, purchasing managers can pinpoint the weaknesses of their buying staff. Those buyers who are price-minded at the expense of quality materials and prompt delivery will be highlighted. An example of this point is brought out in Figure 8.1(a), in which Mr. Joseph Cosgrove is shown as a buyer with a relatively low PPI. The monthly buyer-performance report can be refined for more detailed analysis. Specifically, detailed analyses on price, quality, and delivery can be made for buyers (this is also true for vendors).

Figure 8.1(b)
Multidimensional Analysis of Buyer Performance for the Three Buyers Shown in Figure 8.1(a)

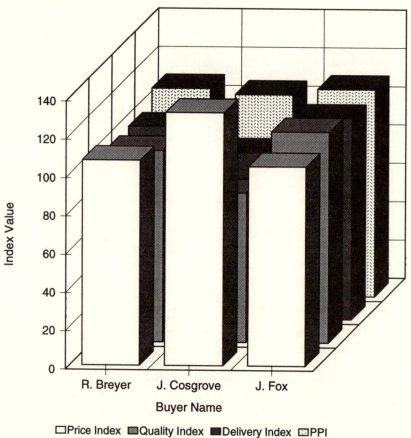

□Price Index ▨Quality Index ■Delivery Index ▨PPI

In addition, both vendor and buyer performance can be evaluated by utilizing multidimensional analysis. As shown in Figure 8.1(b) for buyer analysis, the low value indexes for Joseph Cosgrove stand out more than those shown in a monthly buyer-performance report when comparison is made to other buyers. The relatively high height for the price index and the low height for quality and delivery indexes are indicative of a buyer who is price-minded at the expense of quality and delivery of incoming purchased goods. For a typical manufacturing company, the low index for quality many indicate that the company must spend some time in cleaning up the materials for production and/or spending additional time for machining before the manufacturing process can begin. Needless to say, there is a need for a meeting between the purchasing director and Joseph Cosgrove to sort out these problems, and to determine how to im-

Figure 8.2(a)
A Monthly Purchased-Materials and Parts-Performance Report for a Typical Manufacturing-Oriented Company

Monthly Purchased Materials and Parts Performance Report			For Month Ending 6/30/9-				
						Date of Report	7/2/9-
Purchased Materials/ Part Number	Total Amount Purchased Last Month	Price	Index Quality	Delivery	PPI	Total Amount Purchased This Month	
10772	$18,950.78	98.02	103.50	107.25	101.70	$19,059.75	
17020	4,975.25	105.78	98.25	96.54	101.59	6,205.95	
19203	20,800.50	110.90	93.70	105.90	105.35	20,221.50	
.	.	.	.	.	.	.	
.	.	.	.	.	.	.	

prove the buyer's performance so that his overall PPI can meet the expected 100.

Analysis of Purchased Materials and Parts

Going beyond evaluation of vendors and buyers, there is a need to evaluate purchased materials and parts by purchasing executives. As shown in Figure 8.2(a), a monthly purchased-materials and parts-performance report centers on whether or not the corporation is receiving value for parts purchased. If the *price* index is below 100, this might indicate that prices are rising, and consideration might be given to replacing this purchased raw material or part with another. The *quality* index might also be important if certain finished goods are critical for the maintenance of the company's reputation, especially if difficulty has been experienced in the past. In a similar manner, the *delivery* index might be critical in terms of meeting final customer shipment dates. The monthly purchased-materials and parts-performance report gives purchasing executives an overview of what the buyers are procuring and how effective they are. Equally important, it provides pertinent information for the company's buyers.

An alternative way to view the purchased materials and parts information in Figure 8.2(a) is to reference Figure 8.2(b). In this figure, the performance of the purchased materials by part numbers indicates that there is no one direction in terms of the various indexes. In fact, the established index of 100 or better is not found in all cases, except for the PPI value. Although this final index is favorable, the other indexes may be indicative of problem areas that need to be addressed by purchasing management. Thus, a picture of what these indexes are versus the 100 or better may be a signal for purchasing management to take a

Figure 8.2(b)
Multidimensional Analysis of Three Purchased Materials and Parts Shown in
Figure 8.2(a)

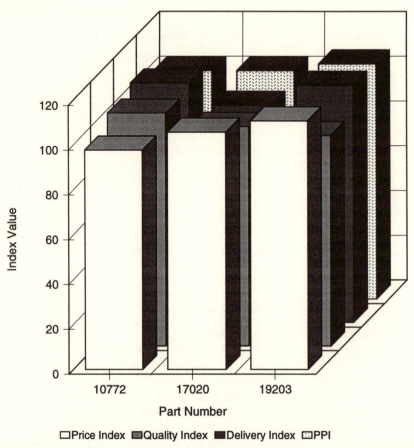

Part Number

□Price Index ▨Quality Index ■Delivery Index ▥PPI

harder look behind these figures, like more extensive analysis of vendor and buyer performance, as well as make-versus-buy analysis.

Product Review Using Value Analysis

For a truly successful evaluation of the purchasing function, it is helpful to employ value analysis. As noted earlier in the chapter, this concept centers on evaluating whether the parts contained in the finished product perform the required function both as efficiently and as inexpensively as possible. Using a value-analysis approach, the appraisal focuses on the function that the part, or the larger assembly containing the part, performs. To illustrate, products of a typical manufacturing-oriented company are dismantled and each part is mounted adjacent to its mating part on a table. The idea is to demonstrate visually the functional relationships of the various parts. Each component is studied by the purchasing-review group under the direction of manufacturing managers as it relates to the performance of the complete unit rather than as an isolated element. A value-analysis checklist contains many questions (see prior section of the chapter) and key ideas for reducing overall costs as well as maintaining the same level of product performance. Answers to these questions will go a long way for a successful review of products that the company is presently producing.

Analysis of Critical Purchasing Areas

For a broad view of the purchasing function, this can be accomplished by having manufacturing managers, working with their purchasing counterparts, evaluate critical purchasing areas via multidimensional analysis. From a very broad perspective, they could include:

- assessment of outsourcing among multiple vendors using a cost/benefit analysis
- analysis if purchasing under uncertainty using statistical methods
- comparison of the results of forming partnerships to buy at lower prices
- analysis of availability of raw materials and parts to meet present and future growth
- the continued quality of raw materials and parts for current products to meet present and future growth
- the capability of obtaining raw materials and parts for new products being developed.

In terms of another perspective that is oriented toward day-to-day operations, critical purchasing areas could include the following:

- measure of idle machines and/or personnel resulting from a lack of purchased supplies
- measure of the extent of successful substitutes of materials and parts
- value of purchase orders subjected to competitive bidding, as a percentage of total orders placed
- ratio of rejected purchases to total purchases
- savings on discounts and quantity purchases.

Attention to the foregoing areas provides manufacturing as well as purchasing managers with the capability to plan and retain control over operations as times change. Of course, it should be recognized that new critical items come into play over time and should be added to the above listing as deemed necessary. As usual, many of the above purchasing areas can be related to a number of recurring and ad hoc ''what-if'' questions to get a handle on these critical areas.

It is up to manufacturing and purchasing managers to raise pertinent questions and answer them in an OLAP-operating mode.

AN OLAP APPROACH TO PRODUCTION PLANNING AND CONTROL

The production planning and control department at the plant level for a typical manufacturing-oriented company is responsible for all physical movements between manufacturing departments and within their respective work centers. This important department coordinates all activities concerning a production order from its initial recording, through inventory layup and manufacturing, to getting the finished goods ready for shipment to customers, that is, direct shipments, or to company warehouses for shipment subsequently to customers. Production planning and control relies heavily upon the plant's database and its communications with all manufacturing work centers. Although daily manufacturing activities are the responsibility of the production planning and control department, they need to be analyzed periodically by manufacturing managers for efficiency and effectiveness just as was performed for purchasing activities (as was demonstrated above). In this manner, manufacturing managers can be assured that short-range manufacturing plans are being implemented on a daily basis as mandated. Before looking at planned and actual manufacturing activities, an overview of manufacturing and their relationship with production planning and control is set forth, along with the utilization of just-in-time inventories and determining the appropriate production planning and control technique.

Manufacturing Partnerships and Their Tie-In with Production Planning and Control

Not too long ago, many large manufacturers, especially in Japan, formed *keiretsu* or company partnerships by grouping the subcontractors who supply them with parts. The result is a production system, distributed among many companies, that has helped manufacturers strengthen their global competitiveness. More recently, however, the subcontracting system has started changing to reflect the structural sophistication in Japanese industries. Automakers, electric machinery manufacturers, and other large Japanese firms, which are suffering from sagging demand and decreasing earnings, are increasingly pressuring subcontractors to cut production costs. If they do not comply, they will be excluded from the keiretsu.

In this new and realistic business environment, many subcontractors are looking for business partners outside their company groups. This presents a good opportunity for subcontractors to become independent. The keiretsu system is evolving from the existing pyramid-type coalition to horizontal or network-type coalitions. In the process, an increasing number of subcontractors are seeking to improve their technology and production to satisfy key manufacturers. Some are pursuing new business partners outside their company groups, while others aim to become independent specialists in processing or manufacturing.

Additionally, a stronger yen encouraged leading Japanese manufacturers to shift production overseas. Consequently, many subcontractors advanced into overseas markets, not only to supply parts to key manufacturers, but also to help train local employees. In the long run, these actions are expected to bring about the internationalization of the Japanese-style production system. Car makers, for example, are working on various cost-cutting programs, including reduction of work hours and model lines, extension of model-change cycles, and increased use of common parts.

In a similar manner, subcontractors have devised plans to streamline operations through layoffs, reviews of production systems, and business mergers with affiliated companies. Small subcontractors are increasingly supplying electric machinery makers and others outside the auto industry. To change their subcontractor status, some parts makers aim to develop and sell original products. These structural changes in the Japanese auto industry have resulted in a current distributed-production system, that is, optimizing horizontal networking among manufacturers and parts makers. This includes a tie-in of subcontractors' production planning and control systems with the systems of large manufacturers.[7]

Utilization of Just-in-Time Inventories

Basically, *just-in-time* (JIT) is a philosophy that is based on elimination of wasteful or non-value-added activity within a company. Its primary goal is to reduce inventory as close to zero as possible and to reduce lead time via reduced setup and reduced lot sizes. While inventory has always been considered an asset in the past, today inventory is a liability. The more excess inventory a company has, the more the root problems that have caused a company to hold excess inventory lie hidden. Manufacturing flexibility is a key aspect of JIT, where quick response to a customer's needs means producting lot sizes when needed. Another addresses the reduction of suppliers with which a company deals rather than having multiple product sources.

Originally, the concept of JIT inventories was used extensively by the Japanese. Now it is used by many companies in the world where the potential during expansionary times has been fully exploited. However, its potential during recessionary times or in declining industries is now just being realized. For example, Corning, which makes kiln-baked parts for catalytic converters in automobiles, has lost 25 percent of its business recently. But this time, no shutdown has been necessary. About 100 jobs have been gradually eliminated, mostly through attrition, leaving more than 800 ceramic workers employed. Thus, it has managed decline. A few years ago, Corning installed JIT-inventory management at Erwin, New York; it is a system that includes supplying its customers with products just a few days after the order is received, rather than the weeks it once took. Corning is now better able to track swings in demand

and avoid getting caught with stockpiles that can take months to work off. Not only does JIT means less handling of inventories, but also profits hold up better than when operations slow.

Skill in managing inventories in times of slack demand, as well as in declining industries, is important to the U.S. economy. Many manufacturers today are keeping inventories lean so that there is little risk that bulging inventories will force them to cut production abruptly and lay off large numbers of workers. The manufacturers include not just Corning but also the automakers and a wide range of companies such as General Electric, Motorola, and Rubbermaid. The net effect of their efforts is that inventories throughout the economy are low not only for the onset of a recession, but they are also low during an expansion and a subsequent contraction in the economy.[8]

Determine the Appropriate Production Planning and Control Technique

Once appropriate manufacturing partnerships have been established, and there are appropriate means to handle just-in-time inventories, there is the need to determine the appropriate planning and control technique over manufacturing operations. Referring to an earlier discussion in the chapter, the focus is currently on client/server-manufacturing systems. Also noted previously, a comprehensive approach to manufacturing that utilizes this approach is *enterprise resource planning*, which is real-time manufacturing software that incorporates the entire supply chain from sales and order processing to production, inventory, and distribution. Related to this approach (ERP) is a manufacturing execution system (MES) that utilizes software to manage shop-floor activities.

Essentially, a *manufacturing execution system* represents the CIM concept at the lower levels of the manufacturing process. It is a set of software applications that can easily integrate into everyday legacy systems and reside on any platform, although the current trend is for PC-based client/server networks. It allows a manufacturer to more effectively produce products on the factory floor by making production visible and information accessible to factory-floor personnel. It is used by operators, setup and tool-room personnel, supervisors, and foremen. An MES can provide information on the following:[9]

1. resource scheduling/allocation and status
2. operations/detailed scheduling
3. dispatch production units
4. document control
5. data collection/acquisition
6. labor management
7. quality management

8. performance analysis

9. process management

10. product tracking

11. maintenance management.

Together these systems allow improved production beyond what is possible with a typical manufacturing system, like MRP-II. MRP-II systems tend to focus on accounting transactions—at best keeping score for the factory floor, but not helping to dispatch production, allocate resources, pace, and otherwise manage production.

In contrast, an MES is the data collection and dissemination of production/process information that makes it truly the new E-mail of the factory floor. It includes such functionalities as resource use, scheduling, quality management, and engineering-change notices. Typically, an MES requires a lot of data-collection points that give users a real-time view of manufacturing. A recent survey of manufacturers who have used MES over the past five years confirms that the technology can be applied successfully to a broad range of shop-floor functions. Respondents cited reduced manufacturing cycle time as a very important MES benefit. The average reduction in production cycle time of surveyed respondents was 45 percent.[10]

Production Planning and Control—Monthly and Daily Bases

Typically, a manufacturing company's products can be produced upon receipt of customers' orders, in anticipation of demand, or in some combination of the two. If goods are being produced to order, a sales copy—in many cases—may actually be the production order (special or regular). The usual arrangement is to have the production planning and control department initiate action on the order, which is then distributed to stock control, shipping, and accounting departments. However, for many companies, products are produced in anticipation of demand. Such is the approach taken below, where the focus is on planning manufacturing activities on a monthly basis at the corporate level, then controlling on a daily basis using one of the current MES software packages at each of the manufacturing plants.

Manufacturing Management Planning Aspects—Monthly Basis. The procedure for determining next-period's sales forecasts (one month hence), after adjusting for finished goods on order and on hand, is shown as the first box in Figure 8.3. Because finished-goods production requirements for the next month provide the necessary input for the manufacturing function, linear programming is utilized to determine what quantity of each product will be produced in each of the manufacturing plants. After next-period production schedules by plants have been computed, the next phase is "exploding" bills-of-materials. The materials planning-by-periods program multiplies the quantity needed of each com-

Figure 8.3
A Manufacturing Planning and Control System on a Monthly Basis at the Corporate Level, and a Daily Basis at the Plant Level

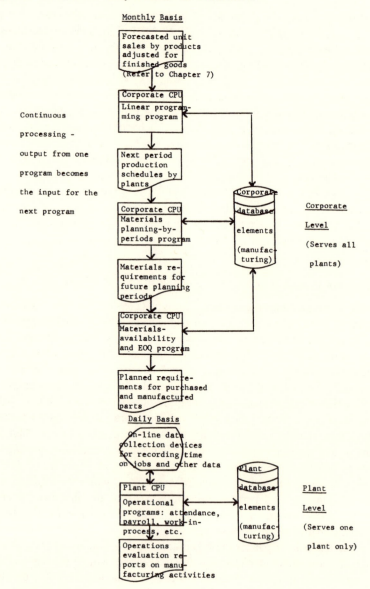

ponent times the number of final products that must be manufactured. Also, it places the component requirements in the appropriate planning period, because some parts will be needed before others. In this manner, parts and raw materials are received just in time for production needs.

The output for the materials requirements by future-planning periods in Figure 8.3 can take two paths. The *first* one is the purchasing of raw materials and parts from outside vendors, and the *second* one is the manufacturing of parts within the plants. The outside raw materials provide the basic inputs for manufacturing specific parts used in the assembly of the finished product. Likewise, outside purchased parts are used in the assembly of the final product. Before materials are to be manufactured or purchased, it is necessary to determine if present inventories and materials on order are capable of meeting the company's needs for future planning periods. At this point, it is important to note that perpetual inventories stored on line have been adjusted to reflect physical counts in order to produce accurate output for the materials-availability and EOQ (economic ordering quantity) program. In this manner, the planned requirements for purchased and manufacturing parts can reflect actual conditions.

Operational Control Aspects—Daily Basis. By no means does the integrated and continuous operating mode stop here for the period under study. Based on established production-monthly quotas that have been translated into planned daily requirements, the MES software provides the means for scheduling production orders through the manufacturing work centers. Additionally, other operational programs that are available to record and control daily activities include attendance, payroll, work-in-process, etc. The output of these programs provides operations evaluation reports on manufacturing activities.

In order to smooth production for each working day, a daily-computerized scheduler is employed at each plant. Before the start of each working day (the program is actually run at the end of the prior day shift and reviewed by the plant's management), the scheduler considers where jobs are backed up or behind schedule, and where production bottlenecks are currently occurring. Based on these basic inputs, the scheduler simulates the activities of the plan for the coming day and determines what will happen as the day begins, thereby alerting the plant superintendent and foremen to critical areas that need attention. Because all data affecting manufacturing activities are entered as they occur, the scheduler feeds back information in sufficient time to control upcoming manufacturing operations. This daily-computerized scheduler also allows the production planning and control department to make adjustments, if deemed necessary, to accommodate last-minute changes which may not have been entered as yet on the plant database. Hence, this approach allows plant management to retain control over the production process.

In summary, monthly programs do not operate individually, but are integrated with daily operations, as shown in Figure 8.3. Sales forecasts (as discussed in the previous chapter) serve as input for finished-goods product requirements which, in turn, constitute input for the next month's production schedules by plant. In a similar manner, this monthly output is input for "exploding" bills-of-materials, forming the basis for materials requirements by future planning periods. In turn, this monthly information is employed for manufacturing orders within the company's plants, and for placing orders with outside suppliers. This input-output approach using the appropriate software at the corporate level and the plant level provides a basis for day-to-day scheduling and dispatching of various manufacturing operations. The manufacturing execution system software, which is assisted by the daily scheduler, is the means for managing on-going shop-floor activities of the plants.

Periodic Review of Production Planning and Control

To determine where a typical manufacturing company stands in terms of its production planning and control system, there is the need to review periodically the information from this input/output approach to monthly and daily operations. This assessment can be in the form of effectiveness and efficiency. That is, manufacturing managers can review present and upcoming manufacturing operations to determine whether or not the company's products are being produced *efficiently* in terms of lowest costs. Similarly, they can indicate whether or not the production of these products are planned properly and, in turn, are scheduled according to the manufacturing plans so that production facilities are being utilized *effectively*.

To assist in this periodic review, plant managers need to be ensured that the present production planning and control system provides factory operating-managers, that is, foremen, with *exception information* as it happens. For example, PCs, located in each manufacturing work center, enable users to enter data into the MES regarding the name and location of goods in process. These keyboard entries, monitored on-line by the plant computer, enable the production planning and control department to know when goods enter and leave a work center. Exception reporting alerts the department when goods are overdue from a specific work center. Delay reasons can also be entered from the individual work-center PC. Prolonged delays, resulting in possible shipment delay, are brought to the attention of manufacturing managers, supervisors, and foremen through exception reports.

The delay reports as entered onto the database alert other manufacturing work centers about trouble areas. The work center(s) can enter "expected remedy" dates so that the rest of the plant can make the necessary changes to the production schedule. In this manner, if noncritical parts are missing (such as power cords), the majority of the work can be performed with the part added later. Or if critical parts are missing (such as the assembly shell), the complete order can be deleted from the daily-run sheet until the part becomes available. Overall, the adherence to set procedures and provision for showing delays enables the plant to operate in an efficient manner.

Going one step further, it is recommended that manufacturing managers pe-

Figure 8.4
An Analysis of Delays per Hour on a Two-Shift Basis During the Past Week for a Typical Manufacturing-Oriented Company

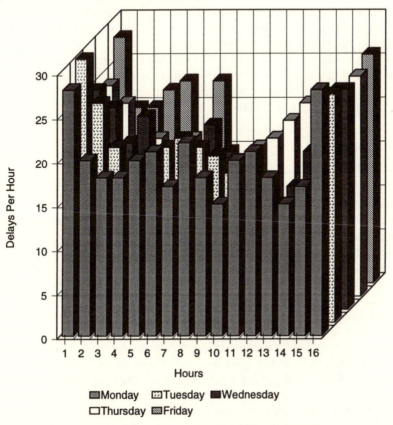

riodically review the results obtained by using MES software in conjunction with the daily-computerized scheduler. Such an approach is found in Figure 8.4, where the results of delays per hour on a two-shift basis are examined. During this past week, using multidimensional analysis, the number of delays were about the same in the first part of the week as in the last part of the week. It may well be that new variables have come into play that were not a problem in the past, or that other factors which are critical to changing the manufacturing work environment, such as new tools and equipment, have not been properly incorporated into the manufacturing process. In addition, manufacturing activities are subject to a wide range of improvements, ranging from a greater use of industrial robots or a better trained workforce. Thus, it is the job of manufacturing managers to analyze thoroughly current operations in order to specify improvements in manufacturing activities that are overseen by production planning and control.

From another perspective, there is a need for manufacturing managers to review those areas that are related to a company's critical success factors, that is, cost control and quality assurance. Because manufacturing costs are under the control of the production planning and control department as is inventory control and quality assurance, manufacturing managers need to review those manufacturing areas that are related directly or indirectly to those important CSFs. By using a CSF approach within an OLAP environment, manufacturing managers can access selected views of information via multidimensional analysis that, much like a pilot using instruments to monitor an airplane, allow them to direct their operations in an efficient and effective manner.

A Problem-Centered Approach to Improve Manufacturing Operations

To demonstrate how the problem-centered approach can be applied within an OLAP environment, consider the following scenario. The production planning and control department starts the production flow initially within the machine shop. Basically, this departmental group performs the following functions for the machine shop: assigns and maintains work-order priorities; monitors and reports work-order status, such as location and quantity; provides a steady flow of work in accordance with the daily requisition plans; and helps identify impeding work flow. Although these functions are performed well by the production planning and control department, there are mixups in the machine shop. In order to get a handle on these mixups, a quality review group which has been formed that includes manufacturing executives has decided to take a problem-centered approach to rectify these day-to-day mixups.

In the *generation* stage (first step), the group looked at problems that are the cause of the mixups in the machine shop. Although production planning and control utilize a computerized approach to scheduling, the data are then handwritten by the production clerks in the machine shop. Based on this mode of operation, the group found that handwritten "move" tickets are often illegible, contain transposed numbers, or are incomplete. In addition, the production clerk may post a copy of the move ticket to the wrong work order. An *evaluation* (second step) disclosed that all of these problems are major causes of mixups in the handling of production orders in the machine shop. In the *validation* stage (third step), all were selected, that is, they were grouped together as the major reasons for the machine shop failing to perform its operations correctly the first time around.

In terms of *establishing boundaries* (fourth step), the group decided that the problems had to be tied together with the computerized approach of the production planning and control department. Hence, the quality review group called on the assistance of the company's systems analysts who were working on an upgraded operating mode. After a thorough discussion between the two groups, the *solution* and *implementation* phases centered on utilizing bar coding. Bar coding has gained increased acceptance in manufacturing industries because of improved coding schemes, decreasing hardware costs, and improved reality of light pens and systems. With on-line data collection systems, machine-shop-floor data are keyed directly to the plant computer using PCs on the machine-shop floor. Machine-shop personnel enter data using alphanumeric keyboards and wand to read the bar codes. The wand scans the employee's badge to record the identification and work-center number, and scans the job ticket to capture the work order and part numbers.

Once the data are entered, an edit check automatically compares the entries to the database. If any discrepancies exist, error messages are displayed before the transaction is accepted. In essence, this on-line computerized approach in the machine-shop's work centers provides for the timeliness of data entry and the immediate data-verification capabilities provided by the on-line data-collection system.

A TYPICAL REAL-WORLD OLAP APPLICATION RELATED TO MANUFACTURING OPERATIONS

To place the foregoing exposition on OLAP into perspective, consider Osram Sylvania Inc. While many of the modules of SAP America Inc.'s R/3 application suite were found to be working well, R/3's distribution planning tools failed to meet its real managerial and operational needs. Undaunted, the company implemented the Demand, Distribution, Manufacturing, and Transportation Planning modules from Manugistics (Rockville, Maryland). The company's managers needed a better way to manage the forecasting and distribution of its finished goods—incandescent, fluorescent, and photo-optical lighting products—which had to be moved from several manufacturing sites to network of distribution centers. Osram Sylvania needs to provide its distribution centers and manufacturing plants with an 18-month forecast for finished-goods customer orders. Essentially, the forecast for finished goods drives all of the manufacturing planning and distribution processes throughout the company. The integration will also incorporate the internal and third-party suppliers because it would be capable of generating purchase requisitions to external suppliers.

This new approach to planning makes the company address the whole supply chain from a single forecast, a single set of numbers. It is a distinct improvement to the business and to the successful management of finished-goods inventory. In the past, the company disbursed forecasting information that separate business units acted upon in different ways, depending upon their needs. There was a forecast developed by the distribution organization, and it did not necessarily connect with the way the company was attempting to plan production. There was a separate forecast driving the manufacturing part of the organization and a statistical forecast being used in part for high-level sales forecasting and general business planning. And that did not relate directly to either of the other two sets of numbers. This new single, unified plan and its use will serve as the basis for planning raw material and component parts through the supplying plants. Overall, manufacturing management will be given more realistic information for everyday operations.[11]

It is recommended that manufacturing management go one step further by implementing an OLAP environment. That is, these managers need to have the capability to evaluate the system to ensure that what was forecasted can be produced during upswings or downswings of the economy. In a somewhat similar manner, a thorough analysis is necessary for products where the manufacturing and distribution lead times are significantly longer than the order-cycle time. For this products, planning is critical because planning may determine whether or not the company makes any money at all. The right combination of planning and scheduling tools enables manufacturing managers to squeeze the optimal throughput from their production processes.

APPLICATIONS THAT CAN BENEFIT FROM OLAP-VR INTEGRATION

The above application that centers on forecasting finished goods and then translating these requirements into daily schedules was enhanced by employing an OLAP approach. Although not required, it can be enhanced further by using a VR approach. More specifically, virtual reality would allow users to fly over the planned forecasts and get an excellent feel for where major or minor changes are taking place. In addition, these forecasts can be simulated and observed in terms of daily-manufacturing schedules such that manufacturing departments that cannot meet their expected demands can see today the need to schedule overtime. As such, a VR approach would assist manufacturing managers in visualizing what operations will be like on a daily basis. In turn, this visualization can be backed up by multidimensional analyses from an OLAP system. This combined OLAP-VR approach can be extended to other areas of the manufacturing function. These include design and engineering plus simulation of a manufacturing facility; these are covered below, along with other areas.

Design and Engineering

Virtual reality is coming of age as far as design and engineering applications are concerned, as companies (such as Bechtel, Boeing, and VPL) design systems for factory controls, construction equipment, and experimental aircraft, among other things. In addition, design and engineering departments which have been utilizing CAD and computerized-drawing tools for years now use interactive, VR-modeling packages that allow the designer, via the computer, to enter the design and walk through the model. For example, using Virtus WalkThrough (available from the Virtus Corporation), participants can walk through the room via mouse control and pass on either side of the contents. Participants can work with a designer and determine what the final room will look like under different conditions. Going one step further, some newer products allow the designer to view the virtual environment through the eyes of a seven-year-old and ask such questions as: Are the shelves the appropriate height? Are the products properly placed for preplanned or impulse buying? Also, similar types of questions can be asked and answered using multidimensional analysis from an OLAP perspective.

In the area of product designing, some companies are using virtual modeling such that marketing works with the product design team to create anything from a new toaster to a new automobile. The design process includes the use of *value analysis*. As such, new products can be designed from an even broader perspective than before. (Typical questions that are useful in value analysis were set forth previously in the chapter.) Once the new product has been designed within a VR-modeling system, a person can actually use the product. Hence, a person can depress the start button of a toaster, for example, and virtually watch the entire cycle of a toaster in producing toast.

Although the person is not actually using his or her hands to turn the toaster on or off, the use of input devices, such as a mouse or an electronic glove, gives the person a realistic simulation of that action. Once there is a working product, the marketing department can let customers test the toaster with new built-in features not found in conventional toasters, as well as suggest changes before it goes into production. In the automobile industry, consumers could, for example, take a virtual ride in a concept car and comment on the styling, placement of controls, color of fabrics, size of seats, and so forth. It should be noted that this approach to test marketing happens before the product is actually built. Although developing virtual-product models is not low in cost, it is usually an order of magnitude less costly than building clay or plastic models or one-of-a-kind prototypes.

Simulation

An important part of the simulation of a new factory has to be in the area of production planning and control. Basically, manufacturing operations are simulated interactively in real time. Included in this simulation can be the important manufacturing concepts set forth earlier in the chapter, such as value analysis and just-in-time inventories, which come under the umbrella of the CIM concept. Also, if reengineering is undertaken, this can be effected through the VR simulation. In turn, the interactive simulation in real time can take into account total quality management such that the final products are of the highest quality. As will be pointed out in Chapter 10, virtual reality can be helpful in training company personnel in the new manufacturing or process control environments, in particular, on new equipment.

An important benefit from using a VR-simulated approach to a new manufacturing facility is that the entire manufacturing process will be transparent to everyone on the design network. Those in manufacturing management will be able to monitor the development of products and anticipate new tooling needs as well as what human resources will be needed in the future. At the same time, they will have control over the parts database from which designers and engineers draw. Similarly, product marketing input on customer reactions to products in development will be fed directly into the network. Overall, manufacturing management, along with those in marketing, will have a better feel for the large expenditures required *before* the fact rather than *after* the fact. Appropriate changes can be made *now* to improve the new factory, thereby having the potential to save a typical company millions of dollars. Also, manufacturing management can utilize an OLAP approach to provide further analyses about the potential savings.

In a similar manner, VR-LAN simulators would be useful to simulate network configurations and patterns that would help determine if a proposed network configuration would provide adequate performance. Analysis of traffic flow, such as cars on a freeway or customers in a shopping mall, is another useful application. Essentially, the basic facilities of older simulation languages, combined with virtual reality and modern object-oriented languages, have valuable practical applications in manufacturing or otherwise.

Other Areas Related to Manufacturing

In the prior exposition on VR-LAN simulators, the focus was on internal operations and not on tieing-in with its customers. Ross Operating Valve Company (Troy, Michigan), for example, typifies a new breed of manufacturer that specializes in rapid product prototyping. The company which produces prototypes and valves has connected its computer-aided design workstations to those of its automotive-industry customers, thereby allowing on-line interactive design. Essentially, there is an exchange of CAD data. When a company is networked with its customers, there is a fast exchange of CAD data that gives a company a real advantage. This type of on-line concurrent engineering could help break down barriers between a company and its suppliers, customers, and even competitors, and go beyond prototyping to manufacturing end products.[12]

Another use of virtual reality is to demonstrate the safety of Volvo cars. The fully immersive VR-crash simulator runs on a Provision system, designed and built by Division Limited, who also developed the software that both recreates the accident and models the interior of the Volvo 850 automobile. Living through the five-minute crash sequence, immersed in VR, each motorist will experience a 25-mph side impact and walk away unharmed. The simulation created by Division Limited is based on Volvo's advertisement and realistically shows the benefits of Volvo's side impact protection system. Division created two complex sets of software for the simulation. First, life-size models of the car and its interior, the road, the countryside, and the collision vehicle were built as a VR environment. Then the animation sequence had to match that of the advertisement. The models are constructed such that the impact and consequent car-body deformation realistically portray actual events while allowing users to experience fully the VR environment.[13] In addition, multidimensional analysis can be used to bring together this information for definitive answers about the car's safety.

SUMMARY

The manufacturing function has and still is witnessing many exciting developments. Automated factories, industrial robots, personal computers, minicomputers, and new processes are important advances in the area of manufacturing. In addition to the employment of advanced-manufacturing methods and machines, newer control systems, such as MES, and mathematical models have helped to bring an entirely new approach to manufacturing. For these advances to be effective in an OLAP approach to manufacturing, a computer-integrated-manufacturing approach should be used. Essentially, after the products are engineered properly, purchasing must buy on an optimum basis and, at the same time, utilize value analysis to ensure good-product profitability. In turn, there is a tie-in of premanufacturing activities with manufacturing operations such that there is a timely flow of raw materials and parts through the manufacturing work centers. The end result is manufactured products for shipment to customers or to finished goods stockkeeping. Throughout the manufacturing process, an OLAP-operating mode can be employed by management to get an overview plus a complete understanding of day-to-day operations. If problems are detected, improvements can be made to the manufacturing process where deemed necessary.

NOTES

1. Dave Holbrook, "Stereo Viewing: Looking into Manufacturing," *Manufacturing Systems*, January 1991, pp. 30–31.

2. Michael Hammer and James Champy, "The Promise of Reengineering," *Fortune*, May 3, 1993, pp. 94–97.

3. Frank Rose, "Now Quality Means Service Too," *Fortune*, April 22, 1991, p. 100.

4. Lura K. Romei, "Quality Becomes Integral to American Business," *Modern Office Technology*, July 1991, p. 10.

5. Mickey Williamson, "Some Simulating Experiences," *CIO*, November 1, 1993, p. 34.

6. Meghan O'Leary, "A New Life for Purchasing," *CIO*, May 1, 1993, p. 32.

7. Ikuo Umebayashi, "New Trends in the Keiretsu System," *The Wall Street Journal*, November 16, 1992, p. A12.

8. Thomas F. O'Boyle, "Last In, Right Out, Firms' Newfound Skill in Managing Inventory May Soften Downturn," *Wall Street Journal*, November 19, 1990, pp. A1 and A6.

9. John Leibert, "Manufacturing Execution Systems," *ID Systems*, October 1994, pp. 40–43.

10. Robert Knight, "MES Challenges MIS," *Software Magazine*, August 1994, p. 28.

11. Eugene M. Grygo, "Planning to Make a Difference," *Client/Server Computing*, February 1996, p. 58.

12. David H. Freedman, "Quick Change Artists," *CIO*, September 15, 1993, p. 34.

13. Products, "Volvo Demonstration Uses VR," *Virtual Reality World*, July/August 1994, p. 6.

9

Accounting and Finance in an OLAP Environment

ISSUES EXPLORED

- How important is it for the typical company to take an accountability approach within an OLAP-operating mode?
- What are the typical newer directions in accounting and finance that underlie OLAP?
- What is so important about integrating financial-strategic planning via CSFs with KPIs and financial ratios?
- How can a typical company benefit from OLAP in the areas of cost accounting and financial analysis?
- How can the integration of OLAP with virtual reality assist accounting and financial managers in real-world companies?

OUTLINE

Accounting and Finance in an OLAP Environment

   Employ an Accountability Approach to Financial Operations

Newer Directions in Accounting and Finance That Underlie OLAP

   A Problem-Finding Approach to Accounting and Finance

   Integration of Financial-Strategic Planning Via CSFs with KPIs and Financial Ratios

   Analysis of a Company's Performance Versus Competition

   Rethinking of Cost-Accounting Approaches

   Using the Internet to Pursue and Realize Profits

   Integrated-Financial Software and Their Tie-In with OLAP Systems

ACCOUNTING AND FINANCE IN AN OLAP ENVIRONMENT

An integral part of an OLAP environment in the areas of accounting and finance is a *vision of the future*. For a typical company, top-level managers must want their companies to be the leaders in their industries, say in five years, or their companies must do this to better service their customers. Vision is not merely financial long-range planning intended to realize more sales, but is a fundamental plan of how the company must change to become competitive or achieve a leadership role. Examples include: Fred Smith's vision when he launched Federal Express; Max Hopper's vision, along with that of several others, when he created American Airlines's Sabre flight-reservation system; and Emil Martini's vision, which helped put a terminal in every drugstore for ordering inventory directly from Bergen-Brunswig. Each of these ideas—radical changes in business operations—was the answer to solving business needs and achieving phenomenal success. In turn, visioning is linked directly to a company's critical success factors (CSFs) and key performance indicators (KPIs). Essentially, CSFs and KPIs are tied-in with a company's financial performance, which is generally captured by the accounting system.

This vision of the future ties-in with the materials presented in the previous chapters. Essentially, the emphasis in Chapter 6 was on the analysis of short- to long-range strategic planning by managers in order to choose objectives and goals, select strategies, develop programs, and set policies. In turn, Chapters 7 and 8 were directed toward the analysis of data related to assuring effectiveness on the acquisition and use of the organization's resources by marketing and manufacturing managers, respectively. This chapter builds upon these prior chapters by centering on financial decisions that are related to short- and to long-range strategic plans. The focus will be on accounting and finance analyses that are essential to carrying out a company's strategic financial plans.

Employ an Accountability Approach to Financial Operations

Because an OLAP system provides relevant financial information to managers for supporting decision making, it can provide them with information for each responsibility center of a company. From this view, it is a responsibility-oriented approach that integrates planning or budgeting with control of performance reporting. Essentially, the focus is on *accountability* of financial performance by the company's managers. Such a system recognizes the significance of flexible budgeting and rethinking cost-accounting approaches, among others, in improving the quality of information provided for all management levels. Generally, it is not too difficult to justify the cost of developing and operating an OLAP system when managers at all levels and their staffs find the information provided to be extremely useful to their planning and control decisions.

Within the framework of an accountability approach to financial operations, finance takes on a new perspective. That is, it goes beyond the role of allowing managers to review current operations. It adds a new dimension by providing a means of synthesizing a myriad of data for answering key managerial questions for one or more areas of accountability. Typically, such questions include: What happens to net profits before federal income taxes if variable costs of producing certain products are decreased by a capital investment? What impact do interest-rate changes have on net profits if funds must be borrowed on the outside? What is the best method—borrowing from a bank, selling stock, or floating a bond issue—for financing large capital projects if future economic conditions are uncertain? Although answering these types of questions generally requires the use of modeling or the use of software packages, an effective OLAP finance system is entirely capable of supplying answers that have far-reaching impact on the company.

NEWER DIRECTIONS IN ACCOUNTING AND FINANCE THAT UNDERLIE OLAP

To better understand a typical company's financial operations, treasurers, financial executives, controllers, and their staffs must enlarge the scope of their thinking. Essentially, this means allowing them to "get the big picture" when reviewing the company's total activities so that there is optimization of resources for the entire company versus one or just a few parts of it. The success which the typical company has in attaining its mission, as well as its short- to long-range goals and objectives, depends on the degree of integration of its operations. Enlargements of the scope of organization activities, as well as the rethinking of traditional accounting and finance activities from a newer view, are set forth in the chapter. This background is helpful to place OLAP applications in their proper perspective.

Newer directions in accounting and finance that underlie OLAP can focus on a wide range of topics. Those which are covered below include: (1) a problem-finding approach to accounting and finance, (2) integration of financial-strategic planning via CSFs with KPIs and financial ratios, (3) analysis of a company's performance versus competition, (4) rethinking of cost-accounting approaches, (5) using the Internet to pursue and realize profits, and (6) integrated-financial software and its tie-in with OLAP.

A Problem-Finding Approach to Accounting and Finance

As a way of demonstrating how an OLAP approach is different from previous system approaches, a logical starting point is in the area of problem finding. Basically, problem finding is able to diagnose more types of important problems that are financially oriented, facing accounting and finance managers as well as top-level executives, than traditional problem-solving approaches. To illustrate the use of problem finding within an OLAP environment, consider the following example. A measurable goal of the corporation is to increase the value of its investments by 25 percent in five years. Top-level executives and the corporate-planning staff, working in conjunction with the corporation's vice president of finance, the treasurer, and the controller, can analyze the problem using OLAP software. By examining each approach to increase investment values, the "bottom line" for each investment approach can be evaluated thoroughly. If the investment's total return does not attain the corporation's goal, the important *variables* can be examined to determine what individual profit contributor(s) is (are) likely to fail to produce its share of gains. The net results are that these analyses are useful to identify future potential investment problems before they happen. In turn, the financial results are quickly calculated based on these problems, and the effect on the aggregrate returns is seen immediately. Typically, this OLAP modeling analysis is helpful to perceive future-investment alternatives and their relevant problems and brings them back to the present time for solution.

From another perspective, after giving consideration to a company's future return on investment, decision makers can evaluate various approaches to increase ROI (return on investment) today and tomorrow. One type of ROI analysis would focus on the company earning more profit without using more capital in terms of cost-cutting methods in its manufacturing plants and warehouses by employing the KISS ("keep it simple, stupid") principle. Another type of analysis would center on using less capital. For example, Coca-Cola uses plastic containers for concentrate instead of costlier metal ones. Also, a company can invest capital in higher-return projects. However, decision makers need to make sure that these projects earn more than the total cost of the capital they require. Thus, newer approaches to increase a company's return on investment must be thought out in advance before implementation.

Integration of Financial-Strategic Planning Via CSFs with KPIs and Financial Ratios

To improve financial decision-making within an OLAP environment, company treasurers, financial executives, and their staffs must enlarge the scope of their thinking and integrate financial-strategic planning via a company's critical success factors (CSFs) with key performance indicators (KPIs) and financial ratios. Basically, this means allowing them to "get the big picture" when reviewing the company's total activities so that there is optimization of resources for the entire company versus one or just a few parts of it. The success which the typical company has in attaining its general objectives and measurable short- to long-range goals depends on the degree of integration of its operations and measurement using KPIs and financial ratios. Enlargements of the scope of organization activities, as well as the acceptance of responsibilities that lie outside the boundaries of traditional finance, are normally found operating in an OLAP environment.

For a company, there are a number of key performance indicators that are useful in determining its viability. Typical ones in marketing include the following:

- ability or inability to make changes to a company's marketing strategies
- increase or decrease in company sales
- increase or decrease in market share
- increase or decrease in customers' satisfaction
- market research on continuing the status quo or bringing new products to market
- acceptance or nonacceptance of new products and services by customers
- increase or decrease in quality of products and services
- improved or unacceptable delivery times
- increase or decrease in sales and operating expenses
- increase or decrease in gross profit and cash flow for a company's products and services.

In a similar manner, a number of KPIs can be developed not only for a company's other functional areas, but also for the company as a whole, which tend to focus on financial ratios. Overall, KPIs are those over which a company has control. The company is able to manage the performance of these areas and make changes when necessary.

Chief among a number of financial ratios that are useful to financial analysts is return on investment. ROI analysis can be used to judge present performance and to evaluate future investment opportunities. Analysts can also use ROI to rate managerial effectiveness and to compare potential profitability of divisions and departments. While the technique of ROI analysis is uncomplicated, the potential applications are varied and valuable. Basically, the ROI equation is: earnings divided by total assets.

A problem in calculating ROI arises in identifying what is meant by earnings or total assets. Although there is no single, correct way to figure ROI, it is customary to use earnings from operations before taxes, sales after returns and allowances for bad debts, and net, year-end book value of assets. It is important that there be consistency and that the same measure of earnings, sales, and assets be used when figuring ROIs for different periods. Also, managers should be prepared for apparent surprises when comparing the company's ROI to another company's; that is, the other company may have used different measures in calculating its ROI.

Going beyond ROI, there are a number of financial ratios that can be applied to a company. Typical ones (which measure some aspect of a company) are:

- capital turnover (management efficiency)
- current ratio (liquidity status)
- investment status (measure of solvency)
- return on assets used (asset profitability)
- average collection period (receivable investment)
- return on sales (operation efficiency)
- inventory turnover (inventory utilization)
- undelivered commitments (days of sales in backlog)
- net worth debt ratio (credit strength)
- acid test ratio (immediate liquidation)
- stockholders' earnings status (percent earnings available).

These financial ratios focus on the overall aspects that assist in financial strategic thinking. They can be calculated as needed and thereby serve as the basis for management by exception where appropriate ranges are assigned to each ratio. For example, the ratio of current assets to current liabilities should be about 2:1. Typically, to calculate these financial ratios, there is a need to interact with a corporate database or data warehouse.

Basically, these ratios provide an insightful look for measuring actual results against the corporate strategic plans (short-range to long-range). Management effectiveness can be measured by the capital turnover ratio, asset profitability, and ROI. In addition, the corporation's performance can be gauged through the return on sales, days of sales in backlog, inventory utilization, and receivable collections.

From a slightly different perspective, these financial ratios can be viewed from the standpoint of a typical manager. Managers know the problem of battling the daily, even hourly, barrage of operating data that assaults their minds. The realization that they cannot track every detail of business comes as their days get longer and their nights get shorter. Like most managers who were faced with this problem, they tried delegating. Yet they still monitored or second-guessed everything they delegated. The net result was that they did not save any time. The most effective way for them to monitor what is transpiring in their companies, then, is to look at the ROI and the financial ratios.

Analysis of a Company's Performance Versus Competition

A most important factor of reviewing corporate financial performance via financial ratios is to assist in giving direction to the organization's top-level managers and its corporate-planning staff for furthering financial strategic thinking. By relating external-environmental factors with internal ones for a typical company, the growth and profitability of comparable firms in its industry are compared to it. This financial analysis gives an indication whether or not the company is increasing its market share and giving a fair return to its stockholders when considering the industry's current state. This overview of financial ratios needs to be supplemented by a more detailed analysis of competitors' financial statements, frequently referred to as *content analysis* of periodic financial statements and annual reports.

Basically, content analysis provides valuable clues to competitors' corporate strategic thinking. It is a source of both financial information and new directions by competition. Content analysis of competing companies can be of real usefulness for getting a handle on specific issues of corporate strategy, and can serve as a primary or supplementary source of information. It can be used to analyze current changes and past correlates of performance, and for more general investigations of questions of interest to top-level executives and their corporate-planning staff.

In terms of a thorough analysis of overall performance and variances that are tied-in with financial ratios, there is a great need to employ graphics. Although financial ratios can be compared on a day-by-day, a week-by-week, a month-by-month, or some other time-period basis, the purpose of this analysis by finance executives is to determine whether or not the company is improving its financial stature. Of equal importance is the fact that financial ratio analysis which uses graphics discloses whether or not financial managers are really managing the company effectively over the short term to the long term.

Generally, "at a glance" graphic presentations of information allow managers to start their thinking processes quickly. The usual method—also the slower method—involves a lot of reading. A "picture" may tell managers immediately what they want to know. Information in this visual aid might otherwise be buried in stacks of computer-generated reports. From another viewpoint, managers may view graphs on a display screen and also employ a paper printout of graphic data to ponder later, as in problem finding. Based on either perspective, computer-prepared graphics are very effective for supporting decision making and getting managers to think about new ways of running their operations.

Rethinking of Cost-Accounting Approaches

To compete in the global markets, U.S. companies must get control of their production costs. The good news is that U.S. manufacturers began meeting that challenge recently with computer integrated manufacturing, automation, robotics, and just-in-time methods (refer to the prior chapter). The bad news is that even with these manufacturing advances, costing systems still cannot compete in high-volume markets. If U.S. companies are doing right things in manufacturing, then why can't they compete? The answer is that U.S. companies have fixed just about everything except their costing systems. Generally, today's product-costing data are wrong, often by extremely large margins. Without more accurate costing methods, the bottom line is a continued competitive crisis. Hence, there is the need to rethink cost-accounting methods for the 1990s and beyond. More specifically, there is the need to take a hard look at activity-based costing, technology accounting, life-cycle accounting, and target costing.

Activity-based costing (ABC) directly relates costs to the resources used to manufacture a product. A starting point is analyzing a company in order to determine all its production and support activities. All costs are then assigned to activities. Next, activities are measured and linked with the products that consume the activities. The total cost of the finished product is an accumulation of the activities required to make the product. In addition to assigning the costs to the products that actually absorb the activities, ABC identifies cost drivers and isolates non-value-added activities. With this information, a company can establish priorities that focus on eliminating or reducing non-value-added activities.

Basically, the ABC method allows a company to identify specifically the activities that are generating costs so that management has a better idea of why budgeted numbers are being exceeded. In essence, the ABC method is a restatement of costs. If a financial analyst looks at the production department section of a profit-and-loss statement in both traditional cost-accounting and ABC-accounting reports, the numbers would be identical on the bottom line. However, they would be categorized differently.

Technology accounting is based on the concept that technology costs, such as plant, equipment, and information systems, should be treated as direct costs, equivalent to direct labor and materials. Today's technology costs, for the most part, are accounted for by amortization (or depreciation) and are included in overhead. The problem with this method of accounting is that conventional amortization methods are time-based, not production-based. A time-based method equates time with cost and often causes amortization of idle machinery to increase overhead costs when there is little or no production. This encourages constant and ineffective production to maintain a desired cost per unit.

Product costs are further affected by the inclusion of the time-based amortization in overhead, which must then be allocated to production. By adopting a direct production-based amortization method, such as units of production, costs are matched more accurately with products manufactured. When determining the number of units over which to amortize an asset, only the planned production of the asset should be considered. Simply using the asset's total lifetime production capacity does not solve the problems associated with a time-based method. Total units used to amortize an asset should be limited by planned production, product demand, and obsolescence of the asset's technology or the manufacturing process. As with activity-based costing, the choice of an overhead allocation method can significantly alter product costing. As technology costs increase as a percentage of total product costs, any misallocation will improperly influence management decisions and possibly the financial results of the company.

Life-cycle accounting accumulates the costs of activities that occur over the entire life cycle of a product, from inception to abandonment by the manufacturer and the consumer. A primary objective of life-cycle accounting is a better match of revenues and expenses. All costs are capitalized as incurred. These costs are charged to earnings as units are sold, based on the total planned number of units to be brought to market. The shortcomings of the traditional cost-accounting model, then, are largely due to the changing manufacturing environment. To remain competitive in today's global marketplace, the time has come for U.S. manufacturers to adopt new cost-accounting methodologies so they know the true cost of their products and make informed cost-management and pricing decisions.[1]

Although the foregoing cost-accounting methodologies are quite useful to assist a company in telling the true story about costs, a more pragmatic way to get a handle on costs is to follow the Japanese. That is, it is necessary to take a look at costs before the fact rather than after. More specifically, a Japanese cost-management system guides and motivates planners to design products at the lowest possible cost, and to give them considerable freedom in introducing new products as well as getting them to market quickly. Like its famed quality philosophy, Japan's cost-management system is ahead of its global counterparts.

American companies developing a new product, for example, typically design it first and then calculate the cost. If it is too high, the product goes back to the drawing board, or the company settles for a smaller profit. On the other hand, the Japanese start with a *target cost* based on the price the market is most likely to accept. Then they direct designers and engineers to meet this target. The system also encourages managers to worry less about a product's cost than about the role it could play in gaining market share. This strategic thinking approach is a big reason why the Japanese so often come out with winning products.

The critical feature of the Japanese cost-management system is its focus on getting costs out of the product during the planning and design stage. That is the point at which virtually all subsequent costs are determined—from manufacturing to what customers will have to spend on maintenance. This target-cost technique, which is used by such companies as NEC, Sharp, Nissan, and Toyota, comes in countless variations. The stripped-down version has several important features. The team in charge of bringing a new product idea to market determines the price at which the product is most likely to appeal to potential buyers. From this crucial judgment all else follows. After deducting the desired profit margin from the forecasted sales price, the planners develop estimates for each of the elements that make up a product's costs: design and engineering, manufacturing, plus sales and marketing. Each of these is further subdivided to identify and estimate the cost of each component that goes into the finished product.

Overall, U.S. companies tend to build a model of the product, determine what it is going to cost, and then ask whether it can be sold at a certain price based on costs. In contrast, the Japanese turn it around, that is, they say, "It's got to sell for X dollars. Let's work backwards to make sure we can achieve it." This is not currently being done by U.S. companies with the same intensity. Western-style cost management, by basing costs on given standards, tends to maintain the status quo. The Japanese approach is dynamic and constantly pushes for improvement.[2]

Using the Internet to Pursue and Realize Profits

Selling on the Internet today is a low-cost approach for a company (or an individual) to pursue and reap profits. One can have a direct connection to the Internet, either using a service such as Prodigy or a no-frills route via a service that provides Internet access only. Whatever service is chosen, there is a need for a "browser," that is, a software program that allows the user to employ a mouse to point-and-click his or her way around the World Wide Web. Browsers, including the popular Netscape Navigator and Mosaic, are often free. Once the individual has an Internet account, he or she logs into the Net, starts a browser, and now can jump from one option to the next. As an example, an investor, after getting on-line, can keep tabs on various stocks by way of a service called Portfolio Accounting World-Wide System (PAWWS). The individual can click the mouse to get the latest quotes, or, by clicking a second time, see a company's most recent financial statements or take a look at how its stock price has moved over the past five years.

Recognizing a potentially significant market for financial services, brokerage houses, investment banks, and discount brokers have gone on-line in a hurry. Companies like Fidelity, Merrill Lynch, J. P. Morgan, and Charles Schwab have opened up new sites for their investors. There are other on-line sources, including the fledgling Microsoft Network and specialists such as the Reuters Money Network and Dow Jones News/Retrieval. But the big three—America Online,

CompuServe, and Prodigy—as well as dozens of investment sites on the World Wide Web are universally available, relatively inexpensive, and good places to start.

Whichever service is chosen, financial bulletin boards and investment forums should be visited first. These popular gathering places are where users talk shop, exchange advice, and interact on-line with a variety of Wall Street gurus. Prodigy's Money Talk bulletin board alone can handle up to 40,000 messages a month. There is a word of warning. Investor forums are fertile ground for operators who talk up cheap, thinly traded stocks, thereby hoping to create enough buy orders to boost the price for a few days. Then they sell their holdings and leave everyone else holding issues that have little or no market.

Integrated-Financial Software and Their Tie-In with OLAP Systems

Today, debate over the benefits of in-house financial-applications software development versus the use of commercial packages seems to be academic. Except in situations where unique financial customization is required, the rationale for in-house development has steadily given way to the persuasive challenge of commercially supplied packages, including OLAP software. The apparent increase in the use of packaged-financial software in a client/server environment is aided by an increasing variety of packages for platforms other than IBM mainframes and DEC minicomputers. Most financial software is now available for all sizes of computers, ranging from PCs to the larger mainframes.

Relationships between financial-software vendors and OLAP vendors are a logical development since integrated products make it easier to share data and reduce maintenance requirements. These relationships offer a particular advantage for OLAP vendors, many of whom are looking to expand market channels and increase their presence in an increasingly crowded segment. However, users want to scrutinize such relationships to determine if they are substantive, providing close integration between financials and OLAP tools, or if they are merely marketing arrangements. If they are substantive, users should be able to access financial data in a free-form ad hoc way.

Because financial-software vendors see the merits of OLAP, they are offering the drill-down technique in their client/server applications. They realize that on-line analytical processing enables users to view multidimensional data and burrow into a data warehouse to extract answers to business questions. The technology goes a long way toward helping users to realize the empowerment promised by client/server computing. Vendors, such as Dun and Bradstreet Software, Hyperion Software Corporation, Oracle Corporation, SAP America Inc., SAS Institute Inc., and SQL Financials Inc., are all marketing OLAP financial-software systems.

Overall, OLAP systems offered today by financial-software vendors are built upon the foundation of integrated-financial software. That is, the basic data of accounting and finance that is accumulated by a typical integrated-financial-software package provides the input for an on-line analytical processing system. Where the accounting and finance data may reside, that is, in a corporate database or a data warehouse, is not important. The important item is that the integrated financial software has data that is available for massaging using OLAP-multidimensional analysis which then can be reviewed by appropriate accounting and finance managers for prompt action if deemed necessary.

ACCOUNTING AND FINANCE AREAS THAT LEND THEMSELVES TO AN OLAP ENVIRONMENT

Today, accounting and finance managers are dealing with a host of disparate financial data and they need an easy way to consolidate these data into financial information that results in meaningful analysis for their users. For example, a controller for a medium-size company wants to streamline her financial procedures so that the company's departments can make better budgeting decisions. An important approach is the utilization of OLAP software to better analyze the current data for more realistic budgets. Other real-world applications that can reap the benefits of OLAP software in the accounting and finance areas include cost-accounting analysis and financial analysis, both of which are covered below.

In addition, an OLAP environment is equally at home in the area of cash flow not only for the short term, but also over the longer term for a typical company. The management of accounts receivables and payables are likely candidates for multidimensional analysis. So too is the area of payroll which, today, is linked to human resource management systems (covered in the next chapter). The source and application of funds is a fertile area for OLAP. In a similar manner, financial statements, that is, balance sheets and income statements, lend themselves to an analysis beyond two dimensions.

AN OLAP APPROACH TO COST ACCOUNTING

Traditional cost-accounting systems are criticized today on the grounds that they do not provide useful information for internal decision making. An important reason given for this lack of usefulness is that the systems were designed to provide cost data for inventory valuation in financial statements rather than for cost management. Other reasons were given in the prior discussion on the rethinking of cost-accounting approaches. However, with recent advances in computer technology—in particular, PC, spreadsheet, and database software—less costly analysis of cost data in different ways is available.

Enlarged View of Cost-Accounting Approaches

To provide information for cost management, there must be an enlarged view of cost-accounting approaches such that they can be flexible enough to analyze costs, including inventory valuation, product costing, life-cycle costing, over-head analysis, quality cost evaluation, direct and indirect labor analysis, and productivity analysis. Most comprehensive accounting systems for supporting cost management must include various types of data, most of which is generated internally. At the most basic level, the data consists of the activities causing the costs, that is, the cost drivers and the costs incurred. As an example, receiving department costs may be caused by the number and size of the deliveries, along with inspection and handling times of these deliveries. If the receiving depart-ment's costs are to be apportioned to the products causing the costs, the cost drivers must be identified and used to trace costs to specific products. When this is done, the cost-accounting system becomes activity based (as discussed previously in the chapter) rather than volume based (like most current cost systems).

One means of developing an activity-based system is to use a database ap-proach, which means recording events, activities, and costs in a computer da-tabase in enough detail so they can be retrieved, analyzed, and summarized in multiple ways as the need arises. Such an approach in reality involves recording some information not required for financial reporting, such as the numbers of deliveries and purchase orders, and the numbers and times of inspections and handling. However, the database of costed activities not only supports the cost-attachment process for product costing, but also provides a useful tool to support planning, coordination, and control across multiple dimensions. On the other hand, a second means to cost activities is one that makes use of virtual reality, which is discussed later in the chapter.

Going one step further, an OLAP approach to activity-based costing provides for a more in-depth analysis of changing costs. This approach not only assists cost management in understanding costs, but also helps to visualize via multi-dimensional analysis how costs affect a company's financial operations. An OLAP environment gives cost management the look and feel of an alternative world. More to the point, costs can be analyzed by cost accountants for a number of products to determine what effect the elimination of certain costs—such as costly training of machine operators or assembly operators—would have on the company. Perhaps senior personnel could act as mentors to eliminate or reduce training costs. Similarly, inspection of assembly operations may be better left to assembly personnel where production-line personnel are permitted to shut down production if there are quality problems. Changes in production activities and their resulting costs, then, are related to the company's financial statements.

The utilization of an OLAP environment can help cost accountants and man-agement determine whether costs incurred in production or nonproduction ac-tivities really benefit the company. From this perspective, a *true cost-benefit analysis* can be undertaken not only for manufactured products, but also for costs related to the marketing and distribution of costs by products and product lines. Thorough analysis gives cost accountants the capability to uncover new relationships that were previously buried in cost figures. Thus, multidimensional analysis can be used for obtaining different costs for different purposes, thereby highlighting problems and exceptions that were ignored or neglected in the past. In light of these comments, the question can be raised: How can a company in these fast-changing times not utilize the latest information systems technology to undertake a periodic cost-benefit analysis of its operations and products manufactured?

Accent on Target Costing

Related to the above discussion about cost-accounting approaches is *target costing*. It represents a powerful force that shifts from cost-led pricing to target costing. Traditionally, companies have started with costs, added a desired profit margin, and arrived at a selling price, that is, cost-led pricing. Sears and Marks & Spencer, as examples, have switched to target costing in which the price the customer is willing to pay determines allowable costs that start at the design stage. Until recently, those companies were the exceptions. Now target costing is becoming the rule. The Japanese first adopted it for their exports. Now Wal-Mart and all the discounters in the United States, Japan, and Europe are practicing this newer approach to costing.

Because target costing is a cost-management technique that lets a company determine how much its customers are willing to pay for a product, and then design the product within certain cost limits that allows for a predetermined profit, multidimensional analysis in an OLAP environment is quite helpful to company managers throughout a company to get a handle on pricing and costing the product. For example, a marketing manager, working with a senior cost manager, could explore the relationship of pricing the product at various levels based upon making the product internally at various costs throughout the marketing and manufacturing processes. In addition, the analysis could include the outsourcing of the product. In effect, company managers would be able to undertake the appropriate pricing-costing analysis for a definitive answer about the product being produced internally or externally.

Although target costing has made its mark on industries in which products require a significant amount of production time, it is equally applicable to services for which the focus is the service-delivery system. As in process-intensive manufacturing, process is inextricable from product. Think of the issues that are important to the delivery of health care and fast-food functions. Services and process-intensive manufacturing diverge in their flexibility; that is, it is very costly to convert a paper machine so that it can produce a grade or weight that was not considered in its initial design. On the other hand, service-delivery systems are a different matter. In customer-responsive service-delivery systems, it is easy to add new services. For example, menus are easy to extend and room services can easily be added. From this view, multidimensional analysis is equally at home in service-oriented industries as they are in manufacturing industries.

It is extremely helpful for companies to practice target costing only if they can manage and control the entire economic chain. Similarly, the same concept applies to outsourcing, alliances, and joint ventures. Any business structure that is built on partnership alliances can benefit from target costing where the focus is on cost containment. Overall, entities, rather than the traditional model of a parent company with wholly-owned subsidiaries, are increasingly becoming the models for growth, especially in today's global economy.

Analyzing Real Profitability of a Company's Products

Once the costs of a company's future products have been properly determined by a cost-management technique, such as target costing, the next step is accumulating costs once the products are manufactured. One approach to cost control or containment is the ABC method set forth previously, that is, the focus is on separating value-added costs from non-value-added costs. With this segregated-cost information, company managers can determine what non-value-added activities can be reduced or possibly eliminated. Although the ABC-costing-method analysis will help in controlling costs, there is still a need to utilize a method to compute the real profitability of a company's products. Such a method is found in direct costing.

Essentially, direct costing segregates variable costs from fixed costs (as opposed to absorption costing which combines them). As such, selling price less variable costs equals contribution to fixed costs and profits before federal income taxes. This value contribution is then subtracted from fixed costs, thereby resulting in the net profit before federal income taxes. Direct costing is concerned primarily with the elimination of arbitrary allocations of common or joint costs. It emphasizes the benefits of tracing costs to individual cost centers and then measuring them. To realize the benefits of direct costing, typically a cost-review group is assigned the responsibility of evaluating product costs and their contributions.

To relate direct costing to multidimensional analysis in an OLAP environment, refer to Figure 9.1. This analysis depicts a comparison among the company's five principal products using direct costing. Similarly, a comparison can be made among the various products in each product line. With an accurate segregation of variable and fixed costs to determine product contribution, the company's managers are able to view important information regarding which products really contribute to overall profits and which do not. In addition, the total contribution of each of the company's product lines can be calculated. It may well be that this cost information, which is reviewed by lower-level managers, should be forwarded to a higher level of management for review. There may be a changing pattern among the products and product lines in terms of total contribution. This capability of the cost-review group, who works with experienced cost accountants, allows the company to detect changing cost trends.

Although direct costing is an effective way of getting at the real costs of a

Figure 9.1
A Comparison of a Company's Five Principal Products Using Direct Costing

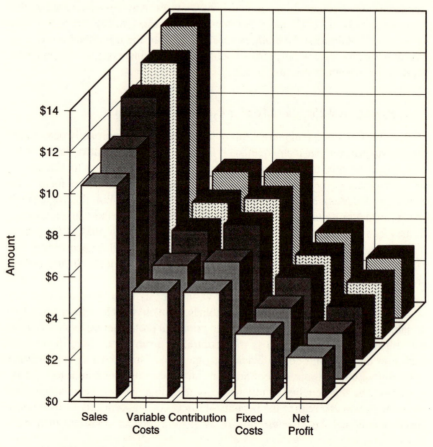

□Product 1 ▨Product 2 ■Product 3 ▨Product 4 ▨Product 5

company, there is the need to go one step further in these fast-changing times. Like the Japanese, American companies need to rethink how they manage their operations. Sometimes, these include making radical changes and setting dramatic targets, whether it is in costs or otherwise. There may be a need to reengineer products—not processes—since product design can account for as much as 80 percent of total production costs. When it comes to product design, it is not what is built into the product, but what can be taken out of it. Basically, simplicity cuts costs and saves time. In addition, there should be a focus on giving customers less, not more, variety which can result in lower prices. Thus, costing is not an island unto itself, but an integral part of most major functional areas of a typical company.

AN OLAP APPROACH TO FINANCIAL ANALYSIS

From an enlarged view of a company, an on-line analytical processing system has the capability to focus on a thorough analysis of financial ratios that tie back to a company's critical success factors for accounting and finance. In addition, a thorough analysis of key performance indicators provides information relating to CSFs, although not treated below. Such an approach integrates planning or budgeting with control or performance reporting, and is based on knowledge of cost behavior and recognizes the significance of costs standards and flexible budgeting in improving the quality of information provided for all managerial levels. It is from this perspective that a financial planning and variance control system is explored below that is tied-in with a financial ratios review.

Linkage of Short-Range Strategic Plans to Variances from Actual

To relate a company's financial activities to everyday operations, the beginning point is short-range strategic planning which forms the basis for monthly flexible-department financial budgets. Actual results are compared monthly to departmental budgeted financial figures. If actual operations are within 5 percent (plus or minus) by individual expense categories, there is no need for action. However, if the amount exceeds the 5 percent limit, appropriate action is undertaken. In cases where there is a need for one or more operational policies, it may be necessary to obtain the involvement of top-level managers.

In effect, a financial planning and variance control system recognizes that individual managers are assigned responsibility and, in turn, will be held accountable for meeting stated budgetary finance objectives. If variances exceed the established norm, there is a need for a drill-down capability that allows the report's details to be examined. Also, operations are reviewed by managers responsible for each major functional area of an organization to ensure that financial organization objectives are being met. Typically, the review is in the form of analyzing financial ratios (such as noted earlier in the chapter), whether they are improving or not improving this month versus last month as well as this year versus last year. (The same can be done for the KPIs noted earlier in the chapter.) Where financial ratios are not improving, there is a need for corrective action by an appropriate level of management. In essence, not only does the above approach provide a linkage to strategic planning at the highest management level, but also there is the capability of assisting finance managers to provide input for modifying strategic plans as well as departmental budgets if deemed necessary.

Figure 9.2
A Comparison of Sales to Net Profit Before Federal Income Taxes Over a Five-Year Period (the Current Year Versus the Past Four Years) for a Typical Company

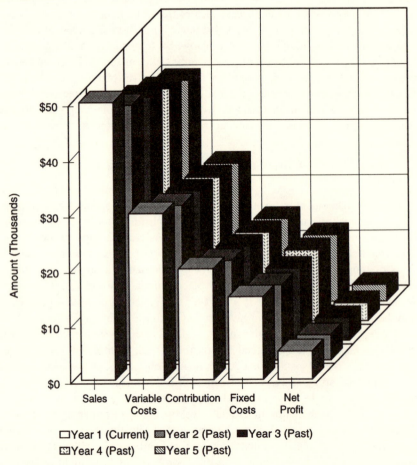

Usage of Multidimensional Analysis to Highlight Financial Trends

To explore a company's overall performance that is tied-in with selected financial ratios, it is helpful to employ multidimensional analysis. As a starting point for an overview of a typical company's financial operations, refer to Figure 9.2. Not only are total sales and related costs and contributions illustrated over five years, but also the net profit before federal income taxes is shown for the same time period. This analysis can be further refined over five years for rising and falling financial ratios that tell more of the story about the company's future—good, bad, or indifferent. Refer back to ROI and financial ratios given earlier in the chapter.

In terms of a shorter-time frame, say this year and last year, financial data and their ratios can be compared on a day-to-day, week-by-week, month-by-month, or some other time basis. The intended purpose of this analysis by accounting and finance managers is to determine whether or not the company is improving its financial stature. Of equal importance is the fact that financial data and ratio analysis discloses whether or not company managers are really managing effectively over the shorter term.

Generally, "at a glance" multidimensional analysis allows managers to start their thinking processes quickly. The usual method—also the slower method—involves a lot of reading. A "picture" may tell managers immediately what they want to know. Information in this visual aid might otherwise be buried in stacks of computer-generated reports. From another viewpoint, managers may view multidimensional analysis on a display screen or employ a paper printout to ponder later. Based on either perspective, multidimensional analysis is a very effective way to support decision making in an OLAP environment, and may signal the need for problem finding to get the company back on track.

Analysis of Capital-Investment Decisions

Capital-investment "what-if" questions from finance managers can benefit from a thorough analysis of financial alternatives or other factors using OLAP software. As a beginning point, the individual preparing the project needs to undertake one or more analyses that focus on looking at the project over its life. This generally entails multidimensional analysis that looks at total sales, total costs, and profits over its life. Because a typical project requires substantial sums of funds for implementation, the cash manager, under the direction of the treasurer, decides on the optimal financing method. After reviewing an analysis of the capital project, the cash manager interrogates the corporate database for financial-structure data, which is primarily of a long-term nature. A financial-structure report is generated for review by the cash manager. This individual is now prepared to make a financing recommendation after considering the current debt-equity ratio, current borrowing rates, interest charges for which the company is currently committed, and current and projected sales as well as other factors pertinent to the decision. Such a report could be prepared using multidimensional analysis.

Once a decision, such as bank borrowing, has been made regarding financing, the cash manager incorporates this information into the analysis of the capital project. The formal report is prepared and then forwarded to top-level managers for review and approval. Typically, for these capital projects, the vice president of the functional area initiating the project, the vice president of finance, the treasurer, and the executive vice president are consulted. When the project is finally approved, a copy of the approval is forwarded to the cash manager, who takes the necessary steps to obtain the funds for implementation. If the project is rejected, it is forwarded with the reasons by the cash manager to the initiating functional area.

Comparison of a Company's Performance to Competition

A most important factor for reviewing a company's financial performance via financial ratios is to assist in giving direction to the company's top management and its corporate-planning staff. By evaluating external-environmental factors as related to internal ones for a typical company, the growth and profitability of comparable firms in its industry are compared to it using multidimensional analysis. For example, an overview of a competitor's current financial position can be compared to the company's own financial picture plus those of other competitors. This financial analysis gives an indication whether or not this one competitor is giving a fair return to its stockholders when considering the industry's current status. This overview of financial ratios needs to be supplemented by a more detailed analysis of competitors' financial statements, frequently referred to as *content analysis* of periodic financial statements and annual reports.

Basically, content analysis provides valuable clues to competitors' corporate strategy. It is a source of both financial information and new directions by competition. Content analysis of competing companies can be of real usefulness for getting a handle on specific issues of corporate strategy, and can serve as a primary or supplementary source of information. It can be used to analyze current changes and past correlates of performance, and for more general investigations of questions of interest to top-level executives and their corporate-planning staff.

As an example, content analysis may disclose that one of the company's competitors is showing improved cost performance, that is, its costs are declining. The appropriate corporate response is for a typical company to get involved in a cost-analysis technique called *benchmarking*, which focuses on what the competitor does and how much it costs him to do it. In the company's lab, analysts tear apart the competitor's products and estimate the cost of designing and producing each part. The analysis extends beyond product costs. To pin down distribution and handling costs, company executives need to order some of its competitor's products, then trace where they were shipped from and examine how they were packed. Typically, cost savings on a particular product start at the earliest stage, with engineering determining the product design. The challenge is to find ways to make engineering more cost-effective without stifling their creative efforts.

A TYPICAL REAL-WORLD OLAP APPLICATION RELATED TO COSTING

A short time ago, Blue Cross/Blue Shield (BC/BS) of Maryland (the Baltimore-based health-care organization) thought its executive information system was just what it needed for top management to view its performance quickly in costs and delivery of service. However, the EIS is gone and the company is rapidly developing its OLAP capabilities because OLAP addresses business problems that typically involve multiple dimensions. Inasmuch as multidimensional queries are difficult for conventional relational databases (which are inherently two-dimensional, composed of tables consisting of rows and columns), top managers at Blue Cross/Blue Shield found OLAP much more suited to long, complex queries that can slice, aggregate, and summarize huge volumes of data in a variety of ways, whereby key trends, isolating problems, and uncovering areas of opportunity can be identified.

To understand better why the change occurred from EIS to OLAP, the director of financial systems (Mark Max) found that EIS was all hard wired, that is, there was no way to change a screen or do anything different. In essence, the data was there, but unless the user was willing to write a new program, a 40- to 80-hours job, the individual could not get at it. Management pulled the plug on the EIS, which was proving too costly to maintain. BC/BS managers and analysts were then forced to rely on such limited data-analysis capabilities as canned reports, stand-alone spreadsheets, and whatever limited information could be culled from the general ledger residing on the mainframe. Basically, managers were massaging the general ledger to come up with profit-and-loss data, which they would input into spreadsheets. The effort produced a summary total but did nothing to help with decision making, because there was no opportunity for real analysis.

For this BC/BS organization, the pressure for better business-management information was growing at the same time that pressure for reform, restructuring, and cost control was impacting the health-care industry. Also, new competitors for health-care dollars were cropping up while Blue Cross/Blue Shield itself was developing new products, such as managed-care programs. To address these pressures, the director of financial systems obtained an evaluation copy of IRI Software's Express multidimensional database which he had previously used when working as a financial-systems consultant at Price Waterhouse. With Express, he quickly built a prototype-budget application, residing on a NetFrame Systems Inc. server, that allowed managers to understand expenses for the first time. Managers were able to find variances over time by cost center or product or any number of criteria. Hence, the company's budget analysts had an effective analysis tool, and managers were finally able to identify and respond to changes. Because of the multidimensional nature of Express, BC/BS could even view results by different organizational hierarchies, allowing managers to make year-to-year comparisons despite reorganizations and the relocations of various cost centers.

The Express budgeting application has two groups of users, including 250 expense-center managers, who use it for monthly-expense reporting, and a small set of sophisticated financial analysts. This latter group was anxious for more than was offered by the application's simple model of time, budget expense, and cost center. So a more ambitious financial-planning system using Express was built. This application allows them to do profit-and-loss planning by product line, market, and cost center over time. Previously, financial analysts attempted this using an Excel spreadsheet, but it required dozens of worksheets for the different months and expense centers. Rollups and aggregations became a nightmare, and the integrity of results was questionable. Needless to say, by putting it in the multidimensional database, it resolved the different dimensions automatically. With the financial-planning application, BC/BS managers are now able to create planning scenarios based on enrollment for its various health-care plans by market. Using current prices, managers can protect revenue while actuaries project various health-care cost trends. The bottom line is that OLAP allows managers to project profit-and-loss based on the expected shift from traditional health-insurance indemnity products to such self-managed plans as the company's health-maintenance organization.[3]

APPLICATIONS THAT CAN BENEFIT FROM OLAP-VR INTEGRATION

OLAP accounting-and-finance applications can benefit greatly from the utilization of virtual reality. Today, companies deal with an incredible amount of data about economic forecasts, market movements, and, in particular, their own operations. Virtual reality has the potential to turn a company's integrated database into a giant simulated structure that is much easier for people to understand. In fact, many of the important new VR accounting-and-finance applications will make great use of the company's database and data warehouses to get a grasp on a company's operations. Reference can be made to the prior sections on cost accounting and financial analysis which are discussed below, plus other areas that can benefit from OLAP-VR integration.

Activity-Based Costing

Using the activity-based costing method, a decision maker can transform dollar amounts and priorities assigned to projects into colorful, interactive worlds that can be explored. As the individual works with one budgeted item or changes an assignment's priority, a ripple takes place in real time. That is, the decision maker can explore how money is spent at all levels of the company, and can make better decisions on how funds are spent. Essentially, VR software is used to create a walk-through scenario of how a company spent its money. Particular attention is given to flagging low-priority activities that were overfunded. Activities are assigned tall or short bars by their spending levels, and color-coded from green to red, to show priority. Exploring this 3-D landscape, managers are able to determine which activities to view, touch, and manipulate. For example, they can focus on tall red bars, indicating low-priority activities with high costs. Touching these bars activated detailed information about the resources consumed. At any point, they could step back to see how resources were consumed for each high-level business process and for the entire company. Hence, VR is a very effective decision tool because it uses size, shape, and color in a 3-D landscape to convey useful information that may have been highlighted from extensive analysis in an OLAP environment.

Stock Market Analysis

One of the most difficult undertakings in the financial world is predicting the movements of the stock market. Much has been written about the strategies employed by mutual funds, pension funds, insurance companies, and individual investors, whether they are large or small. The action of stock-fund investors in the 1987 crash fit the behavior of individuals in bear markets over the last 30 years. Typically, small investors do nothing in the face of a market fall. Once the market rises and investors recover their losses, they then redeem shares and only slowly return to stocks.

Just as individual investors are changing the stock market with their purchasing power, so too are the latest advances in computer technology changing the way stocks are picked. Today, money managers analyze information for thousands of companies and cut the figures by any number of criteria, such as low price earnings ratio, to come up with undervalued stocks to buy. The problem is, too many investment institutions have the same ideas about the kinds of stocks they want to purchase, with the same computing ability to arrive at the stocks to buy. The net result is that these stocks are now overvalued because the institutions have bid up the prices.

To assist market analysts in their never-ending search for stocks to buy and sell under varying market conditions, VR technology has the capability to represent vast amounts of stock market data in an interactive, real-time mode. This capability allows stock market analysts to organize information in new ways and find new relationships that were not apparent before. Typically, the major stocks in one specific industry can be evaluated by the analyst. Or several selected stocks in different industries can be evaluated one against another. Essentially, the analyst can fly over the stocks where the volume of the stock for the day is shown along with the price range of the day. The shape, position, and color of the stocks are dependent on conditions in the market. The stock analyst can assess the behavior of the stocks to help determine whether or not a specific stock would be a candidate for a buy or a sell. From this perspective, virtual reality offers an effective way to condense and streamline financial information for stock market analysts.

Other Areas

Another VR-accounting application that can utilize an interactive, real-time, simulated mode is an analysis of a company's overhead. By virtually flying over the overhead structures of a company's various devices, departments, and the like, accounting and financial analysts can look for exceptions in one part of a company versus another, and possibly highlight for management review why overhead rates are higher in one part of the company versus another. In effect, analysts can navigate through complex overhead data in a graphic way that results in their looking extensively into an alternative world. They can find new overhead relationships that were previously buried in a stack of manufacturing reports that focused on material, labor, and overhead together. In other words, a picture of what constitutes a company's total operations can be broken down for further analysis and possible improvement based on a virtual-world analysis.

Although the VR applications as presented above are designed to give the user a more realistic picture of a complex business environment, visualization techniques could also have been used for the most part. These techniques have been used for years in the science fields, but the advent of faster, more powerful CPUs, and real-time computer-graphics programs along with VR technology encourages accounting and finance experts to try the same approach. Needless to say, a number of ideas have been bounced around. One way, for example, suggests representing a stock as a stalk of wheat. By having a whole field of wheat and having price fluctuations and market trends propagate like wind across the field, program securities would turn a bright orange when they reach a particular price. Stock market analysts could then put on the head-mounted display and goggles and walk up and down the fields and watch the way the market is moving. The net result is that traditional information is presented in a way that does not require a lot of conscious mental processing.

SUMMARY

The main focus of this chapter has been on the application of OLAP to the areas of accounting and finance. However, this exposition was preceded by important newer concepts and views on accounting and finance that underlie on-line analytical processing. The need for newer approaches is necessitated by the environment in which companies operate today. The environment in which financial decisions are made is highly dynamic, complicated, and information intense. Investment banks, commercial institutions, regulatory institutions, and brokerage houses find their staffs increasingly strained in financial times—good and bad. To help streamline operations and keep up with the times, it is necessary to provide the most intelligent, timely, and focused information for these decision makers by using OLAP capabilities. As a result, accountants and financial analysts can view data within a multidimensional framework as a whole or in detail, can see elements in association with each other or individually, and can link those elements. Hence, judgments can be made faster than they could when that data was viewed in numeric form.

NOTES

1. Dennis Peavey and Jim DePalma, "Do You Know the Cost of Your Products?" (New York: Coopers & Lybrand Executive Briefing, May 1990), pp. 7–9.

2. Ford S. Worthy, "Japan's Smart Secret Weapon," *Fortune*, August 12, 1991, pp. 72-75.

3. Alan Radding, "Blue Cross Climbs Mountain of Data with OLAP," *InfoWorld*, January 30, 1995, p. 64.

10

Human Resources in an OLAP Environment

ISSUES EXPLORED

- How important is it to take a broad perspective of the human-resources function within an OLAP environment?
- What are the important newer directions in human resources that affect OLAP systems?
- How can a human-resource-management system be an integral part of an OLAP-operating mode?
- What are some typical real-world examples where on-line analytical processing has been applied to the human-resources function?
- What areas of human resources can benefit from the integration of OLAP with virtual reality?

OUTLINE

HUMAN RESOURCES IN AN OLAP ENVIRONMENT

Related to four previous chapters on business applications of OLAP is the human-resource (HR) function. More specifically, successful companies focus their attention on integrating their short- to long-range strategic plans directly with the plans of the HR department. As such, there is a great accent on human-resource planning and control whereby the HR process centers on three important activities: (1) identifying and acquiring the right number of people with the proper skills, (2) motivating company personnel to achieve high performance, and (3) creating interactive links between overall organization objectives and HR-planning activities. For the human-resource function to be effective in terms of planning and control, it must be capable of providing a good fit among the employee, the task, and the organization unit. If there is a poor fit, the employee will not be as productive as possible, not to mention the cost to management of motivating the individual to at least a satisfactory level of performance. Overall, the underlying thrust of the HR function for a typical company is to provide a good fit for personnel throughout the organization. This is accomplished more easily by allowing human-resource managers to employ an OLAP approach.

With this in mind, the chapter initially looks at a broad-based integration of human resources with other functional areas. Newer directions in human resources that underlie OLAP systems are presented next in the chapter, followed by sample applications of OLAP for personnel selection and placement as well as wage-and-salary administration. Also, the integration of OLAP systems with virtual reality is set forth at the end of the chapter.

Broad-Based Integration of Human Resources with Other Functional Areas

Within a typical OLAP environment, a company's HR managers are concerned with spotting adverse trends in turnover and absenteeism. This responsibility does not end with problem identification. The goal is to determine the causes of these problems and what is actually needed to help the company solve them. HR managers have to be more creative (i.e., proactive) in those areas of its responsibilities, and its staff needs to become involved in providing them with advice that is workable and useful. In addition, HR managers have to become increasingly oriented toward growth and efficiency of the company instead of merely administering traditional human-resource activities. This means greater emphasis upon planning the structure of the future organization and its HR requirements, identifying and selecting the right people to meet those expected needs, developing and utilizing the company's present-day human resources, and assessing and rewarding performance. The purpose of these activities is to ensure growth of both the company and the individual employee.

From this view, there is a need to think in terms of the total company and not the HR department by itself. For an effective OLAP approach, HR activities must be integrated into the company's overall strategic-planning process as well as be related to basic marketing, manufacturing, and finance activities. Instead of a mélange of diverse activities, the HR department must be a broad-based integration of these activities in order to have an effective utilization of the company's human resources. It must be sensitive to the organization's requirements and be committed to making the company more effective. Specifically, the personnel selection and placement function assists in locating qualified employees for full-time and part-time assignments. If in-house personnel cannot be found, this function takes over hiring from the outside. Included in this function is human-resources planning for the short, intermediate, and long run. Additionally, wage-and-salary administration must be concerned with equitable pay for its employees. Wages and salaries must fairly reflect employee positions and skills required. The HR function can best be assisted, then, in the context of an effective OLAP environment by relating its activities from the outset to the strategic-planning process.

NEWER DIRECTIONS IN HUMAN RESOURCES THAT UNDERLIE OLAP

Newer directions relevant to the HR function go beyond its own basic structure within an effective OLAP environment. As examples, production planning and control requires the proper placement of factory personnel to effect the desired level of output. Shipment of finished-goods inventory considers the number of warehouse personnel handling customer orders. Also, payroll-master data provide a starting point in terms of present personnel cost. An effective HR system, then, must relate to other functional areas in order to provide the necessary human resources for accomplishing organizational objectives.

Because the HR function is so all-encompassing, companies need to expand their managerial decision-making processes. Not only is it necessary to develop short- to long-range plans in this area, but also it is extremely important to mesh these plans with other systems encompassing marketing, manufacturing, finance, and other related operations. Competition and technical innovations portend far more than new packaging, engineering, or merchandising programs. The "people element" is indispensable to the typical company. Personnel executives and their staffs must display a high level of analytical ability to provide useful solutions to a wide range of people problems confronting them. To assist in the development of on-line analytical processing systems, newer directions are set forth below. These relate to (1) a problem-finding approach to human resources, (2) the role of human resources in reengineering, (3) accent on human-resource-management system (HRMS) software, (4) finding human resources on the Internet, and (5) training as a prerequisite for a company's rightsizing.

A Problem-Finding Approach to Human Resources

The human-resource function in a typical organization is called upon to assist senior management and its corporate-planning staff in ways that result in more effective use of both human resources and the capabilities of the personnel system. This enlarged perspective necessitates that the personnel decision-process change from problem solving to problem finding. Hence, there is a need to expand on this approach to provide for the impact of human factors on organizational success and productivity. This realization leads to bringing human-resource specialists into corporate planning. Once admitted, these specialists begin to shift the administration's orientation from *reactive* administration to *proactive* management and planning. The organization and its human-resources department begin to think in terms of projected labor needs, five-year hiring plans, anticipatory talent development, employee recycling, productive task distribution, and cost accountability.

Since these issues have for the most part not been seriously contemplated before, the typical organization finds that it has neither the collected data nor the analytical capability to tackle them, and so has turned, in many cases, to outside consultants for assistance. The consultants, in turn, have developed tools to create the forecasts and models that clients are requesting. Only recently have some of these tools begun to appear as software for human-resource-management systems (HRMSs).

The message should be clear. The real value of a human-resource planning system is not after-the-fact analysis, but an anticipatory capability. The critical need is to solve problems before they arise. The human-resources system, then, must be increasingly aware of the significance of the organization's human resources today and tomorrow. It must review the efficient use of existing personnel at its present and future levels of development, assess the level of present and anticipated performance of company employees, and concern itself with the enhancement of the individual's skills and talents currently and in the future in order to improve productivity and overall contribution of the workforce.

From this perspective, there is the need for top management to change its thinking about the company and its employees. Too often, short-term gains are the accepted practice in American business as well as politics. Typically, these short-term gains result in reduced headcount. What happens to a company's jobs that have been simplified, automated, and eliminated? The layoffs in the automotive and computer industries are examples of job functions that have been lost. In prior recessions, when the business climate improved, laid-off employees were brought back. This is certainly not true today. Their job functions have been automated, that is, eliminated. These previous company employees are structurally unemployed. Those who have reaped the benefits of automation are responsible for those who suffer as a result of automation. This structural unemployment is the hidden cost of automation that business and politics must face. What should have been done was that companies should have had in place an educational plan for the year 2000 and beyond. Top management needs to define what job skills will be required in five to ten years, then train and educate the workforce to fill those jobs as needed. Future job-skill needs require long-range HR strategic planning. Failing to manage change today means that the typical company will not be able to react to change at the appropriate times tomorrow.

The Role of Human Resources in Reengineering

Historically, human resources has been an unlikely place to invest significant time and dollars. Although the HR function has been relegated to the bottom of most IT projects, more companies are reengineering their personnel processes. Instead of simply counting heads and administering personnel rules, HR professionals are intimately involved in the strategic side of their business. Companies recognize that their biggest asset is people, and they are finding ways to best manage and utilize this asset. This means that many companies are replacing first- or second-generation HR packages. From an overall perspective, reengineering of human resources centers on improvements in hiring, training, placement, and tracking of employees. The end result should be better employees in the right jobs, reduced turnover, and greater efficiency of a company's operations.

In a typical HR-reengineering undertaking, two things tend to happen. First, reengineering changes jobs that incumbents are not ready to have changed, either because they are not trained to handle the new job requirements or simply because the old familiar ways are more comfortable. Backsliding into old processes is a common pitfall of reengineering. This necessitates continuing communications and training to prevent this from happening. Second, a changed process turns out to be no improvement at all, but rather a focus on automation by itself at the expense of quality or other desired company values. A system that takes the human element out of service-providing functions, such as an automated telephone system that asks callers to push "1" for this, push "2" for that, and so forth, can backfire in many companies.

To help overcome these barriers to successful reengineering, there is a need for HR professionals to plan for technological change that will remake jobs far beyond the work of job redesign and systems implementation. Not only must the new requirements of a changed job be clearly defined and spelled out, but also the HR professionals must take this planning several steps further. More specifically, what current employees have the skills and talents needed to perform successfully in these redesigned jobs? What training will they need? What are their new measures of successful performance? Are the existing compensation plans adequate? How can these employees be motivated in these changed jobs and kept motivated to use the new technology? And, just as important, is this change really an improvement or just a way to do things faster and with less human intervention?

Advanced planning for new technology must consider the appropriateness of any given technology for the tasks to be performed. The major issue of the right system goes beyond technical considerations. The technical issues can be addressed by client/server, enterprise applications, and networked systems that place the various types of computer operations on the appropriate hardware and in the right hands. Currently, it is technically feasible to put data administration on the host server, applications on middleware or PCs, and user presentation and local processing on desktop PCs.

Going beyond these technical considerations are questions of functional appropriateness that are crucial to the success of the new technology. From this perspective, an effective approach to HR-system implementation is one that focuses on the "vision" of the new technology to achieve specific bottom-line results. Technology planners who begin from the chief executive officer's perspective—that is, what will be the total cost of the new technology and what benefits can be expected from its implementation—are in the best position to make the right choices when selecting new technology, and are most likely to succeed in keeping the implementation project right on track. Thus, proper HR-technology planning begins with a business-based mission that is sharply focused on identifiable returns to corporate profitability rather than high-tech solutions to problems of lower magnitude.

Accent on Human-Resource-Management System (HRMS) Software

Because an organization's most valuable resource is its employees, every employee represents an obligation to utilize that resource in the most beneficial way. Also, every employee represents a vast amount of record keeping, not only for the organization's internal needs, but also for governmental (external) needs. In the past, a typical human-resource-management system (HRMS) was performed manually. Hours were spent searching files to locate specific information needed for a list or report. Today, however, performing these tasks manually can bury the human-resources department under an avalanche of details, increasing government and labor union compliance demands, and a growing assortment of employee benefits.

HRMS software is available to fit the needs of most organizations and operate on a wide variety of hardware and networking environments. They are relatively inexpensive, relatively easy to install, and pay for themselves in terms of time saved and penalties avoided. These systems are staking a vital claim in the structure of strategic planning. Human-resource-management systems can be used in a variety of ways to meet internal and external needs. They can track such information as skills, prior employment, and training courses to aid in career path planning. They can be used for recruiting, training, and educating employees. They can track and administer employee benefits and monitor absences.

A most important element related to human-resource-management systems is the planning for human resources, commonly referred to as manpower planning. Human-resources planning is greatly needed because of the decreasing supply of high-talent personnel. The Research Institute of America has stated that management not only is the most urgent need of the future, but will be the most critically short resource. As a result, planning must be aimed toward management development. Not only will management be in short supply, but so will personnel with high levels of technical knowledge. This latter shortage is due to rapid technological change. It is difficult for even a qualified professional to keep abreast of any field, a fact that may cause obsolescence of technical manpower. The increasing shortage of management and technical personnel, together with their high cost, has forced companies to recognize that manpower itself must be considered a resource as important as other corporate resources. To assist in the forecasting process, personnel models are useful in manipulating available human-resource data by using mathematical and statistical models. They provide a simplified and logical view of the levels and flows of personnel throughout an organizational system. They focus on variables considered by managers to be significant and consider assumptions or parameters underlying system behavior.

The role of the HRMS has expanded to include the full range of human-resource functions. One way to justify the investment in HRMS software is to identify the benefits and the costs in each of the areas set forth as follows: human-resources planning, salary planning, pension planning, benefits administration, career planning, management development, training, equal-employment opportunities, applicant tracking, recruitment, skills inventories, time and attendance, and employee directory. Other important areas are: payroll, productivity programs, employee communications, job postings, labor relations, performance evaluation, flexible benefits, and postemployment services. Another way to justify the cost of this software is to focus on its role in performing key functions of greatest concern to top management, such as the planning and implementing strategic changes as well as employee-benefits administration. Typically, a cost-benefit analysis will indicate that investing in HRMS software is a wise move for a company.

Popular HRMS-software packages are set forth in Figure 10.1. Most new HRMS implementations have been on client/server platforms. Client/server systems are less procedure-bound and help companies migrate to process-oriented approaches. A newer direction is a paperless HRMS that creates on-line versions of all HR, benefit, and payroll forms. In this manner, transactions can be automatically routed via E-mail anytime and anyplace. Electronic signoffs speed approvals and ensure that proper procedures are enforced. In effect, hiring, salary changes, applicant reviews, benefits adjustments, and other HR/payroll functions can be completed in less time and for less money.

Typically, selecting HRMS software can be a complex task, especially since purchasing and maintaining it will cost a large company millions of dollars over the lifetime of the system. Selecting the right HRMS is the greatest contribution to improve a company's position in the marketplace and to elevating the role of human resources to a position of strategic partner in the company. Information is power, and the right HRMS will give access to the information needed.

Finding Human Resources on the Internet

The Internet is the latest means by which job applicants and notices for jobs can find each other. Several software providers have begun using the Internet to offer new services to corporate HR departments. Essentially, companies, academic institutions, government entities, professional associations, or individuals use an outward-bound access to services and servers run by these software providers. For example, IntelliMatch provides a worldwide multiple-listing service for jobs and job seekers. It also enables individuals to file resumes in a set format on a World Wide Web site that employers can download for a fee. The prescribed format helps prescreen applicant qualifications. Currently, IntelliMatch offers software for employers to access its database via the Internet and use the company's search engine to find candidates with certain skills. Employers pay only for contacts with the skills that match their needs.

Additionally, this new direction in hiring employees involves HR's participation in intracompany on-line initiatives. More and more companies recognize not only the potential of providing a Web presence to the outside world via its home page that posts job openings, but also the usefulness of implementing an internal Web for posting information, handling routine and administrative transactions, and facilitating company-wide communication. When an organization decides to become involved in the Internet and the World Wide Web, it takes a proactive stance in furnishing information to an external or internal audience.

Figure 10.1
Popular HRMS-Software Packages

Company	Product	HRMS Features
Computer Associates International Islandia, NY 800-225-5224 http:www.cai.com	CA-HRISMA	Personnel, payroll, applicant tracking, defined contributions, benefits, compensation
Cyborg Systems Chicago, IL 312-454-1865 http://www.cyborg.com	Solution Series/ST, HRMS	Personnel, payroll, benefits, applicant tracking, compen- sation, workflow
Dun & Bradstreet Software Atlanta, GA 800-234-3867 http://www.dbsoftware.com	HR Stream	Personnel, recruitment, compensation, payroll, benefits, workflow
Genesys Systems and Services Methueum, MA 508-685-5400 http://www.genesys-soft.com	Genesys Ener- prise Series	Personnel, payroll, benefits, defined contributions
InPower Walnut Creek, CA 800-930-0165 http://www.inpower.com	InPower HR, InPower Pay	Personnel, staffing, compensation, payroll, workflow
Lawson Software Minneapolis, MN 800-477-1357 http://www.lawson.com	Lawson Human Resources System	Personnel, applicant tracking, payroll, benefits
Oracle Corporation Redwood Shores, CA 800-633-0596 http://www.oracle.com	Oracle HRMS	Personnel, payroll, benefits, training administration
PeopleSoft Pleasanton, CA 800-947-7753 http://www.peoplesoft.com	PeopleSoft/ HRMS	Personnel, recruiting, benefits, payroll, agent- based workflow
Ross Systems Atlanta, GA 404-851-1872 http://www.rossinc.com	Renaissance CS Human Re- source Series	Personnel, recruitment, payroll, benefits
SAP America Wayne, PA 800-872-1727 http://www.sap.com	R/3 HRMS	Personnel, payroll, benefits, workflow
Tesseract San Francisco, CA 415-981-1800 http://www.tesseract.com	HRMS	HR, applicant tracking, compensation, benefits, payroll

Training as a Prerequisite for a Company's Rightsizing

Today, there are continuing headlines featuring the *Fortune* 500 companies, most of which are rightsizing. In most cases, the focus is on *downsizing*. The new mantra in corporate America seems to be "Do more with less, be more efficient at what you do, and work smarter throughout the day." In effect, get better at everything done in the workplace. However, some companies are *upsizing* their operations to meet their short- to long-term growth goals. No matter the rightsizing approach taken, there are significant problems facing these companies. The *first* of these problems is that many new workers need training in a growth company, whereas the remaining workers in a downsized company are underskilled and need to be trained to take on new duties and responsibilities. *Second*, there is a need to improve a company's commitment to a total-quality-management (TQM) program such that continuing quality improvements can be made throughout the year. *Third*, the continuing sophistication of newer products and services requires expanded training for company workers at all levels. *Fourth*, whether a company is upsizing or downsizing, there needs to be a renewed emphasis on customers within or outside the organization. *Fifth*, in conjunction with the fourth problem, there should be a team or group effort to meet customer needs as opposed to the individual trying to do the whole job alone. Not to mention others, these problems are reason enough for a typical company to undertake appropriate levels of training for its personnel.

In actuality, training is an obligation that a company owes to its employees and itself for continued existence. Without training, a company can be hobbled by the "check-your-brains-at-the-door" work methods that make no sense in today's business world. If a company wants to build a high-performance and flexible organization, then it has to train its workers. Whether it is large or small, a company that does not train does not gain in the short or long run for its employees or itself, which includes its stockholders.

Today, some of the best training in America takes place at Motorola where its factory workers study the fundamentals of computer-aided design, robotics, and customized manufacturing. This is accomplished not solely by reading manuals or attending lectures, but by inventing and building their own plastic knickknacks as well. The company runs its well-known training programs from Motorola University, a collection of computer-equipped classrooms and laboratories at corporate headquarters (Schaumburg, Illinois). Just recently, Motorola University, which includes regional campuses in Phoenix and Austin, delivered approximately 100,000 days of training to employees, suppliers, and customers. Because this school does not employ many professional educators, it relies on a cadre of outside consultants (including engineers, scientists, and former managers) to teach the bulk of its courses. Their role is to prod, guide, and orchestrate. In a class on reducing manufacturing-cycle time, for example, senior managers break quickly into teams to devise new ways to get a product to market faster.

Motorola calculates that every dollar it spends on training delivers 30 dollars in productivity gains within three years. Since 1987, the company has cut costs by $3.3 billion—not by the normal expedient of firing workers, but by training them to simplify processes and reduce waste. Sales per employee have doubled in the past five years, and profits have increased by about 50 percent.[1]

HUMAN-RESOURCE AREAS THAT LEND THEMSELVES TO AN OLAP ENVIRONMENT

In the continuing battle to meet and beat competition, managers must control labor costs and motivate employees to improve customer-oriented performance and, at the same time, search out new and better ways of doing both. These strategic objectives must be met in the face of shrinking head count and a global environment in which employees are more culturally diverse and located throughout the world. From this perspective, relatively routine tasks of human-resource (HR) record keeping and legal and regulatory compliance are intensified. Such complexity also demands more sophisticated applications of strategies that go beyond simply improving the management of routine tasks. Essentially, company managers have a stake in exploiting appropriate strategies to better manage their human resources.

In light of the foregoing comments, there is the need for managers to understand the impact of human resources on the company today and tomorrow. Essentially, the OLAP applications that have been demonstrated in previous chapters are complementary to those presented in this chapter for human resources. Typical ones in this section that lend themselves to on-line analytical processing for managers at all levels include personnel selection and placement plus wage-and-salary administration. Additionally, the training of new managers for specific functional areas could include the utilization of OLAP systems that are currently in place for their use on the job. In a similar manner, applications that are a natural for OLAP revolve around long-range human resource planning where the focus is on getting a handle on the company's changing workforce. That is, a typical company could be moving in the direction of more specialized technical products and services that require a higher level of basic skills. A thorough analysis of a company's future human-resource requirements would be helpful in deciding whether the present workforce can be retrained or there is need for going outside to recruit a different type of technically qualified personnel. Overall, there are a number of human-resource areas that lend themselves to on-line analytical processing which, in the final analysis, can assist a typical manager in better understanding the ins and outs of the human element.

AN OLAP APPROACH TO PERSONNEL SELECTION AND PLACEMENT

The personnel selection and placement system for either a typical manufacturing-oriented or service-oriented company centers around the recruitment, screening, and selection of employees before and throughout their employment. The initial discussion below focuses on solving human-resource problems before they arise, followed by forecasting human resources, and using an HRMS to assist company managers. In addition, appropriate human-resources information can be passed on to the corporate-planning staff for short- to long-range strategic planning. Within an OLAP-operating mode, multidimensional analysis can be used to measure personnel cost savings, productivity, analysis of lower turnover, and complaints. Also, quantitative measurement encompassing employee morale, interest, and job satisfaction can be undertaken. Whatever the chosen method of measurement, results should then be shared with management at all levels on a regular basis and, if needed, modified to reflect the necessary changes.

Solving Human-Resource Problems Before They Arise

An integral part of the human-resource function is determining employee problems before they arise. These problems can take many directions. As an example, they can center on downsizing. This restructuring in most companies has left human resources with a smaller workforce and yet with equal or greater responsibilities and new demands. Time has become as crucial a resource as talent and money. Human-resources management, then, must review its own work such that problems are anticipated before they arise. Typically, areas to be investigated now revolve around the following. What work must continue to be done? Of that work, which can be done better by searching out efficiencies and economies of scale? Which can be done better by delegating and collaborating with line managers and employees or other functional staffs? Which would benefit most from creative time, talent, and resources? In essence, how can the problems of working harder, smarter, or with more vision be resolved now? Needless to say, the area of training is a major player in solving these problems.

In the area of searching out efficiencies and economies of scale, company managers, assisted by those in human-resource management, could advocate streamlining the processing of employee records, payroll, and benefits by standardizing and eliminating unnecessary paper handling and reporting. This can be accomplished by utilizing a human-resource-management system. In this manner, an HRMS could allow the company to be a low-cost provider for critical administrative work as well as a more accurate and timely provider of HR information. To improve delegating and collaborating with line managers and employees, human resources can collaborate with line managers or others to become more responsive to their needs. For example, HR could replace a merit-pay process requiring product-line managers to follow an imposed standard set of guidelines with a system encouraging human resource and line managers to customize pay-increase plans jointly for their units. While HR contributes the incentive design expertise, line managers contribute their hands-on understanding of customer demands and the rewards that would best motivate employees to achieve those demands. Under an innovation strategy, human resources could allocate 10–15 percent of staff time to exploratory, creative projects with uncertain short-term to long-term payoffs. Perhaps, human resources could reach new customers by providing expertise to other organizations, thereby making human resources a profit center.

Forecasting Human Resources

An integral part of an OLAP-operating mode for personnel selection and placement is forecasting future personnel needs. A workforce simulator can be employed to determine personnel information under varying future conditions. The workforce simulator is a broad-based planning model that takes into account the interaction of different workforce factors. As a starting point, data about the current plant-level workforce—age, work classification, experience, education level, and comparable data—are accessed from the corporate database. A decision concerning a mandatory retirement age is normally included. Also, an estimate of attrition due to reasons other than retirement is set forth. Factors for recruiting new personnel for growth are added, and provisions are made for internal transfers of employees because of promotion or retraining. As such, the workforce-simulation model considers increasing and/or decreasing job levels over time, such as a one-year up to a five-year span. Based on these factors, which can be simulated for one plant, several plants, or the entire company, the results can be graphed and reviewed for comparison over varying time periods.

As shown in Figure 10.2, the company is contemplating a fourth factory in the second year where the increase in employees over the first year (for three plants) is approximately 20 percent. Additionally, net increases in employment are expected to be over 10 percent in the third, fourth, and fifth years. The job classifications used in the illustration are: (1) senior engineers, (2) junior engineers, (3) production planning and control personnel, (4) department foremen, (5) engineering assistants, (6) tool and die makers, (7) machinists, and (8) assembly workers. Over the five-year period, increases in the eight engineering and manufacturing job types are shown in this multidimensional analysis. Hence, the current or base year can be compared to succeeding years, indicating the need for additional personnel in the coming years. Although not shown in Figure 10.2, answers to ad hoc questions based upon different personnel policies of hiring can be answered. For example, the actual number of trained employees would be lower than that required for untrained employees. The net effect of this workforce-simulator model is that it allows a hypothetical test of different personnel policies for review. This approach to human-resource forecasting in an OLAP environment provides human-resource managers with short- to long-range personnel information.

In terms of meeting a company's immediate needs for human resources, say for a manufacturing plant, there is a need for a system that assists manufacturing plant supervisors and foremen in matching current employees to job openings. As suggested earlier in the chapter, an intracompany approach using the Internet could be employed. Or, from another perspective, if one or more job openings go unfilled for two weeks or more, then plant management interrogates the plant

Figure 10.2
Forecasted Personnel Needs for a Typical Company Over a Five-Year Period

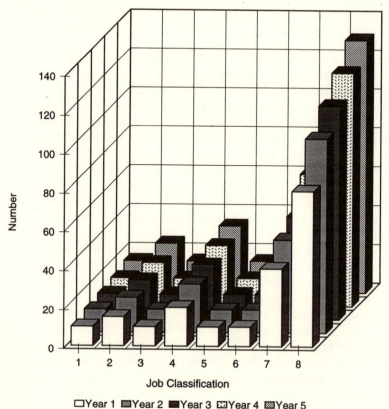

□Year 1 ▨Year 2 ■Year 3 ⊠Year 4 ▩Year 5

database in order to screen possible applicants who might be candidates. If none is available within the requesting plant, the databases at the other plants are interrogated. In either case, an on-line computer comparison in two or three dimensions can be made on the prospective applicants. The output—the job-applicant review profile—becomes the basis for discussion by plant management in terms of a possible transfer of one or more employees. On the other hand, if no one is available internally, or if the available personnel are not interested, it is generally necessary to go outside for recruiting the appropriate factor person-nel. As above, the Internet could be used as a means for recruiting the desired personnel. This access capability is extremely helpful to plant management for high-skill jobs.

The foregoing procedures for matching employees (current and prospective) to job openings is very responsive to the task of meeting the newer skills re-quired in a changing manufacturing environment. Throughout the process, plant management brings certain personal parameters (intuition, past experience, and judgment) to the employee–job matching process. They have the total freedom and flexibility to accept or reject the employees under consideration. With this view, the individual's subjective feelings are integrated with the objective findings via the job-search program.

Using an HRMS to Assist Company Mangers

The human-resource system of a typical company must be able to answer pertinent management questions as they arise. By using an HRMS in an OLAP-operating mode, such questions are answerable with the assistance of three-dimensional analysis if applicable. For example: What is the cost of laying off a shift in a particular plant? The HRMS system is able to provide an answer on the basis of the labor contract. The other parts of the HRMS center on answering questions that relate to the rules, that is, the policies, contracts, and federal regulations that govern the way people within the company can do things. When these rules are incorporated into the system, appropriate questions as posed by managers to make personnel more effective can be answered, and decisions administered properly. If the company has a policy of hiring only people with a particular background at a certain level, for example, management needs to have its HRMS system enforce this. From this perspective, the HRMS serves top-level managers as well as the HR department.

Additionally, the HRMS should allow company managers to produce ad hoc or special reports. The HRMS should be able to provide top-level managers with an answer to such a question as: If a 5 percent increase were given to all salaried personnel employed by the company for over five years of service, a 7 percent increase given to all employees with over eight years of service, and a 4 percent increase to non-salaried personnel, what do salaries look like for the coming year and the following two years, that is, over three years? (This question lends itself to three-dimensional analysis—wage increase, years of service, and years 1 through 3.) The real value of the OLAP system, then, is how its output can be related back to the company's managers at the appropriate level.

Today, an HRMS can assist in providing employees with Employee Self Service (ESS) technology, such as voice-response systems and multimedia interactive kiosks. These technology implementations allow employees to interact directly with their benefit plans, and holiday and sick time programs. Perhaps an even greater benefit (other than reduced costs) is that as employees gain more direct control over their benefits administration, they also gain an increased appreciation of their own overall compensation plan and what it can do for them when needed.

A most important purpose of utilizing an integrated HRMS for company managers is to reduce the costs of routine personnel tasks, especially when employing a local area network. The cost of processing human-resource records should be as low as possible, but it is advisable to offer employees the widest range of fringe-benefit options so that desired employees can be retained. From this enlarged view of HRMSs, how to place all items in their proper perspective can be far from clear. In most cases, work division is not clear-cut. The proper assignment of human-resource work must reveal to company managers how resources might best be allocated to support one specific strategy over another.

In order to undertake an evaluation of different strategies within an HRMS environment, it is helpful to take an OLAP approach. The decision makers would tend to miss important relationships that lie buried in mounds of detail. The individual can navigate through complex data in a three-dimensional graphical way that has not been possible in the past. A "good fit" among the user, the task, and the company can be realized by using an OLAP-operating mode, so that new relationships not envisioned before can be seen to effect employee improvements in productivity throughout the company.

AN OLAP APPROACH TO WAGE-AND-SALARY ADMINISTRATION

Typically, wage-and-salary administration can take several directions since it involves working with selected data and ratios. In many companies, it centers primarily on utilizing various types of wage-and-salary analyses to answer "what-if" questions. In other companies, it includes these analyses and delves into other human-resource issues by evaluating output on the effectiveness of human-resource management in controlling departmental budgets, the backup of key positions in the office and in the manufacturing plants, the amounts paid to factory production workers, the promotability of office and factory employees, the company's progress toward affirmative action, and, in general, the human-resource-department goals and progress toward realizing them. Although all of these areas lend themselves to an OLAP environment, the focus below will be on wage-and-salary administration.

Analysis of Wage-and-Salary Data to Get at a Company's Current Inequities

Within an OLAP operating mode, an annual wage-and-salary survey is useful to make appropriate comparisons. To gain a better understanding of the annual wage-and-salary survey in Figure 10.3(a) (current year only) for a typical manufacturing-oriented company, it is helpful for the company's HR managers to make meaningful comparisons, that is, to compare the industry average to wages and salaries paid in the various manufacturing plants for the current year. For our purposes, three manufacturing plants will be used. The current yearly data is graphed in three dimensions in Figure 10.3(b) for highly technical, technical, and semi-technical personnel. The data in both figures indicate that the company is underpaying and overpaying some of its engineering and manufacturing personnel for the current year. This is easier to see quickly in Figure 10.3(b) than Figure 10.3(a) since the height of the three bars is shown against the industry

Figure 10.3(a)
Current-Year Salary Survey for Engineering and Manufacturing by Job Classifications for a Typical Manufacturing-Oriented Company

| Job Classification | Manufacturing Plants | | | Industry |
	First	Second	Third	Average
Highly Technical:				
(1) Senior Engineers	$52,600	$48,600	$52,800	$51,500
(2) Junior Engineers	39,000	38,600	42,500	40,500
**(3) Production Planning and Control Personnel	40,000	38,500	42,500	42,500
Technical:				
**(4) Department Foremen	41,400	41,100	42,400	42,800
(5) Engineering Assistants	32,300	31,500	34,800	34,400
*(6) Tool and Die Makers	38,700	37,800	39,500	37,500
Semi-Technical:				
(7) Machinists	35,900	35,000	36,800	36,500
*(8) Assembly Workers	32,600	32,200	33,000	32,100

*Above the industry average for all plants

**Below or equal to industry average for all plants

average—the final bar. In addition, comparable analyses could be performed over the last five years to see whether or not these patterns hold true over time. If so, action may be necessary to bring the company's engineering and manufacturing wages and salaries in line with the industry average, as well as with its own manufacturing plants.

Analysis of Wage-and-Salary Data to Resolve Other Wage-and-Salary Issues

Going beyond the above wage-and-salary analysis, many questions can be asked and answered using multidimensional analysis by HR managers. For example, management could evaluate over a five-year period how wages and salaries in a company's plants and warehouses compare to budget, how the cost of wages and salaries compares to sales, and how one plant or warehouse ranks against other plants and/or warehouses and against the company average. Similarly, HR management may want to undertake analyses that focus on present and future personnel problems. The company may want to determine the impact, if any, of wage imbalances because of different costs of living for each of the plants and warehouses, and to determine, given the economic conditions, the impact on employees of adjusting salaries. From another perspective, manage-

Figure 10.3(b)
Multidimensional Analysis of Wage-and-Salary Survey for Engineering and
Manufacturing Personnel During the Current Year Shown in Figure 10.3(a)

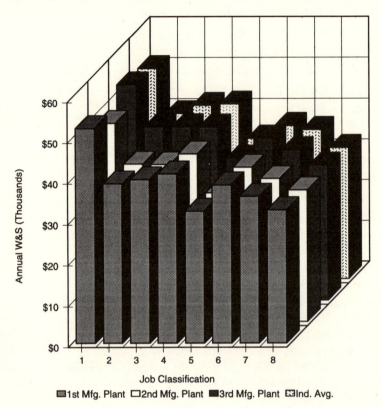

ment might want to know whether or not its workforce will be paid appropriate
fringe benefits in the next two years as well as five years hence. To facilitate
these future evaluations, management needs analyses, such as future wage-and-
salary information, of comparable positions and skills for the plant's and warehouse's geographical area, the estimated future cost of living and consumer price
indices for each plant and warehouse, and the optimal wage-and-salary packages
that the company should offer its workers for certain skills and positions. Thus,
an OLAP-operating mode can be quite helpful to management for understanding
today what wage-and-salary administration problems they might face tomorrow.

In addition, other personnel issues related to wage-and-salary administration
that can be resolved center on evaluating output on: human-resources departmental goals and progress toward realizing them, plant goals and progress toward realizing them, the backup of key positions in the office and the plants,
the promotability of employees, and the company's progress toward affirmative
action. Essentially, human-resource data can be extracted, manipulated, and

graphed to answer specific questions directed toward wage-and-salary administration by HR managers and their staffs. As will be seen below, questions can be of a longer-term nature when top-level management is involved in long-range corporate strategic planning for human resources.

A Problem-Centered Approach to Analyze Future Wages and Salaries

Building upon the foregoing discussion of a multidimensional analysis of wages and salaries, there is a need to bring together top managers in order to address important future problems that should be addressed today for solution. For example, top management of a typical service-oriented company must make sure that the current workforce is being paid appropriate wages and salaries plus fringe benefits. To facilitate this evaluation, top management needs recurring reports such as current wage-and-salary information of comparable positions and skills within each sales-geographical area, the estimated future cost-of-living and consumer-price indices for each sales area, and the optimal wage-and-salary package the company should offer its employees by certain skills or positions. In addition, ad hoc reports are needed to determine if the company paid its employees fair wages and salaries over the past several years; to determine the impact, if any, of wage imbalances because of different costs of living in each of the sales-geographical areas; and to determine, given an economic condition, what will be the impact of adjusting salaries for the employees. Ad hoc wage-and-salary reports need not stop here for the short run, but can be related to future labor costs over the next five years, especially if a company plans to increase its sales significantly. Hence, an OLAP-operating mode can be quite helpful to top management to get a handle today on wage-and-salary administration problems tomorrow. To place this viewpoint into the proper perspective, the discussion to follow will focus on a problem-centered approach to labor costs over the next five years by a typical top-management group.

In the *generation* phase (first step of the problem-centered approach), the top-management group examines the potential labor-cost problems that might arise in the next five years. First, wages and salaries will undoubtedly rise due to the cost of living. Second, the sales growth of the company will affect changes in the wage-and-salary structure. Third, the prior item will affect the company's relations with its unions, that is, the unions will be demanding more with robust sales growth. Fourth, the impact of paying wages and salaries to new employees must be assessed. Additionally, a number of related problems need to be addressed by the top-management group currently. All of the foregoing problems need to undergo a thorough *evaluation* (second step) today by the top-management group to determine what future impact they have on maintaining profitable operations.

In the *validation* stage (third step), the top-management group focused on the company's relationship with its unions. Top management concluded that its future relationship with its various unions is the key factor in meeting its significant increase in sales goals over the next five years, as well as meeting its profitability goals. The *establishment of boundaries* (fourth step) is related to maintaining operations in this country only since the company is not contemplating any foreign operations in the years to come.

The *solution* to this wage-and-salary administration problem centers on utilizing the modeling capabilities of the OLAP software. More specifically, "what-if" questions can be answered for each economic situation (good, average, and bad). Typical questions center on the following: What will be the impact of paying salaries to present employees as well as new employees entering the company? How much will the company have to pay by position and skill? What will be the wage-and-salary structure at each sales office as a result of new hires as well as layoffs? Answers to each of these questions, using multidimensional analysis or otherwise, can be obtained based on certain input parameters and assumptions that can be changed to accommodate ongoing economic conditions.

Even though *implementation* is some time off, the top-management group needs to convey this information to the corporate-planning staff so that it can be an integral part of the company's strategic long-range plans. Overall, a problem-centered approach can help top management understand better its future labor problems that are related to the company's rapid expansion plans and its desire to monitor profitability over the next five years.

A TYPICAL REAL-WORLD OLAP APPLICATION RELATED TO HUMAN RESOURCES

As seen in the prior discussion, a company's workforce today comprises a diverse group of full-timers and part-timers that have a wide range of skills and needs. It is the job of HR managers to enable the company to rightsize at the appropriate times, accommodate flexible schedules, and administer a host of new programs for compensation, benefits, and training. In addition, HR has to keep track of a wide range of legislation and regulations that include EEOC, ADA, FMLA, ERISA, COBRA, and OSHA, not to mention HMOs, PPOs, and 401(k)s. At the same time, the HR department needs to move beyond personnel's administrative legacy and take on a much more strategic role in the company. In many organizations, HR and IS are collaborating on enterprisewide—often client/server based—systems that are designed to provide management with critical information about workforce issues. Many of the analyses needed for this critical information can be obtained from OLAP systems.

For example, new HR technology has helped Holiday Inn Worldwide. Because a hotel's reputation hinges on the level of service provided by its employees, managing human resources for the Atlanta-based chain of almost 2,000 hotels in 60 countries has always been a critical task. Just recently, HR's involvement in establishing strategic direction has expanded with the growing importance of information technology, which includes elements of OLAP. In the past, whenever Holiday Inn looked into a new business venture, financial implications would be the first consideration. Viability from an HR perspective would not be considered until much later in the process. By that time, finance may have spent considerable time and resources looking at deals that had no chance of getting off the ground due to the lack of required personnel skills. However, that has changed because HR can track executives' experience and skills using newer PC-based software—HRSoft Inc. (Morristown, New Jersey).

Newer HR technology is also helping Holiday Inn enhance career development for its top 125 corporate executives and key operational personnel at each hotel. The HRSoft application allows the company to store a detailed resume for each executive, including work history, education, and special skills, in a customized format. A manager can query the database and get a report of all qualified candidates.

In addition, the system also enables Holiday Inn to measure the effectiveness of its career-development program, a capability that would not be possible without the technology. With the system, HR tracks the earliest and latest possible dates on which employees should be moved to another job, based on the opinions of their line managers. Holiday Inn certainly needs to keep track of such progress because over the next four years, the company plans to acquire or convert 1,000 properties.[2]

APPLICATIONS THAT CAN BENEFIT FROM OLAP-VR INTEGRATION

There are a number of human-resource areas that can reap the benefits of a virtual world that is integrated with an OLAP environment. Chief among these are training areas, wage-and-salary evaluation, and job searching. All of these areas are treated below.

Training

In a typical training environment, instructors no longer need to be constrained by the limitations of prerecorded video and film. Different training scenarios can be constructed and then altered by variety. Trainees can have complete freedom to move and interact with the training environment that goes beyond multidimensional analysis. For example, Motorola's three-day advanced training course teaches manufacturing associates how to operate robotic-assembly lines. However, only three facilities (Schaumberg, Illinois; Boynton Beach, Florida; and Singapore) have been outfitted with the advanced-manufacturing equipment laboratory used in the course—a 25-foot by 30-foot replica of the floor-line machinery. Recent tests with virtual-reality software, however, show promising results for cost-effectively expanding this training program to more locations. Using VR to learn operations in a test run, employees become totally immersed in the material, thereby making fewer mistakes than students trained on traditional-laboratory equipment.

For this Motorola training course, programming code was written to add movement so that the model would react correctly. When students turn on a power switch, the corresponding lights or equipment are powered. If the power is not turned on and the students try to start the equipment, there is no response—just as it would be on the actual line. Also, on the virtual line, students hear the same noises they would with the real equipment, and the reactions of activating machinery are identical to real-world events. For example, when a pallet comes to a "lift," the operator hears a sound which lets the individual know that the pallet has been properly raised into position.[3]

As another example, West Denton High School (Newcastle-upon-Tyne), as part of a project funded by the Department of Employment and a number of companies in the United Kingdom, is using desktop VR as a training aid. Students are undertaking projects related to health and safety, foreign-language education, and arts awareness.

In the area of health and safety, West Denton uses a VR program called "Dangerous Environment." Students use the virtual-reality training to author a dangerous environment in a manufacturing firm. As an example, the world includes a bank of lathes, all operated by push-button control. This allows the student to experience how such a piece of equipment would operate in the real world, but without any of the inherent dangers. The lathes faithfully reproduce the characteristics, such as rotation, of the real equipment. Currently, the lathes stop if the student carries out the wrong procedure. In effect, the VR program is designed to reinforce the health and safety training message such that the virtual world is extended to show what happens when something is not done according to the correct procedure.[4]

Wage-and-Salary Evaluation

In reference to the material presented in the first part of the chapter, people learn best when put in control of their own environment and when enabled to solve their own problems. This is especially important since our global knowledge base is doubling every three to five years. If people have interest in their work, the ever-expanding knowledge base will be helpful to this type of person. Of course, today, this knowledge expansion includes the use of virtual worlds to help analyze a company's problems, like those found in the wage-and-administration area. This means going beyond what has been represented to them in two dimensions, or possibly three dimensions, in an MIS-graphical world. Virtual worlds center on giving the user computer-generated environments that simulate real-world wage-and-salary experiences. In effect, the user can navigate through complex wage-and-salary data in an alternative reality.

To better understand this alternative reality when comparing present and future wages and salaries, an analyst could convert the numbers to a 3-D schematic of colored squares that move up and down and symbolize each plant or warehouse as it moves from the current year on up to five years. The analyst may look at the squares which are flashing red representing a particular plant or warehouse. Such situations indicate an increasing cost rate over the coming years, in particular in the later years. In a similar manner, the individual might look at the adjoining plant or warehouse and find that all of the squares are flashing green, which means that the costs appear to be within an acceptable range given the geographical region of the country. In the first case, the analyst can use a mouse to "fly" into the structure and, if outside a specific cost range, help determine what is causing it. This process takes seconds so that the analyst can recognize exceptions, identify potential cost problems, and make appropriate decisions quickly. In such a virtual world, the analyst discovers new relationships that were not evident previously.

Other Human-Resource Areas

Another interesting VR application in this HR area is one that assists high school students before they start a job search. Specifically, a virtual-reality kiosk for junior high-school students would allow them to investigate jobs and careers. The students could navigate through a "job city," and enter buildings and offices to find out more about a variety of jobs. In effect, they find out from an overall standpoint whether or not the jobs interest them. In turn, the students could take on one or more jobs and explore them in more depth through the VR kiosk, as well as by the efforts of their high-school counselors and on their own.

Going off in yet another direction is a VR world designed to help disabled children. The pilot programs at Meadowside School in Liverpool, England, and Shepard School in Nottingham (the United Kingdom's largest school for children with severe learning difficulties) are directed at helping students master vocabulary basics by associating hand signs and symbols with objects. Using the Dobbshire Assessment Scheme, the children's vocabulary skills are ranked incrementally; the children are then started on a program at the next step on the scale. The project gives students a greater degree of control over their environment through communication. Teachers at the schools have worked closely with the Virtual Reality Research Team (VIRART) at Nottingham University to incorporate virtual reality as a new learning tool. VIRART originally started at Nottingham University. Dimension International (Berkshire, England) approached VIRART and asked if it would like to use their Superscape program to work on its projects. VIRART programmers then went to work using Dimension International's beta equipment. The end result was this effort in the schools.

In this pilot program, the Makaton symbol-and-signing system, a technique used for many years to teach vocabulary skills to disabled students, was incorporated into a series of virtual worlds. Through this system, the children have access to interactive, 3-D environments that display images of words, together with the appropriate symbol and sign, rather than just static pages of information. Using the virtual-reality system, it is possible to create a 3-D car, which the child can get into and drive around the virtual world while the 2-D Makaton symbol remains constantly in view. The system helps the child to understand the generic image of a car, associating it with different colors and movements.[5]

SUMMARY

The training and human-resource systems for a typical company are related directly to other systems because all functional areas depend on the human element to accomplish a company's objectives. In terms of data used, human resources rely heavily on the payroll function of the accounting system. Similarly, information available from the manufacturing system, such as technical skills required for a specific job and the apprenticeship requirements for a certain job level, are of great help to the HR function. However, despite this important level of integration, many methods and procedures evolve from the HR function itself. As illustrated in the chapter, the development of an effective HR system centers on providing timely and in-depth management information using multidimensional analysis for changing conditions. Many times, the integration of OLAP with VR systems extends the capabilities of both systems as opposed to each operating independently of one another.

Overall, all of the appropriate information technology in the human-resource area and other functional areas of a typical company cannot replace a sharp person who understands the technology in use and is good at problem solving and problem finding. This probing and proactive approach to on-line analytical processing, complemented by virtual reality, is an important way for a company to beat or, at least, meet competition today and tomorrow.

NOTES

1. Ronald Henkoff, ''Companies That Train Best,'' *Fortune*, March 22, 1993, pp. 62-75.

2. Megan Santosus, ''Human Resources Systems: Personnel Matters,'' *CIO*, May 1, 1995, pp. 46 and 48.

3. Nina Adams and Laura Lang, ''VR Improves Motorola Training Program,'' *AI Expert*, May 1995, pp. 13–14.

4. Andy Tait, ''Authoring Virtual Worlds on the Desktop,'' *Virtual Reality Special Report*, published by *AI Expert* (San Francisco: Miller Freeman, 1993), p. 13.

5. Julie Shaw, ''Getting a Virtual Education,'' *AI Expert*, August 1993, p. 48.

Bibliography: Part III

Abo, T., ed. *Hybrid Factory, The Japanese Production System in the United States.* New York: Oxford University Press, 1994.

Adams, N., and L. Lang. "VR Improves Motorola Training Program." *AI Expert*, May 1995.

Adler, P. S., A. Mandelbaum, V. Nguyen, and E. Schwerer. "Getting the Most Out of Your Product Development Process." *Harvard Business Review*, March–April 1996.

Aley, J. "How Investors Can Use the Internet." *Fortune*, April 17, 1995.

Amer, T. S., and C. E. Bain. "Making Small Business Planning Easier." *Journal of Accountancy*, July 1990.

Ames, B. C., and J. D. Hlavacek. "Virtual Truths About Managing Your Costs." *Harvard Business Review*, January–February 1990.

Anslinger, P. L., and T. E. Copeland. "Growth Through Acquisition: A Fresh Look." *Harvard Business Review*, January–February 1996.

Arthur, J. B. "Effects of Human Resource System on Manufacturing Performance and Turnover." *Academy of Management Journal*, June 1994.

Baatz, E. B. "Making Brain Waves." *CIO*, January 15, 1996.

Barabba, V. P. "The Market Research Encyclopedia." *Harvard Business Review*, January–February 1990.

Barker, Q. "Virtual Reality Market Analysis." *Virtual Reality World*, March/April 1994.

Barr, D. S., and G. Mani. "Using Neural Nets to Manage Investments." *AI Expert*, February 1994.

Bartholomem, D. "Manufacturing, Building a New Future." *InformationWeek*, August 15, 1994.

———. "Blue Collar Computing." *InformationWeek*, June 19, 1995.

———. "Human Resources: More Personnel Choice." *InformationWeek*, March 4, 1996.

Bartlett, C. A., and S. Ghoshal. "Changing the Role of Top Management: Beyond Strategy to Purpose." *Harvard Business Review*, November–December 1994.

Baum, D. "Data Flows from Factory Floor to Executive Suite." *Infoworld*, April 18, 1994.

Bellone, R. "Financial Planning: Forecast Your Clients' Financial Future." *Accounting Technology*, April 1996.

———. "Management Accounting: Guide to Manufacturing Software." *Accounting Technology*, May 1996.

Bennis, W., and M. Mische. *The 21st Century Organization, Reinventing Through Reengineering*. San Diego, Calif.: Pfeiffer & Company, 1995.

Bensaou, M., and N. Venkatramon. "Configuration of Interorganizational Relationships: A Comparison Between U.S. and Japanese Automakers." *Management Science*, September 1995.

Berardi, K. "How to Select an HRIS System." *Solutions*, March 1996.

Berry, W. E. "The HRIS Role in Re-Engineering: Moving from Responsiveness to Active Change." *Solutions*, November/December 1993.

———. "The Technology Trap." *Solutions*, May 1996.

Black, G. "Wellcome Prescribes OLAP for Decision Support." *Software Magazine*, December 1995.

Bleeke, J. and D. Ernst. "Is Your Strategic Alliance Really a Sale?" *Harvard Business Review*, January–February 1995.

Bonoma, T. V. "Marketing Performance—What Do You Expect?" *Harvard Business Review*, September–October 1989.

Bowen, B. D. "Client/Server HR Replacing Patchwork Quilt of Host Applications." *Client/Server Computing*, July 1995.

Bowen, H. K., K. B. Clark, C. A. Holloway, and S. C. Wheelwright. "Reengineering the Lead in Manufacturing, Development Projects: The Engine of Renewal." *Harvard Business Review*, September–October 1994.

Bradenburger, A. M., and B. J. Nalebuff. "The Right Game: Use Game Theory to Shape Strategy." *Harvard Business Review*, July–August 1995.

Breiner, J., and S. S. Rappaport. "How Technology Can Improve HR Customer Service." *Solutions*, April 1996.

Brewer, T. "How to Set Up a Strategic HR System." *Solutions*, January 1996.

Brown, S. L., and K. M. Eisenhardt. "Product Development: Past Research, Present Findings, and Future Directions." *Academy of Management Review*, April 1995.

Burger, N. A. "The Human Resource Information Center." *Solutions*, February 1994.

Burke, R. R. "Virtual Shopping: Breakthrough In Market Research." *Harvard Business Review*, March–April 1996.

Buzzell, R. D., and B. T. Gale. *The PIMS Principles, Linking Strategy to Performance*. New York: The Free Press, 1988.

Bylinsky, G. "The Marvels of 'Virtual Reality.' " *Fortune*, June 3, 1991.

———. "The Real Payoff from 3-D Computing." *Fortune, Special Report*, Autumn 1993.

———. "The Digital Factory." *Fortune*, November 14, 1994.

———. "Manufacturing for Reuse." *Fortune*, February 6, 1995.

Cayton, B. "Open New Windows on Financial Reporting." *Accounting Technology*, July 1996.

Cerny, K. "Making Local Knowledge Global." *Harvard Business Review*, May–June 1996.

Chabrow, E. R. "Retraining: The Training Payoff." *InformationWeek*, July 10, 1995.

Clark, K. B. "What Strategy Can Do for Technology." *Harvard Business Review*, November–December 1989.

Clarke, D. G. *Marketing Analysis and Decision Making: Text and Cases with Spreadsheets*, 2nd ed. San Francisco, Calif.: The Scientific Press, 1992.

Clemons, E. K. "Using Scenario Analysis to Manage the Strategic Risks of Reengineering." *Sloan Management Review*, Summer 1995.

Clinchy, K., and M. Cornetto. "Human Resources: Help for Those Doing the Hiring." *InformationWeek*, March 11, 1996.

Cockrane, J., J. Temple, and J. Peterson. "Shapes and Shadows of Things to Come: A Plan for Forecasting an Organization's Technological Needs and Opportunities." *Information Strategy, The Executive's Journal*, Spring 1996.

Cohn, M. "Fixed Assets Software, Getting a Fix on Fixed Assets." *Accounting Technology*, July 1995.

Cokins, G. *Activity Based Cost Management—Making It Work*. Burr Ridge, Ill.: Irwin Professional Publishing, 1996.

Cole, N. "How Employee Empowerment Improves Manufacturing Performance." *Academy of Management Executive*, February 1995.

Comaford, C. "OLAP Can Transform Your Plans into Profits." *PC Week*, July 17, 1995.

Converse, C. "Accounting Software's Client/Server Architecture Adds Up to Savings." *Digital News & Review*, March 1, 1993.

Cooper, R., and W. B. Chero. "Control Tomorrow's Costs Through Today's Designs." *Harvard Business Review*, January–February 1996.

Cooper, R., and R. S. Kaplan. "Profit Priorities from Activity-Based Costing." *Harvard Business Review*, May–June 1991.

Crowley, A. "Re-engineering Humans." *PC Week*, November 14, 1994.

Davenport, T. "Think Tank." *CIO*, April 1, 1996.

Donaldson, G. "A New Tool for Boards: The Strategic Audit." *Harvard Business Review*, July–August 1995.

Donovan, M. "Ten Tips for Successfully Reengineering Manufacturing." *Enterprise Reengineering*, August 1995.

Drucker, P. F. "The Emerging Theory of Manufacturing." *Harvard Business Review*, May–June 1990.

———. "The Information Executives Truly Need." *Harvard Business Review*, January–February 1995.

———. *Managing in a Time of Great Change*. New York: Truman Talley Books/Dutton, 1995.

Dungan, J. "HRIS Software: 6 Keys to Productivity." *Solutions*, April 1996.

Dunivan, L. "Corporate Rightsizing: An HR Management Guide." *Solutions*, October 1994.

Dyer, J. H. "Dedicated Assets: Japan's Manufacturing Edge." *Harvard Business Review*, November–December 1994.

———. "How Chrysler Created an American Keirestu." *Harvard Business Review*, July–August 1996.

Earls, A. R. "Agile Manufacturing Finds Firmer Ground." *Computerworld*, February 24, 1994.

Eastman, J. R. "A New Age for Marketing Analysis." *Digital Review*, September 25, 1989.

Eccles, R. G. "The Performance Measurement Manifesto." *Harvard Business Review*, January–February 1991.

Edgeman, J. "Fielding Financial Apps." *DEC Professional*, May 1994.

Edwards, J. "A Clear View." *CIO*, November 15, 1994.

Erkes, J. W., K. B. Kenny, J. W. Lewis, B. D. Sarachan, M. W. Sobalewiski, and R. N. Sum, Jr. "Implementing Shared Manufacturing Services on the World-Wide Web." *Communications of the ACM*, February 1996.

Esplin, K. "Running MRP II Applications in Client/Server Configurations." *Client/Server Computing*, March 1994.

Ewing, J. "Quality German (Re)engineering." *CIO*, November 15, 1995.

Fabris, P. "Accounting for Change." *CIO*, August 1995.

———. "Inspired Accounting." *CIO*, August 1995.

———. "Strategic Systems Revisited, Déjà View." *CIO*, October 1, 1995.

———. "Moving the Goods." *CIO*, June 1, 1996.

Finkelstein, R. "MDD: Database Reaches the Next Dimension." *Database Programming & Design*, April 1995.

Flynn, B. B., S. Sakakibara, and R. G. Schroeder. "Relationship Between JIT and TQM: Practices and Performance." *Academy of Management Journal*, October 1995.

Frank, M. "The Truth About OLAP." *DBMS*, August 1995.

Freedman, D. H. "Quick Change Artists." *CIO*, September 15, 1993.

Freichs, D. "Bringing Real Applications to the Virtual Environment." *Virtual Reality World*, July/August 1994.

Frye, C. "With Financial Apps, DBMS Support Often Drives the Sale." *Software Magazine*, June 1994.

———. "Sales Force Automation? Not Without Customization." *Client/Server Computing*, December 1994.

———. "Paper-Heavy Financials Position for Workflow Wave." *Software Magazine*, April 1995.

———. "Financial Toolsets Earning Interest." *Applications Software Magazine*, January 1996.

Gadde, L. E., and H. Hakanson. "The Changing Role of Purchasing: Reconsidering Three Strategic Issues." *European Journal of Purchasing and Supply Management*, March 1994.

Gambon, J. "Information Week 500: Is High Tech a Surefire Cure?" *InformationWeek*, September 18, 1995.

Gardner, W. D. "Mobile Computing: Rebirth of a Salesman." *Communications Week*, April 24, 1995.

Garvin, D. A. "Building a Learning Organization." *Harvard Business Review*, July–August 1993.

———. "Leveraging Processes for Strategic Advantage." *Harvard Business Review*, September–October 1995.

Gatignon, H., and R. R. Burke. *ADSTRAT: Advertising Strategy Decision Support System*. San Francisco, Calif.: The Scientific Press, 1991.

Gilholly, K. "Empower to the People." *Software Magazine*, March 1996.

Glatzer, H. "Client/Server: The Migration Continues." *Solutions*, December 1995.

Goizueta, R., and J. Welch. "The Wealth Builders." *Fortune*, December 11, 1995.

Goldman, S. L., R. N. Nagel, and K. Preiss. *Agile Competitors and Virtual Organizations: Strategies for Enriching the Customer.* New York: Van Nostrand Reinhold, 1995.

Gow, K. "Experience Not Always Preferred." *Client/Server Computing*, May 1994.

———. "Buyers Wake Up to Benefits of Workflow." *Client/Server Computing*, January 1995.

Grant, A. W. H., and L. A. Schlesinger. "Realize Your Customers' Full Profit Potential." *Harvard Business Review*, September–October 1995.

Greenberg, I. "OLAP Tool Makes Hyperion Data More Accessible." *InfoWorld*, July 17, 1995.

Grygo, E. M. "Planning to Make a Difference." *Client/Server Computing*, February 1996.

Hall, B. "Lessons in Corporate Training." *New Media*, March 11, 1996.

Hamel, G. "Strategy as Revolution." *Harvard Business Review*, July–August 1996.

Hamel, G., and C. K. Prahalad. "The Core Competence of the Corporation." *Harvard Business Review*, May–June 1990.

———. "Corporate Imagination and Expeditionary Marketing." *Harvard Business Review*, July–August 1991.

———. "Competing for the Future." *Harvard Business Review*, July–August 1994.

———. "Seeing the Future First." *Fortune*, September 5, 1994.

Hamilton, J. O'C., E. T. Smith, G. McWilliams, E. I. Schwartz, and J. Carey. "Virtual Reality: How a Computer-Generated World Could Change the Real World." *Business Week*, October 5, 1992.

Hammer, M., and J. Champy. *Reengineering the Corporation: A Manifesto for Business Revolution.* New York: Harper Collins Publishers, 1993.

———. "The Promise of Reengineering." *Fortune*, May 3, 1993.

Hammer, M., and S. A. Stanton. *The Reengineering Revolution.* New York: Harper Collins Publishers, 1995.

Hansen, G. "Activity Based Costing—It's Not as Easy as You Think." *Enterprise Engineering*, September 1995.

Hardwick, M., D. L. Spooner, T. Rando, and K. C. Morris. "Sharing Manufacturing Information in Virtual Enterprises." *Communications of the ACM*, February 1996.

Hare, J. "Do-It-Yourself HR." *Solutions*, December 1994.

Harmon, R. L. *Reinventing the Factory II, Managing the World Class Factory.* New York: The Free Press, 1991.

Hayes, R. H., and G. P. Pisano. "Beyond World-Class: The New Manufacturing Strategy." *Harvard Business Review*, January–February 1994.

Henderson, D. "A New Advantage for Market Intelligence." *Computing Canada*, October 25, 1995.

Henkoff, R. "Companies That Train Best." *Fortune*, March 22, 1993.

———. "New Management Secrets from Japan—Really." *Fortune*, November 27, 1995.

Henson, R. "HR Benefits & Technology: Meeting the Globalization Challenge." *Solutions*, February 1996.

Herter, G. "Business Planning Boosts Your Chances." *Accounting Technology*, April/May 1995.

———. "Practice Development, Business Planning Boosts Your Chances." *Accounting Technology*, April/May 1995.

Hills, L. "Business Reengineering Through Client/Server Computing." *Solutions*, April/May 1994.

Himowitz, M. J. "Cyberspace: The Investor's New Edge." *Fortune*, December 25, 1995.

Holbrook, D. "Stereo Viewing: Looking into Manufacturing." *Manufacturing Systems*, January 1991.

Horvath, C. "HR Online: The Future Is Now." *Solutions*, March 1996.

Huselid, M. A. "The Impact of Human Resource Management Practices on Turnover, Productivity, and Corporate Financial Performance." *Academy of Management Journal*, June 1995.

Iacobucci, D. "The Quality Improvement Customers Didn't Want." *Harvard Business Review*, January–February 1996.

Istvan, R. L. "Computing in the Fourth Dimension—Time." *Chief Information Officer Journal*, Summer 1988.

Jacobson, L. "Reading, 'Riting, 'Rithmetic, and Reality." *Virtual Reality Special Report*. Published by the *AI Expert*, San Francisco, Calif.: Miller Freeman, 1993.

Johnson, S. J. "Virtual Reality Takes Architectural Leap." *Computerworld*, June 20, 1994.

Jones, T. D., and W. E. Sasser, Jr. "Why Satisfied Customers Defect." *Harvard Business Review*, November–December 1995.

Jordon, W. C., and S. C. Graves. "Principles on the Benefits of Manufacturing Process Flexibility." *Management Science*, April 1995.

Kamath, R. R., and J. K. Liker. "A Second Look at Japanese Product Development." *Harvard Business Review*, November–December 1994.

Kanter, R. M. "Collaborative Advantage: The Art of Alliances." *Harvard Business Review*, November–December 1994.

Kaplan, R. S., and D. P. Norton. "Using the Balanced Scorecard as a Strategic Management System." *Harvard Business Review*, January–February 1996.

Keenan, W. Jr. "Market Research: Numbers Racket." *Sales & Marketing Management*, May 1995.

Kneer, D. C., and M. G. Bergerson. "Desktop Publishing and Presentation Graphics: Improving Accounting's Images." *Journal of Accountancy*, July 1992.

Knight, R. "MES Challenges MIS." *Software Magazine*, August 1994.

Kolbasuk McGee, M. "Training: Not Just Kid Stuff." *InformationWeek*, January 15, 1996.

Korzeniowski, P. "The CW Guide to Client/Server Financials, Settling Cracks." *Computerworld*, August 28, 1995.

Krioda, C. D. "Deploying Financial Apps on Windows NT." *ENT*, June 1996.

Larson-Mogal, J. S. "An Immersive Paradigm for Product Design and Ergonomic Analysis." *Virtual Reality World*, July/August 1994.

Leibert, J. "Manufacturing Execution Systems." *ID Systems*, October 1994.

Leinfuss, E. "Employees Empowered by Direct Access HRMS." *Software Magazine*, April 1993.

————. "Client/Server HR: Unrisky Business." *Client/Server Computing*, September 1994.

Leong, K. C. "The Ties That Bind." *Communications Week*, April 24, 1995.

Mahoney, D. P. "Virtual Reality on the PC." *Computer Graphics World*, May 1996.

Main, J. "At Last, Software CEOs Can Use." *Fortune*, March 13, 1989.

Malhotra, N. K. *Marketing Research: An Applied Orientation.* Englewood Cliffs, N.J.: Prentice-Hall, 1993.

Markels, A., and M. Murray. "Axing for Trouble, Call It Dumbsizing: Why Some Companies Regret Cost-Cutting." *Wall Street Journal,* May 14, 1996.

Martin, C. T. "Manufacturing Software Suppliers Adopt ERP Focus." *Application Development Trends,* November 1995.

Martin, J. "Ignore Your Customer." *Fortune,* May 1, 1995.

Martinez, E. V. "Successful Reengineering Demands IS/Business Partnerships." *Sloan Management Review,* Summer 1995.

Marvin, M. K. "Expert Systems for Compliance Management." *Solutions,* February 1996.

McFadden, M. "No Small Change." *ENT,* June 1996.

McGahan, A. M. "Industry Structure and Competitive Advantage." *Harvard Business Review,* November–December 1994.

McHose, A. *Manufacturing Development Applications: Guidelines for Attaining Quality and Productivity.* Homewood, Ill.: Business One Irwin, 1992.

McKenna, R. "Real-Time Marketing." *Harvard Business Review,* July–August 1995.

McWilliams, B. "Reengineering the Small Factory." *Inc. Technology,* January 1996.

Mehling, H. "Complex Application Requires Exec IT." *Client/Server Computing,* November 1995.

Merrill, J. R. "VR for Medical Training and Trade Show 'Fly-Paper.' " *Virtual Reality World,* May/June 1994.

Mingle, C. "Strategic Planning: What CPA's Need to Know." *Journal of Accountancy,* July 1990.

Mintzberg, H. "Crafting Strategy." *Harvard Business Review,* July–August 1987.

―――. "The Fall and Rise of Strategic Planning." *Harvard Business Review,* January–February 1994.

Moretti, J. "HRIS: Paving the Way for Change." *Solutions,* January 1995.

Morton, F. J., and D. T. Gallison. "Reengineering Performance Management." *Solutions,* January 1994.

Moshell, J. M., and C. E. Hughes. "Shared Virtual Worlds for Education." *Virtual Reality World,* January/February 1994.

Narus, J. A., and J. C. Anderson. "Rethinking Distribution: Adaptive Channels." *Harvard Business Review,* July–August 1996.

Navas, D. "Electronics Manufacturing." *ID Systems,* February 1995.

―――. "Materials Handling in Manufacturing." *ID Systems,* June 1996.

Nelson, R. R., E. M. Whitener, and H. H. Philcox. "The Assessment of End-User Training Needs." *Communications of the ACM,* July 1995.

Ness, J. A., and T. G. Cucuzza. "Tapping the Full Potential of ABC." *Harvard Business Review,* July–August 1995.

Norton, R. "A New Tool to Help Managers." *Fortune,* May 30, 1994.

O'Boyle, T. F. "Last In, Right Out, Firms' Newfound Skill in Managing Inventory May Soften Downturn." *Wall Street Journal,* November 19, 1990.

O'Leary, M. "A New Life for Purchasing." *CIO,* May 1, 1993.

Payton, D. W., and T. E. Bihari. "Intelligent Real-Time Control of Robotic Vehicles." *Communications of the ACM,* August 1991.

Peavey, D., and J. DePalma. "Do You Know the Cost of Your Products?" New York: Coopers & Lybrand Executive Briefing, May 1990.

Petrozzo, D. P., and J. C. Stepper. *Successful Reengineering*. New York: Van Nostrand Reinhold, 1994.

Pickering. W. "Financial Vendors Drilling into OLAP." *PC Week*, June 26, 1995.

———. "Hyperion to Offer OLAP Tool for Enterprise Financial Suite." *PC Week*, July 17, 1995.

Pimentel, K., and K. Teixeira. *Virtual Reality: Through the New Looking Glass*. New York: McGraw-Hill, 1993.

Pisano, G. P., and S. C. Wheelwright. "The New Logic of High-Tech R&D." *Harvard Business Review*, September–October 1995.

Porter, M. E. *The Competitive Advantage of Nations*. New York: The Free Press, 1990.

Prahalad, C. K., and G. Hamel. "The Core Competence of the Corporation." *Harvard Business Review*, May–June 1990.

Products. "Volvo Demonstration Uses VR." *Virtual Reality World*, July/August 1994.

Quelch, J. A., and D. Kenny. "Extend Profits, Not Product Lines." *Harvard Business Review*, September–October 1994.

Quinn, J. B. *Intelligent Enterprise*. New York: The Free Press, 1992.

Radding, A. "Blue Cross Climbs Mountain of Data with OLAP." *InfoWorld*, January 30, 1995.

Rayport, J. F., and J. J. Sviokla. "Managing in the Marketspace." *Harvard Business Review*, November–December 1994.

———. "Exploiting the Virtual Value Chain." *Harvard Business Review*, November–December 1995.

Reichheld, F. F. "Learning from Customer Defections." *Harvard Business Review*, March–April 1996.

Roberts, B., and L. G. Paul. "On the Line." *PC Week Executive*, November 27, 1995.

Rockhart, J. F. "Chief Executives Define Their Own Data Needs." *Harvard Business Review*, March–April 1979.

Romei, L. K. "Quality Becomes Integral to American Business." *Modern Office Technology*, July 1991.

Rose, F. "Now Quality Means Service Too." *Fortune*, April 22, 1991.

Rothstein, L. R. "The Empowerment Effort That Came Undone." *Harvard Business Review*, January–February 1995.

Santosus, M. "Human Resources Systems: Personnel Matters." *CIO*, May 1, 1995.

Schoemaker, P. J. H. "How to Link Strategic Vision to Core Capabilities." *Sloan Management Review*, Fall 1992.

Shank, J. K., and V. Govindarajan. "Strategic Cost Analysis of Technological Investments." *Sloan Management Review*, Fall 1992.

Shapiro, B. P., V. K. Rangan, and J. J. Sviokla. "Staple Yourself to an Order." *Harvard Business Review*, July–August 1992.

Sharp, K. R. "Selecting Inventory Control Software." *ID Systems*, June 1996.

Shaw, J. "Getting a Virtual Education." *AI Expert*, August 1993.

Sherman, S. "How to Prosper in the Value Decade." *Fortune*, November 30, 1992.

———. "Will the Information Superhighway Be the Death of Retailing?" *Fortune*, April 18, 1994.

Siegman, K. "Money on the Line." *Oracle Magazine*, April 1996.

Simons, R. "Control in an Age of Empowerment." *Harvard Business Review*, March–April 1995.

Smith, H. *Rethinking America*. New York: Random House, 1995.

Smith, J. A. "Database Marketing: Hitting the Target." *Beyond Computing*, July/August 1994.

Smith, P. "Unique Tools for Marketers: PIMS." *Management Review*, January 1977.

Snell, N. "How Hard Is Our Advertising Working?" *EDGE*, January/February 1990.

Stewart, T. A. "Reengineering: The Hot New Managing Tool." *Fortune*, August 23, 1993.

Stuart, A. "Just In Time Planning," *CIO*, November 15, 1994.

———. "The Adaptable Workforce." *CIO*, March 1, 1995.

———. "Knowledge Management." *CIO*, June 1, 1996.

Susman, G. I., ed. *Integrating Design and Manufacturing for Competitive Advantage*. New York: Oxford University Press, 1992.

Tait, A. "Authoring Virtual Worlds on the Desktop." *Virtual Reality Special Report*. Published by the *AI Expert*, San Francisco, Calif.: Miller Freeman, 1993.

Thé, L. "Financial Software Does More Than Just Crunch Numbers." *Datamation*, February 1, 1995.

———. "Retool Human Resources." *Datamation*, June 15, 1995.

Thierauf, R. J. *A Problem Finding Approach to Effective Corporate Planning*, Westport, Conn.: Quorum Books, 1987.

———. *User-Oriented Decision Support Systems—A Problem-Finding Approach*. Englewood Cliffs, N.J.: Prentice-Hall, 1988.

———. *Group Decision Support Systems for Effective Decision Making*. Westport, Conn.: Quorum Books, 1989.

———. *Executive Information Systems: A Guide for Senior Management and MIS Professionals*. Westport, Conn.: Quorum Books, 1991.

———. *Image Processing Systems in Business: A Guide for MIS Professionals and End Users*. Westport, Conn.: Quorum Books, 1992.

———. *Creative Computer Software for Strategic Thinking and Decision Making: A Guide for Senior Management and MIS Professionals*. Westport, Conn.: Quorum Books, 1993.

———. *Virtual Reality Systems for Business*. Westport, Conn.: Quorum Books, 1995.

Tracey, W. R. "How to Weigh the Costs and Benefits of Training." *Solutions*, December 1995.

Tucker, G. F., S. M. Zivan, and R. C. Camp. "How to Measure Yourself Against the Best." *Harvard Business Review*, January–February 1987.

Tufano, P. "How Financial Engineering Can Advance Corporate Strategy." *Harvard Business Review*, January–February 1996.

Tully, S. "The Real Key to Creating Wealth." *Fortune*, September 20, 1993.

———. "You'll Never Guess Who Really Makes. . . ." *Fortune*, October 3, 1994.

———. "Purchasing's New Muscle." *Fortune*, February 20, 1995.

Tyo, J. "Simulation Modeling Tools." *InformationWeek*, July 10, 1995.

Umebayashi, I. "New Trends in the Keiretsu System." *The Wall Street Journal*, November 16, 1992.

Upton, D. M. "What Really Makes Factories Flexible?" *Harvard Business Review*, July–August 1995.

Upton, D. M., and A. McAfee. "The Real Virtual Factory." *Harvard Business Review*, July–August 1996.

Vacco, J. R. "3D World on the Web." *Computer Graphics World*, May 1996.

Valigra, L. "Financial Applications Are a Personal Choice." *Client/Server Computing*, January 1996.

Venkatesan, R. "Strategic Sourcing: To Make or Not to Make." *Harvard Business Review*, November–December 1992.

Wallace, P. "SmithKline Beecham Boosts Budgeting System." *InfoWorld*, January 16, 1995.

Ward, M. "Strategies for Implementing Employee Self-Service." *Solutions*, May 1996.

Weil, M. "Best-in-Class or Single Source? The ERP Decision." *Software Strategies*, March 1996.

Whitney, J. O. "Strategic Renewal for Business Units." *Harvard Business Review*, July–August 1996.

Williams, M. "Back to the Past, Some Plants Tear Out Long Assembly Lines, Switch to Craft Work." *Wall Street Journal*, October 24, 1994.

Williamson, M. "Some Simulating Experiences." *CIO*, November 1, 1993.

———. "To Everything, Turn, Turn, Turn." *CIO*, May 1, 1996.

Winkler, C. "The New Line on Managing People." *InformationWeek*, May 23, 1994.

Worthy, F. A. "Japan's Smart Secret Weapon." *Fortune*, August 12, 1991.

Young, J. "Can Computers Really Boost Sales?" *Forbes ASAP*, August 28, 1995.

Young, S. M. "A Framework for Successful Adoption and Performance of Japanese Manufacturing Practices in the United States." *Academy of Management Review*, October 1992.

Zeidenberg, A. "I Think, Therefore ICON." *CA Magazine*, August 1990.

Index

About the Author

ROBERT J. THIERAUF is Professor of Information Systems at Xavier University, Cincinnati, Ohio. Formerly a staff accountant (CPA) and consultant at Coopers & Lybrand, Dr. Thierauf writes extensively on all facets of information systems, particularly decision support systems, executive information systems, expert systems, virtual reality systems, and information systems management. He is the author of 30 books, twelve published by Quorum.

ISBN 1-56720-099-0

90000>

9 781567 200997

HARDCOVER BAR CODE